THE CONSTITUTION
Written in Sand or Etched in Stone?

Edited by Bill Rhatican

Bloomington, IN Milton Keynes, UK

authorHOUSE

AuthorHouse™
1663 Liberty Drive, Suite 200
Bloomington, IN 47403
www.authorhouse.com
Phone: 1-800-839-8640

AuthorHouse™ UK Ltd.
500 Avebury Boulevard
Central Milton Keynes, MK9 2BE
www.authorhouse.co.uk
Phone: 08001974150

First published by AuthorHouse 4/11/2006

ISBN: 1-4259-2035-7 (e)
ISBN: 1-4259-2034-9 (sc)
ISBN: 1-4259-2033-0 (dj)

Library of Congress Control Number: 2006901618

Printed in the United States of America
Bloomington, Indiana

This book is printed on acid-free paper.

This work is published in part through grants from the Virginia Professional Educators, an affiliate of the Association of American Educators, and from the West Potomac High School Parents, Teachers and Students Association.

AN INTRODUCTION

When the Founding Fathers convened in Philadelphia in 1787 to write a constitution for the new American government, they were not of one mind on such contentious issues as the powers to be allocated to the national government and on the relative powers of the newly created "co-equal" branches of the new government. They argued over the relative merits of a strong national government versus strong state governments. They argued over the roles each of the three new branches of the federal government might play. And then, after they had finished their deliberations, the very document they, themselves, had created was jeopardized by an uprising among the founders themselves. Many believed the new Constitution should be defeated unless written guarantees were included, guarantees protecting the people from the very government they had just created. Thus, the Bill of Rights was born.

As we have seen, both of those debates continue today, two centuries after they began. States' Rightists argue against the infringement of the national government on prerogatives of the states. And the neo-Federalists contend that the national government has the right and the responsibility to provide for <u>all</u> American citizens, regardless of their geographic location.

As recently as the Senate Judiciary Committee hearings on the nomination of Judge Samuel Alito to the United States Supreme Court, we have also seen the debate over the relative powers of the executive and the legislature burst on the public stage. Many of the questions of Judge Alito reflected the senators' concern about an "unlimited" and "all powerful" executive branch.

As a teacher of Advanced Placement (AP) United States Government at West Potomac High School in Alexandria, Virginia, I seek to challenge my students to go beyond the test-preparation elements of the class and to explore the universal themes of the American political experiment. Each year, I invite my students to select a topic within a general theme of my choosing and write an essay on the topic. Actually, it's more than an invitation. It's a course requirement and has been for three years. This year, I selected the Constitution of the United States. Each student was to choose an aspect of that marvelous, revolutionary document, explore its background and write about its relevance for today's American society.

What you are about to enter may be a new world for you, one with a view of American history and constitutional debate that may encourage you, annoy you or completely turn you off. Whatever your reaction to the essays enclosed herein, these are the thoughts of a new generation of Americans, high school seniors all, many of whom will be in college in the fall, pursuing individual interests and careers.

What they all demonstrate, however, is a powerful understanding of the U.S. Constitution and its relevance to the America we find today. Not all of the essays submitted were selected for this publication. The selection of a topic relevant to the Constitution was entirely each student's. The essays are theirs, with some modest editing from my wife, Leslie, and me, primarily to help clarify a point or to provide for consistency among the essays.

In short, I do hope you enjoy these works by high school seniors, each of whom has demonstrated a keen awareness of the importance of this incredible document and the Bill of Rights it spawned.

An especially heartfelt expression of thanks goes enthusiastically to Rima Vesilind, principal of West Potomac High School, for her unstinting support of this effort over the years. She clearly understands the value of preparing our students not only for the end-of-year tests the students must prepare for but also for the challenging academic world they will enter after graduation. A very special thanks, too, should go to our school's outstanding Graphic Arts Department, one of its teachers, Michael Iacavone, and his student, Jeremy Bogdan, for his exciting cover design and to my wife, Leslie, without whose efforts this book would never have made it into publication before graduation. A special thank you also to Ronald Johnson, who was unusually helpful.

TABLE OF CONTENTS

The Argument

Two Antagonists

The Issues

The Issues Over the Years

THE ARGUMENT

Federalism

The Battle Still Rages
By
Zac Knitter

A simple reading of the Constitution would lead no one to believe that the federal structure that exists today could come to be. Since the debate over ratification in the late Eighteenth Century, the question has been posed as to how much power the national government should possess under the Constitution and, essentially, what the role of federalism is. The framers intended the national government to be stronger under the Constitution than it was previously under the Articles of Confederation, yet the extent of federal power they would have desired is more subject to debate. Federalists advocated the ratification of the Constitution and a powerful national government as the centerpiece of a successful United States. Anti-federalists were more skeptical of the Constitution for fear that it would encroach upon the liberties and freedoms of the individual state governments. After examining the federal structure that exists today, it is difficult to say that the Anti-federalists were incorrect in their prediction, for, it appears as though the federal government has almost usurped all powers granted to the states by the Tenth Amendment (also known as the reserve clause).

The Tenth Amendment offers the foundation for what is known as the doctrine of "states' rights"- the idea that states hold individual liberties as do all citizens. For the Constitution to be ratified by the states, it was necessary that the Bill of Rights (including the Tenth Amendment) be added as a result of anti-federalist criticism of the Constitution's possible creation of an all-powerful national government. The Bill of Rights was written not simply to ensure ratification of the Constitution, but, more notably, to guarantee that the federal government would not encroach on the rights and liberties of individuals or of the states. Through the ratification of the Constitution with the Bill of Rights, the states acknowledged their compliance with the structure of the federal government as outlined within the Constitution under the expectation that the states would be reserved those powers not specifically granted to the federal government (nor prohibited to them) on grounds of the Tenth Amendment. Therefore, by advocating the Tenth Amendment, the principle of states' rights was created as a fundamental part of the Constitution and the federal system.

Federalism, as it originally existed under the Constitution, is often considered dual federalism; meaning that the state and federal governments are supreme in their selective spheres. Where these two spheres overlapped, the national government would be considered dominant (due to the supremacy clause in Article IV). As time has progressed, however, a transition has been made from dual federalism into what is referred to as cooperative federalism. The analogy has been made that "dual federalism" represents a layered cake, with defined lines between the two that concern powers, whereas "cooperative federalism" appears to be more of a marble cake in which the powers are more intertwined and it becomes difficult to distinguish which government should hold power in certain matters[1]. Much to the surprise of Hamilton and Madison, who agreed that it would be the state governments (if any) that would tip the scale of federal power[2], it has been the powers of the national government which have expanded the most since the ratification of the Constitution. This transition of federal power did not occur as the result of any single event. It has been the combination of rulings by the Supreme Court regarding interpretation of the "elastic" and "commerce" clauses, as well as historical events like the Civil War and Franklin Delano Roosevelt's New Deal that have altered the federal structure of the United States from "dual federalism" to "cooperative federalism".

At the heart of the evolution of federalism is, of course, the Constitution. Within the wording of the Constitution, the debate over federal structure is represented by the seemingly conflicting elastic clause in Article I and the reserve clause (Amendment X). Although the Tenth Amendment grants the states "numerous and indefinite"[3] powers, it is meaningless without Article I, which established the premise that, as Madison states in *Federalist No. 45,* "The powers delegated by the proposed constitution to the federal government, are few and defined."[4] By specifically listing what

Congress can do, rather than what it cannot, Article I established what Roger Pilon calls the "doctrine of enumeration"[5]; the premise that the only powers granted to the national government are those specified within the Constitution. The doctrine of "enumeration" represented the focal point of dual federalism because the doctrine made clear distinctions between what the federal government was permitted and what the individual state governments were reserved. However, even when read in context with the reserve clause, Article I leaves Constitutional loopholes for the national government to increase its power by means of the elastic clause (also referred to as the necessary and proper clause) and the commerce clause.

The elastic clause (Article I, Section 8, Clause 18) is the central cause for the inception of implied powers. After the initial fight for ratification, the Constitution developed into an interpretation war as the debate between Federalists and Anti-Federalists over the constitutionality of the First Bank of the United States brought to light the contrasting views of the loose and strict constructionists. In the end of the argument over the First Bank, it was the Federalists and loose constructionist who had won and the creation of the First Bank of the United States was dubbed constitutional by Chief Justice John Marshall's ruling in McCulloch v. Maryland in 1819. However, the lasting significance of the loose constructionists' victory was its effect of securing the premise of implied powers as precedent for the extension of federal authority beyond those powers enumerated in the Constitution. Not only was Marshall's ruling the birth of implied powers, but it was also used as justification for implied powers to be granted under the Constitutional premise of the elastic clause. Although the elastic clause can be stretched to defend a wide variety of legislation (especially with regard to economic policy), its greater value comes from its effect of constitutionally justifying implied powers, not to mention the more important precedent it set by allowing for the expansion of federal power beyond the exact text of the Constitution.

The doctrine of states' rights suffered its first blow at the hands of the Supreme Court in 1819 when Chief Justice Marshall declared the creation of the First Bank of the United States constitutional. As stated previously, the case ended the doctrine of enumeration through the recognition of implied powers. Although both the Alien and Sedition Acts and the Court's decision in McCulloch were factors leading toward the concept of implied powers, Marshall's decision provided a written justification for the expansion of federal authority, thus enabling further grasps at power by the national government. This expansion of federal power came at the expense of the states' rights by taking power away from the states and transferring it into the hands of the national government, shifting the federal structure slightly from that of dual federalism towards cooperative federalism.

As a side note, it is also often recognized that Marshall's ruling in McCulloch created the doctrine of supremacy, in which the national government is supreme to the states "within its sphere of action"[6]. Yet, Marshall merely iterated the supremacy clause within Article IV, he did not single handedly create the supremacy of the national government as some would suggest. Regardless of its effect on national supremacy, Marshall's decision in McCulloch v. Maryland laid the foundation for the expansion of federal power within the (implied) confines of the Constitution, making the federal government increasingly able to encroach on states' rights.

Yet, even before the ruling in McCulloch, the federal government encountered resistance to the escalation of its power after Congress passed the Alien and Sedition Acts in 1798. The Alien and Sedition Acts did nothing short of trample the First Amendment rights in the name of strengthening the federal government and national defense. It was in outrage against these acts that Thomas Jefferson and James Madison wrote the Kentucky and Virginia Resolutions, creating the foundations for the doctrine of "states' rights". Jefferson and Madison, both strict constructionists, wrote that the national government had overstepped the boundaries enumerated within the Constitution. Jefferson writes,

> "...the friendless alien has indeed been selected as the safest subject of a first experiment; but the citizen will soon follow... [T]hese and successive acts of the same character, unless arrested at the threshold, necessarily drive [the] States into revolution..."[7]

Jefferson's direct attack on the outreach of federal power through the Alien and Sedition Acts clearly provided the groundwork for the states' rights doctrine to develop. The principle of states' rights possessed room for growth of the doctrine through further or increased encroachment on the sovereignty of individual states. It would be Jefferson's words and his idea that "where powers are assumed which have not been delegated [to the national government], a nullification of the act is the rightful remedy"[8] which would be used to justify the secession of the Southern states during 1860 and 1861. The belief that states indeed possessed all sovereignty not enumerated to the federal government, reflected in the principle of states' rights and strict constructionism would continually lose influence after it was conceived in the Virginia and Kentucky Resolutions. However, the resounding implication of the federal government encroaching upon the liberties of the individual states is that the encroachment illustrates the beginning of the transition from dual federalism into a more cooperative federalism, in which the powers of the national government not only supercede those of the states but become interconnected with the jurisdiction of the states in the federal structure.

After the ruling in McCulloch v. Maryland, the framework was established for the extension of the implied powers of the national government, and the principle of states' rights was about to suffer again at the hands of the Supreme Court . The trend of federal growth received possibly its most significant support from the Court's interpretation of the commerce clause in Marshall's ruling in Gibbons v. Ogden[9]. Marshall declared commerce to include virtually all commercial activity in his decision and also set a precedent that the powers of the federal government could be expanded over the states to include interstate commerce. The loose definition of commerce given by Marshall later came to be critical in justifying some of Congress's legislation regarding economic regulation (as opposed to economic promotion) most obviously during FDR's New Deal[10].

Although the "elastic" clause has served as the basis for the expansion of federal power and, consequently, the transition from dual to cooperative federalism, the bulk of federal power stems from the commerce clause (Article I, Section 8, Clause 3). The commerce clause, and its loose interpretation by the Supreme Court, has arguably served as the most significant grant of power to the national government. Ever since Gibbons v. Ogden (1824), Marshall's broad definition of "commerce" has acted as an open channel for Congress to pass virtually any legislation with the intent of regulating commerce. As it is now defined, commerce includes the Internet, radio, and even insurance transactions, giving the national government an ambiguously large amount of influence through legislation[11]. The span of federal clout under the commerce clause is so extended that in Wickard v. Filburn (1942); the Court ruled that "growing wheat on one's own land for one's own consumption" was considered to affect interstate commerce[12]. The Supreme Court has been incredibly far-reaching in its interpretation of the commerce clause, thereby making the clause a very powerful tool for the national government.

Due to the interpreted extent of the commerce clause, it has become almost effortless for Congress to justify legislative abilities that (according to the Constitution) should be reserved to the states by their absence from Article I. Thus, the federal structure has been influenced by the interpretation of the commerce clause (due to the extensive amount of power it grants to the federal government). By granting the federal government more power, the commerce clause allows for further encroachment by the national government on the rights of the respective states and, once the federal government has the ability to interfere with the powers delegated to the states, the federal structure is altered toward a more cooperative, coercive, or even a unitary federal system.

Despite the clearly influential role of the judicial branch in the conversion from a dual federal structure toward a cooperative federal structure, history has also had a part in this exchange of power. The Civil War was the physical manifestation of the (written intellectual) conflict between the national and state governments and FDR's New Deal created the welfare state, redefining and further expanding the powers of the national government.

The Civil War was the physical victory of national power over state sovereignty. The victory of the Union over the Confederacy solidified the supremacy of the national government forever in American history, for the Union was the federal government and represented a more integrated force than the Confederacy and its loose alliance of states.[13] More than a mere victory for the federal government, the Civil War silenced all qualms regarding the Constitution as a governmental structure and any questions of legitimacy surrounding it. The Constitution had prevailed over the outdated Confederacy, the intellectual child of the Articles of Confederation. So, the Civil War not only physically affirmed what had already been established by the judicial branch, but also symbolically increased the control of the national government over the states and strengthened it through victory.

After Franklin Delano Roosevelt was elected to the presidency in 1932, he started economic relief programs known popularly as the New Deal to assist in the recovery from the Great Depression including the AAA, WPA, NRLB, FDIC, FCC, TVA, Social Security, and multiple others. The overall purpose of the New Deal was to improve the condition of the American people who had fallen victim to the Great Depression by creating a welfare state. Yet, the creation of a welfare state required an increase in spending and a larger scope of legislation and government in general. Indeed, many of the programs of the New Deal were ruled unconstitutional because they were found to violate the restrictions of the national government under the commerce clause. In 1937, however, the Supreme Court reversed its stance on federal power under the commerce clause in NLRB v. Jones & Laughlin Steel Corp., stating that the national government had the right to regulate anything that affected interstate commerce.[14] The expansion of federal capability as a result of the Court's ruling led to the success of several New Deal programs (still around today) at the expense of state sovereignty. The New Deal programs created a welfare state but also gave the federal government a level of power it had never previously held, at the expense of the states, because it was now possible for the national government to regulate the entire economy and author very specific and targeted legislation. The effect of the creation of the welfare state is that the principle of dual federalism had become extinct as federal power had usurped states' rights. Further, the dual federalism that existed in the early years of the Constitution had been replaced by a cooperative federalism that enabled the federal government to intervene in relatively any state affair deemed necessary.

Although there have been vast numbers of laws created under the premise of the commerce clause and the expansion of federal power, many recent Supreme Court rulings have actually served to limit the powers of the federal government with regard to the regulation of commerce. For one, in U.S. v. Lopez, the Court ruled that the Federal Gun-Free School Zones Act (1990) overstepped the boundaries placed on the national government by the commerce clause, stating that guns in school zones and commerce are two separate entities and it is, therefore, unconstitutional for the national government to enforce such a law. Interestingly enough, the act was passed and remained in effect for five years without even mentioning a Constitutional basis for it. Other constraints have been placed on the extension of federal power in cases such as Printz v. U.S. and Mack v. U.S., in which the Court ruled that the national government has no authority to order state officials to carry out federal regulatory programs. The more recent rulings of the Court in Lopez, Printz, and Mack all illustrate that the national government can transgress even its implied powers. More importantly, the rulings in support of limiting the extent of the national government show a possible reversal in the trend toward cooperative federalism in favor of states' rights and toward a return to a dual federal structure.

In National League of Cities v. Usery, the Supreme Court also ruled in favor of states' rights by striking down provisions of a federal law that sought to regulate minimum wage to state and municipal employees. However, showing that the trend toward cooperative federalism and possible unitary status was not in danger of ending, the Court overruled its decision in Usery in Garcia v. San Antonio, mentioning that Usery's decision was "unworkable" in lower courts. The overruling of Usery shows that the established trend of building a stronger national government (at the expense of the states) outweighs state sovereignty and decision-making, not to mention that the dual federalism that kept the state and national governments equal in respective influence is extinct.[15]

Both the roles of Supreme Court rulings and history have been shown to cause the consolidation of power into the hands of the national government, yet there remains an indirect method with which Congress can control state governments. For example, both the Motor Voter Act and the Highway Funding Act withheld federal funding unless states agreed to comply with the laws. By withholding federal funds and using other indirect methods of influencing state governments (such as crossover sanctions and cross-cutting requirements), the national government clearly maintains its supremacy even when it may not be constitutional for it to do so. As mentioned earlier, the Court found it unconstitutional to force state workers to do federal tasks so the federal government uses its most powerful resource – money – to coerce the states to comply, since the states cannot afford what is necessary to maintain their successful operations without federal funding.

The current federal system revolves around the national government, which is entirely contrary to the beliefs of the framers. In the Federalist Papers, both Hamilton and Madison believed that, under the Constitution, the states would have the most influence on the people. Yet, it is mostly federal laws that concern the people now and the national government that appears to have the bulk of influence in American society. Also, Madison states in Federalist No. 45 that,

> "The state governments will have the advantage of the federal government, whether we compare them in respect to the immediate dependence of the one on the other; to the weight of personal influence which each side will possess; to the powers respectively vested in them; to the predilection and probable support of the people; to the disposition and faculty of resisting and frustrating the measures of each other."[16]

There is an apparent difference between the United States Madison believed in and the U.S. that exists today. It appears as though the reality of the cooperative federal structure is almost the exact opposite of the state-centered federalism Madison espoused. Undoubtedly, Madison could not have imagined the complexity of the current federal system in the United States, but it is nevertheless interesting that the statement is almost laughable because of its sheer fallacy. To think that the state governments could ever even be considered equivalent with the national government is nearly impossible but to honestly believe the states to be the better is preposterous due to the amount of influence that the national government currently possesses. The purpose of focusing on the contrast between Madison's vision of the U.S. and the actual body is that Madison's vision was of a dual federalism, whereas the current federal structure is almost unitary due to the sheer amount of power it has over the state governments. Madison's intention was to highlight the power that states should possess, yet today his words only show the power that the states lack due to the evolution of federalism.

The federal structure of the United States as it exists today is not reflective of the Constitution, especially with regard to the Tenth Amendment. According to the document, it is the states which shall be regarded as the most influential to the people through the possession of all rights not prohibited them nor guaranteed to the federal government. In spite of this, is has been the federal government which has emerged superior to the states with respect to power and influence. In addition, the transition of the federal structure from dual federalism to cooperative federalism is evidence of the decreased influence of the doctrine of enumeration and states' rights on the powers and capabilities of the federal government. In the hands of the Supreme Court, the Civil War, and FDR's New Deal, states have lost almost complete sovereignty to the federal government under the title of cooperative federalism.

Bibliography

Exploring Constitutional Conflicts. "Tenth and Eleventh Amendment Limitations on Federal Power"; Available from http://www.law.umke.edu/faculty/projects/ ftrials/conlaw/tenth&elev.htm. Internet; accessed 9 October 2005.

Hamilton, Alexander, Jay, John and Madison, James. The Federalist. Indianapolis, Indiana: Liberty Fund, Inc., 2001.

Jefferson, Thomas. "The Kentucky Resolutions of 1798"; Available from http://www.constitution.org/cons/kent1798.htm. Internet, accessed 12 November 2005.

Pilon, Roger. "On the First Principles of Federalism"; Available from http://www.cato.org/pubs/policy_report/pr-nd-rp.html. Internet, accessed 9 October 2005.

[Wattenberg Textbook, Government in America]

Wikipedia. "Tenth Amendment to the United States Constitution"; Available from http://en.wikipedia.org/wiki/Tenth_Amendment_to_the_United_States_Constitution. Internet, accessed 9 October 2005

Federalists and the Anti-Federalists
A Strong National Government
Or
Strong States

By
Margaret Lawrence

The year was 1787 and fifty-five delegates were gathered in the sweltering heat during a humid summer, in a state house located in Philadelphia, Pennsylvania. These men were responsible for creating a system of government that would last throughout time and keep the general welfare of the people in working condition. During the Constitutional Convention, controversies arose as to which way of governing would be the best. Should the state be governed by the people and the national government, the national government be between the state and people, or should the people and the national government work hand-in-hand with the state government? Division arose and, from the split, two political factions were formed: the Federalists and the Anti-Federalists. The Federalists included John Jay, Alexander Hamilton and James Madison who, along with many others, were in support of a strong national government and weaker state governments. The Anti-Federalists, including George Mason, Patrick Henry, and Richard Henry Lee, wanted strong state governments and a weak national government. However, in order to understand the philosophies behind the factions, one must take a closer look at the men responsible for the creation of the factions.

The men of both factions added tremendous political strengths to each of their respective points of view. James Madison was a man from Virginia, known today as the 'Father of the Constitution'[17] because his persuasive arguments helped to influence some Anti-Federalists to join the Federalist side. Madison is also known for his hard work and emergence as the House of Representatives leader.[18] Another major contribution of Madison was the Bill of Rights, which helped move many Anti-Federalists to ratify the Constitution because he had reassured them that the national government could not become too powerful and diminish the rights of the people.

Another Federalist was Alexander Hamilton, who was so strong in his belief in Federalism he had his own branch known as the Hamiltonians. Hamilton was unwavering in his fight to keep the central government alive and fought to remove crippling limitations on its powers.[19] Hamilton's philosophy "rested on the notion of the 'public good', the superiority of a government which got its power from the consent on the governed, and finally emphasis on an energetic government."[20] The third key Federalist was John Jay, author of five Federalist papers (numbers: two, three, four, five, and sixty-four). Jay would later become better known for the Jay Treaty, an agreement that Britain would leave the American ports alone and the British would pay retribution for damaging American ships during the war of Independence.

One of the key Anti-Federalists was George Mason, "the chief architect of the Virginia Declaration of Rights, a model for so many other states."[21] He was also responsible for some of the Anti-Federalist papers; in one, entitled "Objections to the Proposed Federal Constitution," Mason "continually spoke out in favor of the rights of individuals and the states as opposed to the federal government. He also spoke out strongly against a 10-mile-square Federal district that"[22] would become the District of Columbia. Patrick Henry, a man from Virginia, was another staunch Anti-Federalist. He was a strong critic of the Constitution and wanted the strongest possible government to be in the hands of the states, not in the national government. He feared that the federal government would usurp and abuse power and he demanded amendments to limit those powers[23]. Richard Henry Lee was another Anti-Federalist known for speaking out against the ratification of the Constitution. He was the author of the Anti-Federalist papers one to five and had helped frame the Declaration of Rights of the Colonies.[24] His Anti-Federalist papers were known was the Letters from the Federal Farmer.

The Anti-Federalists were adamant in their view that there should not be a strong national government because they feared that, if there were, then it would usurp the rights of the individual. The Ant-Federalists' political view was shaped by the "geographic, social, political isolation caused by poor communication and vastness of the new republic."[25] The Federalists were unyielding in their fight to have a strong national government because they feared that if America had a weak national government then the states would "encroach upon the rights of the Federal government or shake off the restraints laid upon them by the Constitution."[26]

Madison, Hamilton and Jay had one primary idea to attract the support of the American people in their fight for a federalist government. They wrote this in the Federalist Papers, eighty-five documents that listed numerous reasons why the American people should be in support of a strong national government and a weaker state government. The Federalist papers' "purpose was to provide supporters of the Constitution with a kind of handbook of argumentation they could use in debate."[27] The pen name for many of these papers was Publius, a Latin name which means common man. Perhaps, when the Federalists chose Publius as the surname for their papers they were trying to appeal to the "common folk," who would, in turn, vote for the ratification of the Constitution. They wrote these papers under assumed names and published them in numerous states. New York was the first to receive these papers since that state was gripped most strongly by the Anti-Federalists. The Federalists wanted to distribute their papers in the states that had the strongest opposition to federalism, including Virginia, Pennsylvania, and Massachusetts.

Meanwhile, the Anti-Federalists, Mason, Henry, and Richard Henry Lee, were also hard at work writing papers - these, however, in opposition to the Federalist position. These papers were also anonymously signed with Latin names, as well, such as Brutus, and Cato or Cato's Letters. Cato's Letters are Anti-Federalist papers numbers three, five, and seven. Brutus signed papers numbers one through sixteen. Perhaps, they chose the name Brutus because he was the one who killed Caesar and wanted to overthrow the Roman government. They wrote eighty-four documents and handed them out in various states, trying to convince the American people not to allow the Constitution to be ratified. The Anti-Federalists "rejected the Federalists' proposition that civic harmony could or would prevail at the national level or than a consensus upon a nation public good could be realized."[28]

However, these two political factions were more complex that a group of men handing out leaflets urging people to vote yea or nay on the ratification of the Constitution. Both parties had ideas on how to form and run the government and how the people should be represented. The Federalists believed that "uniting the states under a central government was necessary to prevent the states from fighting amongst themselves. They also believed that unity would provide the states with security against the ambitions of foreign governments."[29] On the other hand, the Anti-Federalists, summed up by Amos Singletary, "believed that a stronger state government and a more remote national government would inevitably increase the power of the aristocracy."[30] The Federalists and Anti-Federalists both had opinions on how the new executive branch would be operated and how much power that particular branch would receive. While debating the Constitution, these two parties battled it out to see which idea and political faction would win.

The Constitution had been written, and all that was left was to ratify it. In order to ratify the Constitution, nine out of the thirteen states were needed. Pennsylvania, Delaware, New Jersey, Georgia, Maryland, South Carolina, New Hampshire, and Connecticut had all passed the Constitution within their states. Massachusetts soon followed and ratified the Constitution on February 6, 1788. However, this did not mean that the Constitution was ratified. In order for the Constitution to be ratified, either Virginia or New York had to ratify it. Both New York and Virginia were torn between the Federalists and the Anti-Federalists and the success of the Constitution depended on either state ratifying it. Therefore, the Anti-Federalists and the Federalists worked feverishly to sway the people one way or another.

One question arose, how the people should be represented in the government. The Anti-Federalist believed that the people should have an equal representation, all Americans would have a say as to the inner-workings of the government. One Anti-Federalist stated "the essential parts of a free and good government are a full and equal representation of the people in the legislature...a full and equal representation."[31] Another Anti-Federalist thought it important that "there ought to be an increase of the number of representatives, and secondly the election of them ought to be more secured."[32] The Anti-Federalists also believed that the government would not work well if it only represented the population that lived in the hub of the country. So, they wondered what about the people who lived on the outskirts of the country? In order for the government to work well, all the people needed to have representation - both those who lived in the hub of the country and those who lived on the border of the wilderness. The Anti-Federalists believed that the House of Representation should be "properly increased in number; the elections shall remain free...and the elections of representatives be annual,"[33] assuring that the people of the United States would have an up-to-date representative.

The Federalists, on the other hand, believed that the House of Representation should not depend on the states. They thought that if the House of Representation were left to the states then the House "would have rendered too dependent on the State government that branch of the federal government which ought to be dependent on the people alone."[34] Madison believed that "the states must remain individually independent and sovereign; or two or more Confederacies must be formed among them."[35] The Federalists also sought to have a biennial election for the House of Representatives. They thought that having a biennial election would make the House of Representatives more dependent on the people and reflect the peoples' emotions better. The Federalists also felt that having a biennial election would benefit the people, stating that "with less power, therefore, the federal representatives can be less tempted on one side, and will be doubly watched on the other."[36]

If one were to have the states operating by themselves, yet under the same leader, it would be very easy for another country to come in and destroy what little 'union' they had. This was one major fear of the Federalists and one for which they fought, along with a strong national government. The Federalist knew that the states had separate laws, pertaining to different aspects of daily life. The Federalists wondered how to unite these different states, with their different laws, and make the House of Representatives work. They believed that having a biennial election for the representatives would make it easier to "judge the elections, qualifications, and returns of its members...for simplifying and accelerating the process in disputed cases, so great a portion of a year would unavoidably elapse, before an illegitimate member could be disposed of his seat."[37]

A second debate between the Federalists and the Anti-Federalists was on the topic of the judiciary branch. Such questions arose as to how the judiciary branch should run and how much power the judiciary should have. The judiciary was new to the colonists, and they were fearful of giving this new branch too much power. The Judiciary Act of 1789 set up the Judiciary branch, establishing three basic pillars that we have come to know today: the Supreme Court at the top of the scale with district courts for each state then in the Union at the bottom. There were two additional courts, one for Virginia and the other for Massachusetts. Finally, between them, there were three circuit courts consisting of "two Supreme Court Justices and a local district judge sitting together."[38]

The Federalists took the stand that the Judiciary should extend to all the laws in the United States, "secondly, to all those which concern the execution of the provisions expressly contained in the articles of the Union: thirdly, to all those which involve the peace of the confederacy, fourthly, to all those which originate on the high seas, and, lastly, to all those in which the state tribunals cannot be supposed to be impartial and unbiased."[39] They believed that the judiciary branch was vital because if there were not such an entity, the courts of the thirteen colonies would create contradictions and confusion. One can imagine the confusion that would arise when one state would pass laws on a particular subject while a neighboring state would refute it.

The Federalists believed that, once the judiciary was created, confusion on the courts would subside and order would prevail. This was to assure the common people, as well as themselves, that multiple courts weren't needed to operate a government. Another reason the Federalists believed that having a judiciary would be important was to limit the number of territorial quarrels between the states. The Federalists drew from past experiences to help support their stand on the judiciary branch. They also thought it necessary that the judges hold their offices in good tenure and that the courts be completely independent. The Federalists held the view that, because the judges were to be independent, they would protect the "Constitution and the rights of the individuals from the effects of ill humors in the society"[40] and serve as a balance to the legislative branch.

The Anti-Federalists viewed the judiciary in another light, altogether. They wrote five papers, all under the pen name Brutus, objecting that the judiciary branch should not have supreme power, arguing that this was unhealthy for the government. They felt that, without power over the judiciary, the mistakes of judges would not be corrected and that the judges' ruling would be final. They also felt that without power over the judiciary, that branch might become unruly and so independent that any form of legislature or law made to control or remove judges would fail. They felt that the judiciary was "(I)ndependent of the people, of the legislature, and of every power under heaven."[41]

Another Anti-Federalist objection to the proposed judiciary branch was that the judges could not be removed except for treason or high crimes. Bad judicial judgment would not be enough to remove a judge from the court, something the Anti-Federalists wholeheartedly opposed and thought should be changed. A third objection to the judiciary branch was that it had a power greater than that of the legislative branch. The judiciary was allowed to decide upon the meaning of the Constitution, the very source of power for the legislative branch. The Anti-Federalists feared that the judiciary would limit the power of the legislative branch and only allow the legislature certain powers. For instance, if the legislature were to pass a law considered unconstitutional by the judiciary, that law would become null and void. However, the Anti-Federalist did agree that the legislative, judicial, and executive branches should be made separate of each other and be accountable for their actions.

Anti-federalists still feared that the judiciary would become too powerful because there would not be any other power as a check. Another complaint the Anti-Federalists had with the judiciary branch was that the judiciary could come to a decision on a question pertaining to the fairness of the Constitutional laws, thinking that this would allow the government to explain the law based on the spirit on the law rather than the law itself. This, again, reflected a fear that the judiciary would have the utmost control because there would not be any outside power to correct their errors.

The Anti-Federalists also held the opinion that the men who held high positions would feel that they had a right to hand down their jobs to their successors or heirs as if they were royalty.

The Anti-Federalists and the Federalists also argued over the executive branch, including the presidency and vice presidency. It was crucial to the Anti-Federalists that the president not have too much power and diminish the rights of the people; yet, at the same time, it was critical that the president not be weak, allowing foreign states and countries to take advantage of his vulnerabilities.

Federalist 67 stated that the President should have the right to nominate judges to the Supreme Court, ambassadors, other public ministers, and all other officials whose positions were not stated in the Constitution.[42] If a vacancy were to arise in the Supreme Court, the Federalists felt that the President of the United States should have the power to fill that vacancy while the Senate was adjourned. The Federalists believed this was a good idea because it allowed the president to appoint officers in a way that would complement his other appointments, chose appropriate persons and to make the length of the appointment consistent with the Senate's term, thus, allowing the Senate to choose a permanent person to fill the seat. Allowing the president to make a temporary appointment until the next meeting of the legislature is "an express power given, in clear and unambiguous terms, to the State Executive, to fill casual vacancies in the Senate by temporary appointment."[43]

The Anti-Federalists, however, saw this in another light. They felt that the very concept of the executive branch was not a very good idea. They believed that the executive branch, with its rules and regulations for electing a president and vice president, would lead to danger if the president stayed longer than one year. They felt that Article two, section One of the Constitution was too vague, leaving the election of the president and the vice president to be left wide open. The Anti-Federalists were frightened that the new executive branch would become too powerful and would, in turn, lead the new executive to seek even greater powers for himself.[44]

The Anti-Federalists also believed that the president would be unsupported when the Senate went to recess, making the President vulnerable because he would be lacking the advice and counsel he would normally receive from the Senate. The Anti-Federalists also felt very strongly that there should not even be a vice president. They felt that having a vice president would compromise the senate, "thereby blending the executive and legislative powers," which was considered very dangerous. If there were to be a blending of the two branches, the vice presidency would be dangerous to the people's rights. The Anti-Federalists warned the American people about the executive branch saying "beware that the advocates of this new system do not deceive you by a fallacious resemblance between it and you own state government, which you so much prize."[45]

The final debate involved the Senate itself. The Federalists thought that it was important that a Senator be thirty years of age and have been a citizen for nine years. The senators, the Federalists felt, should have equal representation because in a "compound republic, partaking of both the national and federal character, the government ought to be formed on a mixture of the principle of proportional and equal representation."[46]

The Federalists recognized the "portions of sovereignty remaining in the individual state"[47] and felt that having a Senate would help to protect the government from the "emotionalism" of the representatives in the House.

Any law, then, to be passed, would have to go through the House of Representatives, on behalf of the people, and then the Senate, representing the states. The Federalists acknowledged that this method of legislation could, at times, have both positive and negative results but that, overall, was more helpful than harmful. They wanted the senate to act as another branch of the legislative assembly when a problem arose, acting as a check and balance within the legislative branch on the power of the House.

The Federalists wanted a senate that would not "yield to the impulse of sudden and violent passion, and to be seduced by factious leaders into intemperate and pernicious resolutions."[48] Finally, the Federalists wanted the senate membership to change little over the years to allow for new ideas.

The Anti-Federalists agreed that the senate should be "the apportionment of members of the Senate among the States not according to numbers, or the importance of the States."[49] They were, however, displeased that they could not add other principles that would allow the states to have more power secured to them within the government.

The first objection that the Anti-Federalists had to the senate was the duration of the senatorial term, thinking that, as proposed, it was too long and that the very creation of the senate reflected representation for the aristocracy. The Anti-Federalists also feared that if the men in the senate stayed too long, they would forget what made them who they were. The Anti-Federalists also believed that the men should "remain some time in office to acquire"[50] experience but that if they stayed too long they would think of themselves as above all others and more important than the ones who appointed them. This echoes the Anti-Federalists' fear of one person or entity having too much power over a particular person or group. A four-year term was more than enough in the Anti-Federalists view. The Anti-Federalists believed that "a rotation of the senate...would be of great use."[51] This would make sure that the men staying in the seat would not become too comfortable and try to "influence their friends into staying in office."[52]

The Federalists and Anti-Federalists each had many important views and opinions relative to the Constitution. Each faction had a view on each branch and expressed it forcefully throughout the debate over the ratification of the Constitution. And, while Hamilton, Jay, and Madison could justifiably feel a sense of pride that the Constitution was adopted and their faction's beliefs had overcome those of the Anti-Federalists, one must acknowledge that the battle continues to the present day in Congress and elsewhere in the United States.

Bibliography

Faber, Doris and Harold. <u>The Early Years of the United States The Birth of a Nation</u>. Charles Scribner's Sons, New York. 1989

Finseth, Ian. <u>The Rise and Fall of Alexander Hamilton.</u> <http://xroads.virginia.edu/~CAP/ham/hampltcs.html#2>

Haskins, Robert Bryan . <http://home.earthlink.net/~haskman/history.htm#VI>

Hamilton, Alexander. Federalist No. 52, 67, and 80.

Madison, James. Federalist No. 52

Meyers, Marvin. <u>The Mind of the Founder Sourced of Political Thought of James Madison.</u> University Press of New England. 1973

Miller, John C. <u>The Federalist Era.</u> Harper and Row Publishers. 1960

Morris, Richard M. <u>Witnesses at the Creation Hamilton, Madison, Jay, and the Constitution.</u> Holt, Rinehart, and Winston New York. 1985

Sharp, James Roger. <u>The New Nation Crisis American Politics in the Early Republic.</u> Yale University Press. 1993

Storing, Herbert J. <u>The Anti-Federalist Writings by the Opponents of the Constitution.</u> University of Chicago Press. 1981

<www.odur.let.rug.nl/usa/B/gmason/gmas05.htm> 11/3/05

<www.lexrex.com/bios/phenry.htm> 11/3/05

<www.stradfordhall.org/richard.html?HISTORY> 11/3/05

Two Antagonists

Alexander Hamilton

"Federalist Extraordinaire"
By
Vincent Genuario

Alexander Hamilton was one of the great men of the eighteenth century and, by far, one of the great Founding Fathers of the United States. Both his wisdom and impact on this country live on to this day, reflecting his powerful impact on our Constitution and on this nation's first president.

Hamilton was born in 1755 on the island of Nevis, part of the British West Indies. He was the illegitimate son of a poor merchant who moved the family to what is now the Virgin Islands and, shortly after, deserted his wife and two sons. This, however, would not hold Hamilton back. His mother and a Presbyterian clergyman were responsible for providing Hamilton with a basic education.

At about the age of 12, Alexander's mother died, forcing him to get a job. In order to support himself, Hamilton became an apprentice clerk at Christiansted at a mercantile. His apprenticeship there gave him great skill and experience with commerce, a skill that would later come in handy as Secretary of the Treasury. Even as a young boy, Hamilton was noticed for being very intelligent. He excelled as an apprentice and, at age 15, was already the manager at a trading house. In his free time he would write. While the manager at a trading house, his piece about a hurricane that had just passed through the area was so good it was published by the local newspaper, The Royal Danish American Gazette. A proprietor recognized his intelligence and ambition and funded an education for Hamilton.

In 1772, Hamilton traveled to New York City and attended Barber's Academy while staying at the home of William Livingston, another supporter of Hamilton's education. In 1773, Hamilton transferred to King's College, which would later be renamed Columbia University. Hamilton loved it there. The American Revolution, however, interrupted his studies and success in college.

During college, Hamilton was part of a cadet group and yearned for war to break out. As soon as it did, he joined the army and first saw action at Trenton as a captain of an artillery regiment. His courage and intellect were noted and, through some connections, Hamilton was able to work his way into General George Washington's Army. He was appointed as an aide for General Washington, who was not very confident in his own abilities to thoroughly explain himself in his letters. He, therefore, needed someone who possessed that ability. Hamilton was perfect for the job and was to be Washington's secretary and letter writer.[53]

Hamilton was given the rank of lieutenant colonel. He was very useful to Washington because he possessed the ability to listen to what Washington wanted to say and turn it into a series of letters exactly the way Washington wanted it. He served in the military for four years, during which time he was able to distinguish himself, made important contacts and developed a good reputation that would later help him emerge as a fine public man. However, he grew very tired of his job for Washington, wanted to see real action and dreamed of the battlefield and glory. His wish was granted during Washington's campaign at Valley Forge, but Hamilton wanted more, and constantly bothered Washington to transfer him to fight. Hamilton was too valuable and Washington was always able to talk him out of it. Finally, the two got into an argument and Hamilton announced his resignation.

After his resignation, he went back to New York and practiced law. Throughout this time, Hamilton pushed to be accepted back in the war effort, as a colonel of his own regiment. His wish came true just in time for the end of the war. He was moved to the Continental Lines and earned his glory at Yorktown against Cornwallis' army.

After the war, Hamilton went back to New York to practice law. That same year, he was elected as a delegate to Congress. He read the law, managed to write his own manual for legal studies and, after a sufficient amount of time and experience, Hamilton was admitted to the New York bar. He did, however, grow tired of simply practicing law and wanted to move up in the world as a public man.

In 1786, Hamilton won election in New York as a representative, a major step in his political career giving him power to make a difference. With the help of James Madison and John Dickinson, the three sought to assemble their colleagues at a convention to form a new Constitution that would unify the states. After the outbreak of Shay's Rebellion, politicians began to agree that there needed to be a more unified country with a new Constitution.

Many well-known politicians of the day attended the convention - Thomas Jefferson, Patrick Henry, and George Washington. Hamilton and Jefferson were completely opposite people, not only in terms of ideology but also in their personalities. Hamilton was a crisp little man, while Jefferson was much taller and very lean. Hamilton was much more outspoken and was known for giving his opinion on everything even when it was not wanted. Jefferson, on the other hand, was much more quiet. The two did not like each other and got into many debates. They did, however, respect each other and, to many people's surprise, Hamilton would later support Jefferson for President. Politically, Jefferson was much more Anti-Federalist while Hamilton was a firm Federalist. Unlike Jefferson, Hamilton would not be of much influence during the convention. This was not the case later during the ratification process.

During the convention, Hamilton had great difficulty making an impact with his vote since two delegates at the convention from his state, John Lansing and Robert Yates, almost always neutralized—by one voting against and one not voting—or cancelled out Hamilton's vote. Frustrated, Hamilton did not speak very often and returned to New York often to take care of personal business. On June 29, Hamilton left the convention but later returned to Philadelphia to resume work until the Constitution was signed. Hamilton came often enough to get many of his views heard and on record, much of which assisted other Federalists get their views across and their points made.

On June 18, Hamilton delivered a five-hour-speech to the convention in which he stated his support for a strong national government. He said he believed that men do not honor authority and, therefore, must be led by the national government. He held the British military and its strong economy in highest regard and agreed with pretty much everything about the English Constitution, calling it "the best of the world." He was often called monarchical and, while he admitted that his policies turned a little towards a monarchy, he completely supported independence from Britain.

In his speech, he supported the idea that there should be a senate to act in place of the House of Lords of England. He argued that the President should serve a life term because it would replicate the greatness in the English Constitution. However, he completely disagreed with any election process of the President that did not involve the people. Hamilton believed extreme governments were the worst, whether an extreme monarchy and an extreme democracy.

In his speech, Hamilton wanted to get his fellow framers in the mindset of the importance in "stability and permanency" for a government. He vocalized his belief that in order to gain the respect of foreign powers, a government needed both if it were to survive.

Hamilton believed that the major division in the country was between the North and South, not large and small states. He wanted states to be reduced to administrative districts, with the national government having a veto over legislation in the states. He also wanted the national government having power to create state courts. He did not expect most at the convention to agree with his ideas; but he would have been pleased if he were able to get them to consider his side. William Samuel Johnson of Connecticut later said that everyone praised Hamilton's speech but no one supported him.

In the end, a Constitution was produced that reflected all of the time, effort, and brilliance of the framers and, actually, much of Hamilton's philosophy. It clearly gave the central government much more power than state governments. Hamilton was, however, disappointed with the compromised Constitution, feeling it incorporated few of his ideas and was too democratic. Yet, believing that rejection of the Constitution would lead to civil war, he supported adoption of the document. He also believed he had found a wonderful loophole in the "necessary and proper clause." It was with this clause that Hamilton felt the very strong central government would have more power. However, the first act following the proposed Constitution was to get it ratified.

Ratification was no easy task and Hamilton had to work very hard to get the Constitution ratified. New York was a pivotal state and, in order for it to vote for the Constitution, the people needed some persuasion. Hamilton organized and led a campaign for the ratification in New York, constantly arguing with the political leadership of the state who opposed ratification. He argued quite a bit, particularly, with the governor of New York at the time, George Clinton. Clinton, along with other leaders of New York, proved to be very influential. The odds for a while were very much against Hamilton and the Constitution. The people needed to be persuaded to support the Constitution and Hamilton would collaborate with James Madison and John Jay to write the *Federalist* papers. [54]

The *"Federalists"* were a series of essays written by Hamilton, Madison, and Jay. About two - thirds of the essays were written by Hamilton under a pseudonym to persuade people to read his side of the argument, become much more aware of the issues involved and ratify the Constitution.

In *Federalist 9*, Hamilton argued against splitting the country up into many little commonwealths. In *Federalist 80*, Hamilton supported the idea of federal courts having authority over state statutes. In Federalist no. 81, Hamilton supported the separation of powers. Throughout the essays, Hamilton constantly defended the rich and powerful.

In *Federalist 72*, Hamilton argued there should be no limit on the number of terms a president could serve. He argued that the president would gain wisdom in serving his country. The *Federalist* papers would become a major factor in support of the new Constitution. Things went smoothly for awhile and then there was a crisis. In order for the Constitution to be passed, a compromise was struck, satisfying people who feared the central government would have too much power and demanding that citizens could fall back on their rights. It was due to this concern that the Bill of Rights was introduced and the ability to amend the Constitution made possible. After that compromise, the Constitution was ratified, laying out the provisions for the new government.

Now, a president would need to be put into office. [55] George Washington was appointed the first President of the United States and it was up to him to choose the members of his cabinet. From the end of the Revolutionary War to Washington's inauguration, Hamilton had become increasingly involved in politics. However, nobody ever thought Hamilton would be on Washington's list for cabinet members. Washington knew Hamilton's intellect and ability. Hamilton was a financial master and perfect for Secretary of Treasury to which he was appointed in 1789. Washington would also appoint Thomas Jefferson as his Secretary of State. This would prove to be a very interesting combination because Hamilton and Jefferson were complete opposites ideologically. Jefferson was part of the Republican Party and was opposed to Hamilton's Federalist beliefs.

Immediately after Hamilton was appointed Treasury Secretary, he got right to work. The country was still new and needed leadership to get it on its feet. Hamilton dreamed of an American empire that would prosper with the help of an energetic government. As Treasury Secretary, Hamilton proposed a national bank, supported a pro-business economic program and took steps to strengthen the new national government. These were not his only contributions, but they were among his greatest.

The country was millions of dollars in debt due to the Revolutionary War and the Articles of Confederation were not able to solve this problem. Many people overlooked the nation's debt and did not believe it to be too great. Hamilton completely disagreed and knew that, in order to gain any credit and become a world power, the United States would have to eliminate this debt. His first steps as Secretary of the Treasury were to pay back all of the debt that the country owed. Hamilton wanted to have the central government pay the debts of all the states.

Hamilton was a supporter of a pro-business society and wanted to have a very prosperous economy. He came up with a program for the country to become a prosperous economic world power and first proposed a national bank, an ingenious idea to pay back the national debt. It set a precedent for a capitalist society that prospered due to business. Hamilton also set up a system of taxation to help pay off the national debt. The ultimate purpose of the bank and the tax system was to strengthen the central government.

One of the Hamiltonian beliefs was that it is the duty of the federal government is to promote a multi-industrial capitalist economy and promote the births of new types of industry. Hamilton wrote in <u>The Report of Manufactures</u>, "Capital is wayward and timid in lending itself to new undertakings, and the State ought to excite the confidence of capitalists, who are ever cautious and sagacious, by aiding them to overcome the obstacles that lie in the way of all experiments."

Hamilton's program for the country favored the wealthy class. He was one of the first believers in the "trickle down doctrine," give to the rich and everyone will get their share. He did, however, admit to hating rich men. His capitalist beliefs were below his nationalist beliefs. He intended to have the federal government diversify the economy by developing commerce and industry.

Hamilton wanted a free economy but he also wanted the national government to promote entrepreneurs to invest and benefit the national welfare. The way he did it was clever, and it worked. He believed in using bounties, premiums, moderately protective tariffs, and other aids for entrepreneurs and new industries to develop industry. There would be federal inspections of domestic manufactured goods to protect consumers, which would enhance the reputation of American goods in foreign markets.

After studying Adam Smith's <u>The Wealth of Nations</u>, Hamilton believed that manufacturing was more important than agriculture. Agriculture was important but the country that manufactured most of its own products had an advantage. He believed free trade was good, but it was better for the country not to be dependent on foreign countries for anything, mainly weapons of war. He believed it was good for the government to protect new American industries and promote them until they were at the same level as foreign industries.

The ultimate goal was to strengthen the Union of the United States by making the United States "one nation, indivisible, bound together by common wants, common interests, and common prosperity," said Hamilton. As the Secretary of the Treasury for Washington, Hamilton took steps to strengthen the federal government.

He believed that conflict between states and nations was inevitable. He believed neighboring countries were "natural enemies." Hamilton believed the national government should have military forces strong enough for foreign affairs and domestic disputes. He believed that the success of a government depended on strong executive and judicial branches but his ambitious plan still had to pass the Congress. [56]

Jefferson and Hamilton met one day to discuss a deal. James Madison came to this meeting, opposed to Hamilton's strong central government and thinking Hamilton's refunding plan was poorly constructed. Madison believed the poor man would suffer from Alexander's plan and did not believe the "trickle down doctrine" would work. Jefferson did not agree with Hamilton's plan either but Hamilton needed his support.

Hamilton knew he would be able to get northern votes for his plan but, for it to pass, he would need some southern votes. Jefferson was very influential when it came to southern Congressmen. If Hamilton could get Jefferson's support, then he knew he would gain the votes necessary to get his plan passed. The two decided to strike a deal.

Jefferson knew a few southern congressmen who, if he told them to, would vote for Hamilton's plan. The deal was that if Jefferson got those southern votes for Hamilton, Hamilton would agree to have the capital of the United States moved to the Potomac River. Both men agreed and Hamilton's refunding plan passed through Congress. Later, Jefferson would complain that it was an unfair trade.

Throughout his term as Secretary of the Treasury, the Republicans in Congress tried hard to drive Hamilton out of his position. Finally, in 1795, Hamilton left his position. Politics wasn't out of his life as he continued to write many pieces on important issues of the day and even drafted George Washington's Farewell Address (1796) at the end of Washington's last term as President. Hamilton did not support John Adams during his re-election of 1800 even though Adams was a fellow Federalist. Instead he supported his long time rival, Thomas Jefferson. [57]

Hamilton spoke very poorly of Aaron Burr's candidacy for President although Burr, too, was a Federalist. Enraged by such attacks on him, Burr challenged Hamilton to a duel. The duel took place on July 13, 1804, and Hamilton died of his wounds the next day. His death was an atrocity and very untimely, impacting many people who respected him and followed him. The Federalist Party would fall a few years after Hamilton's death and many of the Hamiltonian beliefs began to dwindle. A few people such as John Quincy Adams, Daniel Webster, and Henry Clay kept his dreams and ideas alive but his beliefs lost influence gradually until the end of the Civil War, when the federal government was strengthened once again. Hamilton was a great model to both conservatives and liberals. His ideas and actions during his lifetime have affected many great people over the years. Among the great people impacted by Hamilton's beliefs and ideas was George Washington. When Hamilton drafted Washington's Farewell Address, the composition was a collaboration of ideas between the two. In the speech, there was a warning to stay out of European Wars. Isolationists in the twentieth century used the address as the authority for the U.S. to stay out of World War I as well as World War II. What these contemporary isolationists did not take into account, though, was why Hamilton and Washington supported that belief. They supported it, not because they believed in appeasement, but because of the time and what was going on in the new country. Washington and Hamilton knew the U.S. republic was very weak and in great debt, completely incapable of entering a war between England and France. The country just could not afford it.

Washington and Hamilton had a great relationship and each impacted the other in some way. Washington's army during the war and presidency would have been completely different without Hamilton. Later, another president would emerge as a dominant follower of Hamiltonian beliefs - Abraham Lincoln. [58]

Lincoln was one of the largest figures in the Hamiltonian tradition. While Lincoln is known as the "Great Emancipator," his greater goal was to preserve the Union. This is a belief that he shared with Hamilton. He believed his task as president was to preserve the Union and help his republican cabinet members enact Hamilton's economic procedure.

In Lincoln's anti-slavery and pro-Union speeches it appears as though Lincoln was using Jeffersonian rhetoric. Lincoln uses the quote: "All men are created equal," which comes from Jefferson in the Declaration of Independence. This was, however, a political move in order to gain Democratic Jeffersonian votes in the South. With just that sentence, Lincoln could pretend that he was making an addition to Jefferson's belief in human equality. Therefore, he could be seen with some of Jefferson's beliefs that almost the entire south was set on. The truth was that Lincoln did not agree at all with states' rights, agrarianism, or strict construction of the federal constitution. Lincoln was the Great Nationalist.

Lincoln and Hamilton were in the same boat as far as preserving the Union. Both were in danger of a civil war. Lincoln's Civil War happened, while a Civil War was dodged during Hamilton's time. But, both were able to save the Union. Lincoln's Union won the war, while Hamilton helped get a Constitution ratified that the majority of the country approved. Lincoln agreed with Hamilton's belief of a strong national military and a dominant industrial society. Lincoln was able to put the nation on the road to being dominant in industry and having a powerful military for the twentieth century. Lincoln used arguments from Hamilton and Washington to save the Union.

Before the Civil War began, President Lincoln delivered his speech, "The Myth of State Sovereignty," to Congress July 4, 1861. In his speech, he argued the Constitution has yet to change and the states have the same powers they did since the Constitution was ratified. "The states have their legal status in the Union, and they have no other legal status," Lincoln said. He argued that seceding from the Union was against the law and would result in revolution. He argued that the Union and not the individual states produced their independence and their liberty. The Southern states, obviously, did not agree with Lincoln. However, his speech still held relevance and was an outstanding example of the Hamiltonian belief in a strong central government. Later, another one of our great presidents would emerge and bring with him Hamiltonian beliefs - Theodore Roosevelt. [59]

Theodore Roosevelt was a philosopher statesman of American Democratic Nationalism. Teddy's "Square Deal" passed the Food and Drug Act, interstate commerce reform, and conservationist steps that included preserving national parks. During his presidency, Teddy grew concerned about the national unity due to mass immigration where classes separated. His concern for the national unity was something both he and Hamilton had in common.

Theodore Roosevelt is, however, most famous for his speech, "The Big Stick." His "The Big Stick" speech was given on September 2, 1901. In this speech, he delivered the famous line for which he best known, "speak softly and carry a big stick." He went on to say that anyone who "blusters" and "lacks civility" will need to back up their words. And, if they cannot back up their words, then they must stay quiet. However, neither of the two types of people can ever be efficient.

The purpose of the speech was to make clear to the American people and to foreign nations that the U.S. meant to do justice and that anything the U.S. says it is going to do will be backed up. He also meant to make it clear that any injustice done to the U.S. would not be tolerated. However, the U.S. will stay moderate. Roosevelt went on to say that this is the attitude of a self-governing people. The speech relates to Hamilton because Roosevelt believed the U.S. should stay moderate. Hamilton was a firm believer in moderate governments as the most efficient. Roosevelt also shared the Hamiltonian belief in strengthening the national government in order to contend with foreign governments.

There was also a Supreme Court Case that ended up ruling in favor of Hamilton's beliefs. [60]In 1819 the case of *McCulloch v. Maryland* went to the Supreme Court. The issue was whether the state of Maryland could tax the national bank. The bank's cashier, James McCulloch, refused to pay and the issue went all the way to the Supreme Court.

John Marshall ruled in favor of the national bank, citing the implied powers of the national government along with the "necessary and proper" clause of the Constitution. During the court case, Marshall quoted Hamilton and said. "Necessary and proper should be broadly construed to mean not indispensable, but appropriate." The implied powers, given to the federal government, were the loophole Hamilton had found. Looking back, it is evident that the U.S. could not have developed into such a complex and great society without the doctrine of implied powers. It is what made the federal government supreme to state governments. It made it possible for this country to be much more efficient and have a unified country. [61]

Looking back, it is evident that Alexander Hamilton has affected our country to this day. Hamilton was extremely intelligent with an extraordinary ability to write. He was born a bastard to a poor family outside of this country. His intellect and ability to write was noticed at a young age. He was given the opportunity to travel to this country for an education. He made political connections and fought in the American Revolution as an officer for George Washington. Washington admired him and could count on him for good advice. After the war, Hamilton was part of the Constitutional Convention. His contributions included organizing and shaping the Constitution, leading the fight to get the Constitution ratified and, after its ratification, developing a national economic plan for the new nation. Hamilton transformed the government into a much more energetic entity that promoted a capitalist society full of entrepreneurs and prosperous industries, ensuring the credit necessary to become a world power. The spirit of the Hamiltonian beliefs lived on through some of our greatest presidents to this day, including Washington, Lincoln, and Theodore Roosevelt. Hamilton was an amazing politician and person from whom we all can learn.

George Mason

Hero
To The
Anti-Federalists

By

Margaret Bradley

By simply signing the Constitution, George Mason could have projected himself to the level of other Founding Fathers, such as his friends George Washington and Thomas Jefferson who both went on to become president. Yet, his act of not signing was a protest against a Constitution he felt gave the national government too much power and the people too little. The impact of his protest is still being felt today and is greater than any impact he could have made if he had been elected president.

George Mason was a man who valued human rights above all else. He "had been the leading figure in the convention which had prepared Virginia's founding documents at Williamsburg in May and June of 1776."[62] It was there he wrote Virginia's Declaration of Rights in 1776. Virginia was the first state to draft a Bill of Rights, and it quickly became a blueprint for Thomas Jefferson's Declaration of Independence and other bills of rights. It even became a blueprint for the nation's own bill of rights.[63] He was very concerned with preserving the individual rights and liberties of citizens, which is apparent in the Virginia Declaration of Rights. "All men are born equally free and independent,"[64] and, "certain inherent natural rights, of which they cannot, by any compact deprive or divest their posterity,"[65] are just two excerpts that emphasize the importance of individual rights. Both ideas were repeated in Jefferson's Declaration of Independence.

George Mason was both "influential and highly respected in the public affairs of Virginia."[66] He was a private man, but his talents did not go unnoticed by his peers. He was chosen to be a delegate at the Annapolis Convention in 1786 but was too ill to serve. He was, however, able to serve as a delegate at the Philadelphia Convention.[67]

From May 29 to September 17, 1787, he met with the other delegates to write the Constitution. He was one of the few delegates who were able to attend every single meeting.[68] It is apparent Mason was dedicated to his work, but he did not go to Philadelphia without hesitation.

"It is easy to foresee that there will be much difficulty in organizing a government upon this great scale, and at the same time reserving to the state legislatures a sufficient portion of power for promoting and securing the prosperity and happiness of their respective citizens. Yet, with a proper degree of coolness, liberality, and candor I doubt not but that it can be effected." [69]

He took his position as a delegate seriously and knew it would be a challenge. He did not go into the Constitutional Convention with a plan not to sign the finished document; he went with a plan to stick up for what he believed was right because he knew it was going to be a challenge. It was this dedication to his cause and his strong belief in individual rights that made him so highly respected by his peers. He seemed to be aware of the influence the new Constitution would have and is quoted as having said, "The happiness or misery of millions unborn," was weighted upon their decisions at the convention.[70]

Throughout the convention, Mason was very vocal; he gave at least a hundred and thirty-six passionate speeches in the five short months he was there.[71] He made several objections to the proposed Constitution, most of them being based on basic human rights. Along with his objections, Mason made three major proposals: that a Bill of Rights be added, that slavery be ended and that a two-thirds majority be needed in Congress to pass navigation acts.[72] Unfortunately, none of these proposals was passed, but all are examples that George Mason was a man who stuck to his beliefs and fought for them.

Mason proposed an end be put to slavery because he was morally opposed to it, although he did own several hundred slaves who worked at his home, Gunston Hall Plantation.[73] He objected not only for moral reasons; he believed slaves took jobs away from white immigrants who wanted to be in America and were willing to contribute to the nation.[74] Mason objected to putting something so morally incorrect and on its way out (he knew slavery would not last much longer) in a document as important and final as the United States' Constitution.[75] He lashed out at the convention when the three-fifths compromise, under which each slave would count as three-fifths of a person when it came to counting population for representation in the lower house, was mentioned. He went against his own southern, slave holding state on this issue and sided with the northern states. The idea of counting slaves as only three-fifths of a person went against Mason's idea of all men being created equal, which he wrote in Virginia's Declaration of Rights. In Mason's mind, slavery should only be mentioned in the Constitution if it were in the context of giving the federal government power to limit its increase.[76]

Mason may have disagreed with many from his state, and from the south in general, when it came to the issues of slavery and the three-fifths compromise, but he fought to make sure the northern states were not given an unfair advantage over the southern states in either house of Congress. Along with other delegates, Mason argued a two-thirds majority was needed in Congress rather then a simple majority. James Madison summed up this argument in his example that showed, conceivably, eighteen members from just Virginia and Pennsylvania alone could pick the next president since they would comprise a simple majority.[77] Mason's fear was that sectional interests would control Congress, so in order to protect his own southern state he wanted, at the least, a two-thirds majority required for navigation and trade laws. It worried him that a simple northern majority in Congress would regulate trade and jeopardize the southern economy.[78] If two-thirds majority were not required then a few rich merchants in the northern cities such as New York and Boston would be able to monopolize a few southern agricultural staples and reduce their value.[79] Or the North would continue to grow as a commercial and manufacturing center and taxes would be put in place that would destroy the Southern economy.[80]

Giving one person too much power concerned Mason. He believed the majority of the power should fall in the hands of the people, and giving too much power to one person, the president, would result in another monarchy. "He considered an Executive during good behavior as a softer name only for an Executive for life.

And that the next would be an easy step to hereditary Monarchy."[81] There was no constitutional council, or group of advisors set up so the President could very easily become "a tool to the Senate."[82] To fix this, there should be a six person council set up in order to advise the President. The group would represent the whole country: two from the south, two from the north, and two from the east.[83] This is very similar to the President's cabinet today, except the group of advisors that Mason proposed was to be selected by the Senate rather than the President. Mason was hesitant to give the President too much power since it, in turn, took power away from the people. He disagreed with giving the power to grant pardons for treason to the President because he worried this would allow the President to hire someone to commit a crime for him and then pardon them. The power to declare war was another presidential power that he opposed. He once again felt this was too much power to grant to one person but his objections went unnoticed. He was, however, able to get the number of votes needed to override a presidential veto lowered from three-fourths to two-thirds.[84] This was a major accomplishment because it took some power away from the president and set up more checks and balances in the government.

As much as Mason was opposed to allowing the president to have power he was even more opposed to allowing the Senate to have power. Mason objected to the whole idea of the Senate. He found it unfair to the people that the house that they did not elect, the house that was appointed by other leaders, was the house with the most power. He felt the majority of the power should be placed in the House of Representatives since the people directly elected them.[85] The Senate should not have power to control money because money would allow them to gain too much power and influence and "should the latter (the Senate) have the power of giving away the people's money, they might soon forget the source from when they received it. We might soon have an aristocracy."[86] He also argued having an unelected group just sitting for so long would "destroy any balance in the Government."[87] Having the Vice President serve as the president of the Senate linked the legislature and executive branches too closely and once again destroyed the balance in the government.

The biggest objection and the largest proposal Mason made at the Philadelphia Convention was that there swas no Bill of Rights and one should be added. Mason had written Virginia's own Declaration of Rights and it was important to him that citizens' individual rights were protected by the national government. He brought this up several times at the convention but each time he was told that since each state had its own bill of rights a national bill of rights was not needed.[88] Mason argued back that since the federal government was to be supreme, a state bill of rights would do the citizens no good.[89] His arguments went ignored, so on September 12, 1787, near the end of the convention, Mason and Elbridge Gerry from Massachusetts proposed that a committee be set up to draft a bill of rights.[90] Mason pleaded that it would take less then two hours for the committee to draft a bill of rights since they could just base it on the states' various bills of rights but their proposal was shot down unanimously.[91] Gerry's fellow delegates from Massachusetts abstained from voting out of respect for Gerry but all the delegates from Virginia voted down Mason's proposal for a bill of rights.[92]

Following the rejection of their proposal for a bill of rights, Mason and Gerry fought for another Constitutional Convention. "This Constitution has been formed without the knowledge or idea of the people. A second convention will know more of the sense of the people, and be able to provide a system more consonant to it."[93] They believed that the states should look at the Constitution as it stood then, make any suggestions or complaints, and then the convention could meet again to revise the Constitution and take into consideration these suggestions. Edmund Randolph, also of Virginia, made this proposal to the convention on September 15 but it too was shot down.[94] Gerry and Mason refused to sign the Constitution. Fifty-five men in all contributed to the United States Constitution but only thirty-three signed it. Few representatives attended every meeting, thirty-six attended the signing and of the thirty- six only three men refused to sign: they were Elbridge Gerry, Edmund Randolph, and George Mason. Mason was the only person who had shown up to every meeting of the convention yet refused to sign.[95]

Following the convention, when he returned home to Virginia, Mason's fight against the Constitution was far from over. He found when he returned many of his fellow statesmen had labeled him an anti-federalist and an ex-patriot because of his refusal to sign the Constitution. Mason argued back that, "in this important trust, I am truly conscious of having acted from the purest motives of honesty, and love to my country, according to that measure of judgment which God has bestowed on me, and I would not forfeit the approbation of my own mind for the approbation of any man, or all the men upon earth."[96] He may have gone against popular federalist beliefs but he did what he truly believed was right.   Mason was determined to be a member of the Virginia ratifying convention; he was able to get nominated for a seat by Stafford County, which was known for having fewer federalists then the rest of Virginia.[97] At the ratifying convention, Mason had hoped he would have the support of fellow Virginian and fellow non-signer, Edmund Randolph. Randolph had supported Mason at the Philadelphia convention but things were not the same at the ratifying convention. Randolph believed he had to sign the Constitution at the Virginia convention because Virginia was the largest state and was home to the strongest leaders, and he believed without Virginia's support the Constitution would fail.[98] Virginia ended up ratifying the Constitution, once again without Mason's signature.[99]

Mason returned home to Gunston Hall disappointed. His "primary concerns about government, both Virginia's and the new nation's, were aimed at preserving the rights and liberties of individuals above all else. While he wanted a strong nation, he feared giving the government too much power."[100] He had fought so hard to protect the individual rights and liberties of the citizens. He had served his country so well, showing up to every meeting at the convention, making hundreds of speeches. He had fought so many times for what he believed was right. Through his passionate proposals to add a bill of rights, another convention would be held so the citizens could have a say in their government. He flat out refused to give too much power to one branch or have slavery supported by the national government. Mason was an idealist; he felt if they were going to be given the opportunity to create their own government from scratch, they should make it perfect. He did not believe it could be done in such a short amount of time, the convention only lasted five short months. Creating a Constitution that was going to govern generations and generations of people in just five months time left a lot of room for mistakes, and Mason realized this. That is why he pushed for a second Philadelphia convention. They needed time to let the Constitution sit, to think it over, to let others examine it and give their opinion. Mason entered the convention with knowledge of the impact of their actions; he knew the Constitution they were writing was going to govern the country for centuries.

Though he showed much determination and dedication at the convention, Mason was unable to get his three main proposals passed. He had proposed that a bill of rights be added, a two-thirds majority be required to pass navigation acts in Congress and, finally, that an end be put to slavery. All three upheld Mason's dedication to individual rights and liberties of citizens. He proposed the bill of rights in order to protect those individual rights and liberties of the citizens. The two-thirds majority was proposed in order to protect the southern economy and the finances of the southern people. And the proposal to end slavery was, of course, to protect the rights and liberties of an oppressed group of citizens. Mason pushed these proposals in both the Philadelphia Convention and once again in the Virginia Ratifying Convention yet, despite his best efforts, Mason failed both times.

Although Mason was unable to get a bill of rights added on his own, his protest had caused uproar among many citizens. Following the ratification of the Constitution a series of papers were written entitled the Federalist and the Anti-Federalist papers.[101] The Federalist papers argued if they added a bill of rights they would forget some rights and it was ridiculous to have to list inherent rights, while the Anti-Federalist papers argued that it was a necessary part of the government in order to protect the citizens' individual rights.[102] Along with the Anti-Federalists, Mason had also gained the support of several states. Although all the states ratified the Constitution, five states (South Carolina, Massachusetts, New Hampshire, Virginia, and New York) included suggestions that a bill of rights be added.[103] The support did not stop there. James Madison, who had won a seat in Congress, finally became convinced that a bill of rights was necessary and presented Congress with his own draft of a bill of rights on June 8, 1798. The draft was based on Mason's Virginia Declaration of Rights and it took Congress nearly two years to pass it.[104] Although it was Madison who finally was able to get the Bill of Rights incorporated in the Constitution, it is Mason who receives credit for writing it. The Supreme Court frequently cites Mason when interpreting the Bill of Rights.[105] It was finally passed in 1791, a year before Mason died, which meant he was able to see at least one of his proposals added to the Constitution.[106]

The only one of Mason's main proposals not to make it into the Constitution was his proposal to end slavery. This was the most controversial proposal Mason made at the convention. Not only was Mason a delegate from a southern state, where the economy was directly dependent on slave labor, but he was a slave owner as well. Being a slave owner did not stop him from being morally opposed to slavery. He refused to allow something so morally wrong even to be mentioned in the Constitution except if it were outlawing it. He was the only southern delegate to oppose the three-fifths compromise because it promoted slavery in the south and because it was morally wrong to count someone as only three-fifths of a person. Mason did not live to see an end to slavery or even an end to the slave trade, but both happened not too long after his death. In 1808, Congress prohibited the continuation of the slave trade and the end of slavery altogether followed shortly.[107] On January 31, 1865, immediately following the Civil War, the Thirteenth Amendment was proposed to outlaw slavery and was ratified on December 6, 1865.[108] Although he did not live to see it, and he is rarely given credit for being one of the original objectors to slavery, one of Mason's major proposals to the Constitution had finally been incorporated.

Mason's third major proposal for the Constitution was never incorporated, but one of his major objections was. Mason had always objected to the upper house of Congress, the Senate, being selected from representatives from each state rather than from the people directly. He believed that it was unfair to give the house that was not directly elected by the people more power. While many of his contemporaries feared giving the people too much power because they were not educated and informed enough to make good decisions, Mason feared giving the central government too much power. The last thing he wanted was to have the new government turn into an aristocracy or another monarchy.[109] And, in Mason's mind, allowing the Senate to be picked rather then elected by the people was getting awfully close to an aristocracy. Mason's fears became true; the Senate soon became full of corrupt political organizations and special interest groups. Citizens soon became dissatisfied with the process for electing senators.[110] Finally, on April 8, 1913, the Seventeenth Amendment was ratified, allowing for the direct election of senators.[111] It may not have been one of Mason's major proposals to the Constitution but it was one of his major objections, and it is a way in which his legacy lives on today.

George Mason was a man ahead of his time; he was able to look outside of the here and the now to see how his actions would influence generations to come. He could have signed the Constitution and raised himself up to the level of other Founding Fathers and become a president or a vice president or even a senator but he chose to do what he believed was right. He went into the convention hesitantly, knowing it would be a challenge, but truly honored at the opportunity to serve his country and to make his mark on the new government. He fought hard to represent the citizens of the United States as a whole and not just the citizens of Virginia. He went against the people of his own state in order to stand up for a group that was ignored and suppressed, slaves. He wanted all citizens to be able to enjoy the same rights and freedoms, which is why he fought so hard to get the Bill of Rights added to the Constitution.

Although he may not have seen many of his ideas carried out in his lifetime they were not forgotten, and the effects of them are still being felt today. He was a forward thinker who was able to see the problems arising in the future. One of the reasons he gave for not signing the Constitution was that "it is at the present impossible to foresee whether it will, in its Operation, produce a Monarchy, or a corrupt Aristocracy, it will most probably vibrate some years between the two and then terminate in the one or the other."[112] He refused to sign his name to a document because he was unsure of where it would lead. He wanted desperately for the new government to succeed.

George Mason was a perfectionist. He would stand for nothing less then a perfect government.

"We came equals into this world, and equals shall we go out of it. All men are by nature born equally free and independent. To protect the weaker from the injuries and insults of the stronger were societies first formed;...Every society, all government, and every kind of civil compact therefore, is or ought to be, calculated for the general good and safety of the community. Every power, every authority vested in particular men is, or ought to be, ultimately directed to this sole end: and whenever any power or authority whatever extends further, or is of longer duration than is in its nature necessary for these purposes, it may be called government, but it is in fact oppression." [113]

This quote from Mason sums up his feelings about the government. He felt the government's purpose was to serve and protect the people and that the government should benefit all of its citizens, not just a few. Mason strove to help the other Founding Fathers achieve a government that was able to do so. When they were unable to achieve such a government, at least in Mason's mind, he was unable to give them his support.

George Mason could have been a better known Founding Father if he had gone along with the majority at the Philadelphia Convention and signed the Constitution, but instead he went against the majority and left an even stronger legacy. It is amazing to think that some of the objections and proposals to the Constitution went on to become major issues in the United States government even after he died, and that he is still quoted today when courts are attempting to interpret the Bill of Rights. His ideas still have an impact on citizens of the United States today. George Mason could have had a high political career like many of the other Founding Fathers but by standing his ground and sticking up for what he believed was right he left an even greater legacy then any of the other Founding Fathers.

Bibliography

"About the Founding Fathers," Oak Hill Publishing Company, http://www.constitutionfacts.com/Founding_Fathers/AboutFF.htm (accessed October 28, 2005).

Carter Pittman, "Our Bill of Rights and How it Came to Be," http://www.constitution.org/gmason/amd_gmas.htm (accessed October 20, 2005).

Donald Senese, <u>George Mason and the Legacy of Constitutional Liberty</u> (Fairfax: Fairfax County History Commission, 1989).

Edmund Morgan, <u>The Birth of the Republic 1763-89</u> (Chicago: The University of Chicago Press, 1992)

"George Mason Quotes," Gunston Hall Plantation, http://gunstonhall.org/geogemason/quotes.html (accessed November 4, 2005).

Gunston Hall, "George Mason and the Constitution," Gunston Hall, http://www.gunstonhall.org/georgemason/constitution.html (accessed October 25, 2005).

Helen Hill Miller, <u>George Mason the Man Who Didn't Sign</u> (Board of Regents of Gunston Hall, 1987).

"Notes on the Amendments," The U.S. Constitution Online, http://www.usconstitution.net/constamnotes.html (accessed October 20, 2005).

Pauline Maier, <u>American Scripture</u> (New York: Alfred A. Knopf, 1997).

"Popular Election of Senators," http://www.gpoaccess.gov/
constitution/pdf/con028.pdf (accessed October 22, 2005).

Robert Ferris and James Charleton, <u>The Signers of the Constitution</u>
(Flagstaff: Interpretive Publications Inc, 1986).

Robert Rutland, <u>The Papers of George Mason 1725-1792 Volume
III</u> (Chapel Hill: University of North Carolina Press, 1970).

THE ISSUES

Freedom of Religion:

Our Forefathers' Original Intent
By
Emily Macklin

Children in the United States of America grow up knowing two important documents of our nation: The Declaration of Independence and the Constitution of the United States. While the Declaration of Independence declared that America was an entity separate from Britain, the Constitution set up the government of the new nation, creating a new nation where the people had rights and freedom. Our Founding Fathers also allotted different powers to the three branches of the federal government and added a Bill of Rights, guaranteed individual liberties to the nation's citizens.

The first amendment of the Constitution guarantees the freedom of worship, of speech, of the press, of assembly, and of petition of the government. These were spelled out by the writers of the Constitution because they knew what it was like to have them taken away. They had once lacked these rights under the monarchical authority of Great Britain and they wanted to ensure that each citizen of the United States would be able to have these personal freedoms. Amendment I of the Constitution reads:

> Congress shall make no law respecting an establishment of religion or prohibiting the free exercise thereof; or abridging the freedom of speech, or of the press; or the right of the people peaceably to assemble and to petition the government for a redress of grievances.[114]

There have been many disputes about all of these individual freedoms, but Freedom of Religion is perhaps the most controversial and prevalent of them all. Religion played a large role in our forefathers' lives, as we know from the letters and other pieces written by them, during their deliberations and discussions of what became the First Amendment. The wall of "separation of church and state," as laid out by Thomas Jefferson, for example, is a very divisive subject today, but it is important to look at its significance during the time the Founding Fathers were writing the Constitution and the First Amendment.

After reading their works, some people claim that many of the Founding Fathers were atheists, agnostics, and deists – not Christians. Since atheism is the belief that there is no God, agnosticism is the profession that nothing can be known beyond what is visible and tangible, and deism is the belief in an impersonal God who is no longer involved with mankind, it seems as though there was no religious affiliation in any of the Founding Fathers. This, however, is a very erroneous assumption that can easily be refuted by looking at the Founding Fathers' lives.

One quote that many use to make the assertion that our Forefathers were not religious is when John Adams wrote in 1817 to Thomas Jefferson that it "would be the best of all possible worlds if there were no religion in it."[115] If read out of context, one would presume that Adams was adamant about a separation of church and state and wanted nothing to do with religion or anything that dealt with religion. But, if one examines the entirety of the letter, one will end up with a very different conclusion. In the beginning of the letter, Adams described two ministers and discussed a typical conversation they would have with each other regarding the relationship between government and religion. During one particular discussion, Adams' Latin schoolmaster, Joseph Cleverly, declared that he would want to have only one religion if he were a monarch. Adams' parish priest, Lemuel Bryant, responded by saying "Cleverly! you would be the best man in the world if you had no religion."[116] Through this, Adams illustrates the common intolerance between Christians of different denominations. The next part of the letter is where the true feelings of Adams' view on religion are expressed:

> Twenty times in the course of my late reading have I been on the point of breaking out, "This would be the best of all possible worlds, if there were no religion in it!!!" But in this exclamation I would have been as fanatical as Bryant or Cleverly. Without religion this world would be something not fit to be mentioned in polite company, I mean hell.[117]

It is obvious that those who claim that Adams was an atheist are therefore sorely mistaken. If the entire letter is read, the fact is evident that Adams felt exactly the opposite of what he is quoted to have said. He even used the word "hell" to describe a place without religion. A man with no religious beliefs would probably not have spoken so strongly against this.

The strong religious convictions of many of the Founding Fathers are shown in their extensive involvement and leadership in various religious associations. John Quincy Adams was the Vice-President of the American Bible Society and a member of the Massachusetts Bible Society. Alexander Hamilton proposed the formation of the Christian Constitutional Society, which spread the concept of a Christian government to other countries. John Jay was the President of the American Bible Society and a member of the American Board of Commissioners for Foreign Missions. John Marshall was Vice-President of the American Bible Society and an officer in the American Sunday School Union. Countless other signers of the American Constitution and many early government leaders in the United States had important leadership positions in similar religious organizations.[118]

When the first Congress was held in 1774, our Founding Fathers' religiousness became evident when they requested Reverend Jacob Duché from Christ Church in Pennsylvania to open each session with prayer.[119] Many of the members of Congress were very pleased with this decision to include Reverend Duché. John Adams, in a letter to his wife Abigail, stated that he had never heard "a better prayer or one so well pronounced...for America, for the Congress, for the Province of Massachusetts Bay, and especially the town of Boston. It has had an excellent effect upon everybody here."[120] Silas Deane, a prestigious attorney and a member of the First Continental Congress, said that Reverend Duché's prayer "was worth riding one hundred miles to hear."[121]

Later, when the first Constitutional Convention was held in the late 1780s, Benjamin Franklin, who was largely considered the least religious of all the Founding Fathers, delivered a speech on June 28, 1787, requesting daily prayer at the opening of each session. There had been quite a few problems between large and small states dealing with how each state would be represented in the new government and he suggested that the delegates of the Constitutional Convention resolve their differences through prayer:

> "In this situation of this Assembly, groping as it were in the dark to find political truth, and scarce able to distinguish it when presented to us, how has it happened, Sir, that we have not hitherto once thought of humbly applying to the Father of lights [God] to illuminate our understandings?... To that kind providence we owe this happy opportunity of consulting in peace on the means of establishing our future national felicity. And have we now forgotten that powerful friend?" [122]

Franklin knew that the only way the disputes between opposing parties would cease was if they remembered all that God had done to help them arrive at their situation and if they sought His guidance once again. He believed that "without [God's] concurring Aid, we shall succeed in this political Building no better than the Builders of Babel." Due to lack of funds to pay for local clergymen to act as chaplains, his request for daily prayer was not granted, but it shows the very real presence of religion in all of the Founding Fathers' hearts.[123] Because they held religion in so much esteem, they made sure that when they were creating the Bill of Rights and guaranteeing all of the individual liberties to the people, they included freedom of religion.

It is obvious that the Founding Fathers were religious, but what did they mean by stating that "Congress shall make no law respecting an establishment of religion or prohibiting the free exercise thereof?"[124] By examining the words in the Freedom of Religion clause in the First Amendment, one can determine that it was created in order to encourage denominational pluralism, or the healthy coexistence of the various Christian denominations. It was not established for complete pluralism of multiple religions. The Freedom of Religion clause in the First Amendment states that "Congress shall make no law respecting an establishment of religion, or prohibiting the free exercise thereof."[125] "Congress" is usually interpreted to mean the "federal government," and "respecting" can mean "having anything to do with." An "establishment" in those days was the "government support of a single church or government preference of one creed or denomination over another."[126] Therefore, if the Freedom of Religion clause is translated literally, it would say that "The federal government shall make no law having anything to do with supporting a national denominational church, or prohibiting the free exercise of religion."[127]

In this day and age, people take this section of the First Amendment to mean that the Christian religion should not be tolerated or encouraged by the government. By looking at the words of some of our Forefathers, however, the original intent appears quite different. The Constitution was based on many of the state constitutions and, in a few, such as New Hampshire, New Jersey, North Carolina, and Connecticut, they made it obvious what they cared about regarding religion. New Hampshire's stated that "every denomination of Christians...shall be equally under the protection of the law."[128] New Jersey's declared that "There shall be no establishment of any one religious sect...in preference to another."[129] North Carolina's said that "There shall be no establishment of any one religious church or denomination...in preference to any other."[130] Connecticut's Constitution asserted that "each and every society or denomination of Christians in this State shall have and enjoy the same and equal powers, rights, and privileges."[131] Obviously, these states cared little about any other religion and more about the protection of Christianity's many different denominations.

Supreme Court Justice Joseph Story bluntly states in his Commentaries on the Constitution in 1811 that, "The real object of the [First A]mendment was not to countenance, much less to advance, Mohammedanism, or Judaism, or infidelity, by prostrating Christianity; but to exclude all rivalry among Christian sects."[132] Although the Founding Fathers recognized the different religions in their nation, they specifically preferred Christianity and sought to protect the various denominations within Christianity. James Madison termed the word religion to mean "the duty we owe our Creator," [133] which indicates a special preference to Christianity and the God of Christianity over all other religions and their deities, and shows that when the Founding Fathers were protecting "religion," they were protecting Christianity and Christianity only. In a letter written to fellow-signer of the Declaration of Independence Benjamin Rush, Thomas Jefferson explains that the First Amendment was created to prevent the federal establishment of a single national Christian denomination. He makes it obvious that he did not intend to allow the government to limit, restrict, regulate, or interfere with public religious practices.

> [T]he clause of the Constitution which, while it secured the freedom of the press, covered also the freedom of religion, had given the clergy a very favorite hope of obtaining an establishment of a particular form of Christianity through the United States; and as every sect believes its own form the true one, every one perhaps hoped for his own, but especially the Episcopalians and Congregationalists. The returning good sense of our country threatens abortion to their hopes and they believe that any portion of power confided to me will be exerted in opposition to their schemes. And they believe rightly."[134]

Supreme Court Justice Robert Jackson once said, "Freedom of Religion was first in the Bill of Rights because it was first in the forefathers' minds; it was set forth in absolute terms, and its strength is its rigidity."[135] The rigidity of Freedom of Religion, however, has waned and changed drastically over the years. The infamous "wall of separation between church and state" is a very controversial subject that has been altered over time and has seemed to develop into a fundamental right on its own. It was first seen in Thomas Jefferson's response to a letter written by the Danbury Baptists in Virginia in 1801, in which they stated:

> Our sentiments are uniformly on the side of religious liberty: that religion is at all times and places a matter between God and individuals, that no man ought to suffer in name, person, or effects on account of his religious opinions, [and] that the legitimate power of civil government extends no further than to punish the man who works ill to his neighbor. But sir, our constitution of government is not

specific... [T]herefore what religious privileges we enjoy (as a minor part of the State) we enjoy as favors granted, and not as inalienable rights.[136]

In this letter, the Danbury Baptists expressed their serious concerns with the concept of the First Amendment. They felt that when the First Amendment gave people "free exercise of religion," the right was government-given, not God-given. This, therefore, meant that there was a possibility that the government might someday attempt to regulate religion. Jefferson had the same opinion as the Danbury Baptists on this subject, and his view can be seen in his return letter to them on January 1, 1802, where he assured them that the government would not interfere with the free exercise of religion.

"Believing with you that religion is a matter which lies solely between man and his God; that he owes account to none other for his faith or his worship; that the legislative powers of government reach actions only and not opinions, I contemplate with sovereign reverence that act of the whole American people which declare that their legislature should "make no law respecting an establishment of religion or prohibiting the free exercise thereof," thus building a wall of separation between Church and State." [137]

Thus the "separation of church and state" was created. Today, the common misconception is that what Jefferson meant was that religion should have no part in governmental affairs. In reality, his original intent was quite the opposite. In his Second Inaugural Address in 1801, Jefferson said that "In matters of religion I have considered that its free exercise is placed by the Constitution independent of the powers of the General [federal] Government. I have...left them, as the Constitution found them, under the direction and discipline of the church or state authorities."[138] In another quote, he said that "Certainly, no power to prescribe any religious exercise or to assume authority in any religious discipline has been delegated to the General [federal] Government. It must then rest with the States."[139] Although he was adamantly against the federal government's interference with religion, he did not oppose similar actions made by the individual states.

In one of his letters to the Methodist Episcopal Church in 1808, Jefferson stated that "[O]ur excellent Constitution…has not placed our religious rights under the power of any public functionary,"[140] and in a letter to Samuel Miller in 1808, he declared that "I consider the government of the United States as [prohibited] by the Constitution from intermeddling with religious expression."[141] By Jefferson's definition, the "separation of church and state" meant that there should be a wall of separation around the church to protect it from any infringements by the federal government, not a wall around the government to protect it from religion.

Jefferson was not the only Founding Father with these opinions. James Madison said that "There is not a shadow of right in the general [federal] government to intermeddle with religion…This subject is, for the honor of America, perfectly free and unshackled. The government has no jurisdiction over it."[142] In his Commentaries on the Constitution, Supreme Court Justice Joseph Story stated that "the whole power over the subject of religion is left exclusively to the State governments to be acted upon according to their own sense of justice and the State constitutions."[143] These quotes show that the only purpose of the First Amendment was to prevent the federal government from usurping this specific state power. The "separation of church and state" is a misunderstood statement, especially after observing the Congressional records from June 7 to September 25, 1789. These records log months of discussions and debates between the ninety Founding Fathers dealing with the First Amendment. Not once is the phrase "separation of church and state" mentioned. Clearly, it was not an important subject on their agenda.

Freedom of Religion in the First Amendment is no longer what Jefferson and the Founding Fathers meant it to be. It was originally meant to restrain the federal government from limiting the exercise of religion while, at the same time, allowing the individual state governments to do whatever they wished regarding religion. Its purpose was to protect religion from the government, not the government from religion. There have been a few Supreme Court Cases that deal with Jefferson's letter to the Danbury Baptists and his declaration of a "separation of church and state." The first one was Reynolds v. United States in 1879, and it is clear that those Supreme Court members understood Jefferson's original intent.

In Reynolds v. United States, George Reynolds, a Mormon living in the Utah Territory in the 1870s, was married to both Mary Anne Tuddenham and Amelia Jane Schofield. This act was in accordance with the Mormon practice of polygamy, where males were married at the same time to more than one female. At that time, polygamy was against the law in all United States and Territories, of which Utah had become in 1848. Reynolds was accused of a violation of the Federal Anti-Polygamy Law and was tried for bigamy. Since the Mormon Church held polygamy to be a religious duty of all male members, he believed that it was protected in the Utah Territory and all other states by the First Amendment, which was translated to mean that "Congress cannot pass a law for the government of the Territories which shall prohibit the free exercise of religion."[144] The question that the Supreme Court had to answer was "whether the law now under consideration comes within this prohibition."[145] By a 9 to 0 vote, the Court declared Reynolds guilty and, after examining Jefferson's letter to the Danbury Baptists, concluded that:

> Coming as this does from an acknowledged leader of the advocates of the measure, it [Jefferson's letter] may be accepted almost as an authoritative declaration of the scope and effect of the Amendment thus secured. Congress was deprived of all legislative power over mere [religious] opinion, but was left free to reach actions which were in violation of social duties or subversive of good order.[146]

In this opinion, the Supreme Court published Jefferson's complete letter, and then broke it down to its initial meaning. The Supreme Court Justices made sure that they completely understood what Jefferson meant by the "separation of church and state" before they made a conclusion. Their summary of Jefferson's original intent was that:

> [T]he rightful purposes of civil government are for its officers to interfere when principles break out into overt acts

against peace and good order. In thi[s]...is found the true distinction between what properly belongs to the church and what to the State."[147]

In this court case and in others such as Commonwealth v. Nesbit and Lindenmuller v. The People, the Supreme Court identified actions, even when in the name of religion, that the government had authority to intrude upon. Such unconstitutional activities include human sacrifice, polygamy, bigamy, concubinage, incest, infanticide, and promotion of immorality.

The second Supreme Court case that addressed Jefferson's letter to the Danbury Baptists and his phrase "separation of church and state," was the 1947 Court Case Everson v. Ewing Board of Education. It was the first to misinterpret the phrase, thus leading our nation into the quandary it is in today. This case dealt with New Jersey's Student Transportation Law, which allowed district boards of education to make contracts for the transportation of school children living in remote areas to and from school, both public and parochial. After the Ewing Board of Education passed a resolution authorizing the repayment, from public tax money, of transportation fares, Arch Everson, a taxpayer from that school district, sued the Ewing School Board. He claimed that the authorization of the use of public tax money to pay for the transportation to and from a parochial school was in violation of the First Amendment's Establishment Clause.[148]

After the trial court found that the New Jersey State Legislature had incorrectly enacted the School Board's Reimbursement Resolution, the School Board appealed to the New Jersey Court of Errors and Appeals, which reversed the lower Court's decision. Everson then appealed to the United States Supreme Court which concluded, by a vote of 5 to 4, that New Jersey's Student Transportation Law was, in fact, in violation of the First Amendment. They decided this because of the Fourteenth Amendment, which stated that "No State shall make or enforce any law which shall abridge the privileges or immunities of citizens of the United States."[149] The Supreme Court Justices in Everson v. Ewing Board of Education took this Amendment to mean that the state governments, along with the federal government, could not establish nor prohibit the practice of any religion. The Court said that "The broad meaning given the Amendment by these earlier cases has been accepted by this Court in its decisions concerning an individual's religious freedom rendered since the Fourteenth Amendment was interpreted to make prohibitions of the First applicable to state action abridging religious freedom."[150] This declaration means that:

> "Neither a state nor the Federal Government can set up a church. Neither can pass laws which aid one religion, aid all religions, or prefer one religion over another. Neither can force nor influence a person to go to or to remain away from church against his will or force him to profess a belief or disbelief in any religion. No person can be punished for entertaining or professing religious beliefs or disbeliefs, for church attendance or non-attendance. No tax in any amount, large or small, can be levied to support any religious activities or institutions, whatever they may be called, or whatever form they may adopt to teach or practice religion. Neither a state nor the Federal Government can, openly or secretly, participate in the affairs of any religious organizations or groups and vice versa."[151]

This assertion made by Supreme Court Justice Hugo Black conflicts directly with the original intent of the Founding Fathers when they wrote the First Amendment's Freedom of Religion clause and when Jefferson stated that there should be a "separation of church and state." Justice Black makes a statement when he said "In the words of Jefferson, the clause against establishment of religion by law was intended to erect 'a wall of separation between church and State'"[152] Although he is correct in quoting Jefferson, Black does not completely understand the full implications of it.

This decision by the Supreme Court said that "The First Amendment has erected a wall between church and state. That wall must be kept high and impregnable. We could not approve the slightest breach."[153] After this declaration, the Supreme Court, along with other lower courts, began striking down religious activities and expressions which had previously been constitutional for over 150 years. After the court cases Engel v. Vitale in 1962, Abington v. Schempp in 1963, and Commissioner of Education v.

School Committee of Leyden in 1971, a verbal prayer offered in a school is unconstitutional, even if that prayer is both voluntary and denominationally neutral. The court case Lowe v. City of Eugene in 1969 made it unconstitutional for a war memorial to be erected in the shape of a cross. It is unconstitutional if a Board of Education uses or refers to the word "God" in any of its official writings after the 1976 decision of Ohio v. Whisner.[154] All of these cases have intruded upon many Americans' practice of religion.

Would the Founding Fathers of our Constitution have supported and encouraged these decisions made by the United States Supreme Court? "Congress shall make no law respecting an establishment of religion or prohibiting the free exercise thereof."[155] These sixteen words were supposed to have protected Christianity from the impeding role of the Government. They were written by pious men who cared about their God and wanted the future citizens of the United States to be able to worship Him without restrictions. Whatever happened to the original wall of separation, created by Thomas Jefferson in his letter to the Danbury Baptists, assuring them that their religion would be protected from Government? Why is Christianity, the main religion of our Forefathers, being punished and restricted by our Government? The answer is unclear, but it is unmistakable that we must hurry to preserve this important yet diminishing right.

In his Democracy in America in 1835, Alexis de Tocqueville wrote that he "[does] not know whether all Americans have a sincere faith in their religion – for who can read the human heart? but I am certain that they hold it indispensable to the maintenance of republican institutions. This opinion is not peculiar to a class of citizens or to a party, but it belongs to the whole nation and to every rank of society."[156] We must not consent to a world unsympathetic towards the religion of our forefathers. We must fight to restore Christianity to the same level of esteem in which they held it.

Bibliography

"Amendment I," The Declaration of Independence and the Constitution of the United States of America. Washington, D.C.: Cato Institute, 2000.

"Amendment I (Religions.)" The Founders' Constitution, 2000. <http://press-pubs.uchicago.edu/founders/tocs/ amendI_religion. html> 27 October, 2005.

Barton, David. Original Intent: The Courts, the Constitution, & Religion. Aledo, TX: WallBuilder Press, 1997.

Coates, Sr., Eyler Robert. 1999. <http://etext.virginia.edu/Jefferson/ quotations/ jeff1650.htm> 1 November, 2005.

Drinan, Robert F. Can God and Caesar Co-exist? New Haven, CT: Yale University Press, 2004.

Epps, Garrett. To An Unknown God: Religious Freedom on Trial. New York, NY: St Martin's Press, 2001.

Fisher, Louis. Religious Liberty in America. Wichita, KS: University Press of Kansas, 2002.

Harrison, Maureen and Steve Gilbert. Freedom of Religion Decisions of the United States Supreme Court. San Diego, CA: Excellent Books, 1996.

Kramnick, Isaac and R. Laurence Moore. The Godless Constitution. New York, NY: W.E. Norton & Company, 1996.

"Religion and the Founding of the American Republic." Library of Congress. 27 October, 2003. <http://www.loc.gov/exhibits/religion/ religion.html> 14 October, 2005.

Schaaf, Gregory. Franklin, Jefferson, & Madison: On Religion and the State. Santa Fe, NM: CIAC Press, 2004

Sherrow, Victoria. Freedom of Worship. Brookfield, CT: The Millbrook Press, 1997.

Whitehead, John W. The Second American Revolution. Westchester, IL: Crossway Books, 1988.

Peaceable Assembly

Just As Important Today?
By
Shannon Smith

The freedom of assembly is a First Amendment right granting Americans the right to peaceably gather. It is an important piece of the First Amendment, which defines inalienable personal rights of expression, and the Bill of Rights, which protects Americans from encroachment by the government. The freedom to assemble guaranteed to Americans by the First Amendment is defined by the statement, "Congress shall make no law respecting...the right of the people to peaceably assemble." Though this freedom has limitations, it does include the freedom of association. This freedom is not directly stated in the Bill of Rights or the Constitution, but is explicitly linked with the freedom of assembly.[157] Association includes the right to be free from compelled association, and gives us the right to join and gather with any group we desire, as long as it is peaceful.[158] The freedoms of assembly and association have become increasingly important and necessary as our nation grows and its citizens become more concerned and questioning of the government and its leaders. As Americans become more involved in government affairs and policies, they become more active with their political opinions and actions. They also become more aware of what their rights are and how to exercise them.

The freedom of assembly was intended to protect political expression. Our Founding Fathers exercised the aspects of free assembly many times during the colonial and revolutionary periods.[159] They gathered in town squares and gave speeches denouncing the king and British rule, formed liberty groups such as the Loyal Nine, and circulated information among several states describing their groups' problems and grievances with the current government. These founding fathers, men like James Madison and George Mason, were the primary leaders in America once the war was won and a new form of government was in demand. It was these men and other representatives of the thirteen colonies that joined together, "in general congress assembled" in 1776 to petition for a redress of grievances against Great Britain and the king, and declare their independence.[160] These representatives did not soon forgot that peaceful assembly and protest were important agents of expression, and were tools that led to our country becoming independent and free.

The United States Constitution was adopted in September 1787, and did not include a Bill of Rights. George Mason, a delegate to the convention from Virginia, called for a document that would give personal liberties and freedoms, to be included. However, his proposal was quickly shot down by a vote of 10-0, and the convention presented the finished Constitution to the states for ratification without any guarantee of personal rights. The lack of a Bill of Rights hurt the federalist cause, and hindered the passage of the Constitution. Critics cried out, "There is no Bill of Rights!" Some states, like Massachusetts, had to promise an addition of a Bill of Rights to get the Constitution passed.[161] Agreements like this helped the ratification process, and the Constitution went into effect in 1788.

The Constitution set up a bicameral Congress as the central law - making body in America when it was ratified. Congressman James Madison, from Virginia, drafted fourteen personal rights to be passed as the Bill of Rights. He submitted the list to Congress, and ten of his amendments were sent to the states to be ratified.[162] Virginia was the ninth state to ratify the document, guaranteeing its passage. Though Americans of the eighteenth century responded passively to the passage of the Bill of Rights, the freedoms it included became more precious as time went on. This was especially true when the Fourteenth Amendment passed to protect the civil liberties of recently freed slaves by prohibiting states from denying privileges to any United States citizens. The amendment's Due Process clause clearly states that state and local governments cannot infringe on the protections of the Bill of Rights.[163] With the freedoms in the Bill of Rights further protected, the right of peaceable assembly became increasingly more important after 1868.

The first instance of a United States Supreme Court case involving freedom of assembly occurred in 1876. This case, United States v. Cruikshank, tested the validity of the amount of protection the government will give to the freedom to assemble. A lynch mob was charged with threatening the peaceful assembly of two African American citizens. The mob was convicted of interfering with assembly rights, but the case was eventually dismissed on a technicality.[164] However, during the case proceedings the Court stated that, "the very idea of government, republican in form, implies a right on the part of its citizens to meet peaceably for consultation in respect to public affairs and to petition for a redress of grievances."[165] Though this case was dismissed and never resolved, it was a landmark for the freedom of assembly. United States v. Cruikshank went in favor of those in the case who were assembling peacefully, indicating the seriousness the Supreme Court took, and will take in the future, in reference to cases protecting individual rights.

The Supreme Court case DeJonge v. Oregon was the next instance in which assembly was addressed in the United States. This case was brought about by the Red Scare that swept the country after World War I. Communism was a great fear during this time because of the relatively new Bolshevist following in Eastern Europe. The Communist Party took control of Russia in 1917, and as it spread to surrounding countries, the U.S.S.R. began to form. Communists tried to fight the capitalist system, which is based on property ownership, and is the system in the United States.[166] They hoped to achieve equality through government ownership of property. Fears of this anti-capitalism spread to the United States and were thrown at the labor movement when strikes occurred. The American Communist Party was founded in Chicago in 1919. Hundreds of Russians who were thought to be subversive were sent out of the country when Attorney General A. Mitchell Palmer ordered raids throughout the country.[167]

In the case DeJonge v. Oregon, which occurred in 1937, Dirk DeJonge challenged his arrest and conviction which occurred when he was participating in a communist protest. Though the protest was peaceful, he was arrested because of Oregon's criminal syndicalism law, which outlawed organizations that advocated violence and potential government overthrow.[168] Criminal Syndicalism laws were passed by many states to attempt to thwart a Communist takeover in the U.S. The state of Oregon felt that communist organizations fell into this criterion. The Supreme Court overturned DeJonge's conviction because Oregon was unlawfully trying to limit the freedom of assembly, as well as association. Chief Justice Charles Hughes stated that, "peaceful assembly...however unpopular the sponsorship, cannot be made a crime."[169]

A similar outcome was reached in the case Hauge v. CIO in 1939. A New Jersey Mayor, Frank Hague, used his position to attempt to stop labor meetings because he felt they were of the communist nature. When the case reached the Supreme Court, it ruled against Hague because the ban on labor meetings violated the first amendment's freedom of assembly.[170] In both of these cases, though it was unpopular, the Supreme Court ruled in favor of the right to assemble. The rulings show that the protection of personal liberties is absolute when those exercising these rights are following the law.

The mass demonstrations of the 1950s and 1960s Civil Rights movement further stretched the use of the right to assemble and associate, and tested how the Supreme Court would respond to more controversial cases. The case of the NAACP v. Alabama in 1958 concerned an official members list of the Alabama chapter of the NAACP.[171] Alabama state officials were trying to force the NAACP to release the members list to the public. The organization refused to release any names for the obvious reason that its members would be subject to violence, harassment, and more discrimination. The Supreme Court sided with the NAACP, agreeing that releasing the list would violate the member's right to associate and assemble with any group they pleased. The case Shelton v. Tucker (1960) is similar. This case dealt with an Arkansas law that required teachers to file lists of organizations they belong to or had belonged to in the past year. This law was made in effort to discover NAACP members. As teachers who refused to divulge their various memberships were fired or refused contracts, the case Shelton v. Tucker came up in the Supreme Court.[172] The Supreme Court found that the Arkansas law violated the freedom to associate, and struck it down.

Also in Alabama, the Supreme Court stuck down an assembly permit law allowing a city to deny parade permits to groups it disagreed with. The law stated that the city could refuse permits based on "judgment of the public welfare, peace, safety, health, decency, good...be refused." This meant that any gathering the officials felt "violated" this law, they could prevent.[173] This law was used most often by Birmingham politicians to stop Dr. Martin Luther King Jr. and other Alabama Civil Rights advocates from protesting.

Marches and protests in Columbia, South Carolina, in 1961 led to the arrest and conviction of many African American students, who were charged with breach of the peace. Around 180 students marched on the capitol to take a stand against discrimination. Their protests drew several hundred onlookers, and though there was no conflict between the two groups or threat of violence, police grew nervous and ordered the protesters to disband. The student protesters refused to disperse because they were holding a peaceful protest, however they were still arrested. The Supreme Court overturned the convictions the protesters received in Edwards v. South Carolina (1963). The court agreed that the protesters were breaching peace according to South Carolina state law, but then went on to say that the law was too broad, and was unconstitutional. South Carolina's law violated the people's right to exercise free speech, assembly, and petition. The Justices wrote that, "these petitioners were convicted of an offense so generalized as to be...not susceptible of exact definition....And they were convicted upon evidence which showed no more than that the opinions which they were peaceably expressing were sufficiently opposed to the views of the majority..."[174]

Similar circumstances occurred, and a similar outcome was reached in the case of Cox v. Louisiana (1965). Reverend B. Elton Cox organized and led a demonstration in Baton Rouge in 1961. Cox and his fellow protesters were to march a short distance, from the capitol to a courthouse where a few African American students were being held after they were arrested for trying to dine in a whites-only eatery. The protesters waved signs, gave speeches, and sang, all the while acting completely orderly and peaceful. When Reverend Cox began urging his followers to try and eat lunch at the whites-only counters, police stepped in and demanded an end to the march. Police then proceeded to launch a tear gas canister at the crowd to force it to disperse. They arrested Reverend Cox for disturbing the peace, and he was convicted. However, the Supreme

Court overturned his conviction because it found the Louisiana law concerning breaching the peace to be too broad. Their law, like that of Alabama's, "penalized persons who were lawfully exercising their rights of free speech, assembly, and petition."[175] According to the Supreme Court, convicting Reverend Cox under the current Louisiana law violated the First Amendment.[176] Both the Cox case and the Edwards case were decided in favor of those peacefully exercising their right to assemble.

Another Civil Rights protest spawned conflict that reached the Supreme Court, but this instance occurred in the more integrated, northern state of Illinois. Demonstrators in Chicago were marching for the desegregation of Chicago public schools in a residential area near the mayor's home. Neighbors and other residents of that area became quickly aggravated by the protesting, and complained to police. To avoid potential violence, the Chicago police ordered the demonstrators to abandon their march. When some refused, they were arrested and convicted of disorderly conduct, even though the march was peaceful and nonviolent. The Supreme Court voted unanimously to overturn the convictions in Gregory v. Chicago.[177] Because the protest had been peaceful, the Court explained that the conviction of the protesters violated the due process clause of the Fifteenth Amendment. The Court also wrote that, "a march, if peaceful and orderly, falls well within the sphere of conduct protected by the First Amendment."[178]

The major exercise the freedom of assembly received during the decades of the Civil Rights movement shows just how important and necessary peaceable assembly is to Americans. Africans Americans who had finally had enough of segregation and racism were able to make changes to our government by protesting and demonstrating. Even though their positions were unpopular in many states and to many people, their right to assemble was protected by the Supreme Court because it is guaranteed in the First Amendment. This is much like the cases that arose early in the twentieth century concerning Communist Party activity. Though this party's ideology was very unpopular, they had a right to peacefully express their views through protests and marches.

During the Civil Rights movement, because African Americans were active, many unconstitutional state laws were overturned. The very broad laws of Alabama and Louisiana actually punished people for exercising their First Amendment rights. Because this was brought to the Supreme Court's attention, these states could no longer get away with convicting people who voiced views of the minority. The Supreme Court was also able to strike down the Alabama law that allowed city officials to use their discretion in confirming or denying who could get a permit to protest. This action limited the influence that state politics could have on demonstrations. The mass protesting of this era forced the Court to narrow the government's jurisdiction on stopping public protest.[179]

The women's movement of the 1970s and 1980s led to more conflict and more rulings dealing with the freedom to assemble. Thousands of women (and some men) gathered in Washington D.C. on November 20, 1971, for a massive pro- choice demonstration put on by the National Abortion Action Coalition. The demonstrators marched around the capitol, gave speeches, and held a concert.[180] It was people exercising their right to peaceably assemble, like this, which lead to governmental action regarding abortion. The ruling in the famous Supreme Court case Roe v. Wade (1973) legalized abortion in the United States. The right to have a safe, legal abortion was a huge gain for women's rights advocates. However, ever since Roe v. Wade, pro choice and pro life Americans have been fighting over the controversial decision which stated that a woman had the freedom to end an unwanted pregnancy. Pro life protests at abortion clinics are common, and still occur today. Advocates of life gather at medical clinics and vocally protest against abortion with chants and signs. They approach women going into the clinic for procedures and attempt to talk them out of their abortion, offering other alternatives. Protesters also approach clinic doctors and staff, and often berate them for allowing what they consider to be murder, to happen. The confrontations between patients or doctors and protesters can get very loud, angry, and sometimes violent.[181] These protests are an instance in which protecting the protester's right to free assembly and speech, as well as protecting the patient's right to safety and privacy presents a difficulty.

In the 1994 case Madsen v. Women's Heath Center, regulations and restrictions were established for protests at medical clinics. Madsen originated in Florida, where a state court established many boundaries for anti-abortion protesters because the protesters were harassing patients and doctors attempting to get into the medical center. The Supreme Court ruled that the Florida state court ruling violated the First Amendment with some of its regulations; those concerning a three hundred foot "no approach" zone surrounding the clinic.[182] However the Supreme Court upheld the thirty-six foot buffer zone for the clinic, which would allow people to easily access the clinic driveway. It also upheld the restriction on sound devices and chanting during working hours, because they disturb patients and doctors in surgery.[183] The no approach zone was denied because that restriction would go against the First Amendment rights of free assembly and speech. Not allowing the protesters to peacefully express their views near the clinic violates the First Amendment, but subjecting patients and doctors to messages that could be violent or hurtful would be violating their safety and privacy. The small buffer zone established by Madsen will keep people who need to access the clinic away from harm, but still allow pro life protesters to express their views.

There have been several other notable cases in history in which the right to assemble has played a prominent role. The major controversy between the National Socialist Party of America (American Nazis) and the very Jewish population of Skokie, Illinois, is one example. In 1977 the National Socialist Party of America tried to hold a march in the town of Skokie, which is a suburb of Chicago. Since a high percentage of the community of Skokie was Jewish, the people believed the march would be disruptive and tried not to allow it.[184] Despite the hateful message that the Nazi party would be displaying if they were allowed to march through the streets of a Jewish community, their march was allowed to proceed. The American Civil Liberties Union got involved when Skokie tried to deny the National Socialists a permit and made sure that a court order was given to allow the march. Though many people cannot imagine this ironic and hateful act occurring, the National Socialist Party was acting within their rights when they decided to march in

Skokie. The First Amendment and the Bill of Rights must protect all American citizens, whether or not their views are considered acceptable. Though the Nazi march ended up not happening due to a lack of support needed to carry it out, the permission being granted is enough to show that the right to assemble is taken very seriously. Americans who desire to express their views need only to organize a peaceful assembly, and gain the correct licenses.

There is a very fine line between protecting American' freedom to assemble, and keeping order and peace in a community. [185] As seen in the case of Skokie, Illinois, and the National Socialist Party of America, someone's right to assembly could have easily sparked violence and endangered the community's order. Judges also need to be protected from protests and picketing outside courtrooms, so that they are not influenced by outsiders' opinions.[186] Since the government must protect our rights, courtroom judges, and keep order throughout the country, there are guidelines and a system for Americans organizing and participating in protests, marches, and parades.

Common law statutes state that a gathering of three or more people can constitute an assembly. If these people have an illegal purpose for their meeting, or their meeting breaches the peace, then their assembly will be unlawful, and they could all be charged.[187] Even without the commission of an illegal act, an assembly for an unlawful purpose can constitute breaking the law. Unlawful assembly is generally a misdemeanor. To be legal, assembly must occur in an appropriate time, place, and manner.[188] The manner is the most obvious; the assembly must be peaceful, and cannot in any way disrupt order or safety. Time and place are harder to determine. The place must be a public forum, and the time must be when the government has opened that forum for the public to use. The Supreme Court has recognized that a public forum includes streets, parks, and "any property that government has opened for use by the public as a place for expressive activity."[189] However, the government can impose further restrictions on the use of public forums, and not all places open to the public can be considered a public forum when the First Amendment is concerned. Privately owned shopping centers are open to the public so that consumers can purchase goods, but people cannot necessarily gather and protest in a shopping center.

This was seen in the case of Lloyd Corporation v. Tanner (1972). The Lloyd Corporation was the owner of a private shopping center in Portland, Oregon. When protesters in this mall began to hand out literature with information concerning their organization, completely unrelated to the shopping center, they were asked to leave, and did. Although the Lloyd Corporation's mall was open to the general public in hopes to attract shoppers, the mall did not have to open its doors to protesters handing items out that were unrelated to shopping. The corporation had a strict policy in effort to prevent this. Because the Lloyd Corporation's shopping center was private, the petitioning was unrelated to the shopping center, and the protesters had "adequate alternative means of communication" outside of the shopping center, they could not exercise their right to assemble within the center.[190] The Court ruled in favor of the corporation, showing that the government does not have the power to designate permits in all areas. The power our government has over time, place, and manner in First Amendment activates is complicated; the exercise of that power does not extend to certain areas, and must be reasonable and neutral.

Neutrality is the key in assigning permits for parades, protests, and other assemblies as well. Cities and towns are allowed to grant permits for assembly under the precedent that they are granting then fairly and equally, and not basing the decisions on the views and politics of the group. The permits are given by the chief of police, mayor, or other municipal officer.[191] The statutes requiring neutrality in permit granting prevent discrimination like that which occurred in Alabama and other southern states during the Civil Rights movement. These states denied assembly permits to African Americans who desired to protest against segregation. The permit system also prevented the discrimination that took place in New York in 1948 at the hands of a Police Chief. A city ordinance allowed the chief of police to permit or deny the use of sound amplification devices in gatherings at his discretion.[192] The chief of police chose to deny a permit to a Jehovah's Witness minister, explaining that people had complained about the volume of his Sunday speeches. The court held that the denial by the police chief violated the Jehovah's Witnesses First Amendment rights of free assembly, speech, and religion, and that the city ordinance was unconstitutional.[193]

The case of Cox v. New Hampshire (1941) also displays the usage of the permit system. Mr. Cox was one of many Jehovah's Witnesses convicted of parading in a residential area of New Hampshire without a permit. Cox tried to challenge his conviction and say his right of assembly was violated; however the Supreme Court rejected this argument. The court agreed that the New Hampshire permit laws were not discriminatory, but that they prevented people from parading around residential streets and interfering with traffic.[194] This case is a good example of the regulations that Americans must follow when exercising their right to assemble, and a good example of the proper procedures that must be taken to gain an assembly permit. It shows that the system is as fair as possible, and that neutrality works.

Free assembly allows Americans to have collective political expression. Free association allows Americans to join and congregate with whomever they choose, and prevents compelled association. These rights ensure that no one is forced to support ideals they disagree with, and ensures that they can express ideals with which they do agree. [195] Because the rights of free assembly and association are protected by our government, Americans can gather in Washington D.C. to protest against a war that the current administration supports and not worry about the consequences. They can picket in front of an abortion clinic espousing their religious beliefs, and demonstrate in front of a slaughter house or meat packing factory to support animal rights. The United States is full of people with differing ideologies, ranging from leftists who believe in no government and no God, to the radical Christian right. As Americans become increasingly more educated, they are more aware of the inequalities in the world, and are also aware of what they can do to express how they feel about them. This explains why Americans who were tired of the hierarchy of the capitalist system turned to communism and were not afraid to advertise their views. This explains why African Americans who were tired of being disenfranchised and tired of being complacent about segregation chose to act by demonstrating and protesting. This explains why women began demanding equal rights, including the right to have a safe and legal abortion, and to be given the same jobs, salaries, and opportunities as men. The activism of the past century shows that Americans have become more politically knowledgeable and aware, and better able to use their First Amendment rights. As our country matures and Americans become more politically savvy, the freedom to assemble only becomes more important.

Bibliography

Anne and Heidi, "Women's March on D.C.," Documents from the Women's Liberation Movement, 29 November 1971, < http:// scriptorium.lib.duke.edu/wlm/wom/> (7 November 2005)

Chairman Warren Burger, The Bill of Rights and Beyond, (Washington D.C.: The Commission on the Bicentennial of the U.S. Constitution, 1991), 22

David G. Savage, The Supreme Court and Individual Rights 4th Edition (Washington D.C.: CQ Press, 2004), 46, 47

Jethro Liberman, A Practical Companion to the Constitution (London: University of CA Press, Ltd., 1999), 196

Judy Madsen et al. v. Women's Health Center, Inc. et al Supreme Court of the United States, 512 U.S. 753 1994

Kris Palmer, Constitutional Amendments 1789 to the Present (Farmington Hills, IN: Gale Group Inc., 2000), 20

Lloyd Corporation v. Tanner Supreme Court of the United States, 407 U.S. 551 1972

Lorraine Glennon, The 20th Century: An Illustrated History of our Life and Times (North Dighton, MA: JG Press, Inc., 1999), 138

Richard Hanes and Daniel Brannen, Supreme Court Drama Volume 1 (Canada: UXL, Gale Group, 2001), 7

Roger Newman, The Constitution and its Amendments Volume 2 (New York: Macmillan Reference USA, 1998), 88

Roger Newman, The Constitution and its Amendments: Volume 3 (New York: Macmillan Reference USA, 1999), 60

Saia v.The People of New York Supreme Court of the United States, 334 U.S. 558 1948

"Skokie, Illinois" Wikipedia, the Free Encyclopedia, 4 November 2005 <http://en.wikipedia.org/wiki/Skokie,_Illinois> (5 November 2005)

U.S. v. Cruikshank et al. Supreme Court of the United States October Term, 1875

The First Amendment
And
Protection for Vulgar and Distasteful
Language

By
Alex Miller

"I honor the man who is willing to sink
Half his present repute for the freedom to think,
And, when he has thought, be his cause strong or weak,
Will risk t'other half for the freedom to speak,
Caring naught for what vengeance the mob has in store,
Let that mob be the upper ten thousand or lower."
- James Russell Lowell[196]

All it takes is a word, one word to put people in an uproar. Something so simple a concept as words can divide a society, pitting people against each other. It may not always be popular, but the First Amendment protects free speech and with that comes protection for the most repugnant and crude of acts. As members of a democratic state, people must allow free speech and the means one chooses to express oneself to flow with as few restrictions as possible. The freedom of speech is a staple of American society.

The First Amendment has had a turbulent history with multiple interpretations; differences in individual standards of what constitutes free speech and the shifting of its powers all affect its role in society. It may not be apparent, but the protection of what others consider distasteful, or do not necessarily agree with, helps ensure the protection of all opinions and views. The quote by Voltaire, "I do not agree with what you have to say, but I'll defend to the death your right to say it" best sums this up. By protecting free speech in all forms, values essential to the United States are served and held.

As expressed in University of Missouri-Kansas City Prof. Linder's Introduction to the Free Speech Clause, the First Amendment holds certain values that are achieved by protecting the freedom of speech.

Free speech makes possible the discovery of truth. As the poet John Milton said, "Let her [Truth] and Falsehood grapple: who ever knew Truth put to the worse in a free and open encounter?"[197] By allowing free speech to flow openly without restrictions, truths and falsities will go head to head and the truth will prevail.

The political process is advanced when there is a protection of free speech. Citizens will be more interested in participating, knowing that they will be heard. This also applies to candidates and advocates of more controversial policies who are more capable of expressing their positions when not restricted.

Unrestricted speech creates a more flexible and stable community. In a society where angry and alienated citizens have the freedom to speak their mind, there will be more stability as people will be less inclined to resort to acts of aggression. Allowing citizens to speak freely and vent lessens tension between citizens and creates stability in the state.

Free speech enables individuals to express themselves, find self-fulfillment through creating an identity and connecting with others. In this way, freedom of speech becomes a facet of human dignity.

Checking abuse of governmental power is a focal point of the United States political system. Those who are part of the government, as well as citizens, need to be vigilant to watch for abuses of power. As Watergate demonstrated, freedom of the press makes it possible for citizens to learn about misuse of power. In 1972, police discovered that five burglars had broken into the Democratic National Committee to adjust bugging equipment that had previously been installed. The Watergate investigation turned up connections to the White House and found a series of political crimes running much deeper than previously thought which led to the president's downfall. When issues are identified, people can do something about it when they vote.

Promoting tolerance is important in a diverse country with people of vastly different backgrounds. In the United States, where customs, traditions and cultures come together and intertwine, the assurance that all citizens can express themselves as they see fit without abuse from others is of the utmost importance. Promoting freedom of speech and expression, especially through the practice of extending protection to speech that many would find distasteful, even personally upsetting, teaches people to become more tolerant in other parts of life. Moreover, a more tolerant society is a better society. While there still are disagreements between people, exposure to different views does not necessarily create agreement with or liking other views, but helps lead to understanding.

Protecting free speech in all its forms creates a more vibrant and interesting society. A community where free speech is treasured and defended creates a society that is energized and creative, where its citizens satisfy their wants and needs in a diverse environment that encourages an array of lifestyles and interests.

These values are an essential part of the First Amendment as well as components of an open society. The values of society manifest themselves not only in everyday situations but also in the law. Sometimes they hold more influence than at other times, but just as the First Amendment is effected by interpretations and different trial rulings increasing or decreasing its powers, so too is it by social attitudes and the function of the different values.

Congress shall make no law respecting an establishment of religion, or prohibiting the free exercise thereof; or abridging the freedom of speech, or of the press, or the right of the people peaceably to assemble, and to petition the Government for a redress of grievances.[198]

The court system is one of the central battlegrounds for free speech. The argument of speech covers a vast area of law. In addition to the First Amendment, the Fourteenth Amendment, Section One, also covers speech, to an extent. While the First Amendment guarantees the protection of free speech, the Fourteenth guarantees equal protection and treatment under the law to all citizens. The Fourteenth Amendment more clearly defines the First Amendment and who falls under its protection. The First Amendment, among other powers, protects free speech and the Fourteenth Amendment guarantees all are equal under the law, the first is strengthened by the latter.

Some cases are more famous than others and attract the public's attention. These cases range from dealing with cursing to just plain lewdness.

The People v. Lenny Bruce

A cultural icon of the 1950s and 60s, Lenny Bruce's "underdog, idealistic humor took on every American sacred cow."[199] Nothing was sacred. Nothing was taboo for him, from religion to sexuality to politics. In his standup routines, Lenny Bruce delved into why certain words were dirty and then deflated the arguments. Rough, brutal, raw, Lenny was a fresh voice in the nightclub scene, turning standup on its head. Bruce began his standup career in the 50s working the "strip clubs of southern California where Bruce began to develop the iconoclast edginess that would be his trademark."[200] Working the burlesque houses, Lenny had a freedom that few, if any comedians achieved.

> Four years working in the clubs—that's what really made it for me—every night: doing it, doing it, doing it, getting bored and doing different ways, no pressure on you, and all the other comedians are drunken bums who don't show up, so I could try anything.[201]

Bruce made his national television appearance on the Steve Allen Show on April 9, 1959, with the introduction, "the most shocking comedian of our time, a young man who is skyrocketing to fame—Lenny Bruce!"[202] On February 3, 1961, Bruce reached his peak, performing what many considered his best show, to a packed house at Carnegie Hall. That fall his troubles began.

His arrest record began piling up for drug charges or obscenity. The first of many cases was for a performance at the Jazz Workshop in San Francisco, violating California's obscenity law only a week after being arrested in Philadelphia on a narcotics charge. Albert Bendich, who specialized in First Amendment law, represented Bruce. He represented Bruce alone, being turned down by the co-counsel he hoped would help him. Though the odds were against them and most thought they were going to lose the suit, Bendich proved otherwise stating that Bruce's humor "was in the great tradition of social satire, related intimately to the kind of social satire found in the works of such great authors as Aristophanes and Jonathan Swift."[203]

Victory was short lived for, in 1962, he faced another charge for violating the obscenity law, this time for a show in West Hollywood. Less than two weeks after the West Hollywood charges, Bruce was facing charges in Chicago. On top of these charges, he was then arrested for a show in Los Angeles. The West Hollywood and LA trials ended in a deadlocked jury, but he was not as lucky in Chicago and was sentenced to a year in jail. Free on bail, Bruce tried to do a show in London while his appeal was pending, only to be deported. In June, a California court ordered Bruce to attend a rehab center in Chico, California for his drug addiction. Bruce moved to New York City in March, 1964, after another arrest in California, believing it was "the last refuge for controversial brand of humor."[204]

Now past his prime - both physically and artistically, Lenny Bruce was no longer the hip Lenny he once was in the 50s. He became more and more obsessed with his drug busts and obscenity charges. Later that March, Bruce started performing regularly at Howard and Ella Solomon's Café Au Go Go in the Village for $3,500 a week. On March 31, 1964, Herbert Ruhe, a former CIA agent and now license inspector for the city of New York, sat in on Lenny's set. Throughout the performance, sitting only a row from the stage, Ruhe jotted down words he considered vulgar, adding "his own editorial comments, such as 'philosophical claptrap on human nature.'[205] The day after the performance, Inspector Ruhe presented his report on the show to Richard Kuh, the man who would later lead the prosecution against Bruce. On April 2, a transcript of his show was submitted to twenty-three grand jurors, who indicted Bruce for violating Penal Code 1140-A, "which prohibited 'obscene, indecent, immoral, and impure drama, play, exhibition, and entertainment… which would tend to the corruption of morals of youth and others.'[206] The next day at the Café Au Go Go, Lenny Bruce and Howard Solomon were arrested shortly before his performance.

"Bruce hired as his attorney Ephraim London, one of the nation's leading First Amendment lawyers"[207] and Martin Garbus, a young associate who was a fan of Bruce's work. In Garbus' eyes, the arrests of Bruce were "public exercise of hypocrisy,"[208] facing prosecution because of "his attacks on religion and public figures, rather than because of his use of dirty words."[209] In Richard Kuh's opinion, however, Bruce's shows consisted of "cumulatively nauseating word pictures interspersed with all the three- and four-letter words and more acrid ten- and twelve-letter hyphenated ones, spewed directly at the audience" unredeemable by artistry or cogent social criticism.[210]

The opening of the Café Au Go Go trial was June 16, 1964. The court, overwhelmed by the number of people who showed up in support of Bruce, had to move the trial to a "larger courtroom with twenty-foot high ceilings."[211] Instead of a jury, the trial was before a three-judge court, the presiding judge being John Murtagh. The prosecution relied heavily on Inspector Ruhe's account of Bruce's performance. Ruhe presented his interpretation of Bruce's act, to which Bruce responded, "I'm going to be judged by his bad timing, his ego, his garbled language."[212] After the prosecution rested and the court reconvened, "the defense moved to dismiss on the grounds that the prosecution had not presented sufficient evidence to provide a violation of Penal Code 1140."[213] London and Garbus argued that

"the prosecution's case rested largely on Bruce's coarse language, and that the Supreme Court precedent required the prosecution to show that the defendant's words had inspired 'lustful and lecherous thoughts.' The court denied the motion. Justice Randall Creed dissented, saying that although he found Bruce's performance 'distasteful,' he did not think it made 'the grade as to hard-core pornography'"[214]

Bruce's case relied profoundly on the testimony of expert witnesses. Out of the group of witnesses assembled by the defense, Dorothy Kilgallen, was their most noteworthy. Because of her role as a regular panelist on the television show What's My Line, Kilgallen was a household name. Kilgallen's testimony was thought to be particularly influential because, in Garbus' words, she was "considered by many to be a spokesperson for the more prudish elements of the entertainment world."[215] On the stand, Kilgallen appeared calm and at ease, saying she had "enormous respect" for Bruce. She described him as "a brilliant satirist, perhaps the most brilliant that I have ever seen. [His] social commentary, whether I agree with it or not, is extremely valid and important, and I have enjoyed his acts on several occasions."[216]

Of the witnesses put together by the prosecution, the most scathing came from sociologist Ernst Van den Haag. Describing Bruce's acts as a "sort of diarrhea—instead of defecating on stage in the literal sense, he does it through orality", the only people who would find Lenny Bruce's performances acceptable would be the patients of "mental hospitals". However, during London's questioning, he disputed Van den Haag's authority as an expert on community standards when it was brought to light that he had not been to a nightclub in twenty years. When the defense rested, Bruce asked to address the court, to provide evidence he thought was being withheld. London was set on not letting Bruce testify; even going so far as to leave the courtroom before Bruce withdrew his plea. The verdict was not to be given for another 90 days. During this time, Bruce fired his lawyers and prepared for the decision.

On November 4, 1964, the court announced its decision. Lenny Bruce, standing alone, asked the court to reopen his case. His motion denied, Murtagh announced the court's ruling; both Lenny Bruce and club owner Howard Solomon were found guilty of all charges. Bruce remained free on bond while appealing the court ruling. Bruce would never see his final hearing, or any other involving his appeal. On August 3, 1966, Bruce was found dead in his home in Hollywood Hills, California of a supposed heroin overdose. After his death, one of his many prosecutors, Assistant D.A. Vincent Cuccia of New York lamented his part in the case:

> There was community pressure . . . in the sense that the overwhelming percentage of the population wanted Lenny Bruce prosecuted and they wanted him punished because his words were offensive and his ideas hurt the Establishment. He said things that the Establishment didn't want said. For that reason, I feel, there was a compulsion to prosecute and punish him. And we did. He didn't harm anybody, he didn't commit an assault, he didn't steal, he didn't engage in any conduct that directly harmed someone else. So, therefore, he was punished, first and foremost, because of the words that

he used . . . At the time, I was given a job to do, I was wrapped up in the prosecution of it and was oblivious to some of the things we were doing . . . I wouldn't have anything to do with his prosecution now.[217]

It took 39 years for Bruce's name to be cleared. In 2003, a group of people campaigned to persuade New York Governor Pataki to give Lenny Bruce a full pardon. On December 23, 2003, the first posthumous pardon was granted in New York's history. Governor Pataki declared it "a declaration of New York's commitment to upholding the First Amendment",[218] how ironic, or, rather, how sad.

Hustler Magazine v. Jerry Falwell

Another such case that gained widespread media attention was Hustler v. Falwell. Jerry Falwell sued Hustler Magazine and publisher Larry Flynt for libel and the intentional infliction of emotional distress. The reason for this suit was a satirical Campari ad. The "advertisement 'parody' which, among other things, portrayed respondent [Falwell] as having engaged in a drunken incestuous rendezvous with his mother in an outhouse."[219] The jury disregarded the libel charge as the parody could not "'reasonably be understood as describing actual facts ... or events,' but ruled in his favor on the emotional distress claim."[220] Flynt appealed, but the Court of Appeals affirmed the decision. The case was taken to the United States Supreme Court in December, 1987, and was decided in February 1988. The Supreme Court overturned the lower court's ruling with a decision written by Chief Justice William H. Rehnquist:

'Despite their sometimes caustic nature, from the early cartoon presenting George Washington as an ass down to the present day, graphic depictions and satirical cartoons have played a prominent role in public and political debate' throughout the nation's history and that the First Amendment protects even 'vehement, caustic and sometimes unpleasantly sharp attacks.[221]

Parody and satire are not solid grounds for libel suits unless, by using the Sullivan standard,[222] "actual malice" is found.

"Outrageousness" in politics and social interactions is such a subjective matter that there cannot be one standard to define it. If there were, juries would be able to decide based on their own opinions, their personal tastes, and their dislike for particular expressions/actions and not on the facts. It would be impossible to consistently award damages for libel, negating the first and fourteenth amendments.

Cohen v. California

On April 26, 1968, Paul Cohen was arrested for disturbing the peace. His offense, wearing a jacket with "Fuck the Draft" printed on the back. His jacket was deemed a violation of California's "Vulgar Speech" law. Saying he used the f-word on his jacket to emphasize his deep feelings about the Vietnam War and the U.S. Selective Service program, and that the word made his statement more powerful, his choice of words fell under First Amendment protection. The Los Angeles County Municipal Court convicted Cohen for violating the California Penal Code, sentencing him to thirty days in the county jail. Cohen appealed to the California Court of Appeals, but the ruling was upheld. Appealing to the California Supreme Court, his case was denied to be heard.

Cohen claimed that the State of California did not have the right to punish him for expressing his anti-war views, whether they were considered vulgar or not. He argued that the First Amendment protected his use of curse words in protest and public display. Cohen appealed to the Supreme Court of the United States on February 22, 1971. The court's decision was announced on June 7, 1971.

The decision, 5-4 in favor of Cohen, read by Associate Justice John Harlan, stated that a state could not ban the simple act of "communication." However, there are specific exceptions to this rule, such as the right not to be subjected to objectionable or offensive speech in one's own home. Cohen's situation did not fall under one.

The constitutional right of free expression is powerful medicine in a society as diverse and populous as ours. It is designed and intended to remove governmental restraints from the arena of public discussion, putting the decision as to what views shall be voiced largely into the hands of each of us, in the hope that use of such freedom will ultimately produce a more capable citizenry and more perfect polity and in the belief that no other approach would comport with the premise of individual dignity and choice upon which our political system rests.[223]

Finally, and in the same vein, we cannot indulge the facile assumption that one can forbid particular words without also running a substantial risk of suppressing ideas in the process. Indeed, governments might soon seize upon the censorship of particular words as a convenient guise for banning the expression of unpopular views. We have been able... to discern little social benefit that might result from running the risk of opening the door to such grave results. It is, in sum, our judgment that, absent a more particularized and compelling reason for its actions, the State may not, consistently with the First and Fourteenth Amendments, make the simple public display here involved of this single four-letter expletive a criminal offense. Because that is the only arguably sustainable rationale for the conviction here at issue, the judgment [of the court] below must be reversed.[224]

FCC v. Pacifica Foundation

On October 30, 1973, a twelve-minute portion of comedian George Carlin's act, Filthy Words, played on WBAI, a New York radio station owned by the Pacifica Station. Before the segment was aired, a warning to listeners was played telling them the act contained language that some might find offensive. An angry parent complained to the Federal Communications Commission after his son heard the broadcast.

Congress granted the FCC regulatory powers over public airwaves, but not censorship. An order sent to Pacifica dated February 21, 1975, deemed the language in George Carlin's act "offensive, indecent, vulgar, and shocking"[225]and that sanctions would be imposed, including fines or even license revocation if any more complaints were made. Pacifica appealed to the United States Court of Appeals, which overturned the FCC's order. The FCC appealed and took it to the Supreme Court. Arguments began on April 18, 1978, and a decision was made and announced July 3.

In a 5-4 decision, the Supreme Court overturned the Court of Appeals ruling. In their defense, Pacifica had explained that the segment was played during a program on society's attitude toward language and that a warning was played first.

> Pacifica characterized George Carlin as "a significant satirist" who "like Twain and Sahl before him, examines the language of ordinary people... Carlin is not mouthing obscenities; he is merely using words to satirize as harmless and essentially silly our attitudes towards those words."[226]

The question at hand was not whether Carlin's act was indecent, but whether the government had the power to regulate content if it did not possess the power to censure. If the First Amendment protected George Carlin's monologue, the act could not be regulated based on its contents, as the degree of its offensiveness was subjective, giving no adequate reason for suppressing it. Though the FCC does not have the power to censure to a certain degree, it did have the power to regulate in the matters of this broadcast because of two main reasons. First, radios can enter almost everyone's home, in a sense taking away the privacy of one's home. People have the right not to have to put up with what they consider offensive or objectionably wrong within their own homes. Second, with radio, there runs the risk of children listening to questionable content. Expression such as Cohen's jacket (Cohen v. California) may be incomprehensible to children; a radio broadcast such as "Filthy Words" can widen a child's vocabulary in an instant. Cohen's jacket may not be as easy for children to comprehend because it is written and the word would likely be unfamiliar with the child, unable to fully process the message. The radio broadcast on the other hand could introduce new words at a much faster rate. By hearing the words instead of trying to read it, children are more likely to remember them and repeat the words even if the child's understanding of the words are less than accurate or not at all. In this case, the Commission decided in a matter of context, a matter of nuisance and not the words specifically.

A "nuisance may be merely a right thing in the wrong place - like a pig in the parlor instead of the barnyard. We simply hold that when the Commission finds the pig has entered the parlor, the exercise of its regulatory power does not depend on proof that the pig is obscene."[227]

There have been successes and losses in the fight for the freedom of speech. Many have fallen in their struggles, some harder than others, but through each effort, the freedom of expression has been secured for others. At the heart of the First Amendment is the idea that we can express our beliefs without fear of persecution, express our views no matter how unpopular, mock those in power without facing litigation; it cuts to the core of the values of the United States. As Larry Flynt himself wrote, "If the First Amendment will protect a scumbag like me, then it will protect all of you. 'Cause I'm the worst."[228]

Bibliography

Bernstein, David E, You Can't Say That! the growing threat to civil liberties from antidiscrimination laws. Cato Institute, Washington, D.C. 2003

Frank Collins and the National Socialist Party of America v. Albert Smith, President of the Village of Skokie, Illinois, (1978)

Harrison, Maureen, Gilbert Steve, ed. "Cohen v. California", Freedom of Speech Decision of the United States Supreme Court. Excellent Books, San Diego. 1996.

Hustler Magazine and Larry C. Flynt v. Jerry Falwell, 485 U.S. 46, (1988).

Kamen, Al. Court Bars Damages To Falwell: public Figures' Obligation to Prove Libel Is Affirmed, Washington Post. 25 February 1988.

Linder, Doug. Introduction to the Free Speech Clause of the First Amendment.

http://www.law.umkc.edu/faculty/projects/ftrials/conlaw/ firstaminto.htm (2000-2005)

Linder, Doug. The Lenny Bruce Trial.http://www.law.umkc.edu/ faculty/projects/ftrials/bruce/bruce.html (2003)

Taylor, Stuart. Court, 8-0, Extends Right to Criticize Those in Public Eye: Rules to Protect Speech Extended in His Case Against Magazine, New York Times. 25 February 1988.

Freedom of the Press

By
Leah Withers

   Free press is a canon of American society. Along with a free market, democratic government, and constitutional rights, free press forms the basis for what makes America great. American press (moving beyond the English instituted, Parliament regulated press) began in 1690 when Benjamin Harris opened a coffeehouse/book shop in Boston. From there he published a four page newspaper titled *Publick Occurrences, Both Forreign and Domestik*.[229] The paper was shut down only four days after the first edition was released because Harris had not received a license from the British authorities for his newspaper and several of the articles were found to be insulting to the British and their allies. The next and much more successful attempt was by Boston postmaster John Campbell. Campbell started the *Boston News-Letter* in 1702 and gained the approval of British authorities before printing each story[230]. His paper lasted for 72 years – the first continuously published newspaper in America. Over the years, the press gained its liberties slowly and grudgingly from British rule and during the revolution, the American press played a huge role in spreading the word and calling for troops. Indeed, Thomas Paine's *Common Sense* pamphlet and John Dickenson's Letters from a Farmer in Pennsylvania to the Inhabitants of the British Colonies are credited with swaying the American colonists toward revolution.

   While the Founding Fathers were concerned with denying government censorship of the press, throughout American history the greatest censor has been the press itself. The American press relinquishes its own constitutional freedom through self censorship to the detriment of the people. The mass media has edited and censored itself and left the American people blind and uninformed. The press has often faltered in insuring American liberty by not maintaining a constant vigil to keep the people informed. For every "The Jungle" written there is another opportunity for sensational, significant reporting that the press lets slip.

The only one to blame for these travesties is the press itself. The government is not, in general, forcing the press to stay quiet about anything, and if and when it does, the press has the right and power to fight back. No, this is an enemy from within and thus it is more deadly. The press is not suppressed but self-driven. These failures are adding up to hurt the public. How can a farmer in Iowa know what his country's government is doing if the press can not be trusted to truthfully tell him? The press has failed to inform us on so many subjects - The Mobil Oil/Rhodesian connection (1976), injustice at Greensboro, North Carolina, after a Ku Klux Klan and Nazi attack (1981), U.S. agencies conducting radiation tests on humans for 30 years (1986), Inslaw software theft- a Justice Department Conspiracy (1991), U.S. chemical industry fights for toxic ozone-killing pesticide (1995) - to name just five from the past 30 years[231]. The people are fed a certain stream of information that the mass media determines, rather than a wide range of all the new information available.

The press has the freedom, the right, and above all the responsibility to inform the people on any and everything so that the people may be educated enough to maintain the most democratic society. The press is indisputably leaving this cause to follow one of corporate gain. This shift in mission is hurting the people. We will explore the actual freedom of the press, why and how the press self-censors, the patterns in press self censorship, the press' disservice to the American public, and finally, the epitome of good journalism - muckraking.

Providing accurate information is crucial to any open society because knowledge is power. A free press was so coveted during British rule it is not surprising that, when the Founding Fathers set up our government, one of their first concerns was providing for a free press. The First Amendment in the Bill of Rights states that, "Congress shall make no law...abridging the freedom...of the press..." Overtly, this gives the American people the right and freedom to have a press and for that press to not be constrained by the government. This freedom ties into the 'Freedom of Speech' which has, through law, been interpreted to also guarantee to the public a right to know - the freedom of information. The free press' duty in a democratic society is to act as the people's watchdog over the government. The Founding Fathers felt strongly that a free press must be defended. Thomas Jefferson, third president of the United States, said, "The basis of our government being the opinion of the people, the very first object should be to keep that right (full information of government affairs.)"[232] This poignantly states the altruistic belief behind the press, and although the press' freedoms have been clarified and protected over the years, they have also been called into question and limited in some ways.

The fact remains that the press' freedoms were left so vague by the Constitution that, paradoxically, the clearest definitions of its freedoms are the constraints placed by the government. The press' constitutional freedom has not been clarified to give it greater access to events than any other citizen. "The [Supreme] Court thus far has refused to draw any constitutional distinction between speech and the press, or ... the 'organized media,' in part, perhaps, because there is no principled way of doing so."[233] Because any citizen has the potential to be just as much a member of the 'press' as a member of the organized media, the First Amendment cannot be used to give reporters rights to more information.

What the Constitution has achieved is insuring that any governmental constraints placed on the press are spawned from clear moral and societal objections. Should a magazine be allowed to print lies? Should a book be allowed to ruin someone's reputation? Should television, such a powerful influence, especially on the young, be allowed complete freedom with the programs it chooses to air? Shouldn't the government have the right to fight against newspapers leaking secrets vital to national security? These issues have all been addressed and continue to be addressed through our history.

Should a magazine be allowed to print lies? Should a book be allowed to ruin someone's reputation? These two are tied together because media lies are almost always made to hurt someone. Libel is a written, printed, or pictorial statement that damages a person by defaming his or her character or reputation. Defaming is defined as falsely communicating information that injures a person's reputation by lowering the community's regard for that person or by otherwise holding an individual up to hatred, contempt, or ridicule. Libel laws exist to protect people from the press; thus, the media may not print lies and ruin a reputation. But this is not to be read that the media can never speak ill of a person, because this happens every day. The distinction was made in the landmark libel case, New York Times Co. v. Sullivan.[234] The case was an appeal by the New York Times of a case decided by the Alabama Supreme Court. In that case the court had ruled in favor of L. B. Sullivan, a Montgomery city commissioner who supervised the police department and who had brought libel action against the Times for running a pro-civil rights advertisement which made allegations that peaceful demonstrations in the city hade been confronted by a "wave of terror" instigated by the police of Montgomery. The ad also listed some examples of specific police cruelty, some of which were found later to be spurious. The Times appealed the case to the Supreme Court arguing that they were right in assuming the accuracy of the charges and thus for not verifying them, and that they had the right to run the ad under the First and Fourteenth Amendments. The Court voted unanimously to reverse the lower court's decision. Justices William J. Brennan, Jr. said this of libel action brought by a public official against critics of his official conduct, "the Constitutional guarantees require ... a federal rule that prohibits a public official from recovering damages for a defamatory falsehood relating to his official conduct unless he proves that the statement was made with 'actual malice' – that is, with knowledge that it was false or with reckless disregard of whether it was false or not."[235]

Should television, such a powerful influence, especially on the young, be allowed complete freedom with the programs it chooses to air? This question deals with the issue of obscenity. Obscenity is a term used to describe something that is indecent, lewd, or offensive in behavior, expression, or appearance. No overlaying judgment can be made on what is or is not obscene because standards differ from person to person and region to region. Most obscenity cases brought to the Supreme Court are decided on an individual basis as the individual's right of free expression is weighed against society's responsibility to protect the morals and welfare of the community. The grandest and most far reaching case was that of Miller v. California (1973) in which the Supreme Court ruled by a narrow margin that individual states may ban books, magazines, films, or plays if they are offensive to local standards.[236] In Chief Justice Warren E. Burger's remarks, the specific guide lines for determining what is obscene were laid out. First, would the average person, applying contemporary community standards, find the work as a whole appealing to prurient (sexually arousing) feelings; second, does the work depict or describe sexual conduct in a strongly offensive way; and third, does the work, as a whole, lack serious literary, artistic, political, or scientific value. Needless to say, there were many questions about this decision and, in 1987, the Supreme Court changed the guidelines listed in Miller v. California writing that juries must now apply a national standard in deciding whether a work has redeeming value, rather than some local standard.

Shouldn't the government have the right to fight against newspapers leaking secrets vital to national security? Through document classification, the government does keep a tight rein on information that could be detrimental to national security. But this is not to say that the government can hide everything it wishes. The Supreme Court may order the release of any documents and almost all classified documents must be released after seven years. For example, in 1971, the 'Pentagon Papers' were leaked to the New York Times and the Washington Post. President Richard M. Nixon and the Justice Department desperately tried to prevent the publication of the papers and, in fact, got a temporary restraining order that prevented the papers from publishing the information. The Times quickly took the case to the Supreme Court where it was decided by a 6 to 3 vote that the papers could release the story and 'be free to publish news.'

The free press still remains a questioned entity today. Does the Constitution give us the freedom to print anything, no matter how irresponsible, or does it simply mean we are free from government censorship? The courts have shown an analysis combining both lines of thinking. The press is free to speak, just as any citizen is free to speak without government infringement. But the press also has a responsibility to be honest, informative, and decent.

I maintain that the press' biggest enemy, the most voracious proponent for censorship is, in fact, the press itself. The press self censure more than any court case has decided they should, more than any law has demanded they do so, and more than the people ever wanted them to. The question is why. Why do the press self censure? The press self censure for four main reasons: money, politics, 'follow the leader' phenomenon, and problems with a specific story.

Money is an enormous motivator for the press. The rose tinted dream that the press are the people's eyes and that they fight for us by educating us is just that - a dream, as far as main stream news goes ('main stream news' refers to any large news agency: The New York Times, The Washington Post, The Los Angeles Times, CBS, CNN, NBC, Fox, etc.). Rather, the giants of news are self serving enterprises, motivated, like any other corporation, by money. Hence, the press self censure due to money mostly under the simple motivation of wealth accumulation. Seven corporations control our mass media. The New York Times owns itself as well as other newspapers; The Washington Post owns itself and Newsweek Magazine among other newspapers; Viacom owns CBS, UPN, MTV, BET, and Paramount Pictures and others; Time Warner owns CNN, AOL, HBO, Warner Bros. Pictures, Time, Life, and People, and others; Disney owns the expansive Disney franchise, ABC, ESPN, A&E, Lifetime, E!, Miramax and Touchstone Pictures among others; General Electric owns NBC, CNBC, MSNBC, USA, Bravo, and Universal Pictures and Studios and others; finally, News Corporation owns Fox, Fox News, FX, 20th Century Fox, The New York Post and others. All of these businesses are exactly like any other business except the commodity they sell is news. They are, thus, motivated not by what the people should know, but by what the people want to know. They will then overfeed stories simply because they capture the people's interest and not tell us stories that they think will bore us. This is causing severe harm to the American people who, for example, should know who the Secretary of Defense is and what he or she stands for, but rather are more interested and thus are fed all about the latest celebrity divorce. What is newsworthy is no longer an issue of its importance to the American public, but its appeal to the American Public. Comedian John Stewart wrote in his book America, A Citizens Guide to Democracy an equation for news coverage of a kidnapping: y=Family Income x (Abductee Cuteness/Skin Color)^2 + Length of Abduction x Media Savvy of Grieving Parent[3], where y=minutes of press coverage.[237] In addition, the media also self censures stories that may become financially detrimental. Million dollar law suits have tamed the news' wild side.

Politics is another motivator for news self censorship. News agencies, once again self serving, may choose not to report government actions that, if the public became aware of, would anger them against the agencies. Partisan news is now the norm, and only adds to self censorship. A liberal news program may only report the goods of liberal politicians and the grievances of republican politicians, and republican news does the same but vice versa. What often gets lost in the divide is the truth. There are also instances where there is direct pressure from the government on the press to report or not to report a certain story. For example, in 1961, The New York Times' reporter Tad Szulc wrote an article revealing that the United States was about to launch an invasion of Cuba using CIA trained Cuban exiles.[238] Word of the article reached President Kennedy before it was published and he promptly called James Reston, The Times' Washington bureau chief, and asked him to kill the story. Eventually, a heavily edited version of the article was published with no mention of the CIA's involvement, or that the invasion was imminent. Kennedy was later quoted as saying to the Times Managing Editor Turner Catledge that, "If you had printed more about the operation, you could have saved us from a colossal mistake."[239]

Another reason some stories are not reported is that they have not been 'blessed' by the 'bigger fish' in the press world. Many of the smaller 1,500 or so daily newspapers get their leads on stories from the bigger newspapers, resting comfortably under the protective shadow of the giants (their judgment in reporting is less likely to be challenged if it coincides with the Post or the Times.) World news, in particular, is very difficult to find in smaller papers if it were not in a bigger one first because the bigger papers have the resources to put reporters around the world.

The final significant reason the press self censures a story is if the story is problematic. Sometimes, a reliable source cannot be found (an eye witness is not deemed to be reliable) to support the story through testimony. Also, a story would be difficult to report because it does not have an easily identifiable beginning, middle, and end (example: acid rain is never ending). Tieng into the media's desire to give the public what it wants, a lot of stories are cut because they are termed too complex for the general public (example: because no one would understand the savings and loan crisis anyway, why report it?) Another reason for non-reporting is if a story is too old, or has already been covered. At that point, many news agencies will say 'why bother?' But then they are ignoring their duty to keep the public informed.

The press self censure for capitalistic, corporate reasons. The mass media once had a duty to the public, now they have a duty to their stock holders. The smaller press agencies are stunted by the larger ones, and the TV news is just a flashier face slapped on the same print news.

The U.S. press uses many different tools to self censure – to keep the public uninformed for the reasons described above. Chiefly used is story or fact omission, bad reporting and tainted reporting. Bad reporting is characterized by face value transmission (no fact check or passing on someone else's story), false balancing (not reporting all sides of a story), or simply lying. Tainted reporting is that which is colored by political bias. All are used, whether intentionally or not, to censure our news and keep the people in the dark.

Story omission is the greatest way the press self censures. Completely ignoring an event or situation and not informing the public about it is the press' easiest tool for maintaining its own agenda. Omission is easier and simpler than lying and harder for angry citizens to prosecute. Non-reported stories number in the thousands and so many are crucial to America and the world. Omission mostly occurs because the "powers that be" don't want a certain story reported, (see description of Bay of Pigs media cover up above). Americans have come to rest on the belief that anything not reported is insignificant, and that the press can be trusted to report everything that should be reported. But that has been proven false time and time again. For example, in 1965, the Indonesian military – advised, equipped, trained, and financed by the U.S. military and the CIA – overthrew President Achmed Sukarno and the Indonesian Communist Party, killing over half a million people in what has been termed the greatest act of political mass murder since the Nazi Holocaust.[240] And yet, the story was not even mentioned for three months and then only in passing in Time magazine. When it was finally reported in The New York Times (5 months after the uprising) the small, no-detail article praised the Indonesian military for "rightly playing its part with utmost caution."[241] The American people in general are then left knowing nothing of the fact that our government supported mass murder. The article was most likely censured because it would be highly embarrassing to the country and would reflect horrifically on the democratic movement. But one can be sure that if the roles were reversed and it were a communist regime overthrowing a democratic ruling party and killing hundreds of thousands it would be front page news for weeks.

Bad reporting is another tool the press uses for self censorship but in a less drastic way than omission. In bad reporting, a story is reported but facts are changed, un-researched, or simply wrong. Everyday, in all newspapers, there will be a list of corrections from the last edition. Most are mistakes that the editor didn't see until after the paper hit the presses or that readers called in to report. But many mistakes are left because so many are an intentional skewing of stories to hide or exploit certain angles.[242]

Face value transmission is a very common reporting inaccuracy, particularly in smaller papers and in political reporting. Face value transmission is what occurs when facts or stories are passed from source to the public without the press checking the facts. For example, in the early 1950's, it took four years before the press stopped blindly passing Senator Joseph McCarthy's allegations around the nation and actually began to investigate and then to report the truth. So often, politicians' accounts on domestic and foreign policy are passed directly from their press agents to the people;[243] the press is supposed to be the people's watchdog on the government but all they generally do is act as the government's megaphone to tell the country whatever it wants.

False balancing, another censoring tool, is seen when only one or two sides of a story are presented to the public. Our country had been lulled into thinking that in almost all stories there are at most two sides, be it liberal v. conservative, democratic v. socialist, industrial v. environmental, etc. Thus, the press at most presents us with two sides on a given story even though almost all stories have three or four or more interpretations.

Lies are the mass media's last resort in self censuring. The press lies when they want to make up stories, cover up stories, or change stories. For example, in 1996, the San Jose Mercury News ran an in-depth series about CIA-contra cocaine shipments that were flooding East Los Angeles.[244] The article was based on a year-long investigation that was supported by hundreds of documents, witness statements, and depositions. Oddly enough, no large media agencies picked the story up for several months until it had gained enough fame on the Internet that it could no longer be ignored. The media then began an assault on the story claiming there was no evidence to support the story's claims, that the Mercury News series was bad journalism, and that the real problem was the public's propensity to be hysterical, gullible, and susceptible to conspiracy mania. Lies were spread discounting the story and the paper itself. Eventually, the valid and significant piece of informative journalism was completely discredited and slandered.[245]

Tainted reporting is by far the most common and 'main stream' form of media self censorship. There was a time when a canon of good journalism was being non-biased; now party based reporting is the norm. Each media's political bias is determined by two main factors – what the boss believes and what the target populace believes (once again catering to the people rather than informing them.) Stories are tainted by political bias in the manner in which they are presented or, as the case may be, not presented.

Two ways information is skewed is through framing and labeling. Framing refers to the presentation of information – by using emphasis and other embellishments mass media can create a desired impression without resorting to explicit advocacy and without departing too far from the appearance of objectivity. Framing is achieved in the way the news is packaged, the amount of exposure, the placement (front page versus hidden in the middle), the tone of presentation (sympathetic versus derogatory), headlines, photographs and other accoutrements. In this way, a politically biased newspaper can turn the public's opinion to its side covertly, by perhaps having flashier color pictures go along with a story they want the people to believe and having no pictures and an insulting tone accompany a story they want the people to ignore or be against.

Labeling is a more overt form of framing in which subjects are illustrated with non-descript labels that work to make the reader draw certain conclusions. Common positive labels include "stability," "The President's firm leadership," "a strong defense," and a "healthy economy."[246] These are literary gems because they are un-detailed and can be stuck in front of any subject and immediately the subject looks good. Some negative labels are "conspiracy theories," "civil disturbances," "all-white," "un-supported," etc.[247] Perhaps the most common label is used by the press on itself. The liberal and conservative press like nothing more than labeling each other as biased.

Press censorship is not some sort of nationwide, time expansive conspiracy to keep the people in the dark but there are patterns to the cacophony. A statistical analysis of the top 200 stories from 1976-1995 reveals that, while there are some variations from year to year and from election to election, in general, there has been a systematic omission of certain types of issues.[248]

Top 200 Censored stories from 1976-1995

Rank	Subject matter	Number of stories	percentage
1	Political	64	32.0%
2	Corporate	37	18.5%
3	International	30	15.0%
4	Military	28	14.0%
5	Environmental	15	7.5%
6	Health	13	6.5%
7	Media	7	3.5%
8	Economic	5	2.5%
9	Education	1	.5%

There were also patterns of censorship in relation to which political party held the White House. There were significantly more political, international, and military stories exposed by the alternative media during the Reagan and Bush Sr. administrations and more corporate and environmental subjects exposed during the Carter and Clinton Administrations.[249] This pattern is difficult to explain satisfactorily. It is possible that there just happened to be more reason or opportunity to expose political, international, and military matters while Reagan and Bush were in power and Carter and Clinton were more effective in monitoring these sectors during their administrations (and conversely with corporate and environmental subjects while Carter and Clinton were Presidents.) More likely, however, is that the alternative news media was more interested in investigating political, international, and military issues during republican administrations and corporate and environmental issues during the democrats' incumbency.

These patterns reflect an extremely alarming reality: the one subject that should be the press's greatest priority to report honestly and completely to the public is the most censored and susceptible to bias squabbles – Politics. The press is supposed to be our watchdog, but 32% of the 200 top stories censored in the past 30 years are political in nature. How can we have faith in our government if we don't honestly know what it is really doing?

What the press is not telling the people is not insignificant, but rather key stories and events that the people should know about. An informed and edified populace is the foundation for a powerful country. The spread of national news unifies the country and protects against the divergence of different sections of the country. The people can keep tabs on the government, holding it accountable to them only through reading or watching the news. New Englanders can feel tied to the problems of the southwest by knowing what is going on there. When a disconnect of news happens – a story is untold, an event uncovered – repercussions occur.

Every year from 1976-1996, a group called Project Censored has released a book of the top 25 censored stories from that year. In 1978, the group included the story of the Law Enforcement Intelligence

Unit (LEIU) as the sixth most censored story.[250] The LEIU links the intelligence squads of almost every major police force in the United States and Canada. Its members are police officers who work for state and city governments, but it is a private 'club,' meaning that it is not a government agency in its own right and is not federally funded. Thus it is not answerable to citizens the way a government agency would be. Its members are loyal to the LEIU above their own particular agency and so the LEIU cuts across vertical lines of authority of local government. Most alarming is that the LEIU is a private club and, therefore, not subject to freedom-of-information laws. They withhold their files from the FBI, all other federal agencies and, in fact, any non LEIU member. Ex-members of the LEIU admit to illegal wiretapping, breaking and entering, and spying on people to gather information for their files. Put simply, the LEIU is our nation's police force's secret tool to gather information they can't gain through legal means. And yet, prior to 1978, no major news source had even mentioned the subversive organization. The small alternative paper, the San Francisco Chronicle, published an article called "Leaks to the Mob: U.S. Police Network's Big Problem" on November 25, 1978. Before that, only Penthouse had mentioned it in "America's Secret Police Network" (1976.) Because the mass media has refused to pick up this story that has potential political repercussions, the American people are, in general, left in the dark about a secret agency that has been known to spy on them. Unfortunately because few people are really aware of the scale on which the LIEU functions it will continue to do the dirty work of our police force with the possibility of abuse to American citizens.

The LEIU is merely one example of clear harm to the people that the press' self-censorship is causing. Other examples include Jimmy Carter's connection to the Trilateral Commission, an alliance of several hundred top political and economic leaders from North America, Japan, and Western Europe whose main goal is to insure the economic advancement of its members in those sectors (censored story of 1976.) Another example is the United Nations' findings after intense investigation that the U.S. was guilty of violating the United Nations Universal Declaration of Human Rights and its Standard Minimal Rules on the Treatment of Prisoners (censored story of

1979.) A third example is the refusal of the Wall Street Journal to print the in-depth, three-part investigation of its reporter Mary Williams Walsh that exposed how CBS News broadcast biased news coverage of the Afghanistan War (censored story of 1989.) Stories such as these add to the ignorance of the American public to their detriment.

Journalism's golden era was that of the muckrakers. Journalists like Ida Tarbell and Upton Sinclair were the epitome of what reporters should be. The muckrakers exposed transgressions and injustice, educated the people, and moved society forward by helping people hold wrongdoers accountable. The muckrakers were not part of some enormous news conglomerate. The reporters were more concerned with getting all the grit of the news than with how much money their company would get next quarter.

The muckrakers did immeasurable good for the American people because of their willingness to report on any and everything. Lincoln Steffen's *The Shame of the Cities* exposed municipal political corruption to the public; Ida Tarbell's *The History of the Standard Oil Company* led to the disbanding of the giant monopoly; Upton Sinclair's *The Jungle,* a powerful exposé of the meat packing industry, led to legislative changes and the first Pure Food and Drugs Act; and Rachel Carson's *Silent Springs* was a leading instigator of the modern environmental movement by exposing the rampant misuse of chemical pesticides.

These writers did exactly what the mission of the press states: to inform the people on any and everything so that the people may be educated enough to maintain the most democratic society. Because of their works, lives were saved, justice was insured, and democracy was furthered.

The American press today has rejected the ideals held up by the Founding Fathers and the Muckrakers. Journalists sold their rights for money and gave up their righteous mission for cheap corporate gain. The American press relinquishes its own constitutional freedom through self censorship to the detriment of the people. The press was given the responsibility to inform the public. The press was given the freedom to carry out that responsibility in any manner necessary. Over our history, the Courts have insured and upheld these freedoms, but our press turns away in greed. The press has not informed the public of so many issues that effect our lives daily: acid rain, the LEIU, CIA drug involvement, U.S. Government policy concerning the international sale of pesticides, the list goes on and on. The press has lost sight of the nobility of its work and the people are paying the price.

Bibliography

Cockburn, Alexander, and Jeffrey St. Clare. <u>White Out</u>. 1st ed. Vol. 1. London: Verso, 1998.

Evans, J. E. <u>Freedom of the Press</u>. 1st ed. Vol. 1. Minneapolis: Lerner Publications Company, 1990.

Farish, Leah. <u>The First Amendment</u>. 1st ed. Vol. 1. Springfield, NJ: Enslow, Inc., 1998.

"Indonesia's New Phase." <u>The New York Times</u> 22 Dec. 1965. 17 Oct. 2005 <http://pqasb.pqarchiver.com/nytimes/>.

Jensen, Carl, and Project Censored. <u>20 Years of Censored News</u>. 1st ed. Vol. 1. New York City: Seven Stories P, 1997.

Lindop, Edmund. <u>The Bill of Rights and Landmark Cases</u>. 1st ed. Vol. 1. New York City: Franklin Watts, 1989.

Lowenthal, David. <u>Present Dangers</u>. 2nd ed. Vol. 1. Dallas: Spence Company, 2002.

Phillips, Peter, and Project Censored . <u>Censored 2005</u>. 1st ed. Vol. 1. New York City: Seven Stories P, 2004.

Stewart, John. America. 1st ed. Vol.1. New York City: Warner Bros, 2004.

The Second Amendment
– The Original Intent

By
Kelsey Morrison

"Quemadmodum gladius neminem occidit, occidentis telum est."
"A sword never kills anybody; it is a tool in the killer's hand."
~Seneca, Letters to Lucilius[251]

Sound familiar? It should. Charlton Heston made a similar statement at a NRA meeting; "Guns don't kill people. People kill people." This stems from one of the most controversial issues today; the Second Amendment in the Bill of Rights. This Amendment states;

> "A well regulated Militia, being necessary to the
> security of a free state, the right of the people to
> keep and bear Arms, shall not be infringed."

Throughout American history, there have been many debates about the true meaning, or interpretation, of the Second Amendment: did the founding fathers write this Amendment with the intent of a collective or individual right? This question has beset some of the brightest political and academic minds all through the nation's history.

The history of the Second Amendment began in England in 1066 and became a reality in Richmond, Virginia, in 1788, with the ratification of the Constitution. The Constitution is based on English Common Law or the English version of the Bill of Rights. Before the Norman Conquest of England, the English relied on militia rather than a standing army for maintaining order and providing military security from foreign empires. The people also had "police responsibilities." In other words, they were obligated to pursue criminals and join a body of people, known as a posse. The idea for forming a militia, as opposed to a standing army, carried from England to America at the time the founders were creating two of the most important documents in American history: the Constitution of the United States, and the Bill of Rights. The latter is where history turned to reality for the Second Amendment.

The Constitution was struggling; it needed ratification from at least nine states, but only eight had consented at the time. Virginia was the best, and last, hope for the Federalists to win the fight for ratification. However, there was much opposition from anti-Federalists, especially Patrick Henry and George Mason.

Virginia was nearly half black and half white, half Federalist and half anti-Federalist. The white population lived in utter fear of slave insurrection and the main slave control was the militia. "James Madison wrote the Second Amendment to assure the southern states that Congress would not undermine the slave system by disarming the Militia, which was then the principal instrument of slave control throughout the South," declares Carl T. Bogus Law Professor, Roger Williams School of Law.[252] The militia was so crucial that southern states refused to send their militias to defend against the British.

Mason and Henry questioned the Constitution because it gave Congress unmatchable control over the militia. "I ask, sir, what is the Militia? It is the whole people, except for a few public officials," said Mason, suggesting Congress might use its power over the militia to do "indirectly what it could not do directly."[253]

"They tell us ... that we are weak – unable to cope with so formidable an adversary. But when shall we be stronger? ... Will it be when we are totally disarmed, and when a British guard shall be stationed in every house? ... three million people, armed in the holy course of liberty ... are invincible by any force which our enemy can send against us," added Patrick Henry.[254]

The militia of that time is very similar to the present-day National Guard. Americans believed that the militia would provide military security and police power, similar to what it did in England. The militias were organized by the states which could arm them and direct them for the purpose of enforcing the law, fighting a foreign power or stopping a rebellion. The American militia was also expected to protect liberty in the case of domestic unrest or an uprising leading to tyranny. Article 13 of the Virginia Constitution, adopted in 1776, states:

A well regulated Militia, composed of the body of the people, trained to arms, is the proper, natural and safe defense of a free State; that Standing Armies, in time of peace, should be avoided as dangerous to liberty; and that, in all cases, the military should be under strict subordination to and governed by the civil power.[255]

In some colonies, every adult male was obligated to join a militia. "When the framers wrote the Second Amendment, they did not see it as giving the private citizen a right to have arms for his or her own sake. Rather, the purpose of the amendment was to assure that citizens would have a right to be armed so that they could become part of a militia," says Herbert M. Levine, author of 'American Issues Debated: Gun Control.'[256]

Guns were a necessity during the 17th and 18th centuries. In fact, in 1770, Georgia passed a law requiring its citizens to carry guns to church with them. Guns were not used for sport; they were used for protection from attacks by American Indians and for hunting animals for food and clothing. However, by the 1800s, states began to pass what would be the first gun control laws, laws against carrying concealed weapons.

Virginia barely ratified the Constitution, which, in turn, hurt James Madison's career hopes. Madison, upset with losing a bid to the U.S. Senate, settled for running for a House of Representatives seat. Patrick Henry, along with many other anti-Federalists, was upset with the ratification of the Constitution and gerrymandered Madison's congressional district to include as many anti-Federalists as possible. Henry also recruited James Monroe to run against Madison. Madison won the election, promising he would support adding a Bill of Rights to the Constitution. He included, in his draft, a stipulation that is now known as the Second Amendment.

This history of the Second Amendment is essential because it supports the argument that the Amendment was not written for individuals to have the right to keep and bear arms for personal purposes when, in fact, it is only the militia it defines as having the right to bear arms. The Second Amendment was also to protect the southern states from insurrection because they used their militia to control the slaves. Professor Bogus argues that "the evidence – including an analysis of Madison's original language, and an understanding of how he and other founders drew on England's Declaration of Rights – strongly suggests that Madison wrote this provision for the specific purpose of assuring his constituency that Congress could not use it's newly acquired power to deprive the states of an armed Militia. Madison's concern was not hunting, self-defense, national defense, or resistance to governmental tyranny – but slave control."[257]

The NRA and pro-gun activists, however, have a very different point of view. For example, John R. Lott Jr., a fellow at the University of Chicago School of Law and author of More Guns, Less Crime, on the subject of President Bill Clinton's 1994 "Assault Weapons Ban" believes, "There is no reason to believe banning their guns has reduced crime. On the contrary, taking defensive weapons out of the hands of the law-abiding urban poor may actually encourage crime. More important, except for cosmetic differences or provocative names, all these guns are essentially the same as other legal rifles used by hunters." When interviewed further Lott said, "High crime urban areas and neighborhoods with large minority populations have the greatest reductions in violent crime when citizens are legally allowed to carry concealed handguns."[258] However, the following list compares the total number of people killed by handguns in the United States and five other countries during 1992:[259]

- Australia   13
- Great Britain   33
- Sweden   36
- Japan   60
- Switzerland   97
- Canada   128
- United States   13,495

This list severely discredits the NRA and pro-gun activists' argument that more guns equal less crime. The United States has the highest homicide rate of any Western industrialized country; one person is shot every two minutes, and one person dies from a gun shot wound every fourteen minutes.[260] All of the above countries have gun control laws, the same laws that the NRA is trying to outlaw in the United States. Writer Osha Gray Davidson calculated: "Since 1933, more Americans have died from gun wounds here at home than in all the wars our country has been involved in since – and including – the American Revolution."[261]

One should question what would happen to this country if the NRA were able to have its version of "gun-control" laws. This question is actually an easy one to answer, just take a look at countries in the Middle East – Iraq, Israel, and Pakistan – or South Africa or Brazil with their excessive lack of gun control.[262] Every single day in Brazil one hundred people die, that is 36,000 people a year, from firearm related deaths alone.[263] In South Africa, seven out of every hundred people die from firearms. In Karachi, alone, a small city in Pakistan, over 1,000 people die from firearms each year.[264]

"This idea that more guns equals less crime is flat out wrong. The truth is more guns equals more crime and it's as obvious as the nose on my face," said Matthew Nasanchuk of the Violence Policy Center.[265] In truth, the number of violent firearm crimes in the United States between 1987 and 1992 increased from 150 per 100,000 people to over 270 per 100,000 people.[266]

In November, 1988, a study was published in The New England Journal of Medicine about the effects of gun control. The Seattle-Vancouver study took two neighboring cities to illustrate the impact gun control laws have on crime. Researchers studied firearm-related homicides and suicides in Seattle, Washington and Vancouver, British Columbia (western Canada). Although these cities have similar population sizes and population characteristics in crime statistics, they differ in the number of guns per person and gun control laws. Vancouver's laws are stricter than the gun laws in Seattle and the study determined that Vancouver had a much lower gun-related homicide rate. This study shows that gun control does, in fact, work.[267]

On May 14, 2000, hundreds of thousands of protestors gathered on the National Mall demanding better gun control laws. The Million Mom March is just one example of the majority of American people pleading for gun control laws. At the march, Susan Sarandon, actress and anti-gun activist, reminded audiences that the Second Amendment was written when a musket, not an AK-47, was the weapon of a well-regulated militia. Sarandon stated, "A three-year-old cannot operate a musket as easily as a three-year-old can pull a trigger now. There are guns out there that had nothing to do with our forefathers."[268]

Not only has Susan Sarandon spoken up, but the Supreme Court, in the United States v. Miller (15 May 1939), held that "in the absence of any evidence tending to show that possession or use of a 'shotgun having a barrel of less than eighteen inches in length' at this time has some reasonable relationship to the preservation or efficiency of a well-regulated Militia, we cannot say that the Second Amendment guarantees the right to keep and bear such an instrument."[269]

The gun control laws are so ineffective that the Government Accountability Office found that over a nine-month period last year, 47 of 58 gun applications from terror suspects on federal watch lists were approved.[270] Suspected terrorists aren't automatically barred from legally purchasing firearms inside the U.S. In fact, federal law only prohibits selling guns to a miniscule fraction including convicted felons, undocumented immigrants, and the mentally ill. As if that were not bad enough, the NRA has recently drafted a bill that would give legal immunity to the most reckless gun sellers in America. Dennis Henigan, director of the legal action project at the Brady Center to Prevent Gun Violence, called the legislation "such an egregious piece of special-interest legislation, it's almost shameless."[271] Nonetheless, what is really shameless is that on October 20, 2005, the House of Representatives voted to approve the legislation, and President Bush signed it into law. Wayne LaPierre, the NRA's executive vice president, called the vote "a historic day for the NRA and also for the Second Amendment." F. James Sensenbrenner, Jr., House Judiciary Committee Chairman and Republican representative from Wisconsin, said, "Congress must fulfill its constitutional duty and exercise its authority…to deny a few state courts the power to bankrupt the national firearms industry and deny all Americans their fundamental right to bear arms."[272] Washington D.C. Mayor Anthony A. Williams weighed in, stating, "The entire community in the District is working hard to keep down gun violence. It's discouraging when members of Congress pass legislation that would inhibit our ability to hold accountable those individuals or corporate entities who contribute to the proliferation of firearms that are used in committing crimes."[273] In fact, some of the cases which the Bush Administration has deemed "frivolous" by the passage of this bill include:[274]

- The families of the D.C. sniper victims who won a settlement of just over $2 million from a Washington State gun dealer who could not account for his "missing" assault weapons used by the snipers, and who "lost" over 200 other guns.
- The family of Massachusetts slaying victim Danny Guzman, an innocent bystander shot on Christmas Eve, 1999, is pursuing justice against a Massachusetts gun manufacturer that not only negligently hired criminals to work in his plant, but had such irresponsible security practices that it allowed them to walk out of the plant with guns that carried no serial numbers, one of which was used to shoot Guzman
- New Jersey police officers who won a $1 million lawsuit against a West Virginia pawnshop that knowingly sold semiautomatic handguns for cash to a gun trafficking team.

The NRA is also pushing for business owners to be forced to allow employees to bring firearms to work. The President of the Brady Campaign to Prevent Gun Violence, Michael Barnes, inquires, "Is there no end to this? In state after state, the NRA has lobbied for the right to bring hidden, loaded handguns into churches, schools and bars – and now even chemical plants. Is there any place in America where we shouldn't allow firearms?"[275]

Recent polls, taken during the summer of 2004, show that more than 60% of the public favors the renewal of the "Assault Weapons Ban." A 1999 study by President Clinton's Justice Department suggests the ban made it harder and more expensive for criminals to obtain assault weapons.[276] Even the International Association of Chiefs of Police favored reauthorizing and strengthening the ban but the Bush Administration has turned its back on the pleas.

On October 1, 2005, the American government took a huge leap backwards in protecting the American public from gun violence. On this Saturday in October the Floridian government instituted a new self-defense law. Supporters of the law call it the "Stand Your Ground" law, the opponents call it the "Shoot First" law. This new law allows people to shoot anyone who breaks into their homes, occupied vehicle, or even places of business. Under this law, the intruder, no matter if armed or unarmed, is presumed to have criminal intent, which then "justifies" the return use of force. The Brady Campaign has announced its effort to educate the public, and inform the Florida tourists of the new risks of traveling to Florida. In a press release, the Brady Campaign said, "Individuals who are unfamiliar with Florida's roads, traffic regulations and customs, or who speak foreign languages, or look different than Florida residents, may face a higher risk of danger – because they may be more likely to be perceived as threatening by Floridians, and because they are unaware of Florida's new law that says individuals who feel their safety is threatened or their possessions are at risk are legally authorized to use deadly force."[277] In fact, police, prosecuting attorneys and gun violence prevention advocates worry that the new "freedom" may lead to reckless use of guns on the streets. Before this new law was passed, people in Florida could carry concealed guns in public places, but could only use the guns as a last resort when safely avoiding injury or bodily harm was otherwise unavoidable.

One example of just how controversial the Second Amendment is can be seen by what is going on in the District of Columbia today. Currently, D.C. has two sets of laws applying to firearms. One, passed by Congress, is now part of the D.C. code and regulates the purchase, possession, and carrying of firearms. The second, a much newer one, was passed in 1976 by the D.C. City Council and prohibits the sale of handguns, and requires all firearms to be registered and all owners licensed. It also prohibits anyone from either bringing a handgun into or through the city. Handguns are prohibited in D.C. unless they had been registered by February 5, 1977. Rifles and shotguns may be purchased only from a licensed D.C. dealer, and delivery is not made until the registration certificate is approved by the Metropolitan Police Department. In order to obtain the certificate one must be 21-years-old, pass a vision test or have a valid D.C. license, and not be:

- Convicted of a crime or violent weapons offense
- Under indictment for a violent crime
- Convicted of a narcotics or assault or battery charge within the last five years

- Acquitted of a crime by reason of insanity within the last five years
- Committed to a mental hospital within the past five years
- Found negligent in any firearm mishap

Those living in D.C., D.C. police officers, Delegate Eleanor Holmes Norton, and even the Republican Representative Thomas M. Davis III of Virginia all agree with the gun control laws in place. Not the NRA, nor pro-gun activists, though: They believe the current gun control law is "a Constitutional issue, not a home rule question," says Representative Mark Edward Souder, Indiana's 3rd District Representative.[278]

In fact, Mark Souder is sponsoring legislation to overturn D.C.'s gun control laws. Souder says, "The folly of gun control is shown time and time again in cities that have strict gun control laws. For example, Washington, D.C., has the most restrictive gun control laws in the country … What most people don't understand is just how the D.C. gun laws have stripped its citizens of their rights to defend against violent crime. That is why on September 25, 2003, I introduced a bill which seeks to restore to citizens of the District of Columbia the right to own and possess firearms in their homes and businesses."[279] Souder also states that the city's homicide rate shows that the restrictions on guns are ineffective.

On the contrary, the D.C. homicide rate is at a twenty-year low, and has fallen 55% since 1994. Delegate Eleanor Norton ripped apart Souder's bill, saying it's "ludicrous logic… that gun safety causes murders… I have seen various members of Congress try to do some low-down, dirty, mean things to the people of the District of Columbia, all to promote their own political agendas against the will of the people who live here. That we are here discussing this matter is yet a new low."[280] Thomas Davis III has also spoken against the bill saying, "No one should question the importance of keeping fully loaded assault weapons off the streets of the District. There is an important place for debate on D.C. gun laws – that is, in the chambers of the D.C. Council, not the Congress."[281]

It is also interesting that Mark Souder has taken the following position:

"I don't care that commanding majorities of your citizens support greatly restrictive laws on the possession of handguns. I don't care that all your elected officials do. I don't care that local business groups call the law good for business. I don't care that the courts have said the law is constitutional. Even though you didn't vote for me, I say you have to have free access to guns, whether you like it or not. Because, you know, you might find yourself under the rule of a tyrant who will ignore your opinion and legal rights and you'll need a gun to get rid of them."[282]

Not only does Souder not live in D.C., but in this statement he is telling the people of D.C. he does not care what they want, and he is making himself out to be the "tyrant" he speaks against. "So, here's the question; does Souder not realize that, under the logic of the Second Amendment absolutists, he's justifying D.C. residents shooting him and giving them the means to do it? Karma can be so ironic," says David Vacca, who graduated George Washington University with an M.A. in political science.[283]

However, Souder isn't the only person from Indiana supporting this bill. His fellow Congressman, John Hostettler, Indiana's 8th district Congressman, is also supporting Souder's bill. Although one shouldn't be surprised, this is a man who is serving a suspended sentence for trying to bring a gun aboard a commercial airliner.

The facts prove that the founding fathers intended the Second Amendment as a collective, not an individual right. By doing this they were ensuring that the American government could not become a tyranny. So where are the NRA and the Bush Administration leading the American public? As Seneca said, "A sword never kills anybody; it is a tool in the killer's hand,"[284] and what is a gun other than a tool? A gun is a tool designed to kill. By removing gun-control laws that protect the American public, the NRA is leading them into the same chaos that has overcome Brazil, South America, and many of the Middle Eastern countries. Without these vital gun-control laws, would America's firearm related death toll reach the rate of that of Brazil or South America? Should the American public really sit back and wait to find out? No, instead they should educate themselves on one of the biggest, most controversial issues plaguing America today. One final thought, Mao Tse-Tung, a well-known collectivist and founder of the Chinese Communist party in 1921, once said, "Every good communist should know that political power grows out of the barrel of a gun."[285]

Bibliography

Bogus, Carl T. "The Hidden History of the Second Amendment," Violence Policy Center. http://www.vpc.org/fact_sht/hidhist.htm.

"Firearms Facts," Coalition for Peace Action. http://www.peacecoalition.org/facts/index.html.

"BUSH ADMINISTRATION STATEMENT ON SENATE BILL REPEATS LIES OF THE NATIONAL RIFLE ASSOCIATION," July 26, 2005. The Brady Campaign. http://http://www.bradycampaign.org/press/release.php?release=670.

Centanni, Steve. "DC Gun Law Under Fire," December 2, 2002. Fox News. http://www.foxnews.com/story/0,2933,71750,00.html.

Cornell, Saul. "The Second Amendment Under Fire: The Uses of History and the Politics of Gun Control," January, 2001. George Mason University. http://historymatters.gmu.edu/credits.html.

"Editorial: Lax gun laws serving interests of terrorists," March, 2005. San Antonio Express-News. http://www.mysanantonio.com/opinion/editorials/stories/MYSA2031405.04B.terror-guns2ed.12b210f7d.html.

"Gun Lobby Endangers Workers in its Push to Force Businesses to Allow Guns in the Workplace," August 2, 2005. The Brady Campaign. http://www.bradycampaign.org/press/release.php?release=678.

Egendorf, Laura K., ed. How Can Gun Violence Be Reduced? San Diego: Bonnie Szumski, 2002.

"Firearms and Violence," July 9, 2005. DAWN; the Internet Edition. http://www.dawn.com/2005/07/09/ed.htm.

Hanson, Ottem, and Freya. The Second Amendment: The Right to Own Guns. New Jersey: Enslow, 1998.

Jones, Susan. "Ad Campaign Warns Tourists About New Florida Gun Law," September 28, 2005. CNSNews.com. http://www.cnsnews.com/ViewCulture.asp?Page=%5CCulture%5Carchive%5C200509%5CCUL20050928a.html.

LaPierre, Wayne, and Jay Baker. Shooting Straight. Washington, DC: Regnery Publishing, Inc., 2002.

Levine, Herbert M. American Issues Debated; Gun Control. Edited by Kathy DeVico, Shirley Shalit. Austin, TX: Vaughn Company, Steck, 1998.

Long, Roderick T. "Philosophy Page," http://praxeology.net/seneca.htm.

Lott, John R., Jr. "Clinton Lies About the Assault Weapons Ban," 1998. http://www.tsra.com/Lott2.htm.

_____. More Guns, Less Crime, second ed. Chicago: The University of Chicago Press, 2000.

Malone, Mary. James Madison. New Jersey: Enslow, 1997.

"Map & Graph: Countries by Crime: Murders with Firearms," December, 2005. nationmaster.com. http://www.nationmaster.com/graph-T/cri_mur_wit_fir_cap.

Miller, Marilyn. Words That Built A Nation. New York: Scholastic, 1999.

Miller, Maryann. Working Together Against Gun Violence. The Rosen Publishing Group, Inc., 1997.

Montgomery, Dave. "Interest in Renewing '94 Weapons Ban is Low," August 12, 2004. Detroit Free Press. http://www.freep.com/news/nw/guns12e_20040812.htm.

"Q&A: Brazil Arms Referendum," October 23, 2005. BBC News. http://news.bbc.co.uk/2/hi/americas/4356728.stm.

Sargis, Tom, Jr. "Famous Quotes from Famous Americans (and others...)," October 14, 2005. http://www.ycsi.net/users/gunsmith/quotes.htm.

Souder, Mark. "Issues: Second Amendment," U.S. House of Representatives. http://souder.house.gov/Issues/Issue/?IssueID=664.

Tuomala, S. Marvin. "The Right to Bear Arms," http://www.spiritcaller.net/quotes/guns.htm.

Vacca, David. "David Vacca's Suitcase Full of Good Ideas," September 16, 2005. http://www.radix.net/~vacca/.

The Right To Bear Arms
A Limitless Right?
By
Matt Vennell

"A well regulated Militia, being necessary to the security of a free State, the right of the people to keep and bear Arms, shall not be infringed." This is how the Second Amendment appears in the U.S. Constitution. These twenty- seven words were modified from a longer version of the amendment, proposed by James Madison. The original proposal contained a clause about a person's right to be excused from military service due to religious beliefs, but this clause was removed by Congress. The final version of the amendment to the U.S. Constitution was accepted as a part of the Bill of Rights without any disagreement. On September 25, 1789, Congress adopted this, and eleven other amendments. On December 15, 1791, the Virginia legislature ratified the Bill of Rights, bringing ten of the proposed amendments into the Constitution.[286] Today, in America, the Second Amendment and its meaning with regard to the twenty-first century is one of the most debated political topics. There are many opposing views about the original intent of the Founding Fathers and what the implications of this amendment would be in modern society, compared with the time when the amendment was written. Since the adoption of the Second Amendment, Congress and the Supreme Court have taken measures, usually after large national events involving guns, to make the amendment practical in modern society.

Today, there are two basic schools of interpretation of the Second Amendment's meaning. One can be called the Standard Model, or the Individual's Right Model, and the other can be called the States' Right Model, or the Collective Right Model. The Standard Model's view is that the Second Amendment "protects the right of an individual to own firearms. The 'militia' of the Second Amendment is comprised of the armed citizenry at large, but in no way is the individual right dependent on being in active militia duty." The States' Right Model claims that "The Second Amendment protects the rights of States to keep armed militias. Because the role of militias is served by the National Guard, this protection does not extend to individuals." These two schools of thought have varying opinions on what the intent of the Second Amendment is, and the arguments mostly revolve around a few certain questions. These questions are: What does the word "militia" mean? What does the phrase "the people" mean? and what "arms" are protected by the Amendment?[2]

Understanding the original intent of the Second Amendment, as interpreted by the Founding Fathers, is more easily understood by examining the time in which it was written. Under British rule, King George III had control of the people through his regulated army. This army was formed by the government and was a government body of soldiers. Conversely, a militia was made up of volunteering citizens who were capable of taking up arms. With the memory of King George III's army, the Founding Fathers wanted to make sure that militias could be used by states as a counter balance to the federal army.[3] This would prevent the federal army from controlling the country, and would allow people to take up their personal weapons against the federal government, if it ever became oppressive and tyrannical.

Guns were a large part of people's lives during this time. During the colonial period, people depended on guns for hunting and to protect themselves from threats to their families and property. In Georgia, for example, there was a law passed in 1770 requiring citizens to carry guns to church. After the start of the Revolutionary War, guns were even more necessary in a military sense, and the Second Continental Congress called on the people to "bear arms" in the fight against the British.

At the Constitutional Convention, George Mason was one of the anti-federalists who opposed the new constitution, because he felt it lacked a Bill of Rights. Our Bill of Rights, in the Constitution today, is modeled after Mason's Virginia Declaration of Rights, which was written when he served in the House of Burgesses in Virginia. This Declaration of Rights contained the provision about people's right to "bear arms" as well. In Thomas M. Cooley's, "The General Principles of Constitutional Law in the United States of America (1880)", the period in time when the amendment was written is discussed, with reference to the intent of the amendment. The book argues that the Second Amendment was originally modified from part of the English Bill of Rights of 1688. In this bill of rights, the amendment was a protest against unfair rule of a leader. It was meant to keep the power of any one ruler in check, and to ensure that people could not be made defenseless to an unjust, tyrannical ruler. With regard to the phrase "militia", Cooley's work states that the intent was to allow anyone who was fit to be in any type of militia, the right to personally bear arms. As well as allowing citizens to bear arms, it is noted that the intent of the amendment was also to allow private citizens to be prepared to participate in any actions of an armed militia. While the amendment was insuring that militias could not be disarmed by the federal government, it was also allowing individuals to possess and bear their private arms, to insure that a state militia could function against any threat, if necessary.[4] This said, not only was the amendment intended to allow private citizens to own guns, but to allow them to carry them and practice their use as well. This would insure that people were properly trained, in case the forming of a militia was ever necessary. Thomas M Cooley's view on the original intent of the Second Amendment appears to be consistent with most literature written about the amendment around the time of the writing of the Bill of Rights and the U.S. Constitution.

An analysis of the text and structure of the Second Amendment is interpreted to support the individual's rights to carry guns in a Department of Justice article entitled "Whether the Second Amendment Secures An Individual Right." The article takes the questions about the phrasing of the amendment and explains how it is intended to secure an individual's rights. It points out that the "right of the people" is intended to mean the rights of individuals, not of a State or of militiamen of a State. Since the word "right" and the word "people" are joined together, it is felt that this phrase's intent is to secure the right for individuals, and not necessarily for a government or a body of soldiers. Also, the phrase "the right of the people" appears multiple times in the Bill of Rights and in the Constitution. The First, Fifth, and Ninth Amendments contain the phrasing, "right of the people" and those amendments all have a clear intent to give rights to individual citizens, not solely to the government or to a state organized body.

The words "to keep and bear arms" are argued to apply to individuals as well. It is explained in the article that, while this phrase was used with a military context in the times that the amendment was written, it was not limited to a military context. The words "to keep and bear arms" were used by many people throughout history, including some of the Founding Fathers, to discuss an individual's right to own and posses a gun for a variety of purposes. Also, given this phrase's context, immediately following "the right of the people", it seems more likely to be giving these rights to individuals, not to the state or government.[5]

The words "Well Regulated Militia" can also be used to determine the original meaning of the Second Amendment. In a Department of Justice document, it is shown that there is a difference between a militia and a state or national army. At the time, militias were made up of private citizens, not soldiers of the government. For the most part, militias did not meet or train on a regular basis as a function of the state. They were simply made up of any able-bodied citizens who could arm themselves and unite to provide a common defense for their state. Since militias did not meet and train regularly, it is accepted in this document that the intent would have been for the citizens of a militia to own their own private guns, enabling them to practice and become familiar with their weapons on their own time. Allowing private citizens to own their own guns, for the purpose of practicing on their own time, to be ready for any militia action, would ensure that militias could be called upon to protect a state from foreign invaders or a tyrannical rule. [6]

The best way to determine the original intent of the Second Amendment is to look at documentation by the Founding Fathers. Mason, Jefferson, and Madison, who all had major roles in the writing the Constitution and Bill of Rights, have been quoted at debates over the adoption of the Second Amendment. Madison, the "Father of the Constitution," wrote in Federalist No. 46 (1788), "Notwithstanding the military establishments of the several kingdoms of Europe...

the governments are afraid to trust the people with arms." George Mason was the "Father of the Bill of Rights" and also wrote the Virginia Declaration of Rights. During his push for individual rights in the Constitution, he said "... that people have a right to keep and bear arms; that a well regulated Militia, composed of the body of the People, trained to arms, is the proper, natural, and safe defense of a free state." Thomas Jefferson, in the proposed Virginia Constitution, said that "No freeman shall ever be debarred the use of arms." These quotes obviously point toward the intent of the Founding Fathers as being one of an individual's right, as opposed to a state-only right. These direct source quotes are the best way to discover what the original intent of the Second Amendment was meant to be by the Founding Fathers.

Since the ratification of the Bill of Rights, the Second Amendment has been one of the most questioned amendments in our Constitution. Its intent is constantly debated by different groups in America, and it is the central focus of many groups both anti-gun and pro-gun. Firearms issues are often major factors in elections, and cause national debates whenever the issue of guns and gun control come up in the media.

Over the last two hundred years, the Second Amendment right to bear arms has been questioned thoroughly by both the American people and courts. Cases revolving around the Second Amendment have been brought before the Supreme court many times and have prompted the Court to pass different regulations to meet the requests of different interest groups and different outcries from the American citizens. Legislation has been passed over the last two hundred years, in an effort to protect peoples' Constitutional freedoms and also keep society as safe as possible. With pressure coming from both sides of the gun control argument, the Supreme Court has had to rule on many cases, passing various restrictions and protections for the American people with regard to the Second Amendment right and gun ownership, but has still maintained that individuals have the right to bear arms in America. The intent of our Founding Fathers has been upheld.

Throughout American history to modern times, the story of the Second Amendment follows a somewhat consistent, almost predictable course. Public concern about gun violence, and legislation aimed at preventing it, has consistently coincided with high-profile shootings and threateningly violent social change, either domestic or international.[7]

In the early 1900s, the individual's right to bear arms often became linked to the rising trend of Prohibition related violence. Alcohol consumption had historically been blamed for a variety of social ills since before the turn of the century. Finally, in January, 1919, the Eighteenth Amendment was passed prohibiting the manufacture, sale and transport of alcoholic beverages within the United States. Once passed, it very quickly became apparent that enforcement would be extremely difficult, as routine violations became commonplace. Later the same year, the Volstead Act was passed in an attempt to better enforce the restrictions of the Eighteenth Amendment. Despite both, a lucrative new industry, bootlegging, was born. Al Capone, and others like him, made their fortunes on the newly illegal trade of alcohol. A profitable, and often violent, black market for alcohol was born and flourished. Seemingly in response, attempts to restrict firearms soon began to follow.

A petition to the Illinois State Constitutional Convention of 1922 called for the "suppression of the manufacture, transportation and sale of 'concealable weapons' as far as private individuals are concerned." The petition also proposed amending the state constitution to allow denial of bail to people accused of any crime, even misdemeanors. Neither petition to the court was made into law.[8]

Soon afterwards, in 1924, Congress held hearings on "Firearms and Intoxicants in the District of Columbia" in response to an incident in which U.S. Senator Frank Greene of Vermont had been wounded by a stray shot when police opened fire on bootleggers. Contrary to the hopes of the crusaders, the police, rather than the bootleggers, turned out to have fired the stray bullet. Nevertheless, a permit requirement for carrying handguns was imposed in Washington.[9]

By the mid 1920s, the Chicago gangs were gaining celebrity and notoriety for their brutally violent ways. Al Capone's nearly legendary status as a gangster was almost synonymous with the

Tommy gun. It first made headlines being used by his gang in the April 27, 1926, killing of three men: a bootlegger, a politician and William McSwiggin, Assistant State's Attorney outside a saloon in Cicero, Illinois.

Prohibition violence eventually persuaded Congress to attempt to suppress pistol traffic. There was a 1927 ban on mail-order handguns, through the Mailing Firearms Act, also known as the Miller Act, the first federal legislation regulating firearms.

The repeal of Prohibition in 1933 ended much of the Capone type gangster violence, but not adequately to quiet an anxious nation. Gun violence continued, including a failed assassination attempt on Presidential candidate Franklin Delano Roosevelt, and so Congress passed the National Firearms Act (NFA) of 1934. Public opinion was still calling for further regulation to counter the violence and dangers of the preceding decade. Despite this prevailing fear and insecurity, those who introduced the act in Congress feared that the Supreme Court would later reverse it as unconstitutional, so the drafters introduced the law as part of a tax bill - focusing on the taxation component rather than the regulation aspect.[10] Because Congress had the authority, as granted in Article 1, Section 8 of the Constitution, to make laws concerning interstate trade, firearms legislation frequently focused on economics: buying, selling, taxation and registration. It was anticipated that any national legislation that strayed too far from these boundaries would be more likely to be deemed unconstitutional and overturned.

In the case of the NFA, the registration of certain classes of guns was now required, and a tax was applied to the sale itself. The NFA banned certain types of weapons including sawed-off shotguns with a barrel shorter than eighteen inches long. Also restricted were machine guns, certain rifles, and silencers in general. The registration process included an application, a photograph and fingerprinting, all of which were then forwarded to the Federal Bureau of Investigation for a background check. Final sale of the gun was contingent upon clearance through this process. The owner was then required to keep documentation of the registration on his person whenever carrying the gun.

Amidst the escalation of European unrest, and with the threat of WWII on the horizon, the Federal Firearms Act was passed in 1938. Much like its predecessor in 1934, it was based on the Interstate Commerce Clause of the Constitution and was supposedly to protect American firearms from foreign subversion.[11] It expanded the licensure requirements for manufacturers, dealers and importers of both guns and ammunition. It required them to keep records including names and addresses of all to whom they had sold guns. Finally, it banned firearms sales to known felons who had been convicted of a violent crime. According to some, with its passage, "an indirect goal was accomplished as a right began to be converted to a licensed privilege under the guise of regulating interstate commerce." [12]

The constitutionality of the National Firearms Act was questioned, but ultimately upheld, in a landmark case U.S. vs. Miller in 1939. In the original case, Jack Miller and Frank Layton were arrested in Arkansas carrying an unregistered 12 gauge shotgun with a barrel less than 18 inches long. They were indicted for breaking the 1934 NFA. Their defense included the argument that the NFA was unconstitutional in its restriction of an individual's right to "bear arms." The Supreme Court stated that such a shotgun couldn't have "any reasonable relation to the preservation or efficiency of a well regulated militia" at the time the Second Amendment was written, and, therefore, the Second Amendment doesn't protect any right to have or carry it. [13]

The Gun Control Act (GCA) of 1968 was actually initiated in 1963. Its origins were in a bill prohibiting mail order sales of handguns to minors. Then came the fateful day of November 22, 1963, and the assassination of President John F. Kennedy by Lee Harvey Oswald, using a mail-order military surplus rifle. Not only was the nation grieving for the loss of a President, but there was a growing public awareness of the true lack of control over the sale or possession of firearms despite numerous legislative attempts. Long before the country had adequate time to heal, came the assassinations of two other major leaders of the times: Dr. Martin Luther King, Jr. in April and Senator Robert Kennedy in June. While the GCA had been in development for several years, it had also been held up by ongoing contentious debate. These two high profile murders gave proponents the momentum and public support to quickly pass this major revision of previous legislation.

Through the GCA, came major revision of previous legislation with an impact on both dealers and purchasers. A broader range of dealers were now required to go through the licensing process and for a wider array of firearms. There was more detailed record keeping required of them. There were more restrictions on interstate sales. The groups of individuals restricted from purchasing and owning guns was expanded to include the mentally incompetent and drug users. The defining new element of this legislation was making all mail order sales of rifles and shotguns illegal. Previously, a purchaser had only to sign a statement that he was over 21 years of age for handguns and over 18 for rifles or shotguns.

Ironically, there was dissatisfaction from all directions after passage. Gun owners and dealers wanted to be able to buy and sell through the mail. Dealers didn't like the additional administrative demands of the record keeping. Gun control advocates didn't think the restrictions were imposing enough to make a difference. [14]

The country moved forward through the 1970s without much activity on the Second Amendment legislative front, as other forces and issues dominated the media. The Vietnam War, President Richard Nixon's resignation under threat of impeachment, the continuing civil rights and women's movements momentarily moved to the forefront of the nation's interest and attention.

Then, on March 30 1981, outside the Hilton Hotel in Washington D.C., came the assassination attempt on the life of President Ronald Reagan. Leading up to it was the disturbing trail of purchases by the would-be assassin John Hinckley. He had begun purchasing guns and target shooting in 1979. In 1980, he began taking medication for clinical depression, and, in the fall, he was arrested for carrying handguns in his luggage while preparing to board a plane. Once released, he continued his firearms purchases and bought exploding Devastator bullets, the type he would eventually use in the Presidential assassination attempt. Four men were wounded in the attempt. In addition to the President, also hit were Secret Service agent Timothy McCarthy, D.C. police officer Thomas Delehanty and, most severely, Press Secretary James Brady. Brady was shot in the head and suffered permanent brain damage. His injury and subsequent recovery, at times in the public eye of Washington's political arena, revived concerns over the criminal use of firearms.

Nineteen eighty-six saw passage of three distinct pieces of firearms legislation. The Armed Career Criminal Act strengthened penalties for anyone possessing a gun who was prohibited from doing so by the Gun Control Act of 1968. The Law Enforcement Officers Protection Act banned all manufacture, import, sale or possession of armor piercing ammunition, known as "cop-killer bullets." Ironically, the same year, the Firearms Owner's Protection Act eased some previous restrictions, such as on interstate and mail order sales and dealer record keeping requirements, while raising the penalty for using a gun during the commission of certain crimes: the use of firearms during a drug trafficking crime, the use of a machine gun or silencer during commission of a crime. [15]

A broadly focused piece of legislation, the Crime Control Act of 1990, attempted to put controls in place covering a huge variety of areas. One piece of the legislation introduced the concept of drug free school zones and within its description, made it illegal to possess or fire a gun in such a school zone. With passage of this Act, came a renewed debate over whether firearms legislation fell under local or federal jurisdiction. Was it under federal domain since firearms were often transported across state lines, and so Congress should be able to regulate their use and possession, in this case near public schools? Or, was it under local or state domain to regulate local laws?[16] The Supreme Court decided in a 1995 case United States v. Lopez.

Alfonso Lopez, Jr. had been hired to deliver a handgun to a fellow student. He brought the gun, unloaded, and the bullets into Edison High School in San Antonio, Texas. He was charged with and convicted of violating the Gun-free School Zones Act. The prevailing thought was that "possession of a firearm in a school zone can be expected to lead to violent crime which can be expected to affect economy and traveling in the area as well as to produce a citizenry with less of an education due to the distraction of the violent crime and in the long-term, a weaker economy. Thus, possession of a firearm at a school falls under the jurisdiction of the Commerce Clause." [17]

The Lopez case proceeded through layers of appeals courts until the Supreme Court ruled that the1990 Crime Control Act was unconstitutional. Chief Justice Rehnquist, writing the majority opinion, wrote that Congress had overstepped its bounds. He maintained that carrying a handgun was too far removed from commerce to fall under Congressional domain, as there was no evidence that carrying a gun would affect the economy. Laws concerning guns in or near schools should be left to the states.

During the 1980s and 1990s, while these pieces of legislation were being passed, James and Sarah Brady were still pushing legislation on Capitol Hill to prevent more violence, like the shooting that left James permanently disabled. In 1993, Congress passed the Brady Act. This act is an amendment to the Gun Control Act of 1968, and it imposes a five day waiting limit on the purchase of any hand gun. The purchaser of the gun is subject to a complete background check during this waiting period. This measure was also intended to provide a "cooling down" period for anyone about to commit a crime of passion, allowing them to calm down before acting upon their desire to cause someone harm. [18]

In today's society, there are many acts of gun violence and gun accidents that bring up questions about gun regulations in America. Is purchasing a gun in America too easy? Do regulations on guns need to be more strict? Who should be allowed to own a gun in America? These types of questions all basically refer to the Second Amendment. If you interpret the Second Amendment as guaranteeing an individual's right, then anyone should be able to own a gun, and no one should have the authority to infringe on this right.

Times have changed continuously and drastically since the period in history when the Second Amendment was written. The question raised today, and raised since the ratification of the Bill of Rights, is whether or not people should still have the individual right to own and bear arms. There are many groups consistently vocal and visible, either in favor of private gun ownership or in favor of gun ownership regulation and restriction. Most of the arguments have roots in defining the principal Second Amendment right.

Questions about the intent of the Second Amendment right in America are common in modern media. Debates about the modern implications of the Second Amendment arise following a public gun-related incident, or with new Congressional legislation passed pertinent to the amendment.

In 1992, riots in Los Angeles brought the issue of the Second Amendment and gun control to the nation's attention. After a jury found police officers not guilty of using excessive force on black motorist, Rodney King, the city found itself engulfed in riots. Looting, killing, and arson spread all over southeast Los Angeles and the city was declared to be in a "state of emergency" by the governor. Stores and schools were shut down, as the streets filled with violence. Buildings and cars were being burned. Motorists were reportedly being dragged out of their cars and shot or beaten by outraged mobs.

While guns did not play a role in the original incident, the availability of firearms soon became a significant element in the aftermath. During the chaotic days following the verdict in the Rodney King beating case, gun and gasoline sales were banned. During this period, some shop owners who had their own weapons were able to defend their shops from looters and protect themselves from harm. At the same time, people were shooting police officers and innocent citizens out of rage over the decisions in the Rodney King case.[19]

After the riots were over, the role of firearms as cause or solution to the violence was publicly debated. Should the sale of guns have been prohibited? One argument was that the sales should have been stopped, because people were using the guns to loot and kill. Pro-gun ownership groups said that law abiding citizens were being restricted from using their weapons, and that they were unable to defend themselves, as the Second Amendment allows. In national crises, where guns are involved, this type of debate often surfaces regarding the relevance and role of the Second Amendment in modern society. Most recently, events following Hurricane Katrina in New

Orleans brought up questions about the Second Amendment rights of American citizens. In the horrific aftermath of the Category five storm, many individuals took up arms to defend themselves from crimes being committed in the city. As tensions rose and people, including police officers and medical personnel, were being shot at, some parish leaders put provisions in place to stop the private carrying of firearms by citizens in New Orleans. At one FEMA compound housing displaced residents, an order was put in place banning firearms. In other areas of the city, police and city officials attempted to confiscate any weapons being carried by private citizens. While many people in the New Orleans area may have agreed with these actions, others felt that these confiscations and regulations were an infringement of the citizens' Second Amendment right. The Second Amendment Foundation (SAF), a group that protects individual's rights to own guns, stepped in to take legal action. They said gun confiscation was a violation of a citizen's Second Amendment right to posses a firearm, and a natural disaster was not cause for this right to be taken away.[20] Along with the SAF, the NRA was active in protecting rights in New Orleans. The NRA secured a temporary restraining order in certain New Orleans parishes against the confiscation of firearms by police officers.

The Second Amendment to the U.S. Constitution gives individual's the right to own and bear arms, thus allowing them to form a militia for their state. This insures that a tyrannical national government could not establish a national military that could disarm the states, and control the country. Over the last two hundred years, as more and more gun violence has contributed to national tragedies, gun control proponents have lobbied for tougher legislation on guns, and challenged the intent of the Second Amendment. The other side of the argument, voiced by pro-gun ownership groups like the NRA, has been trying to keep the individual's right to bear arms intact. Throughout history, even as national events, such as school shootings and presidential assassinations have taken place, the Supreme Court has upheld the right of individuals to own and bear arms.

The Second Amendment's interpretation has evolved over the last two hundred years, as society has obviously changed tremendously.

While the Supreme Court has maintained the basic right of individual's to own guns, it has implemented many restrictions on the right to own guns, as a way to meet the outcries of anti-guns groups, and keep society as safe as possible in our modern society. Restrictions on gun ownership today include waiting periods, age limits, background checks, and bans on certain types of weapons. The majority of these legislative measures appear to be the government's way of meeting the demands of as many different interest groups as possible - trying to maintain the responsible citizens' right to bear arms, while keeping the country safe for "the people."

The Second Amendment

An Individual Or Group Right To Arm
By
Steven Aramony

The Second Amendment to the United States Constitution provides
that, "A well regulated militia being necessary to the security of a
free State, the right of the People to keep and bear arms shall not be
infringed." The intended meaning of the Second Amendment is one
of the most frequently and hotly debated topics in American politics.
In the last few decades, courts and commentators have offered what
may fairly be characterized as three different basic interpretations
of the Second Amendment. Under the "individual right" view, the
Second Amendment secures to individuals a personal right to keep
and to bear arms, whether or not they are members of any militia or
engaged in military service or training. Under the "collective right"
view, the Second Amendment is a federalist provision that provides
to states a prerogative to establish and maintain armed and organized
militia units akin to the National Guard, and only states may assert
this prerogative. Finally, there is a range of intermediate views which
is labeled the "quasi-collective right" and these advocates argue that
the Second Amendment secures a right only to select persons to keep
and bear arms in connection with their service in an organized state
militia such as the National Guard and persons may bear arms only
when actively participating in that militia's activities. This paper will
discuss the history of the Second Amendment, the wording of the
Amendment and the issues giving rise to the various interpretations
as to the protections afforded by the Second Amendment. It will
conclude with the thesis that the awkward wording of the Amendment
was intentional as the founding fathers intended not only to confer
upon individuals the right to keep and bear arms but to give support
for the Anti-Federalists belief that there should be continued vitality
for the state militias.

In 1787, the Continental Congress summoned a convention to
propose amendments to the Articles of Confederation. The primary
shortcoming of the Articles of Confederation was that the central

government was too weak. It was generally recognized, however, that the central government was to remain one of limited and enumerated powers, lest the cure be worse than the disease. Instead, the decision was made by the delegates to the Constitutional Convention to draft a replacement compact which offered Americans a unique opportunity to decide the terms by which they would be governed. Thus, the challenge was to design a federal government strong enough to deal effectively with those issues requiring federal control without allowing the federal government to become tyrannical. The delegates differed as to the proper balance. The Federalists favored a strong federal government, whereas the Anti-Federalists were fearful of a strong government and wanted numerous safeguards to protect the people and the states. The Constitution alarmed the Anti-Federalists because, although the federal government appeared to be one of limited and enumerated powers, the Anti-Federalists feared that one day it would infringe upon individual rights. With the exception of limitations on ex-post-facto laws, bills of attainder and peacetime suspensions of habeas corpus, the convention's proposal did little to recognize individual rights. The Constitution also gave the federal government large powers over the militia including the power to provide for the organizing, arming and disciplining of the militia. There was a fear that making militia service so unpleasant the people would demand a standing army or select militia. The states were also forbidden from keeping troops without the consent of Congress. [287] The Anti-Federalists were also very concerned about the federal government's power to maintain a standing army. Such could be used to suppress the American people and, without a militia to defend against the standing army, the states and the citizens would be defenseless. There were no restrictions on the federal standing army but for a two-year limit on any appropriations for that purpose.[288]

In early 1789, it was not clear whether or not the Constitution would be expanded by a Bill of Rights. Supporters of enumerated rights felt that a bill of rights would provide further constraints on the new government, while opponents felt that by listing only certain rights, other unlisted rights would fail to be protected. Many delegates supported a statement in a bill of rights that provided for an individual to be able to keep and bear arms. Delegates from Pennsylvania, lobbyed for adoption of the bill which included a provision that, "the people have a right to bear arms for the defense of themselves and their own state, or the United States or for the purpose of killing game and no law shall be passed for disarming the people or any of them unless for crimes committed ."[289] When New Hampshire voted for ratification of the Constitution, it called for the adoption of a bill of rights which included the provision that "Congress shall never disarm any citizen unless such are or have been in actual rebellion."[290]

Delegates feared Congress would overstep its powers in organizing and disciplining the militia and others feared that a standing army would overwhelm the militia. One delegate wrote:

> The personal liberty of every man, probably from sixteen to sixty years of age, may be destroyed by the power Congress has in organizing and governing of the militia. As militia they may be subjected to fines of any amount, levied in a military manner; they may be subjected to corporal punishments of the most disgraceful and humiliating nature; and to death itself, by the sentence of a court-martial.[291]

The right to bear arms has a tradition with deep roots in American society. In the colonies, the necessities of hunting and defense led to armament statutes. In 1623, Virginia forbade its colonists to travel unless they were well armed and, in 1631, it required colonists to travel well armed. In 1658, Virginia required every household to have a functioning firearm and, in 1673, passed a law providing that a citizen who claimed that he was too poor to purchase s a firearm would have one purchased for him by the government. The right to keep and bear arms was a right prized by the colonists. When Patrick Henry gave his famous "Give Me Liberty Or Give Me Death Speech," he spoke in support of the proposition that a well regulated militia composed of gentlemen and freemen is the only security to a free government. [292] Thomas Jefferson proposed that "no free man shall ever be debarred the use of arms," and Samuel Adams called for an amendment banning any law "to prevent the people of the United States who are peaceable citizens from keeping their own arms."[293] After winning the Revolutionary War, the citizens of the newly established country demanded protections against an oppressive federal government. Central to these fears was the idea that a standing army represented a threat to their liberty.

Amidst this debate, James Madison drafted what ultimately would become the Bill of Rights and proposed it to the Congress on June 8, 1789. When the bill was initially brought to the floor of the Constitutional Convention, the original text of what was later to become the Second Amendment, stated as follows:

> "The right of the people to keep and bear arms shall not be infringed; a well armed and well regulated militia being the best security of a free country; but no person religiously scrupulous of bearing arms shall be compelled to render military service in person."[294]

The proposal was modified so that the militia clause came before the proposal recognizing the right. The Founding Fathers debated the "religiously scrupulous" clause. Some representatives feared that the government could declare people to be religiously scrupulous, and thereby disarm them against their will. This clause was removed. In approving the text, some argue that the Senate indicated its intent that the right be an individual one by rejecting an amendment which would have limited the keeping and bearing of arms to bearing "for the common defense."[295]

As ratified, the Second Amendment to the United States Constitution states that, "A well regulated militia being necessary to the security of a free State, the right of the People to keep and bear arms shall not be infringed.

The documented debate in the House and Senate over the Second Amendment is sparse, especially when compared to debate over other articles of the Bill of Rights. For this reason, contemporaneous writings and speeches of the Founding Fathers are often referenced because who would better understand the original intent and historical context of the Second Amendment than they. However illuminating the historical background of the Amendment may be, it is not necessarily dispositive of what the framers actually intended. Numerous statements were made by them prior to the adoption of the Second Amendment. Thomas Jefferson stated, "No freeman shall ever be debarred the use of arms."[296] He later stated:

"Laws that forbid the carrying of arms. . . disarm only those who are neither inclined nor determined to commit crimes. . . Such laws make things worse for the assaulted and better for the assailants; they serve rather to encourage than to prevent homicides, for an unarmed man may be attacked with greater confidence than an armed man."[297]

John Adams stated:

"To suppose arms in the hands of citizens, to be used at individual discretion, except in private self-defense, or by partial orders of towns, countries or districts of a state, is to demolish every constitution, and lay the laws prostrate, so that liberty can be enjoyed by no man; it is a dissolution of the government. The fundamental law of the militia is that it be created, directed and commanded by the laws, and ever for the support of the laws."[298]

In Massachusetts, Samuel Adams argued that ratification of the Constitution should be conditioned upon a Bill of Rights beginning with a guarantee that the Constitution, "shall never be construed to authorize Congress to infringe the just liberty of the press of the rights of conscience; or to prevent the people of the United States who are peaceable citizens from keeping their own arms."[299]

However, even the founding fathers did not advocate the universal possession of arms. New Hampshire had no objection to disarming those who "are or have been in actual rebellion," just as Samuel Adams stressed that only "peaceable citizens" should be protected in their right of "keeping their own arms."[300]

The scope and meaning of the Second Amendment has been discussed by courts and commentators over the course of American history. The political issues surrounding guns in the United States is an especially contentious political topic in the United States. The degree to which firearms can or should be regulated has long been debated and disagreements range from the practical, does gun ownership cause or prevent crime, to the constitutional, how should one interpret the Second Amendment, to the philosophical, which weapons, if any, does the government have the authority to control? Recent interpretations of the Second Amendment have been characterized by disagreement and uncertainty. The Supreme Court has not decided the issue. However, the Congress and the Department of Justice have weighed in on the issue. The Amendment has been the subject of extensive academic debate for the past two decades. For much of the twentieth century, there were two schools of thought regarding the meaning or interpretation of the Second Amendment, i.e., the individual right view and the collective rights view. Recently there has come into play a third view which is an alterative model which combines some of the ideas of both and is labeled the alterative model.

The first school of thought is referred to as the Standard or Individual Right Model. This interpretation provides that the Second Amendment protects the rights of an INDIVIDUAL to own firearms. The "militia" of the Second Amendment is comprised of the armed citizenry at large, as opposed to an organized militia which was a governmentally controlled body such as a standing army. Proponents of this view argue that in no way is the individual right dependent on being on active militia duty. The phrase to "keep and bear arms" is interpreted by individual rights advocates to mean the retention of personal firearms in the home, the free carrying of them elsewhere and learning how to handle them. The word "arms" is interpreted as anything suitable for militia for military purposes. They argue that the first ten Amendments are all individual rights and the phrase "the people" used in the First, Fourth, Ninth and Tenth Amendments refers to individual rights and that the same interpretation should be afforded the Second Amendment. According to this view, individuals may bring claims or raise challenges based on a violation of their rights under the Second Amendment just as they do to vindicate individual rights secured by other provisions of the Bill of Rights.[301] .

The second school of thought is the States' Right or Collective Right Mode. Under the "collective right" view, the Second Amendment is derived from the concept of federalism and provides to the States a prerogative to establish and maintain armed and organized militia units akin to the National Guard, and only states may assert this prerogative. Under this view, the Second Amendment contains two clauses, the Militia Clause (a well regulated militia being necessary to the security of a free state) and the Right to Arms Clause (the right of the people to keep and bear arms shall not be infringed). It is argued that it's customary in constitutional law to point out that the second clause is controlled by the first clause. This is expressed technically by saying that the independent clause is prefaced by a dependent phrase and that a dependent or subordinate clause is more important than an independent or main clause. This interpretation states that the Second Amendment protects the rights of States to keep armed militias. In this way, the states could be a check on the national government's power. Thus the words "right of the people" in the Second Amendment actually refers to the right of the state. Because the role of militias is served by the National Guard, this protection does not extend to individuals. The phrase to "keep and bear" is interpreted by the collective rights advocates in the military sense that soldiers bear arms and civilians carry them. The word "arms" is interpreted by collective rights advocates as weapons suitable for hunting or self-defense only. This interpretation thus concludes that the Second Amendment protects the rights of citizens to keep and bear those arms needed to meet their legal obligation to serve in the militia.[302]

The more collectively the right to bear arms is interpreted, the more broadly Congress can legislate to restrict the right to bear arms. There are sociological reasons for a collective interpretation. Proponents of gun control argue that the United States remains one of the world leaders in gun-related violence and that regulation on a federal scale would help remove and control the number and type of firearms available as well as regulate who possesses those weapons. Furthermore, because of the diversity of state regulations, getting a weapon is merely an exercise in crossing borders. This being so, allowing the individual states to promulgate their own regulations and requirements effectively subjects all states to the least restrictive state's regulations and requirements. A collective view would simply bestow on Congress a greater ability to legislate gun control laws.[303]

The third school of thought is sometimes referred to as the Alternative Model and at other times, as the quasi-collective right theory. From this perspective, the Second Amendment secures a right only to select persons to keep and bear arms in connection with their service in an organized state militia such as the National Guard. Under one typical formulation, individuals may keep arms only if they are members of a functioning, organized state militia and the State has not provided the necessary arms. Furthermore, they may bear arms only while and as a part of actively participating in the militia's activities. Such a view would allow a private cause of action (or defense) to some persons to vindicate a State's power to establish and maintain an armed and organized militia such as the National Guard. [304]

The controversy as to whether the right to bear arms is collective or individual is largely attributed to the wording and the placement of the Amendment. No one has ever described the Constitution as a marvel of clarity and the Second Amendment is, perhaps, one of the most poorly drafted provisions. [305] Unlike the other amendments in the Bill of Rights, the Second Amendment contains a preamble which states that, "A well regulated militia being necessary to the security of a free State." There is no similar clause in any other Amendment. The Amendment purports to protect the "security of a free State" by way of a state militia. The preamble's wording strongly contrasts with the second part of the Amendment that emphasizes the "people" and states "the right of the People to keep and bear arms shall not be infringed."

Legal analysts who wish to limit the Second Amendment's force focus on its preamble as setting out a restrictive purpose. Those who argue that the right to bear arms is a state's right, argue that the purpose was to allow the states to keep their militias and to protect them against the possibility that the new national government would use its power to establish a powerful standing army and, thus, eliminate the state militias. This interpretation is dismissive of any notion that there is an individual right to keep and bear arms. The right, if there is such, is only a state's right. Some argue that the national government has the power to regulate, to the point of prohibition, private ownership of guns. This is, indeed, the position of the American Civil Liberties Union which reads the Second Amendment as protecting only the right of maintaining an effective state militia and that the individual's right to bear arms applies only to the preservation or efficiency of a well-regulated militia. They would argue that, except for lawful police and military purposes, the possession of weapons by individuals is not constitutionally protected.[306]

Proponents of the individual rights model argue that the preamble is simply explanatory of why the people must retain this right. If the rights of the people were meant to be subordinate to protection of the states, the Amendment would have been constructed differently. Advocates of a collective interpretation argue that the first clause qualifies the second, restricting the protection conferred by the right. To interpret the first part of the Amendment in any other way would rob it of its significance. The right conferred simply protects the states from the disarmament of their militias, known today as the National Guard, by the federal government.

Central to the debate as to the contours of the Second Amendment is the controversy over the proper definition of militia, the people and arms. Individual rights proponents and collective rights advocates define these words differently. Gun control advocates and gun rights advocates have different interpretations as to these terms. Firstly, to what does the term "militia" refer? Secondly, who are "the people?" And, thirdly, what "arms" does the Amendment protect?

The Bill of Rights was ratified over 200 years ago. In that span of time, the meaning of many words has drastically changed. What some may consider the militia today may be far removed from the original meaning. The American militia movement goes back to 1687, a concept vital to the colonies. The colonies lacked an economy which could support a significant standing force. The charter of every American colony included the authority to create militia units separate and distinguishable from troops and all American colonies passed militia laws under the authority granted by their charters. All white able-bodied free males were required by law to belong to a militia by the statutory law of their colony. Whether or not they actually served in militia units is another question since the laws were not vigorously enforced and some colonies allowed religious exemptions. The requirement for service could be met by joining either the colony's official militia or joining, if they would have you, a volunteer militia unit. [307]

The 1792 Uniform Militia Act, which was passed by Congress to organize, arm, and discipline the militia, specified that militiamen must purchase and maintain their own weapons. This resulted in a militia system with very little in the way of central control or support. There were no penalties placed on states that refused to maintain their militias as required by the 1792 act. Therefore, the states let their official militia units all but die out. Most states officially abolished compulsory militia duty during the 1840s, but left the volunteer units alone which would eventually evolve into the National Guard. Subsequent legislation in Congress likewise supports the interpretation of the word militia consistent with the interpretation that the Second Amendment confers rights upon all men and not just those in a formal military component. In the Militia Act of 1792, the second Congress defined "militia of the United States" to include almost every free adult male in the United States. These persons were obligated by law to possess a firearm and a minimum supply of ammunition and military equipment. It is important to remember that the Second Amendment was drafted after ratification of the Constitution that provided in Article I, Section 9 that Congress had the power to raise and support armies with no restrictions except a two year limit on appropriations and that it also gave the power to the federal government to provide for organizing, arming and disciplining of the militia.[308]

Those who believe that the Second Amendment secures the rights of individuals argue that there can be little doubt that when the Congress spoke of a "militia," it was referring to the traditional concept of the entire populace capable of bearing arms, and not to any formal group such as what is today called the National Guard. The purpose was to create an armed citizenry, which the political theorists at the time considered essential to ward off tyranny. Those who believe that the Second Amendment protects the rights of the states argue that the "militia" was not, as the gun lobby claims, simply another word for the populace at large. Rather, membership in the eighteenth century militia was generally limited to able-bodied white males between the ages of 18 and 45, which hardly encompassed the entire population of the nation. They argue that the U.S. Constitution established a permanent professional army, controlled by the federal government. With the memory of colonial history fresh in their minds, many of the "anti-Federalists" feared a standing army as an instrument of oppression. State militias were viewed as a counterbalance to the federal army and the Second Amendment was written to prevent the federal government from disarming the state militias. Those who believe that the Second Amendment was written to protect collective rights argue that in the twentieth century, the Second Amendment has become an anachronism, largely because of drastic changes in the militia it was designed to protect. There is no longer the citizen militia like that of the eighteenth century. They argue that today's equivalent of a "well-regulated" militia is the National Guard which has more limited membership than its early counterpart and depends on government-supplied, not privately owned, firearms. Gun control laws have no effect on the arming of today's militia, since those laws invariably do not apply to arms used in the context of military service and law enforcement and, therefore, laws restricting gun ownership do not violate the Second Amendment.[309]

"The People" is used repeatedly in the United States Constitution, including the Preamble, Article I, and Amendments I, II, IV, IX, X and XVII. Those who believe that the Second Amendment confers rights to individuals argue that it is ridiculous for gun control advocates to argue that the phrase "the people" should mean individuals in every single case except for the Second Amendment, where it means "the states." Individual rights proponents argue that the First Amendment has never been interpreted as giving "the states" the right to peaceably assemble. Nor has the Fourth Amendment been ruled as providing only protection for state officials from unreasonable searches and seizures. Why, then they ask, should the Second Amendment be treated differently? This is especially true since the term "the people" is not found in Article IV which talks about the responsibilities of the states. [310] Finally, the Tenth Amendment reserves powers to, "the States respectively, or to the people." By listing these phrases separately, individual rights advocates argue that the founding fathers must have believed that these terms were different and separate identities. Otherwise, one of the phrases would have been removed from this Amendment. Legal commentators have observed that there is no evidence in the text of the Second Amendment, or any other part of the Constitution, that the words "the people" have a different connotation within the Second Amendment than when employed elsewhere in the Constitution. In fact, the text of the Constitution, as a whole, strongly suggests that the words "the people" have precisely the same meaning within the Second Amendment as without. And, as used throughout the Constitution, "the people" have "rights" and "powers," but federal and state governments only have "powers" or "authority," and never "rights."[311]

Proponents of the states rights and some collective rights models argue that the phrase "bear arms" only applies to members of the militia carrying weapons during actual militia service. Advocates of the individual rights model argue that "bear arms" refers to any carrying of weapons, whether by a soldier or a civilian. There is no question that the phrase "bear arms" may be used to refer to the carrying of arms by a soldier or militiaman. The issue is whether "bear arms" was also commonly used to refer to the carrying of arms by a civilian. Additionally, there are numerous instances of the phrase "bear arms" being used to describe a civilian's carrying of arms. Early constitutional provisions or declarations of rights in at least ten different states speak of the right of the "people, citizen or citizens" to bear arms in defense of themselves and the state," or equivalent words, thus indisputably reflecting that under common usage "bear arms" was in no sense restricted to bearing arms in military service.[312]

In 2004, the Justice Department under Attorney General John Ashcroft issued the first formal written position taken by an executive branch specifically regarding the Second Amendment and concluded that the Second Amendment protects an individual right to bear arms. The opinion stated:

> The Second Amendment secures a personal right of individuals, not a collective right that may only be invoked by a State or a quasi-collective right restricted to those persons who serve in organized militia units.[313]

In 1982, a bipartisan subcommittee of the United States Senate investigated the Second Amendment and reported its findings, which included the following opinion:

> The conclusion is thus inescapable that the history, concept, and wording of the second amendment to the Constitution of the United States, as well as its interpretation by every major commentator and court in the first half century after its ratification, indicates that what is protected is an individual right of a private citizen to own and carry firearms in a peaceful manner. [314]

The United States Supreme Court has never directly ruled on the meaning of the Second Amendment, despite having had a variety of opportunities to do so. This has left supporters on all sides of the debate open to interpret the actions of the court as they see fit. The Supreme Court's most important decision on the meaning of the Second Amendment, United States v. Miller, grew out of the enactment of the National Firearms Act of 1934. [315] Miller and a co-defendant were indicted for transporting an unregistered sawed-off shotgun in interstate commerce. The Supreme Court found that it could not take judicial notice that the use or possession of a short-barreled shotgun in this case had any military purpose or could be used to contribute to the common defense and thus could not say that the weapon was protected by the Second Amendment. But the Court did not indicate that National Guard status was in any way required for protection by the Amendment, and, indeed, defined militia to include all citizens able to bear arms. The Court stated that the Second Amendment's purpose was to assure the continuation and render possible the effectiveness of the militia which it defined as a body that was comprised of all males physically capable of acting in concert for the common defense and who were expected to appear for occasional training bearing arms supplied by themselves and of the kind commonly used at the time. The meaning of the decision has been debated by all three sides in this controversy. Supporters of the individual rights read Miller to support the right of individuals to privately possess and bear their own firearms, while supporters of the States' right model read Miller as endorsing the view that the Second Amendment exists specifically to assure the continuation and render possible the effectiveness of the militia. It has been said that the holding of the case was limited to the meaning of arms in the Second Amendment and whether a sawed-off shotgun is among the arms protected by such. Some have argued that the Court's decision to address the substance of this challenge to his indictment, as opposed to summarily concluding that only states could bring such a challenge, appears to be inconsistent with a collective rights view. After the Supreme Court opinion in United States v. Miller, most, but by no means all, lower federal courts have interpreted the protection of the Second Amendment as a collective right. Surprisingly, the Supreme Court has stayed relatively silent on the issue, never stating clearly whether the right is collective or individual.

The debate as to whether the Second Amendment guarantees an individual or a collective right is not only a constitutional issue but a political one as well. Second Amendment agreements tend to run counter to traditional political debates. Liberals who usually try to read individual rights as broadly as possible strain mightily to read this one narrowly. Conversely, conservatives who are generally strict constructionists are looking for a more expansive interpretation of the Amendment as found in the individual rights approach. Many liberals have adopted the collective theory and they argue that the Second Amendment's words "right of the people" mean "a right of the state" and overlook the impact of those same words when used in the First and Fourth Amendments. The "right of the people" to assemble or to be free from unreasonable searches and seizures is not contested as an individual guarantee. Still when it comes to interpreting the Second Amendment, they ignore consistency and claim that the right to "bear arms" relates only to military uses. They argue that the right conferred by the Second Amendment simply protects the states from the disarmament of their militias (now known as the National Guard) by the federal government.[316] These commentators contend, instead, that the Amendment's preamble regarding the necessity of a well regulated militia to a free state means that the right to keep and bear arms applies only to a National Guard. However, the fact that the National Guard wasn't even created until more than a century after the adoption of the Bill of Rights seriously compromises the idea that such a limited system is what the framers of the Constitution had in mind. Such a reading fails to note that the framers used the term "militia" to relate to every citizen capable of bearing arms and that the Congress established the present National Guard under its own power to raise armies.

Those who believe that the Second Amendment confers rights to individuals argue that the preamble is simply explanatory of why the people must retain the right to bear arms However, by way of analysis, if the rights of the people were meant to be subordinate to protection of the states, one would think the amendment would have been constructed to just say that. Individual rights proponents argue that the amendment guarantees individuals the right to possess arms for their own personal defense. This argument is quite appealing, given the fact that the development of a professional police force came well into the nineteenth century and that, during this time period, guns and other arms were routinely used for protecting and hunting on a daily basis. As the country expanded into unpopulated areas, guns were a necessity for food and protection. Perhaps, neither the collective nor individual school of thought is correct insofar as their claims to entirely explain the Second Amendment and both are correct, insofar as they purport to offer partial explanations. Perhaps, the Second Amendment was not intended to recognize only a single principle, but rather, like the First, Fourth, Fifth, and Sixth amendments, it was intended as a composite of constitutional provisions. Its militia component and its right to bear arms recognition have in fact different origins and theoretical underpinnings. To be sure, militia systems and individual armament have always been related concerns with a practical interaction. An armed citizenry was the basis of the militia that the Founding Fathers sought, and the functioning of such a militia was the most obvious political purpose for citizen armament. Such an interaction is hardly unique. After all, the First Amendment guarantees freedom of expression and the right to petition the government. At the same time, neither of the interrelated rights can, perhaps, fully express the purposes of the framers. Supporters of one view may not have disputed the principle of the other, but they certainly disputed the relative importance.

I believe that the Second Amendment to the Constitution had two objectives. The first purpose was to recognize in general terms the importance of a militia to a free state. The second purpose was to guarantee an individual right to own and bear or carry arms. Only by incorporating both provisions could the first congress reconcile the priorities of Anti-Federalists and the Federalists. This approach makes sense. Concluding that there were two purposes for the Second Amendment, " allows us to avoid the pitfalls of the collective rights view, which would hold that the entire amendment was meant solely to protect a collective right to have a militia."[317] To read the recognition of an individual right, the right to arms, as subsumed within the militia recognition is, thus, not only permitting the tail to wag the dog, but to annihilate what was intended as a right. Reading the entirety of the Second Amendment as militia-related confuses the purpose of one provision with the text of another. I believe that the Second Amendment only makes sense if one recognizes its dual nature. The Anti-Federalists desired a bill of rights, a provision calling for increased state power over the militia, and a meaningful expressed limitation of the power of the federal government to maintain a standing army. Also, the Anti-Federalists complaint that resonated best with the people at large was the lack of a bill of rights. The federalists had wanted Congress to have the power to establish a national army and the Constitution provides not only this but also the power to regulate the militia. The prospect of federal power to render the militia useless and to maintain a large standing army combined with the absence of any specific guarantees of individual liberty frightened Anti-Federalists.

Given the political dynamic of the day, the wording of the Second Amendment is exactly what would have been expected. The Federalists had no qualms with recognizing the individual right of all Americans to keep and bear arms. Such was an age-old American tradition. Remember there were no policemen at this time The Second Amendment's preamble represents a successful attempt, by the Federalists, to further pacify moderate Anti-Federalists without actually conceding any additional ground, i.e. without limiting the power of the federal government to maintain a standing army or increasing the power of the states over the militia. Absent a citizenry generally keeping and bearing its own private arms, a militia, as it was then thought of, could not meaningfully exist. The right of individual Americans to keep, carry, and acquaint themselves with firearms does indeed promote a well-regulated militia by fostering the development of a pool of armed and trained citizens who could be called upon to serve in the militia. While standing armies are not mentioned in the preamble, history shows that the reason a well-regulated militia was declared necessary to the security of a free state was because such a militia would greatly reduce the need for a standing army and additionally establishing a declaration of the right of citizens to be able to keep and bear arms. The success of the Constitution in remaining the foundation of American government is based on the fact that successive congresses and courts have been able to interpret it or readapt it to the demands of changing times. It is now, perhaps, time to reexamine the meaning and purpose of the Second Amendment. For over two centuries, the Constitution has remained in force because its framers successfully separated and balanced governmental powers to safeguard the interests of majority rule and minority rights, of liberty and equality, and of the central and state governments. The drafting of the text of the Second Amendment is an example of such and should be so recognized.

The Internet and Ownership of "Ideas"

By
Jackie Fernandez

The Constitution of the United States has given citizens certain rights that supposedly the federal government is not allowed to take away. One such right, one that most citizens know, is the freedom of speech and of the press. According to the Constitution, "Congress shall make no law...abridging the freedom of speech, or of the press." The Constitution also gives citizens a right to property through the Fifth Amendment when stating "nor shall private property be taken for public use, without just compensation".[318] However, within the past few years the rights of property and freedom of speech have come at odds in a new battlefield: the Internet. In recent years, the Internet has been flooded with what is known as "'fanfiction (or as those in the know say, 'fanfic')."[319] Fanfiction are stories created by fans, for fans. On the Internet there are millions of stories written on movies, TV shows, books, games, anime (Japanese animation), etc. that were not written by the original creator. Fans have taken their favorite stories and made these stories their own.[320] Fanfiction is not necessarily new and actually started during the 1970s when Trekkies (Star Trek fans) would write stories for fan magazines. However, fanfiction has really started taking root and becoming popular because of the Internet's speed and accessibility.[321] Fanfiction has been described several different ways. In better lighting, fanfiction has been described as an art, a form of flattery, or as a dream turned to literature.[322] However, on the other side of the fence, fanfiction writers have been labeled as uncreative[323] and, in the worse case scenario for fanfic writers, fanfiction has been described as copyright infringement, and have been called to cease and desist by the original creators.[324] According to the Constitution, as well as copyright law, the original creator of the media that fanfiction authors use (whether it is books, movies, shows, etc.) has a right to his/her property. In that aspect, fanfiction writers are on the wrong side of the law since they have committed copyright infringement and, thus, could face charges, lawsuits, and fines.[325] However, fanfiction writers can invoke their First Amendment rights, arguing that their work is a form of freedom of speech, thus, they are protected by the very same Constitution that would call them criminals. [326] The real issue is whether or not fanfiction should be allowed to flourish under the Constitution. On one hand, it goes completely against copyright law and is the misuse of another's property. On the other, it is called freedom of speech and the press. However, since fanfiction is not doing any sort of harm to the original creators' works and no money is being made, there seems to be no reason why it should be taken from the Internet or from magazine pages, despite the fact that fanfiction and fanfiction writers might not be completely following the law.

Copyright infringement has been defined as "the unauthorized use of copyrighted material in a manner that violates one of the copyright owner's exclusive rights, such as the right to reproduce or perform the copyrighted work, or to make derivative works that build upon it."[327] Since fanfiction is basically the "derivative works" of pre-existing stories, then it most certainly is copyright infringement, as well as a violation of the Fifth Amendment. Fanfic writer, Shirou Shinjin (that is a penname, as he does not wish his real name to be used) does not bother to deny this accusation. "Oh it most certainly is copyright infringement," Shinjin writes about his stories and other fanfiction, "We're (fanfiction authors) taking another person's (or frequently, company's) property, and doing with it as we please. Even worse if the characters in question happen to be trademarked."[328] So, if fanfiction truly is copyright infringement, and copyright infringement is punishable by lawsuits and fines, why has fanfiction been allowed to thrive? And it is thriving –rapidly.

Welcome to FanFiction.Net (fondly, or not so fondly, known as FF.Net or FFN to those who know about the world of fanfiction). Nearly every fanfic author and reader knows about FF.Net. It is probably the biggest of all fanfiction archives, with innumerable stories and authors; and it grows bigger every day. To give an idea how large the archives are, here is the basic set up of FF.Net: The archives are broken up into eight categories, "Anime," "Book," "Cartoon," "Comic," "Game," "Misc.," "Movie," and "TV Show." In turn, these eight categories are broken up into smaller categories, listing the specific show, book, movie, etc. The category "Anime" alone has about 360 different categories. Some of those smaller categories only host a handful of stories, such as "Mermaid Saga", which hosts 11 stories. Others host hundreds of stories, such as "Spirited Away" with 998, and then there are the categories that have thousands of stories, such as "Rurouni Kenshin" with 12,440 stories. (Please note that these categories mentioned are not the smallest nor are they the largest sections in FF.Net's archives.) Most categories lean towards the hundreds and thousands range. Of course, the numbers given here will be, more likely than not, different within the next twenty-four hours since new stories are posted daily.[329] Then there are those who encourage new writers to post their writing of fanfiction on websites such as FF.Net. These people argue that fanfiction gets younger generations interested in reading and writing, which, in turn, brings up the number of fanfiction writers.[330]

Consequently, it is obvious that fanfiction is quite alive and is doing quite well, but since it has already been established that fanfiction is indeed copyright infringement, why have the various companies, directors, and writers who own the original work not sued the growing army of fanfic writers and made some money or, at the very least, tried to stop its growth? Some authors and publishers have asked that archives stop publishing fanfics on their work. FanFiction.Net, for example, does not allow submissions of fanfiction on the work of P.N. Elrod, Raymond Feist, Terry Goodkind, Laurel K. Hamilton, Robin Hobb, Dennis L. McKiernan, Robin McKinley, Irene Radford, Anne Rice, Nora Roberts/J.D. Robb, or Archie Comics in accordance with these people's wishes.[331] Anne Rice, in particular, is notorious among fanfiction writers for not allowing any sort of fanfiction on any of her work, including her famous vampire series. "I do not allow fanfiction. The characters are copyrighted. It upsets me terribly to even think about fanfiction with my characters. It is absolutely essential you respect my wishes," Rice once wrote on her website. Of course, her wish was respected, especially after her lawyers became involved, forcing most, if not all, Anne Rice fanfiction off the Internet. Not all original owners feel that fanfiction is intolerable. One of the reasons why fanfiction has been allowed to flourish is because many of the original creators are completely at ease with fanfiction or any other sort of fan-media. Some even encourage it. George Lucas, for example, has held a fan film contest on his own masterpiece, Star Wars, offering up a $2000 prize.[332] Manga (Japanese comics) artist, Nobuhiro Watsuki, is well known among his fans to be a rabid fan himself, and enjoys reading doujinshi (fan comics) done by his fans on his series, Rurouni Kenshin. In fact, Watsuki likes doujinshi so much that he even helps doujinshi artists on their work, contributing a few pages to doujinshi himself.

In a section of fanfiction world dedicated to books, the top three authors whose work it is to write fanfiction are J.K. Rowling, J.R.R. Tolkien, and Tamora Pierce. [333] J.K. Rowling said on fanfiction, "I've read some of it...I find it very flattering that people love the characters that much." Even if J.K. Rowling did try to stop fanfiction about Harry Potter to make its way on the Internet, she would have a hard time doing to, considering on FanFiction.Net, the Harry Potter Section is among the larger sections, with stories ranging in the hundreds of thousands, and that if she tried to ban fanfiction, it would more likely backfire causing people to become even more interested in fanfics on Harry. Not to mention the fans who write fanfiction are also the ones who buy the merchandise and several copies of the book, and it would hurt sales if Harry Potter fanfiction writers decided to go on strike, giving further reason why Rowling would not ban fanfiction on her books. Luckily, J.K. Rowling is leaving fanfiction and its writers alone for now.[334] However, she does not condone fanfiction on her work that is either sexually explicit or is trying to make money.[335] Tamora Pierce, the third most written about in the book section of fanfiction world, has a take on fanfiction that is actually a bit surprising. At one time, Pierce was a fanfiction author herself, writing stories on Tolkien's work as well as penning tales on Star Trek since she was "totally in love with Mr. Spock."[336] Many fanfiction writers are in similar situations as Pierce, seeing as that many fanfiction writers "have used the medium as practice before embarking on an original story of their own."[337] One fanfiction author, Mere Smith, found her "Buffy the Vampire Slayer" fanfiction coming to life when she became part of the staff of Buffy spin-off "Angel." "It's just so odd because I've been in both places," Smith commented on how she is both fanfiction writer and original creator.[338] Other writers, such as Shirou Shinjin, started writing fanfiction because they were fans of fanfiction and wanted to try their hand at it themselves.[339] However, by no means are fanfiction writers "frustrated novelist(s) who can't think up plots or characters on (their) own." Fanfiction authors are more creative than people give them credit for. For instance, "West Side Story" is a complete rip-off of Shakespeare's "Romeo and Juliet" which in turn is a complete rip-off of the myth of Pyramus and Thisbe.[340] In that respect, many fanfiction writers are more creative than Shakespeare since at least they create new plots and use different angles in their stories in fanfiction world.

Fanfiction does not really have a set of standards. The genre is notoriously filled with typos, poor stories, chat speak, and terrible grammar. This is understandable considering every fanfic author is an amateur. Many fanfic authors, about one third, are young, still in their teens.[341] Fanfiction.Net, however, does restrict the website by not allowing authors under the age of 13 to join.[342] Older writers, college students and some writers in their fifties, also write fanfiction.[343] There are fanfiction authors who hold themselves to a standard and there are some really good pieces of literature in fanfiction with descriptive narratives and amazing plots. Some stories are so good that readers get confused on which is the original work and which is fanfiction. Most fanfiction writers carefully study what they are writing about to make sure it follows canon (the original work), whether it is by book-marking and making notes in Harry Potter books or watching an episode of a show ten times.[344] Fanfic writers, even the poor ones, have no desired to be "flamed" or given a bad review, so they try their best at fanfiction, even if it is full of typos and bad grammar. Feedback, good or bad, is easy to come by since reader reviews come in almost instantaneously thanks to an online review box. Fanfic authors' love for their chosen series, movies, etc. is clearly shown in their work, even if their writing resembles more of an online chat than a story.[345] It is this care, whether clumsy or elegant, towards honoring the original work that proves that fanfiction authors are not really criminals out to destroy the hard work of the original creators; they are fans being fans.

Many people have confused fanfiction writers with plagiarists. In reality, fanfiction writers are anything but, and it is an insult to a fanfiction author to be called a plagiarist. When asked the difference between a plagiarist and a fanfiction author, Shiro Shinjin writes, "A plagiarist is someone who takes another's work and claims it as their own. Fanfiction authors notoriously take pains to disclaim that they don't own the characters they are writing for."[346] Plagiarism is taken very seriously by fanfiction writers and the webmasters and administrators of fanfiction websites. In both FF.Net and another archive, MediaMiner.Org, one of the easiest ways for a writer to get kicked off the site and get all his/her stories taken down is by plagiarizing a story. Nearly every fanfic has a disclaimer in the author notes. Some disclaimers are very serious, others humorous, some long, and some short. There are even disclaimers that are small poems or short skits. However, they all have the same message: "This is a fanfiction; I do not own the original story."[347]

While most fanfiction authors do realize that, on some level, what they are doing is copyright infringement; they do not think of the consequences or even think that what they are doing is wrong. The main reason why they think this way is because of one simple fact: they do not make any money from their stories. When asked if he ever thought of the repercussions of writing fanfiction, such as getting sued, Shirou Shinjin replied, "Not especially. I've always operated surreptitiously under a pen name, and have made fair efforts to protect my actual identity. But even if it came down to it, I don't think it would be worth suing me... corporations only tend to sue if you're threatening their profits, and my stories have never been that popular."[348] While several fanfiction authors, including Harry Potter writer, Christina Teresa, would enjoy having their fanfiction published, they doubt the possibility of it happening because of the legal issues.[349] In the interview, Shirou Shinjin also mentioned that while fanfiction is, indeed, copyright infringement "the distinction is that fanfic authors aren't doing it to make money from someone else's intellectual property - they're doing it for love of the medium and the characters. So whilst fanfiction is copyright infringement to the letter of the law, I think as far as the spirit is concerned, we aren't doing anything wrong."[350] His statement about how no one would sue fanfic authors because there is no money involved echoes J.K. Rowling's stand on fanfiction; that she finds the stories flattering and that she will only battle fanfic authors if they are trying to make money from her characters or if there is sexual content. It is the respect and love that fanfiction writers put into their favorite books and shows that makes it very hard to think of fanfiction as copyright infringement.

There are other reasons why fanfiction is still going strong. As mentioned earlier, fanfiction could also be interpreted as a form of freedom of speech. According to Louis Brandeis, a former U.S. Supreme Court Justice, "the general rule of law is that the noblest of human productions -- knowledge, truths ascertained conceptions, and ideas -- become, after voluntary communications to others, free as the air to common use."[351] Fanfiction is most certainly ideas and fanfiction authors correspond with each other often, leaving reviews, editing each others work (known as betaing or being a beta), and by asking each others' opinions on certain aspects of their stories and the original work they are writing the fanfiction on.[352] Copyrighted work is also ideas and communications, thus making it fair game for fanfiction writers to use. In that sense, fanfiction is a very free form of art and technically is not doing anything wrong.

One argument in favor of fanfiction, made by Stanford University law professor, Lawrence Lessig, says that "copyright now acts as a brake, stifling creativity, smothering innovation and squandering the democratic potential of the Internet." Lessig is the leader of the "free culture" movement. He argues that since copyright covers so many bases, those with copyrights can control the culture. The motto of the "free culture" movement is "What's at stake is our freedom -- freedom to create, freedom to build, and, ultimately, freedom to imagine." Copyright originally was supposed to encourage writers to create books "with the goal of cultivating a rich public domain." Copyright was also supposed to be a short term, lasting fourteen years, and it could only be renewed once. Now, the copyright term in the United States is about ninety-five years. Copyright also gives the original creator sole rights over "derivative" and "transformative" work, and fanfiction falls under that umbrella.[353] Lessig's argument brings to light the idea that perhaps fanfiction is not in the wrong, but copyright is. If this is the case, then perhaps the growth of fanfiction is justified, and in fact should be growing more and that fanfiction writers should also use fanfiction as a medium of free speech more. In the meantime, according to this argument, copyright law should be suppressed.

Many fanfiction writers do not realize that copyright law technically forbids them from writing fanfiction, and that the writing/publishing of fanfiction is a right solely held by the original creator. "I tend to believe that the person who wrote the story 'owns' the story," fanfic author, Shirou Shinjin writes on the issue of who owns a fanfic, "Provided it is an original idea (ignoring the question of the characters), then it is something they have created, and should be able to lay claim to."[354] This sentiment is echoed by many other fanfiction authors who write in their disclaimers and author notes that while they might not own the copyrighted characters, they do own the plot, the idea, and any OC (original characters of theirs) used in the story, and ask other fanfiction writers to please e-mail them first before using their original trimmings to their fanfiction in other fanfiction.[355] Interestingly enough, some fanfiction authors claim that their work is copyrighted, and that claim is staked without laughter or paradox.[356] Fanfiction writers as of yet, do not have to worry about original creators stealing their work. There have been no reports of an original creator taking a fanfiction and claiming it as their own. In fact, most original creators are very careful when it comes to fanfiction. Take for instance this real situation. Some staff members of the TV show "Buffy the Vampire Slayer" have read some fanfiction on the show. However, they always stopped reading a story once it started to head towards a direction that was similar to the show, rather than risk being blamed for stealing a story.[357]

Going back to copyrighted fanfiction, there is also "fanfiction" that is being not only copyrighted but published. These "published fanfiction" are modern adaptations of famous literary works. Sequels or spin-offs of famous stories like Peter Pan, James Bond, or Sherlock Holmes not done by the original creator are out there. There are more than enough Sherlock Holmes adaptations out there now, including A Slight Trick of the Mind, by Mitch Cullin and Final Solution: a Story of Deception, by Michael Chabon. In the case of the Peter Pan sequel, Captain Pan, the hospital which owns the copyright to the original story has extended their copyright to the author of Captain Pan, but there are unauthorized sequels in print.[358] These authors seem strangely lucky, as compared to most fanfiction authors. While these writers, whether or not their sequels are authorized or not, can put their real names on their work and not worry about it or be embarrassed. Most fanfiction authors hide behind a pen name and do not generally like to give out their real name or tell the people that they see everyday that they have written fanfiction. On the Internet, the need to be anonymous is a must. However, embarrassment about their writing is always a key factor, as well as the belief that most people wouldn't be able to understand why they write fanfiction unless they themselves are a fanfiction author or reader. One fanfiction author, Rhiannon, mentioned that since her fanfiction is based on dreams, most people wouldn't understand her, save for her best friend, Eileen. [359]

Fanfiction writers are also protected in the clause in copyright law that allows "fair use" of copyright material.[360] One could argue that fanfiction is "fair use" of copyrighted material since no money was ever made, disclaimers are attached, and the writers are all fans honoring their favorite media rather than people who download the copyright material. Fanfiction has never taken away from company profits like downloading or buying bootlegged copies of DVDs has. Henry Jenkins, author of several books about how fans act, when talking specifically about J.K. Rowling's Harry Potter series says that "There's no question that J. K. Rowling is the author of the original work, but Hogwarts [Rowling's imaginary wizarding school] may have room for more stories than she wants to write. And she might not be the best writer for every possible story set in Hogwarts."[361] Fanfiction fills in the gaps of stories that the original writer might leave. In fact, that is the main reason why so many fanfictions are started; fanfic authors want to fill in the gaps using their own ideas. Not only that, they want to continue on with a story that has been finished or want to look through the eyes of certain characters and try to figure out how they think.[362] This is why the majority of fanfiction writers, about eighty percent, are female, since women are more likely to want to fill in the gaps in stories.[363] One of the most common gaps that fanfiction authors want to fill is romantic undertones in the original work that are never fully realized. One example is the Scully and Mulder pairing from the TV show, The X-Files. While the actual TV show never fully explores the potential of the pair's relationship, there are fanfiction authors who have and have tried to persuade the show's real writers into incorporating the romance between Scully and Mulder.[364]

Fanfiction is a bit more versatile than originally thought. There is one other defense of fanfiction and that defense comes in the form of school work. There have been arguments that fanfiction is no "different from a school assignment requiring one to craft a missing chapter of Homer's Odyssey or an alternate ending to Jane Austen's Pride and Prejudice."[365] School teachers assigning such work might not realize it, but they are not just encouraging their students to break the law, but forcing them to. In fact, it is not uncommon to see in FanFiction.Net's archives a short story or poem that the author claims to have been used for an English assignment.[366] So if schools are allowed to have students write fanfiction, there is no reason for fanfiction authors in the privacy of their home not to write fanfiction.

Fanfiction is creating new stories from pre-existing copyrighted material. It breaks copyright law. It breaks the Fifth Amendment of the U.S. Constitution in regards of use of property. It is also a form of freedom of speech and of the press. It is a form of flattery. It is an art form. It is technically illegal, but no one is going to do much about it. There is no point to try to destroy the world of fanfiction at the moment. The copyright owners still are making a profit and are not loosing any money to fanfiction authors. Fanfiction writers go on their merry way, trying to avoid conflict with the original owners by writing disclaimers, respecting and honoring the original creators, and staying ignorant to how much trouble they could potentially be in legally with their fanfiction. For the copyright holders to go off and try to tear down fanfiction would be too much effort on their part. Fanfiction writers have no money to give to fend off the lawsuits, but they do purchase the merchandise, thus the copyright holder makes a profit. Yes, fanfiction is controversial, but not controversial enough to start a war over.

Bibliography

Abas, Zoraini Wati. 2003. Helping kids to pick up writing skills. New Straits Times. September 25, sec. Outlook Web Watch.

Amendments to the Constitution. 2004. United States House of Representatives. http://www.house.gov/Constitution/Amend.html (accessed September 2005)

Copyright Infringement. 2005. http://en.wikipedia.org/wiki/Copyright_infringement (accessed October 22, 2005)

Buechner, Maryanne Murray. 2002. Pop Fiction Stars and storybook characters are inspiring more teens to write for the Web. Is this a good thing? Time. March 4.

Cha, Ariana Eunjung. 2003. Harry Potter and the Copyright Lawyer. The Washington Post. June 18, sec. A.

Chandler-Olcott, Kelly and Mahar, Donna. 2003. Adolescents' anime-inspired "fanfictions": An exploration of multiliteracies. Journal of Adolescent & Adult Literacy. April 1.

Chicago Citation Style. B. Davis Schwartz Memorial Library. http://www.liu.edu/cwis/cwp/library/workshop/citchi.htm (accessed October 21, 2005)

Chicago Manual of Style. 2005. The University of Chicago. http://www.chicagomanualofstyle.org/cmosfaq.html (accessed October 21, 2005)

Dilucchio, Patrizia. 1997. Multimedia: Get with the Programs of the Cultish World of Fan Fiction, Stars of Competing TV Shows Mix It Up—and Censors Don't Exist. Entertainment Weekly. September 26.

Darbyshire, Peter. 2005. Classic characters never die: They're just reinvented by modern-day writers. Vancouver Providence. September 11, sec. Unwind.

Gray, B Allison. 2005. Good Conversation! A Talk with Tamora Pierce. School Library Journal. March 1.

Interview with the author. Shinjin, Shirou. October 22, 2005. E-mail interview.

Junion-Metz, Gail. 2005. Scare Them into Writing. School Library Journal. October 1.

Kenshinny. 2003. Normal Doujinshi Page 3. Fortune City. http://members.fortunecity.com/kenshinny/id73.htm (accessed September 2005)

Lee, Kylie. 2003. Confronting enterprise slash fan fiction. Extrapolation. April 1.

Li, Xing. 2005. FanFiction.Net. Fanfiction.Net. http://www.fanfiction.net/ (accessed September 2005)

Mayo, Tracy. 2003. Taking Liberties with Harry Potter Thousands of Spin-offs of J. K. Rowling's Novels - Many with Graphic Sex – can be Read on the Internet. But Why Is This Fan Fiction, Often of Questionable Legality, Allowed to Flourish? The Boston Globe. June 29, sec. Magazine.

MediaMiner.Org. 2005. MediaMiner.Org. http://www.mediaminer.org/fanfic/ (accessed September 2005)

On the extraordinary growth of fanorama and why it is here to stay. 2003. The Spectator. June 14.

Plagiarism. 2005. Wikipedia. http://en.wikipedia.org/wiki/
Plagiarism (accessed October 22, 2005)

Potter, Andrew. 2004. Will it be free, or feudal? National Post. May
15, sec. Books.

Salamon, Julie. 2001. The cult of Buffy. New York Times Upfront.
May 5.

Schulz, Nancy. 2001. The E-Files. Washington Post. April 29, sec.
G.

Scodari, Christine and Felder, Jenna L. 2000. Creating a pocket
universe: "Shippers," fan fiction, and The X-Files online.
Communication Studies. October 1.

Washingtonpost.com. 2005. The Washington Post. http://www.
washingtonpost.com/?nav=globaltop (accessed October 10, 2005)

Weeks, Linton. 2004. iT was a dark+stormy Nite... The
Washington Post. February 1, sec. Style.

Due Process and Juvenile Justice

By
Maureen McCusker

Imagine the fate of a twelve – year - old convicted of murder after a two-day trial, sentenced to death and sent to the gallows at the age of 13 years and 8 months; or the fate of a ten-year-old prisoner who died in a penitentiary after being accidentally scalded in a huge tub of coffee. Then there was the eight-year-old child put in the same jail cell with a sixty-five-year-old adult and the young vagrant who was forced to work eight hours a day manufacturing brass nails and then attend school four hours a day. These events occurred in the nineteenth century --- in the United States.[367]

These instances were very common occurrences in the U.S. prior to the Progressive Era. Along with the civil rights movement, the women's suffrage movement and the campaign against child labor came a change in society's views of juvenile delinquents during the Progressive Era. Although this alteration was due mostly to new, radical views of the social and political reformers, research by many psychologists had changed the way that people viewed and understood minors. They were no longer seen as miniature adults, but as children with "less than fully developed moral and cognitive abilities."[368] The focus changed from a desire to punish delinquent juveniles to a desire to rehabilitate them. In 1824, a group of social reformers built the New York House of Refuge, a detention center that focused on improving child behavior as opposed to penalizing the juveniles for their behavior.

Although the reforms made during the Progressive Era made huge advances for juveniles and their rights, juveniles were still not given legal protection similar to that found in adult court. In one situation, a father sought a writ of habeas corpus from the Pennsylvania Supreme Court to fight against his daughter's involuntary commitment to one of the institutions for youthful offenders. The court denied the writ and said it would be an "extreme act of cruelty" to release the girl; additionally, the court refused to inquire into the proceedings for commitment, the duration of the commitment or the conditions of the school.[369] With this decision, the concept of "parens patrea" or "father of the country" came into play to justify the court's informality and paternalism in dealing with children in the system.

About seventy-five years later, beginning in 1899, the reformers' work paid off as states began to take children out of adult jails and began to put them in juvenile reformatories.[370] The Illinois Juvenile Court Act created a special court for neglected, dependent or delinquent children under the age of sixteen and determined rehabilitation to be the primary purpose of that court. The proceedings were very informal and might consist of the judge having a conversation with the juvenile to gain his trust and then asking questions about the offense. One judge at the time described the court's preferred proceedings; "The judge... seated at a desk, with the child at his side, where he can on occasion put his arm around his shoulder...The judge, while losing none of his judicial dignity will gain immensely in the effectiveness of his work." [371]

Now, imagine a sixteen-year-old boy sent to criminal court for trial without any hearing to determine whether this was in his "best interest." Imagine the situation where a fifteen year old boy is caught making an obscene phone call to a neighbor and is sent to a juvenile correctional facility for a period not to exceed his twenty-first birthday. These events occurred in the twentieth century in the United States.

With these two situations, the attitude that had governed juvenile proceedings into the middle of the twentieth century began to erode. In the mid-1960s, society began to question the validity of the juvenile court's philosophy which seemed to favor informality over due process. These two situations evolved into two landmark Supreme Court cases, Kent v. United States (1966) and In Re Gault (1967). [372]

Prior to these court cases, the Fifth Amendment of the Constitution did not apply to juveniles.   The 5th Amendment states:

> 'No person shall be held to answer for a capital, or otherwise infamous crime, unless on a presentment or indictment of a Grand Jury...nor shall [a person] be compelled in any criminal case to be a witness against himself.'" [373]

Nor were they protected under the Fourteenth Amendment. .

> "The Amendment states, 'No State shall make or enforce
> any law which shall abridge the privileges or immunities of
> citizens of the United States; nor shall any State deprive any
> person of life, liberty, or property, without due process of
> law; nor deny to any person within its jurisdiction the equal
> protection of the laws.'"[374]

This Amendment made certain that everyone was equal under
the law, and no person would be deprived of due process. This
included everyone except for juveniles until In Re Gault and Kent
v. U.S.

The Kent v U.S. court case brought juveniles a step closer to equal
rights in the courts. In 1966, a sixteen-year-old boy was accused of
rape and robbery. Although he was not given a trial, his case was
moved to a criminal court. Kent's lawyer believed that the juvenile
courts had no right to move a youth to a criminal court without a
court hearing. He took it to the Supreme Court, which ruled that
juveniles must be given a fair trial.[375] This was a significant court
case because it established very important procedural rights in the
juvenile courts. Also, it brought the Fifth Amendment to minors.
At the conclusion of the hearing, Justice Abe Fortas expressed the
concern,

> "While there can be no doubt of the original laudable
> purpose of juvenile courts, studies and critiques in recent
> years raise serious questions... There is much evidence
> that some juvenile courts lack the personnel, facilities and
> techniques to perform adequately as representatives of the
> State in a parens patriae capacity. There is evidence, in fact,
> that there may be grounds for concern that the child receives
> the worst of both worlds: that he gets neither the protections
> accorded to adults nor the solicitous care...postulated for
> children."[376]

One year later, in 1967, juveniles would be even closer to being legally equal.

In 1967, a fifteen-year-old Arizonian, Gerald Gault, made several vulgar phone calls to a neighbor. The neighbor complained and the police arrested the boy. The police did not inform Gerald's parents and when they came home, they were worried because they did not know where their son was and eventually found out from a friend that he had been arrested. At the trial, the court did not follow standard court procedures or due process laws. Neither Gerald's father nor the accusing neighbor, Mrs. Cook, was present, nobody was sworn in, and there was no recording of the trial. The judge committed Gault to the State Industrial School for six years until he turned twenty-one. If an adult had committed the same crime, he or she would have received no more than a $50.00 fine and two months in jail under then-prevailing court procedures. Gault's counsel filed a writ of habeas corpus, but was denied by the Arizona courts. The case was then taken to the Supreme Court.[377]

At In Re Gault, the Supreme Court found against the Arizona Supreme Court only after Gault's attorney argued that the Arizona code was contrary to due process rights, which included:

"(1) Notice of the charges with regard to their timeliness and specificity,
(2) Right to counsel,
(3) Right to confrontation and cross-examination,
(4) Privilege against self-incrimination,
(5) Right to a transcript of the trial record, and
(6) Right to appellate review."[378]

The Court found that juveniles were entitled to due process under the Fourteenth Amendment and that, "neither the Fourteenth Amendment nor the Bill of Rights is for adults alone."[379] Justice Fortas again ruled, saying,

"It would be extraordinary if our Constitution did not require the procedural regularity and the exercise of care implied in the phrase 'Due process.' Under our Constitution the condition of being a boy does not justify a kangaroo court."[380]

This was probably the most important court case for juveniles because it set a standard for youth to be afforded the same legal safeguards as adults. In 1967, many believed that, from that point on, juveniles could and would have the same due process rights as adults in a court of law.

Sadly, many juveniles today are treated very similarly to the way that Gerald Gault was in 1967 before the enforcement of juvenile due process by the ruling of In Re Gault. "The mysterious phrase 'due process' means nothing more or less than the right to procedures that are fundamentally fair."[381] This fairness, enforced by the rulings of In Re Gault and Kent v. U.S., is not upheld today as too many juveniles are going without "due process" in their trials, if they receive any trial at all.

Inconsistency in juvenile court commitments to due process can be seen in numerous decisions made by the U.S. Supreme Court. While the Court determined that juveniles must be proven guilty beyond a reasonable doubt, in 1971 the Supreme Court refused, 6-3, to require a trial by jury for juveniles in McKeiver v. Pennsylvania. In the court's main opinion, Justice Harry A. Blackman said a "fully adversary proceeding would put an effective end" to the positive aspects of juvenile courts: "fairness…concern…sympathy and… paternal attention."[382]

Looking at the Supreme Court during the 1970s and 1980s, law Professor Nat Stern assessed that many of the rulings seemed to reflect assumptions that did not support the rights of juveniles. For example, in supporting a parent's right to institutionalize a minor in a mental hospital without a hearing, it would appear that the Court determined that a minor's constitutional rights did not stem from his rights as an autonomous human being, but rather from his position in a family structure. [383]

Outside of the Supreme Court, in local courts, juvenile unfairness is even more prevalent. Even though law in the Gault decision requires it, few trials ever take place. "Probably fewer than 5% of petitioned juveniles undergo a trial, even with its requirement of legal proof."[384] This means that probably 95% or more of all juvenile courts are breaking the law by not carrying on a trial. Even worse, these courts, where "justice" is enforced, are getting away with violating the law by refusing juveniles' due process rights.

On April 18, 2002, the In Re J.L.D. court ruling proved to the Texas Juvenile courts that the juvenile courts had violated the due process rights of a juvenile girl, J.L.D., by trying her twice for the same crime. In 2002, J.L.D was found guilty of assault and sentenced to twelve months probation. While on probation, though, the juvenile assaulted someone for the second time and thus was taken to trial again. The juvenile courts found J.L.D guilty of the assault that J.L.D. committed while on probation and ordered that she be committed to the Texas Youth Commission (TYC) for an indefinite period of time. The prosecution also reverted back to the very first of the two assaults and sought to extend her probation because of it.[385]

 J.L.D.'s attorney then took this case to the Texarkana Court of Appeals where he objected to the court ruling by saying that the Texas juvenile courts had infringed upon the juvenile's due process rights by practicing double jeopardy. He claimed that the juvenile courts had tried her twice for the first assault by first putting her on probation, and then extending it.[386] The Texarkana Court of Appeals stated,

> "...The substance on J.L.D.'s argument on appeal is that the court violated her right to due process by twice using one act to modify her community supervision. We conclude that the juvenile court violated J.L.D.'s due process liberty rights when it modified a previous disposition."[387]

Violation of liberty due process rights of juveniles happens often due to double jeopardy and many lawyers do not do anything about it for a number of reasons.[388] Luckily, J.L.D.'s attorney could and did do something.

Although the Gault decision did not require a counsel, it allowed juveniles the right to have them, but many lawyers for juveniles are insufficient for a number of reasons. Typically, after juveniles file formal court petitions, initial appearance hearings take place. Many juveniles at this time admit to their crimes and thus do not need counsel while others request counsel and "...go outside the courtroom for 5 to 10 minutes to talk with an attorney, and then come back in to admit their offenses or request a continuance of the case."[389] Five to ten minutes with an attorney is definitely not enough time to sufficiently talk about an offense.

"Most urban juvenile courts are serviced by public defenders who establish reputations as strong advocates for the juveniles, although their heavy workloads place real constraints on case investigations and time available for the conduct of trials." As a result, defense attorneys very frequently ask the prosecuting attorneys to dismiss the case and try to compromise with the prosecutor on a plea bargain.[390] It is unfair for the juvenile to be without a fair trial just because his attorney is too busy. It is a violation of a juvenile's due process civil liberties to be denied a fair trial.

Even though the In Re Gault decision guaranteed juveniles the same due process protection under the Fourteenth Amendment as adults, the trials in juvenile courts are far from being that. The trials go on without a jury, the delinquents are often double jeopardized, and the right and ability to counsel is hardly a right as the attorneys are often inadequate to defend their clients.

In the past twenty years, we have seen the public grow increasingly concerned with juvenile crime and demand increasingly punitive responses. Certain classes of offenses have been removed from the juvenile justice system and offenders are automatically transferred to the criminal justice system. Between 1992 and 1997, all but three states changed laws in one or more of the following areas:

"Transfer provisions: Forty-five states have made it easier to transfer juveniles to the criminal justice system

Sentencing authority: Thirty-one states gave courts expanded sentencing options

Confidentiality: Forty-seven states modified or removed the confidentiality provisions of juvenile court cases."[391]

In response to the large increase in violent crime between 1989 and 1993, "in the mid-1990s almost every state changed its juvenile laws." In addition to "a) removing more juveniles from juvenile court jurisdiction and placing them in criminal court; b) increasing the severity of court dispositions; and c) reducing the confidentiality of juvenile proceedings and records,"[392] many schools increased school security. The schools probably thought, and currently think, that they were protecting the students, but what they may not have known is that much of what school security did went against youths' rights protected by the Fourteenth Amendment, even though many court rulings found these acts constitutional.

Schools continue to infringe upon students' freedom of expression without abiding by the Fourteenth Amendment. This amendment clearly states, "nor shall any State deprive any person of life, liberty, or property, without due process of law." The freedom of expression is a liberty plainly given to youths by the Gault decision, yet schools are permitted to take this liberty away from juveniles without any due process. In 1969, just two years after the Fourteenth and Fifth Amendments began to apply to juveniles, the Courts partially took this right away. In Tinker v. Des Moines Independent School District, the courts recognized that schools could limit free speech rights of youths.[393] From then on, all schools could take away a right guaranteed to all other Americans in the Bill of Rights without giving the juveniles their guaranteed due process and fair trial, another right guaranteed to minors by the Fourteenth and Fifth Amendments of the Constitution.

In 1988, the Courts ruled that a school possessed the ability to censor the contents of a high school newspaper if the school found it necessary.[394] A school newspaper is, like the Constitution, created for the people (students) by the people (students). It is a way for students to express their creativity and their views. Censoring these newspapers not only confines the creative originality of an adolescent's mind, but also encroaches upon a youth's rights. This censorship violates one's freedom of expression and of the right to due process as the students have no right to a just trial against the school; they just obey the laws that are infringements on their rights and creativity. Fethro K. Lieberman, author of The

<u>Evolving Constitution</u>, expresses a similar viewpoint in dealing with censorship of school newspapers by the school by saying, "The irony of an educational system that teaches democratic values by censoring newspapers escaped the court majority entirely."[395]

Another occurrence of a juvenile rights violation at school took place much more recently, in 1996. In Burlington, Vermont, a male high school student was gay and "was sent home because he continually wore a dress to school."[396] The school thought that it was within its own legal right to send the juvenile home because of his behavior, but it was not. All citizens are entitled to freedom of expression, even high school students. The homosexual boy was expressing himself through his clothing, which was not inappropriate.[397]

A school should not be allowed to violate someone's rights of expression, not even a juvenile, without due process of the law, and that is the law guaranteed to all citizens of America through the Fourteenth Amendment, the Fifth Amendment, and the In Re Gault decision.

In 1972, the U.S. Courts ruled in Wisconsin v. Yoder, that when Amish children are fourteen years old, their parents could remove them from public school without the child's consent.[398] If the child wants to stay in school, he or she should not, according to the Fourteenth Amendment be deprived of a liberty that he or she has and should be able to attend school. But because the Amish child is under the guardianship of his or her parents, then he or she has no right to sue his or her parents or take it to court,[399] a violation of the Fourteenth Amendment.

"Although they never met one another, Steven Roach, Douglas Thomas, and Glen McGinnis will forever share a grim page in United States history."[400] All three of these boys were seventeen-years-old when they committed a crime, a crime that killed them. All of them were put to death in January of 2000 for murder crimes. [401] Since 1976, "when the U.S. Supreme Court's holding in Gregg v. Georgia made it clear that the death penalty was not always... an unconstitutional punishment," twenty-one youth executions have been carried out. Texas is responsible for thirteen of the twenty-one executions. [402]

Until the late 1980s, juvenile death sentences were not clearly constitutional, but were still carried out. The two landmark court cases relating to juvenile capital punishment were Thompson v. Oklahoma (1988) and Stanford v. Kentucky (1989). The Thompson v. Oklahoma verdict was that the execution of a person for a crime that he or she committed under the age of sixteen-years-old is unconstitutional.[403] The latter of the two court cases, however, held, in 1989, that "the imposition of capital punishment on individuals for murders committed at the age of 16 or 17 does not constitute cruel or unusual punishment in violation of the Eight Amendment."[404] When determining the age for which capital punishment was legal, the Courts did not try to relate this age boundary to any studies of maturity or emotional development. The Courts conducted no tests to make sure that 16 is the best age for capital punishment,[405] and many people today are arguing that it is not because of new findings proving that youths are not mature at sixteen-years-old.

"Dieter, a representative from the Death Penalty Information Center in Washington, adds, 'Teenagers are somewhat there, but they are not fully in adulthood. We recognize that by saying that they cannot vote, can't serve on a jury, buy alcohol, be drafted. There are a lot of lines we draw for which 18 is a bright line.'"[406] The certainty of limitations on underage teenagers is proof that minors are not mentally or emotionally mature.

Some think that the death penalty will have a preventative effect on teenagers, but Doctor Streib, a lawyer and law school dean at Ohio Northern University, disagrees. He says that this view ignores the way troubled teens really think. "They are impulsive, they don't plan ahead. They think they are immortal, they don't fear death. Treating them like adults just assumes that they think like adults."[407] Adults plan ahead and very often fear death. This is completely different from the mindset of "troubled teens." Thus, teens should not be treated in the same manner as adults. They should not be killed for their actions if the minors are not mature enough to see what they have done. The focus of the courts should not be to impose "what has properly been called the 'ultimate penalty in criminal law'"[408] on juveniles on order to get retribution. The focus should be more so on bettering the teens and facilitating maturity so that teens will not commit such treacherous acts as murder ever again.

"...proposing a particular age or set of conditions as appropriate for full punishment should be accompanied by the advancement of a theory of maturity- a set of assumptions that should be tested against other legal principles that implicitly or explicitly make assumptions about how and when adolescents reach adulthood."[409]

The U.S. Supreme Court, itself, showed its views of adolescents' maturity in some of its own cases. One included Eddings v. Oklahoma.

"[A]dolescents, particularly in the early and middle teen years, are more vulnerable, more impulsive, and less self-disciplined than adults. Crimes committed by adults may be just as harmful to victims as those committed by older persons, but they deserve less punishment because adolescents may have less capacity to control their conduct and to think in long-range terms as adults."[410]

Even though the Supreme Court claims that juveniles should not be treated like adults because of their mental immaturity, they still try them as adults in many murder cases where sometimes the youths are sentenced to death.

In Schall v. Abrams, the Supreme Court, quoting from Wayburn v. Schapf, said,

"Our society recognizes that juveniles in general are in the earlier stages of their emotional growth, that their intellectual development is incomplete, they have had only limited practical experience, and that their value systems have not yet been clearly identified or firmly adopted."[411]

Despite the way our society and our own Supreme Court views juvenile maturation and its impact on their actions, when it comes to dealing with major crimes, where the decision-making process of juveniles is most affected by incomplete maturation, our society and the courts treat juveniles like adults by giving them adult sentences. They believe that at the time of the major crimes, and only at that time, the youths had finished growing emotionally, had completed their intellectual development, had a great deal of experience, and had a firm value system. It is completely unfair to the juvenile to think in that way.

A fair trial is an important part of the Fourteenth Amendment and part of the due process rights that the In Re Gault decision gave to juveniles. It is fully unjust to call individuals minors and to deprive these individuals of the right to vote, the ability to be on a jury, and the ability to smoke because of their immaturity and underdevelopment and then change this belief and consider the minors adults if they commit a serious enough crime. This transformation of views is unfair to the juvenile and leads to an unfair trial, contrary to the provisions of the Fourteenth Amendment.

The right to due process guaranteed to juveniles in the Fifth and Fourteenth Amendments and by the court cases of In Re Gault and Kent v. United States is very often violated by numerous means, including the absence of a jury, a poor legal definition of an adult, and incompetent and overworked lawyers.

People can take one of two stands on juvenile rights. They can consider juveniles adults and take all those over sixteen-years-old to criminal court to try them as adults, or people can consider juveniles as minors and try all those under eighteen in juvenile court as minors. Today, our society is in the middle. Depending on the crime, some sixteen and seventeen-year-olds are being considered adults but still do not have some of the rights that adults have. But America cannot stand in the middle forever. It must take a side. It must decide whether to punish juveniles as it does adults, put them in jail or on death row, and give them all rights of adults or it must institutionalize juveniles and work to positively mature and develop within them firmly based values.

"If the problem is really that some person and/or community has/have been harmed and suffered loss by an offender, why are victims and community representatives not directly involved in the sanctioning and the rehabilitation process, and why isn't restoration of juvenile victims the primary focus of sanctioning?"[412]

No matter what the crime, the focus of juveniles should be restoration through institutions, not punishment through death.

Bibliography

Fagan, Jeffrey and Zimring, Franklin F. The Changing Borders of Juvenile Justice. Chicago: University of Chicago Press, 2000.

Feld, Barry C. Justice for Children. Boston: Northeastern University Press, 1993.

Fireside, Harvey. The Fifth Amendment. Springfield, NJ: Enslow Publishers, Inc., 1998.

Grisso, Thomas and Schwartz, Robert G. Youth on Trial. Chicago: University of Chicago Press, 2000

http://www.youthrights.org/inregault.shtml

http://www.juvenilejusticefyi.com/history_of_juvenile_justice.html

http://www.tjpc.state.tx.us/publications/reviews/02/02-2-13.htm

IN RE GAULT, 387 U.S. 1 (1967)

Jost, Kenneth, April 23, 2003. "Children's Legal Rights." CQ Researcher. Page 339-354. Retrieved October 24, 2005 from SIRS Researcher.

Leiberman, Fethro K. The Evolving Constitution. New York: Random House, Inc., 1992

Maryam, Ahrajani, Youth Justice in America. Washington D.C.: CQ Press, 2005

Monk, Linda R. The Words We Live By. New York: The Stonesong Press, Inc., 2001.

Pardeck, John T. Children's Rights: Policy and Practice. New York: The Haworth Social Work Press, 2002

Richey, Warren, Feb. 1, 2000. "Teens and the Death Penalty: In Executing Youths, U.S. Stands Alone." Christian Science Monitor News Service. Retrieved October 24, 2005 from SIRS Researcher.

Roberts, Albert R. Juvenile Justice Sourcebook. New York: Oxford University Press, 2004

Shepherd, Robert E, Dec. 1999. "The Juvenile Court at 100 Years: A Look Back." Juvenile Justice. Page 13-21. Retrieved October 24, 2005 from SIRS Researcher.

Snyder, Howard N. and Sickmund, Melissa, Dec. 1999. "The Juvenile Justice: A Century of Change." Juvenile Justice Bulletin. Page 1-20. Retrieved October 24, 2005 from SIRS Researcher

White, Susan O. Handbook of Youth and Justice. New York: Plenum Publishers, 2001

The Fourth Amendment And Students

By
Kristen C. Merek

"The right of the people to be secure in their persons, houses, papers, and effects, against unreasonable searches and seizures, shall not be violated, and no Warrants shall issue, but upon probable cause, supported by Oath or affirmation, and particularly describing the place to be searched, and the persons or things to be seized."[413]

One intrinsic part of human nature is, and has always been, a person's love of his privacy and his belongings. This human characteristic proved instrumental in the Founding Fathers' creation of the Fourth Amendment in the Bill of Rights, which they drafted to limit superfluous searches that would invade citizens' privacy and seizures that would result in the loss of their personal belongings. The drafters saw the rights of privacy and property as so paramount, that they added this amendment, which specifically protected those rights. However, public schools, which have increasingly relied on the expansion of the doctrine of in loco parentis to discipline students, have begun to draft certain policies that have restricted the Fourth Amendment rights of their students. These policies have been supported by the Supreme Court (even when they have been ruled unconstitutional by lower district courts), which has led to the Fourth Amendment being rendered hardly applicable to minors in a school setting.

The Fourth Amendment is one of the ten that make up the Bill of Rights, which was added to the Constitution in 1791, after being ratified by the states as a way to assuage the fears of the Anti-Federalists, those who thought that the new government created by the Constitution would hamper the natural rights of the citizens of the United States.[414] This particular amendment is interpreted today as a safeguard for the people against unfounded searches and seizures of property, and its creation was spurred, as the creation of the entire Bill of Rights was, by a wish to prevent the government created by the Constitution from assuming the type of authoritarian control that the British government exerted over its American colonies before they became independent.

In the years leading up to the Revolutionary War, American colonists felt increasingly oppressed under the thumb of the British government as it continued to expand its law enforcement authority over its subjects. The colonists began to feel that their natural rights were under attack by Britain in many ways, especially through the Crown's issuance of writs of assistance. These omniscient warrants were given to British customs officials in the colonies by Parliament and basically granted them free reign to search for smuggled goods and those who smuggled them. An official possessing a writ of assistance could enter any home at any time and could seize any property at their inclination or make any arrests they deemed necessary.[415] This was seen by the colonists as an abuse of power by the British Crown, and was possibly alluded to in the Declaration of Independence when it states that King George III "sent hither swarms of officers to harass our people..."[416]

The creation of the Constitution showed the Founding Fathers' realization that the government had a duty to aid and protect its citizens; the creation of the Bill of Rights illustrated their consciousness of the fact that citizens should be protected from their government. The egregious infringement on colonists' civil liberties under British rule through the use of writs of assistance was surely on the framers' minds as something that the general public of their new nation should be protected from when they convened to draw up the Bill of Rights. Thus, when the debate came to the Fourth Amendment, hardly a single qualm was raised. Additionally, the protection against capricious searches was nothing new to these early politicians; after independence was declared, the state constitutions of Virginia, Pennsylvania, Maryland, North Carolina, New Hampshire, and Massachusetts all included some form of law against tenuous search and/or seizure. The Massachusetts Declaration of Rights was the earliest document to use the expression "unreasonable searches and seizures", and thus is believed to have served largely as the foundation for the Fourth Amendment.[417]

Thus, by passing into law the Fourth Amendment, the newly formed states assured the sanctity of a man's possessions and dwelling by outlawing open-ended warrants like the writs of assistance. However, the Founding Fathers wished that the Constitution could remain flexible and able to change slightly as times dictated. Thus, if the Founding Fathers were to see the Fourth Amendment in application today, they might barely even recognize the law they helped to create.

This is because society has changed greatly in the over 200 years since the Bill of Rights was passed, and more things have come into play in the categories of "search" and "seizure", such as wiretapping or drug testing or the search of a motor vehicle. The Founding Fathers knew that people valued their property and the sanctity of it, which was one of the main reasons behind the drafting of the Fourth Amendment, and that fact has not changed to this day, which may be one of the reasons why the Fourth Amendment is one of the "most heavily litigated components of the Bill of Rights"[418] at present. The Supreme Court has been able to direct the scope of the amendment's power greatly throughout the many cases they have heard concerning search and seizure, and have helped shape the law into its present interpretation.

The Amendment states that search warrants must be obtained on "probable cause," which is not a phrase that lends itself to easy definition. Over the track of history, courts have come to take it to mean that the police must obtain a search warrant from a judge (or even a magistrate or officer of the court, ruled the Supreme Court in United States v. Lefkowitz[419]). The Supreme Court has ruled that the official who issues the warrant must be neutral and unbiased about the situation to protect the rights of the accused, and stated in Johnson v. United States, that they wish to impose an independent party between the suspect and the police instead of having the suspected criminal be "judged by the officer engaged in the often competitive enterprise of ferreting out crime."[420] Before this unbiased official can issue the warrant, they must know that the police's wish to search is based on evidence or information that would make a rational person suspect that further evidence or proof of crime would be found in the place to be investigated. When deciding to give a warrant, the Supreme Court has also ruled that the official take into account a "staleness limitation," which means that, just because a person was seen committing illegal activities from or in their house two weeks ago, does not mean that evidence of that illegal activity would still remain; police must convince the official that evidence they are seeking is likely to be found on the premises to be searched.[421]

The amendment also states that the warrant must "describe the place to be searched and the persons or things to be seized." The police cannot simply say, when requesting a warrant, that they or another witness watched a criminal run into a hotel lobby, and thus they wish to search the whole building and all of the rooms. That one account is not enough "probable cause" to suggest that the criminal would still be inside the hotel; they must designate a specific room. Searches are also restricted by the objects that are being searched for. If the warrant states that the police are looking for a stolen TV, they couldn't look in places like drawers or under mattresses, where the contraband item could not possibly be hidden. However, if they are searching for the TV and see what may be contraband or evidence lying about in "plain view", they can seize it; they cannot, however, open drawers or overturn mattresses to bring about that "plain view."[422]

The framers intended the Fourth Amendment to limit warrant use and property searches, but Supreme Court rulings have identified over twenty instances where search warrants are not necessary to conduct search and seizure. Anyone can be arrested (have their person seized), and their clothing, purses, briefcases, suitcases, or any other carried items searched without a warrant. People can be detained on the street and frisked, have their cars stopped, searched and impounded, and be stopped at customs and be searched (or even strip-searched), all without the use of a warrant and based solely on probable cause. No warrant is needed to search when consent has been given; the police may search a house without a warrant when consent is given by a person in position to do so, such as the head of the household or spouse, but not a landlord. The police, when in "hot pursuit" of a suspect, may enter and search houses without a warrant. In the recent expansion of law enforcement's "war on drugs," the Supreme Court has upheld drug searches committed without warrants, and have also ruled that airline passengers who fit a specific "drug carrier profile" may be detained and questioned, and that employees in sensitive government work positions can be compelled to submit to drug tests. The Supreme Court has justified all of these exceptions by stating the people's need to have the police enforce the country's laws effectively. These, and all other exceptions to the need for a warrant, occur in situations where the long and often arduous process of obtaining a search warrant would interfere with the ability of law enforcement to efficiently implement the laws of the country. [423]

The Supreme Court in the past several decades has also heard many cases concerning Fourth Amendment rights, and the possible infringement thereof, of public school students. This has most probably been caused by the expansion of the use of the doctrine of in loco parentis as a disciplinary tool in public schools. In loco parentis, which in Latin, literally means "in the place of the parent," has been in practice for many years in United States public schools. Practically, in loco parentis means that the school and its officials assume a parental role over their students in the absence of the students' actual parents. This means that the schools and their officials are to be concerned with the physical, moral and mental well being of their students and are responsible for providing sound academic training.[424]

Minors who have not been emancipated from their parents lack some intrinsic rights given by the Constitution to citizens of the United States. When not emancipated, thus, still under the authority of their parents, minors lack the freedoms of privacy and even the freedom of coming and going as they please; they are subject to the rules placed on them by their parents. Thus, states the doctrine of in loco parentis, when parents place their minor children in public schools to be educated, the teachers and school officials assume those parental controls over the students entrusted to them, and act in loco parentis, in the place of those children's parents.[425]

One of the first, and most persistently raised, questions regarding the nature of in loco parentis dealt with how the Fourth Amendment applies to minor students while they are in school. Parents have the right (and often exercise it) to search their child's belongings when they suspect the child is breaking their rules or even on a whim and also to seize their children's belongings either for punishment or because the belonging is something the parent has forbidden the child from having. When parents place their children in the care of public schools and their officials, does this omniscient right to search and seizure of minors' belongings transfer to these people acting in loco parentis? Can these teachers and administrators, who have no power of enforcement outside their schools, perform searches on their students that even police officers could not perform because of the restrictions of the Fourth Amendment? Does the Fourth Amendment apply in public schools to minors?

The first case to truly set a precedent for the Constitutional implications of in loco parentis was Tinker v. Des Moines Independent Community School Dist. (1969). In this case, Christopher Tinker, his sister, and several friends decided that, in protest of the Vietnam War, they would wear black armbands to school during the Christmas season. They were asked to remove their armbands in school, refused, and were suspended until after New Year's. The Supreme Court ultimately ruled that the wearing of the armbands was "closely akin to 'pure speech'"[26] and was protected under the First Amendment, because the principal failed to show that the wearing of the armbands would in any way significantly hamper order and discipline in his school.

Although this case did not specifically deal with the Fourth Amendment rights of public school students, it did set the standards for the application of Constitutional rights to minors in public schools. The Court stated in its decision that these students did not "shed their rights... at the schoolhouse gate,"[27] and, thus, did acknowledge that, although the school was acting in a parental fashion by trying to keep order and discipline, that the students were not devoid of their Constitutional rights simply because of the application of in loco parentis.

Sixteen years later, the Supreme Court reached another landmark decision regarding public school students' Constitutional rights in the classroom. However, it did not acknowledge simply that the students enjoyed certain rights in school, regardless of in loco parentis. The Supreme Court's decision in the case of New Jersey v. T.L.O. stated that school officials were exempt from many of the restraints set forth by the Fourth Amendment,[428] and could, in a school setting, commit searches and seizures that not even police officers and other public officials are allowed to commit.

In this case, a high school teacher found two teenage girls smoking in the bathroom, which was against the school's policies. One of these girls, when taken to see the assistant principal, denied that she was smoking. The assistant principal then demanded to see her purse, where he discovered much more than he was looking for. Her purse not only contained a pack of cigarettes, but also marijuana, a pipe, a large amount of money, and two notes that implied that she was selling marijuana. Later, she was taken to the police station where she confessed that she was, indeed, selling marijuana. When the state brought charges against her, her lawyer moved to suppress them because they were based on evidence discovered in a search of her purse that he stated violated her rights under the Fourth Amendment.[429]

The New Jersey Supreme Court ruled that the Fourth Amendment does apply to searches committed by school officials, and that the girl's Constitutional rights were, in fact, violated by the search of her purse. However, when the state of New Jersey appealed that decision to the United States Supreme Court, the ruling on the case was reversed.[430]

Although the United States Supreme Court ruled that the Fourth Amendment applies in public schools because, in spite of in loco parentis, school administrators are acting as government representatives, it also ruled that, because of in loco parentis, and the administrators' commitment to the well being of their students, they are not subject to the Fourth Amendment "restrictions to which searches by public authorities are ordinarily subject".[431] In essence, the Court said that pubic school officials have more leeway to infringe upon the Fourth Amendment rights of their students than actual law enforcement officials would.

Police officers are required, under the Fourth Amendment, to posses a warrant in order to search, or, in the least, need to base their search on a "probable cause" to believe that a crime was committed or that they would be able to find evidence of that crime in their search. The Supreme Court's decision in T.L.O. gave public school officials greater freedom than that to search students and to seize their belongings. The Court ruled that school officials do not need a warrant, nor do they even need "probable cause," to commit searches; they simply need "reasonable grounds" for suspecting that a search will lead to evidence of the student's contravention of school policies.[432] By greatly diluting the Fourth Amendment requirements for lawful search and seizure, even though it realized that school officials were also government officials, New Jersey v. T.L.O. was the first step in the monumental downhill journey of a minor student's Fourth Amendment rights in a school setting.

The narrowing of students' Fourth Amendment rights was continued eight years later in the Supreme Court case Vernonia School District 47J v. Acton (1995). In this case, a small rural school district fell under the pressure of the rising popularity of drugs in U.S. culture, and began to see a spike in drug use by students. Public school athletes were found not only to be a part of the teenage drug users, but often led the advent of the drug culture in the community and frequently boasted that the school could do nothing about it. In an attempt to curb and lessen drug use in their public schools, the district began to offer special classes to make students aware of the growing drug problem and to try to deter the students' use of illegal drugs. When these programs failed to work and instances of student drug use reached epidemic proportions, the district tried another approach.[433]

The Vernonia School District implemented the Student Athlete Drug Policy as a last-resort approach to their growing drug problem. Before this policy was put into practice across the board in its public schools, an input and information meeting of students' parents was held to discuss the proposed policy, to which all parents in attendance gave their undisputed approval.[434] This policy required all interscholastic student athletes to sign a consent form that authorized testing of their urine for illegal substances. It mandated that all athletes would be tested at the beginning of their sport's season, and then each week during the season their names would be placed into a hat and a student under adult supervision would blindly draw out ten percent of the names to have their urine randomly tested. The students would be monitored by same-sex adults while giving the sample and would have to disclose any prescriptions they were taking.[435]

James Acton, who was a seventh grader in the Vernonia School District, had signed up to play football in his public grade school. He and his parents refused to sign the forms because, in James's words, they felt "that they [had] no reason to think I was taking drugs",[436] and thus James was denied participation in school sports. James and his parents then brought suit against the school, seeking relief from the enforcement of the policy upon James on the grounds that the mandated urine tests violated his Fourth Amendment rights.[437]

After an Oregon District Court denied the Acton's' claims, the case was appealed to the United States Ninth Circuit Court of Appeals which reversed the lower court's decision, saying that the mandated drug testing was a violation of James Acton's Fourth Amendment rights. However, when this case was ultimately appealed to the United States Supreme Court, the Court, as in the T.L.O. case, reversed the ruling of a lower court, and ruled the mandatory, random urine tests to be constitutional.[438]

The Supreme Court again, as in the T.L.O. case, stated that Fourth Amendment rights are "different in public schools than elsewhere."[439] The Court's ruling hinges on the determination of just how much privacy a public school athlete can expect once they sign up for intramural sports. They ruled that these public school athletes have a reduced expectation of privacy going into the sports atmosphere because they must routinely submit to mandatory physical examinations and receive vaccinations against certain illnesses if they wish to be allowed to play sports. The Court ultimately concluded that public school student athletes have "reason to expect intrusions upon normal rights and privileges, including privacy."[440]

The Vernonia School District sought to expand its rights in loco parentis to include drug testing in order to discipline students who were breaking both the law and school policy. As unemancipated minors have virtually no constitutional rights because they are still under the power of their parents, their parents could compel them to be drug tested at any time. However, the T.L.O. case did realize that minor public school students do have Fourth Amendment rights while in school, and thus Acton simply additionally restricted those already limited rights.

In the T.L.O. case, the school officials who searched the girl's purse did have exclusive suspicion of the girl's wrongdoing as they had a teacher who claimed to have witnessed the girl smoking in the bathroom. Thus, it was somewhat reasonable to believe that a search of her purse would have turned up the contraband cigarettes. In James Acton's case, however, there was no such individualized suspicion of wrongdoing on his part. There was no one who had witnessed Acton taking drugs, there were no physical or social signs that Acton was taking drugs, there were not even any rumors that could have possibly tied Acton to the drug culture of some of Vernonia's teens.[441] The T.L.O. search was based on an individualized suspicion of wrongdoing, whereas the Acton search was simply a blanket search that applied to all student athletes. In her dissent on the Acton decision, Justice Sandra Day O'Connor writes that the blanket nature of the searches considered "dilutes the accusatory nature of the search"[442] and that suspicion-based testing would have been the best way to help solve the district's drug problem while preserving students' Fourth Amendment rights because

> Searches based on individualized suspicion also afford potential targets considerable control over whether they will, in fact, be searched because a person can avoid such a search by not acting in an objectively suspicious way. And given that the surest way to avoid acting suspiciously is to avoid the underlying wrongdoing, the costs of such a regime, one would think, are minimal.[443]

Also, the Court based much of its ruling on the fact that student athletes also submit to mandatory health physicals and vaccinations. Yes, these examinations and vaccinations are "blanket searches" of some sort, but, as Sandra Day O'Connor also points out in her dissent, they do not necessarily have any significance under the Fourth Amendment because they are not "mandatory" in the same sense that the urine tests were; they are not always required regardless of parental objection. Moreover, vaccinations can hardly be constituted as any type of search because there is no real suspicion, individualized or general, in the giving of a vaccine. The vaccine is given to help prevent an illness; it is not a search for anything, and thus there is nothing about which to be suspicious.[444]

One can clearly see the decline in public school students' Fourth Amendment rights. First, the students were asserted to be in possession of their Constitutional rights in the classroom. Then, those rights were abridged to allow school authorities to conduct searches and seizures solely based on "reasonable grounds" for belief that a search will produce evidence of rule breaking, and not the warrant or even "probable cause" required by law of police officers. Their Fourth Amendment rights were even further abridged by the Supreme Court's ruling in the Acton case, which decided that school officials no longer even needed "reasonable grounds" for suspicion of wrongdoing, but could simply conduct blanket searches of public school student athletes.

The most recent case concerning public school student's Fourth Amendment rights, Pottawatomie County v. Earls, occurred in 2002. In this case, a rural school district in Oklahoma adopted a mandatory drug testing policy similar to that adopted by the Vernonia School District, except that this policy required all middle and high school students who wished to participate in any extracurricular activity, not simply intramural sports, to consent to drug testing. The application of this drug policy was similar to that of Vernonia's, but its scope was much larger, requiring the consent to urine testing of activities from the Academic Team to Future Farmers of America. The parents of two high school students who participated in solely academic extracurricular activities contested the district's testing policy as being against the students' Fourth Amendment rights.[445]

As in both Vernonia and T.L.O., the state's District Court dismissed the challenge. After the case was appealed, the Unites States Court of Appeals for the Tenth Circuit reversed that dismissal and stated that the policy did violate students' Fourth Amendment rights because there was nothing to show the suspicion of drug abuse among any significant number of students who were to be tested under the policy. Then, for the third major case in a row relating to public schools students' Fourth Amendment rights, the Supreme Court reversed a lower court's ruling and upheld the policy as constitutional. The Court held that the school district did not need to justify a drug testing policy by showing any kind of proof that a drug problem was pervasive, or even present, in their schools because of their need to ensure the well being of their students and their need for order to be able to educate their students, which are their responsibilities as stated by the doctrine of in loco parentis.[446]

This most recent case on the Fourth Amendment rights of public school students was used by the Supreme Court to further restrict those rights. There was little or no evidence of a drug problem in this school district[447], and thus there was no particular reason to suspect any wrongdoing, but the school district again expanded their rights in loco parentis, saying that the mandatory tests were indispensable in achieving the order needed to teach the students and to ensure their safety. This decision echoes that of the Acton case in that the Court ruled that no individualized suspicion of wrongdoing was needed, but it went one step further by saying that not even a general suspicion of misconduct on the part of the group to be tested was needed, and it also extended the legality of mandatory drug tests not only for public school student athletes, but for public school students in all extracurricular activities.

The real question raised, not only by Pottawatomie, but by the string of cases that have increasingly restricted the Fourth Amendment rights of students is: where should it stop? If the Supreme Court has continuously upheld school administration practices that increasingly infringe on the students' Fourth Amendment rights, will they go on with this practice? If they have ruled it constitutional to mandate drug tests for all public school students involved in extracurricular activities, would they uphold a policy (if such a one were passed) mandating drug tests of all public school students? The framers of the Constitution abhorred "dragnet" searches,[448] but will the Supreme Court still continue to uphold them as constitutional? Will the doctrine of in loco parentis become so instrumental in the discipline of public school students that all distinctions between parents and school officials become erased by legislation? Although the shrinking scope of students' Fourth Amendment rights in a school setting is undeniable, the answers to these questions spawned by Supreme Court decisions remain to be seen in yet other Supreme Court decisions that are sure to arise as public school officials continue to rely on expanding in loco parentis to discipline their students.

The Founding Fathers drafted and the states subsequently passed the Fourth Amendment to ensure what they felt to be inestimable rights of privacy and property. Public school students, however, have not been able to fully realize their Fourth Amendment rights in the classroom because of the advent of the doctrine of in loco parentis. In loco parentis, which permits school officials and teachers to act in the best interest of students in the absence of their real parents, has been greatly expanded by public school officials as a way to maintain order in their schools. Because of this expansion of in loco parentis, many cases regarding students' Fourth Amendment rights in school have come before the Supreme Court. By siding with the school administrators in every instance, the Supreme Court has caused students' Fourth Amendment rights in a school setting to shrink dramatically and, if they choose to continue the same course of rulings, the Supreme Court could cause public school students' Fourth Amendment rights in the classroom to completely disappear.

Bibliography

Alschuler, Albert. Interview with John Kasich. <u>The O'Reilly Factor</u>. 27 June 2002. Fox News. FOX.

Barker, Lucius J., Twiley W. Barker, Jr., Michael W. Combs, Kevin L. Lyles, and H. W. Perry, Jr. <u>Civil Liberties and the Constitution: Cases and Commentaries</u>. Upper Saddle River, New Jersey: Prentice Hall, 1999.

Edwards III, George C., Martin P. Wattenberg, and Robert L. Lineberry. <u>Government in America: People, Politics and Policy</u>. New York: Longman, 1998.

Melear, K. B. "From In Loco Parentis to Consumerism: A Legal Analysis of the Contractual Relationship Between Institution and Student." <u>NASPA Journal</u> 40 (2003).

Moenssens, Andre A. "Do School Children Have Fourth Amendment Rights?" <u>Forensic-Evidence.com</u>. University of Missouri-Kansas City School of Law. 7 Oct. 2005 <http://www.forensic-evidence.com/site/Police/school_4th.html>.

Newman, Roger K. <u>The Constitution and its Amendments</u>. New York: Macmillan Reference USA, 1999.

Palmer, Kris E. <u>Constitutional Amendments: 1789 to the Present</u>. New York: Gale Group, 2000.

"TINKER ET AL. v. DES MOINES INDEPENDENT COMMUNITY SCHOOL DISTRICT ET AL." <u>Touro: Bringing Law to Life</u>. Touro Law Center. 7 Oct. 2005 <http://www.tourolaw.edu/patch/Tinker/>.

The Right to Privacy

By
Charlotte McMichael

The poorest man may in his cottage bid defiance to all the forces of the Crown. It may be frail - its roof may shake - the wind may blow through it - the storm may enter - the rain may enter-but the King of England cannot enter; all his forces dare not cross the threshold of that ruined tenement.

-Sir William Pitt, Earl of Chatham, on the right of the Englishmen to be secure in his home (1763)[449]

When listing the personal rights included in the U.S. Constitution, many are apt to include the right to privacy. It is the great American assumption.[450] However, unlike the right to bear arms or due process in court, the right to privacy is not explicitly mentioned in the Constitution. The word "privacy" is not even included, leading to a debate of whether or not the right even exists in America. Throughout history, and especially now, the question of the right to privacy has risen in courts and in the minds of United States' citizens across the nation. Most Americans feel that they are entitled to some form of privacy and protection for that liberty. After that conclusion though, the truth becomes unclear, as there is no constitutional representation of that right. The question on many American's minds and one which has remained unanswered for some is: did the drafters of the constitution refrain from stating our right to privacy because it doesn't exist, or did they merely feel there was no need to state what in their minds was already so obvious?[451]

Those who feel that the right to privacy does indeed exist, find it in the Bill of Rights of the Constitution. Some believe it to be protected by the Fourth Amendment, which states, "the right of people to feel secure in their persons, houses, papers, and effects, against unreasonable searches and seizures shall not be violated, and no Warrants shall issue, but upon probable cause, supported by Oath or affirmation, and particularly describing the place to be searched, and the persons or things to be seized."[452]

The Fourth Amendment addresses the rights of the people to have protection regarding their belongings and homes, and states that they can not be searched without reason. Many view this as meaning their right to privacy is protected. However, more and more legal searches are conducted for which neither warrants nor even specific suspicion are required. Examples include drug testing, screening areas at airports, and field sobriety checkpoints.[453]

The Fourth Amendment also includes exceptions which keep it from fully addressing the people's right to privacy. The Fourth Amendment, as confirmed by law, has been violated only if a search or seizure violates an individuals "expectation of privacy."[454] This "expectation of privacy" means that anything is allowed to be searched free of questions, unless it has been protected as "private," such as a house. A house is expected to be private, but something like the area of a house is not. Therefore, an aerial surveillance of someone's house (California v. Ciraolo, 1986), or going through someone's garbage (California v. Greenwood, 1988) would not be considered an invasion of privacy or violation of the Fourth Amendment.[455] The exception of "expectation of privacy" to the Fourth Amendment, allows loopholes to be found and tried, and raises questions of how inclusive the Fourth Amendment is concerning the right of privacy.

Others find the right to privacy in the Fifth Amendment. The Fifth Amendment requires that our life, property, and liberty not be taken away by the government without due process of law.[456] This essentially means being notified of the government's intention of prosecuting or taking people's possessions and giving opportunities to be heard and protect themselves and their belongings.[457] It provided protection against self-incrimination. The Fifth Amendment has been noted as the symbol of the essential need to maintain a constant vigilance for individual rights' protection.[458]

The Ninth Amendment states that the enumeration in the Constitution, of certain rights shall not be construed to deny or disparage others retained by the people. The amendment declared that the people of the United States retained rights which were not clearly stated in the Constitution. Many believe this amendment includes the right to privacy, and recognizes what is not stated in the Constitution; that it grants the right of privacy to the people of the United States. However, if it can be argued that privacy is one of the rights that the Ninth Amendment means, then can the same be argued for any rights, no matter their validity?

The adoption of the Bill of Rights almost did not occur. Many of the Founding Fathers argued against it. The fear was that in listing and detailing certain constitutional rights, the unlisted rights would appear as not important.[459] These fears were brought to the attention of James Madison who responded to the concerns in front of the House of Representatives. His response was the creation of the Ninth Amendment.

> It has been objected also against a bill of rights, that, by enumerating particular exceptions to the grant of power, it would disparage those rights which were not placed in that enumeration; and it might follow by implication, that those rights which were not singled out, were intended to be assigned into the hands of the General Government, and were consequently insecure. This is one of the most plausible arguments I have ever heard against the admission of a bill of rights into this system; but, I conceive, that it may be guarded against. I have attempted it, as gentlemen may see by turning to the last clause of the fourth resolution.[460]

Despite all of these possible references to privacy in the Constitution, there are no outright statements which evidence to an existence of privacy for the people. Any references to privacy which do exist are present in partiality, as there seem to be exceptions to any possible indications of privacy.

The term "right to privacy" did not emerge until 1965, in the Supreme Court ruling in Griswold v. Connecticut.[461] In this court case, the issue was the use of contraceptives, and was the first case dealing with reproductive choices. The Supreme Court ruled that a statute of the state of Connecticut, which banned the use of contraceptives, violated the privacy of married couples.[462] Justice William O. Douglas, while waiting for the majority decision of the

Court, stated that the "specific guarantees in the Bill of Rights have penumbras, formed by emanations from those guarantees that help give them life and substance." He concluded that although privacy is not explicitly stated in the Constitution, it is present in our history and in the minds of the people, and decided that married couples should have the privacy to do what they wish in their homes. In opposition to this conclusion, Justice Hugo Black stated that the judicial reasoning was dangerous. He was actually against the ban on contraceptives, but nonetheless, found Douglas' statement on privacy "imaginative." He claimed that "the government has the right to invade it unless prohibited by some specific constitutional provision."[463] His opinion is circulating still today.

Griswold v. Connecticut was the first time personal privacy had been acknowledged by the Court. The decision was monumental in that it repealed what was considered law and changed it into complete freedom of marital contraceptive use. In a later court case, Eisenstadt v. Baird (1972), the Court extended the idea of Griswold and invalidated a ban on the distribution of contraceptives, even to unmarried couples.[464] While Griswold protected the privacy of married couples, Eisenstadt dealt with the privacy of the individual. The acknowledgment of some sort of right to privacy by the Court led to the still unanswered question of its location in the Constitution.

Possibly the most known Court ruling that dealt with the issue of privacy was Roe v. Wade (1973). The Supreme Court decision ruled in favor of a woman's right to have an abortion, with the Court imposing distinctions between the trimesters of a pregnancy, and imposing more regulation as the pregnancy progresses.[465] Although the Court rejected the bans on abortion, it refuted the idea of abortion with no boundaries, and created criteria which the states could use to ban abortion.[466]

Roe v. Wade created another gain for personal liberties and the right to privacy. A decision that was once controlled by the government was handed to the woman, granting her personal choice in the Supreme Court's decision. However, despite this gain for personal privacy, many are still unsatisfied and believe that they are entitled to more freedom and privacy than what was granted in the reproductive choice Supreme Court cases. Others believe that the rulings of the Court were too lax in that they did not impose enough restrictions. Many people who are pro-life feel that it is the government's responsibility to limit or ban abortions in order to save and protect the lives that abortion takes. Despite the acknowledgment of some sort of privacy by the Supreme Court, the inability to recognize where it exists has caused problems where people are attempting to defend it. Is it possible to defend something that we might not even have?

In addition to the Supreme Court acknowledgement of some type of right to privacy in the reproductive choice cases, privacy was also accounted for in the passage of the Privacy Act by Congress in 1974. The Privacy Act created some control regarding the information on people or personal matters gained by the federal government and how they are used. Through the act, three primary rights are granted to the people. They are: a person's right to see records about themselves, the right to amend the record if it is incorrect, irrelevant, or incomplete, and the right to sue the government for violations including allowing others to see the personal information.[467] The Privacy Act only applies to documents which detail individuals maintained by agencies in the executive branch of the federal government.[468] The Privacy Act does not apply to personal information of an individual that is located under areas such as groups or events, and applies mostly to records that are held by federal agencies. There are exemptions to the Privacy Act. These include records which detail classified information on national security or criminal investigations, or information that may profile a confidential person or subject.[469]

There are countless other examples of where the government has encountered court cases which concerned the right to privacy, or lack thereof. In today's nation, the idea of privacy had been changed and impacted by fields of technology. Technology's steady rise has created a world where the word "privacy" is hardly recognized. In this database nation, every movement made involving technology, such as visiting sites on the Internet, or making a purchase with your credit card, leaves a digital trail.[470] This trail tracks one's schedules, movements, habits and political opinions, making them obtainable to the government agencies and businesses.[471]

In this age of technology, privacy has become one of the most important civil liberties. The unrepressed technology has created a trend of ending privacy. With new technological advances comes an increased risk to privacy. The technology alone is not what is jeopardizing privacy; it is the way it is being used by the people who are using it. Claims of identity theft or invasion of Internet privacy are rampant nowadays. Increased concern over exactly who has the ability to trace a person's technological footprints has arisen.

It has been seen that to even keep one's health and medical information private, it has become a nearly impossible task. Medical records and information are not only at risk of being publicized by the government, but also by individuals.[472] As an example, a state health department worker in Florida using state computers was able to obtain private records and compile a list of 4,000 people who tested positive for HIV. His next step was forwarding it to a local health department and the St. Petersburg Times and the Tampa Tribune, which are two local newspapers in Florida.[473] The individual interceptions of medical records, as with this case, are instances of unauthorized abuse. An individual's privacy in relation to their medical history is disclosed unlawfully. Although these are clearly crimes of unauthorized abuse, authorized abuse of medical records are seen as even worse.

Authorized abuses of medical records occur frequently at the hands of the health insurance companies. The companies disclose patient health information to employers. Another instance where authorized abuse can be found is when companies providing their own health insurance for their workers refer to their personnel departments or medical claims divisions for data that violates one's privacy.[474] It is not uncommon to read about someone who has contracted a virus in the newspaper. In cases such as the West Nile Virus, or Avian Flu, these illnesses are a public health concern. Therefore, when a person is diagnosed with an illness that is considered a public concern, their privacy virtually disappears. Only excluding their name in most cases, their personal medical information may be shared across the nation without their consent.

The issue of the government violating the right to privacy has become a topic of hot debate, especially since the passing of the

USA Patriot Act of 2001. Three days after the terrorist attacks of September 11th, Attorney General Ashcroft proposed the laws that would develop into the USA Patriot Act.[475] The USA Patriot Act was designed to provide the U.S. government with unbounded information on any person they wanted information that was seen as a threat to the nation's security. After the attacks, the government's sole focus was on capturing anyone who was involved in the terrorist attacks, or who were part of the terrorist activities around the world, through all means possible.

> How will we fight and win this war? We will direct every resource at our command - every means of diplomacy, every tool of intelligence, every instrument of law enforcement, every financial influence, and every necessary weapon of war-to the disruption and to the defeat of the global terror network.

-President Bush, September 20, 2001[476]

These words, spoken by President Bush only a short time after September 11, passed through the ears of the people of the United States without any second thought as to what they were conveying. The president was saying that a win in the war would come at the cost of privacy being exploited. By mentioning the use of "every tool of intelligence," he is inferring to the practice of governmental access to any useful information on any possible suspects, no questions asked. It has been said that after September 11th, the people of the United States gave up their personal liberties, and most importantly, their right to privacy, in whatever form it may have existed before.

The USA Patriot Act of 2001 does many things. Actually, it allows the government to do many things. It gives law enforcement officials practically boundless justification for obtaining information on people whom they deem to be cause for concern. This information can be collected through wiretaps or conducting electronic surveillance. The president also has the authority, in a time when the nation is under attack by a foreign entity, to confiscate any property within U.S. jurisdiction belonging to anyone the government thinks is involved in the attacks.

The Patriot Act also keeps a closer hold on financial activities, preventing money laundering and bank privacy, in attempts to break up terrorist finances. The measure encroaches on civil liberties in many areas. It states that it is a crime for any person to give money or any type of support to any group on the State Department's terrorist watch list.[477] The FBI is allowed to trace a person across state lines, and track their telephone calls or computer use with obtained warrants. This is a change from how things were before the Patriot Act. Before, a warrant must have been obtained in every state or phone number where a person could be found. After the passage of the act, only one warrant is needed to be enforced in whatever place the person is found in.[478]

The Patriot Act of 2001 also gives the FBI freedom to monitor and tape any conversation that takes place between an attorney and client in federal custody. The act has also affected the privacy and confidentiality libraries once had. If ordered by the FBI, librarians must hand over information regarding their patrons' computer use and books checked out. The patron will not be informed that their information has been turned over to the FBI, as the librarians are prohibited from telling them.[479]

Some members of Congress have begun to recognize the negativity of the Patriot Act in regards to lost liberties in areas like the public libraries. Rep. Bernie Sanders (D-VT) voiced his concern over the act in a speech he made to the American Library Association in June 2003.[480]

Neither you nor I nor the American people want to see a slow but sure chilling assessment on intellectual curiosity. We do not want to see young people, or any person, hesitate to take out a book on politics, on religion, or history or science because someone in the government might think that the person reading the book might have terrorist tendencies. The truth about the U.S.A Patriot Act, Mr. Ashcroft, is that this is an extremely dangerous piece of legislation that strikes at the heart of what freedom is about and, in fact, allows government agents, in unconstitutional ways, to snoop and

spy on the American people and certainly does allow law
enforcement agencies virtually unfettered access to libraries
and bookstores.[481]

The infringing upon any ideas of security and privacy of the
American people in everyday occurrences, such as visiting the
library, is ominous. It raises the issue of whether we, as Americans,
even have the rights of privacy.

Another area the Patriot Act opens up is in regard to accessing
information on citizens. Law enforcement officials can obtain a
secret warrant, which is known as a "sneak-and-peak," and receive
any information on U.S. citizens.[482] This "sneak-and peak" warrant
gives no advance notice to the citizen whose home or possessions
are being searched. These new warrants are a dramatic change from
the old process, before the act was passed, which gave notice to the
person being searched, and was presented due to reliable information.
Today, if a warrant is granted and a person's premises are searched,
they will not find out until after the search is completed.[483]

In regards to surveillance, the act has changed the once existing
rules and regulations for government officials. With the act, the
government can survey Internet use and email processing of
American citizens. They can do this through an order to the Internet
service providers, and give no notice to the people. The FBI can
also conduct aerial surveillance of people and their homes without
a warrant. They have the ability and clearance to even install video
cameras in places where demonstrations or protests deemed unlawful
are held.[484] It seems that after the passage of the USA Patriot Act,
the American citizens have become vulnerable to the surveillance
practices of the government, whether they are aware of it or not.

One extreme example of this secret surveillance is the Pentagon's
Total Information Awareness program (TIA).[485] The motto of TIA is
"knowledge is power" and just as the name indicates, the purpose is
to collect large amounts of information on citizens and non-citizens
through various means. These include records from federal, state, and
local agencies, to airline ticket purchases and credit card spending.
The motive for this program is to sift through data so as to identify
any possible terrorist activity that may be forming.[486] Americans are
constantly offering up their personal information through every day

life as a consumer without any knowledge of doing so. In cases the Supreme Court has actually stated that when personal information is "voluntarily exposed" to others, the person is accepting the risk that the government may see it also. As expected, Americans reacted strongly to the workings of the program, voicing concern over TIA. The concerns eventually reached through to Congress and the President who passed and signed legislation that would curb the activity of TIA. Now, research that TIA wishes to carry out may not be carried out until specifics of the program, such as the cost are provided to Congress.[487]

The actual passage of the USA Patriot Act is not free from concern either. The Bush administration submitted their antiterrorism proposals on September 19, 2001, to leaders of Congress. On October 1, 2001, what was now a more extensive legislation was presented to the House, which was followed by a similar bill on October 4, 2001.[488] Normally, the House and Senate conduct meetings to resolve any existing differences between the conferees. However, due to the timing and situations (the House and Senate offices had been closed down temporarily due to the anthrax scare); there were very few negotiations that occurred. No hearings, few chances for debate, or chances to discuss negotiating amendments were scheduled. Due to the desire for a speedy passage of the act, controversial issues of the act were unable to be discussed. This was not by all means the fault of solely the Republicans, but was shared by the Democrats in the House and the Senate.[489] Many people in top positions wanted the bill to be passed quickly and efficiently.

Despite questionable contents of the act, and some areas that a few found disturbing and cause for concern, President Bush signed the bill into law on October 26, 2001. All of this happened in barely over a month, from the date of the terrorist attacks to the day it was signed and made law. At the time, it can be imagined that most American citizens were not accounting for their personal liberties that would suffer from the USA Patriot Act, or the abuse of privacy they would experience through its measures. The quick passage of the act was fueled by the emotions of the people and the government officials, leaving little room for concern on preserving civil liberties.

Privacy is the American assumption which has been revised by judges, contested by politicians, and imperiled by technology.[490] It can be attested by many that there are some rights to privacy referred to, somewhere, in the Constitution. After that point though, the idea of privacy's existence becomes hazy. The Supreme Court has said that there is a right to privacy, just that no one can find the word in the Constitution. They claim that even though the word is not present, we know that our Founding Fathers must have been thinking about it. Does that mean that any right or idea not directly stated in the Constitution still exists, because we believe the Founding Fathers had it on their mind at the time of the drafting? It can be agreed that we, as Americans, have been granted some rights to privacy. We have a government that in court will often side with protection of our privacy. However, we also have a government that has created and allowed for programs and actions that have been blatant invasions of our privacy.

The drafters of the Constitution may well have given us the right to privacy in their charter. If only they had spelled it out for us though. Then the debate as to who has the right in certain situations; the citizen whose privacy was violated, or the government, who has the authority to collect necessary information, may not have even started. Instead, we are left with what is similar to the "fog of war." The "fog" represents the unmapped boundary between the rights of the government and the civil liberties of the citizens. Due to this "gray area," the boundary is susceptible to being overstepped. The confusion of whether or not the American people have a right to privacy creates an uncertainty in our society and a fear of governmental actions which may intrude on our privacy. The claim that one's privacy has been violated is the remaining question in the argument. If there is no historical evidence or clear documentation of the right, then its existence remains questionable, and may never be clearly answered.

Unlisted Rights Are Still Ours

By
Emily Rogers

> "The enumeration in the Constitution, of
> certain rights, shall not be construed to deny
> or disparage others retained by the people."

A "constitutional curiosity"[491], that "constitutional joker"[492], the Ninth Amendment is perhaps the most vague and misunderstood ideal in the Constitution. Since its creation by James Madison in 1789, it lay dormant for 176 years. That was until 1965; however, when in the Supreme Court case of Griswold v. Connecticut, it was jolted back to life. Whether "regarded by some as a recent discovery"[493], or confused with the similar and almost equally vague Tenth Amendment, the Ninth Amendment to the Constitution remains quite unknown. Ask most Americans to list their basic rights as provided for by the Bill of Rights and they will almost certainly name freedom of speech, press and religion, right to bear arms, and maybe even freedom from cruel and unusual punishment. Hardly anyone will remember that there are a score of rights, mainly those natural rights emphasized by Enlightenment thinkers such as Locke and Descartes, which are guaranteed them under the Ninth Amendment. Despite the flurry of activity the amendment has seen in the past forty years in such prestigious Supreme Court cases as Roe v. Wade, it is still relatively unknown. The journey of the "forgotten ninth amendment"[494] from its origin as Madison's quintessential solution for the ratification of the constitution, through years of inactivity, to becoming the go-to constitutional citation for judicial activists, has been a fascinating one. Eventually, all Americans will know and cherish the fact that they possess "certain inalienable rights; and that among these are life, liberty"[495] and unenumerated rights.

The creation of the Ninth Amendment is inherently tied to the creation of the Bill of Rights itself. It has even been argued that the amendment was the means by which the Bill of Rights was completed, since it was a task "embarrassing to both parties"[496] as it dragged on. To set the scene, the Constitutional Convention had ended and the original unrevised Constitution had been submitted to the states for ratification. An uproar occurred over the lack of a Bill of Rights in the Constitution as the newly minted Americans feared a return to the tyrannical overthrow of rights from which they had just escaped. Some members of the Constitutional Convention such as Elbridge Gerry and George Mason had foreseen this occurrence and had requested a committee draft a bill of rights before the adjournment of the 1787 convention, believing it would give "great quiet to the people" and could be accomplished "in a few hours."[497] The founding fathers did not listen to Mason and Gerry, however, and the struggle to complete a bill of rights instead delayed the formation of the new government for two years.

Opinions on the Constitution came from all over the thirteen states, in the form of anti-federalist writings, newspaper editorials, personal letters and anonymous articles explaining the Constitution in the hopes of ratification. One such opinion came from John Leland of Virginia, who said: "There is no Bill of Rights. Whenever number of men enter into a state of society, a number of individual rights must be given up to society, but there should always be a memorial of those not surrendered, otherwise every natural and domestic right becomes alienable, which raises tyranny at once."[498] This argument over the lack of a bill of rights soon became the central obstacle in the path to ratification. Following the idealistic days of the American Revolution, the belief that certain natural rights existed and could never be taken away by any government created by man was common. No one was prepared to give up their civil liberties. Even women became involved in the battle, like Mercy Otis Warren who advocated the enumeration of rights, saying that they "ought to be the primary object of all government, and cannot be too securely guarded by the most explicit declarations in their favor."[499]

When the founding fathers finally decided to draft a bill of rights, fears arose as to how a simple enumeration would further constrict the rights of Americans. Alexander Hamilton began the argument by claiming that the particularization of rights would lead to a "pretext to claim more than were granted,"[500] creating a whirlwind of controversy over which rights would be listed. The problem was also raised that rights considered extremely important in the North would be overlooked by the South and vice versa, never amounting to a fundamental list of intrinsically American rights. Even more alarming to some was the thought that those rights not listed in the bill of rights would be relinquished to the government. James Wilson, a proponent of this theory, argued that "an imperfect enumeration would throw all implied powers into the scale of government; and the rights of the people would be rendered incomplete."[501] Madison, himself, who later proposed the Ninth Amendment, even feared this enlargement of federal power, querying, "If an enumeration be made of all our rights, will it not be implied that everything omitted is given to the general government?"[502] The Bill of Rights was quickly spiraling into a huge mess of an oversight for the members of the Constitutional Convention. Noah Webster characterized this frenzy by stating that "the contest for perpetual bills of rights against a future tyranny resembles Don Quixotes fighting windmills."[503]

Affirmative action was taken by James Madison, who embarked on the self-described "nauseous project"[504] of itemizing a bill of rights. The legislatures of each of the thirteen states had sent a total of 124 suggested amendments to the Constitution. Madison had to sort through these and pick out the essential American rights, while making sure not to exclude anything that if implied, could give the government more power. Sifting through the proposed amendments, Madison repeatedly came across suggestions similar to this one from the Virginia Convention, proposed in 1788: "There are certain natural rights of which men, when they form a social compact cannot deprive or divest their posterity, among which are the enjoyment of life and liberty, with the means of acquiring, possessing and protecting property, and pursuing and obtaining happiness and safety."[505] The government certainly had no right to take away these inherent natural rights, but it was doubtful whether that list included only those rights and whether the founding fathers could truly foresee all things that would be considered an inalienable human right in the future of the United States government. Mindful of all these objections, Madison compiled a list of amendments to the Constitution and presented them on June 8, 1789, overcoming personal doubts along the way.

His proposal was a triumph of compromise worthy of Henry Clay, history's "Great Compromiser", and a verbal victory worthy of Benjamin Franklin's famed skill of manipulating words. Madison explained his solution thusly:

> It has been objected also against a bill of rights that, by enumerating particular exceptions to the grant of power, it would disparage those rights which were not placed in that enumeration, and it might follow, by implication, that those rights which were not singled out were intended to be assigned into the hands of the General Government, and were consequently insecure. This is one of the most plausible arguments I have ever heard urged against the admission of a bill of rights into this system, but I conceive that it may be guarded against. I have attempted it.[506]

His attempt was the birth of the Ninth Amendment:

> "The exceptions here or elsewhere in the Constitution, made in favor of particular rights, shall not be so construed as to diminish the just importance of other rights retained by the people, or as to enlarge the powers delegated by the Constitution; but either as actual limitations of such powers, or as inserted merely for greater caution."[507]

Members of Congress at once embraced Madison's solution as a "sweep-it-under-the-rug means of disposing as swiftly as possible"[508] of the problem of the bill of rights. One such member, Justice Joseph Story, wrote that it was adopted "to prevent any perverse or ingenious misapplication of the well known maxim that an affirmation in particular cases implies a negation in all others, and e converso, that a negation in particular cases implies an affirmation in all others."[509] Congress quickly passed the amendment, delighting in its ability to take the wind out of the sails of those critics who would attempt to decry the Bill of Rights as incomplete. Also, the two year delay in the formation of the government had also meant a two year delay in revenues for a government which would now have the power to tax. The United States was still in crippling post-war debt that desperately needed to be repaid. Madison had provided Congress with the "definitive solution"[510] to the dilemma of enumerating rights without endangering those rights omitted. In so doing, Madison "stamped the Bill of Rights with his creativity."[511]

The genius of the Ninth Amendment comes from its intentional vagueness, its "utter lack of specificity with respect to the rights that it protects."[512] However, that is also where its problems lie. Robert H. Jackson, an Associate Justice of the Supreme Court, put it best when he said that the rights guaranteed Americans by the Ninth Amendment were "still a mystery."[513] Considering the controversial struggle from which it emerged, one would think that the Ninth Amendment would have done nothing but stir up controversy from the moment it was ratified in 1791. Those rights would have been declared right away, providing us with a lengthy list of constitutional rights now, 214 years later. Yet no such thing occurred. The Ninth Amendment was left alone for 176 years, perhaps keeping people away with its unknown possibilities, as the unknown is often a terrifying prospect. Yet the Ninth Amendment paved the way for the ideals of equality later expounded in the Civil War amendments and the Nineteenth Amendment by providing unknown rights later to be discovered such as African-American and women's suffrage.

The Ninth Amendment was finally dusted off and put into effect in the 1965 Supreme Court case of Griswold v. Connecticut. Estelle Griswold opened a birth control clinic in conjunction with the New Haven, Connecticut branch of the Planned Parenthood League of Connecticut in 1961. Griswold and physician, C. Lee Buxton, gave a married couple information and medical advice on preventing conception and prescribed contraceptives for the wife's use. Both were arrested and charged with aiding and abetting the commission of a crime according to an 1879 state law that forbade the use or assisting in the use of contraceptives. They were found guilty and Griswold's appeals to the Appellate Division of the Circuit Court and the Connecticut Supreme Court on the basis of violation of her Fourteenth Amendment rights failed. The United States Supreme Court accepted her appeal in 1965 and overturned the previous decisions with a vote of 7-2, invalidating the Connecticut law forbidding the use of contraception. In a landmark court opinion, Justice William O. Douglas cited the penumbras of the Ninth Amendment as the basis for an American's "right of privacy."[514]

Justice Arthur J. Goldberg utilized the Ninth Amendment for the majority of his opinion. After being ignored for 176 years, it was suddenly being used as the majority of the reasoning behind a major Supreme Court decision. Goldberg writes that "while this court has had little occasion to interpret the Ninth Amendment, 'it cannot be presumed that any clause in the constitution is intended to be without effect' (Marbury v. Madison, Cranch). In interpreting the Constitution, 'real effect should be given to all the words it uses' (Myers v. United States)."[515] He defends his position using the Ninth Amendment by stating that, "since 1791, [the Ninth Amendment] has been a basic part of the Constitution which we are sworn to uphold. To hold that a right so basic and fundamental and so deep-rooted in our society as the right of privacy in a marriage may be infringed because that right is not guaranteed in so many words by the first eight amendments to the Constitution is to ignore the Ninth Amendment, and to give it no effect whatsoever. Moreover, a judicial construction that this fundamental right is not protected by the Constitution because it is not mentioned in explicit terms by one of the first eight amendments or elsewhere in the Constitution would violate the Ninth Amendment."[516] Griswold v. Connecticut was, in effect, the first case to enumerate one of the rights protected by the Ninth Amendment, the "right to privacy."[517]

The ruling in Griswold v. Connecticut using the Ninth Amendment to declare the "right to privacy"[518] paved the way for several other high profile Supreme Court decisions. In Eisenstadt v. Baird, the privacy rights of married couples to use contraception were expanded to include unmarried couples. Further expanding privacy rights, the 1973 Supreme Court case of Roe v. Wade was the catalyst for the beginning of the schism over abortion in the United States. The Court found that the "right to privacy"[519] was "broad enough to encompass a woman's decision whether or not to terminate her pregnancy."[520] By this time, the Ninth Amendment was comfortably rooted in controversy once more.

The rediscovery of the Ninth Amendment in privacy rights cases certainly had many supporters. However, many warned of the dangers of too broadly interpreting the Ninth Amendment. The debate over the elucidation of this amendment is reminiscent of the strict constructionist v. loose constructionist debate over the almost equally vague elastic clause in Article I of the Constitution. Strict constructionists believed that no additional powers should be given to any branch of the government if deemed "necessary and proper" because it would throw off the system of checks and balances and concentrate power in one branch over another. Loose constructionists believed that if the clause stated that Congress could make any laws deemed "necessary and proper" then they could do just that, with no repercussions. The Ninth Amendment loose constructionists believe the same thing; "no reason exists to believe that it does not mean what it says."[521] Justice Arthur J. Goldberg is among these, for he believes that "the language and history of the Ninth Amendment reveal that the Framers of the Constitution believed that there are additional fundamental rights, protected from governmental infringement, which exist alongside those fundamental rights specifically mentioned in the first eight constitutional amendments…the Framers did not intend that the first eight amendments be construed to exhaust the basic and fundamental rights which the Constitution guaranteed to the people."[522] Strict constructionists have been slowly building steam, however. Since 1965, they have dissented quietly, but they are increasing in number. After the Griswold v. Connecticut decision, Justice Potter Stewart wrote in his dissenting opinion that the Ninth Amendment "was intended to make clear that the adoption of the Bill of Rights did not alter the plan that the Federal Government was to be a government of express and limited powers, and that all rights and powers not delegated to it were retained by the people and the individual states. Until today no member of this Court has ever suggested that the Ninth Amendment meant anything else."[523] He obviously believed that the Ninth Amendment had one purpose, of which the Founding Fathers all agreed. Justice Hugo L. Black warned even further of a loose interpretation of the Ninth Amendment, saying that reading too far into it "would make this Court's members a day-to-day constitutional convention."[524] These arguments continue today. Current Supreme Court Justice Antonin Scalia decries loosely interpreting the Ninth Amendment because he says it leads to judicial activism. Supreme Court justices are there to interpret, not make, the law; legislation should be left to Congress. This brings up the concern that Constitutional oddities such as the Ninth Amendment are a "license for judicial subjectivity" and a "lure to judicial activism."[525] Justice Byron White concurred, saying the decision in Roe v. Wade was "an exercise of raw judicial power". The debate still rages; is the Ninth Amendment a safeguard of our natural rights or is it a vehicle for changing the law when the judicial branch disagrees with it?

Supporters of the Ninth Amendment remain vocal today. Nothing is more indicative of this than the fact that the Ninth Amendment is "being used as a litmus test at new judge confirmation hearings."[526] Senators Joe Biden, Herb Kohl and Arlen Specter grilled current Chief Justice John Roberts in his confirmation hearings this year as to his positions on the "right to privacy"[527] and the Ninth Amendment. Roberts, a savvy constitutional theorist, carefully avoided denouncing either principle, or the cases in which privacy rights were decided, stating that they were "settled as precedent."[528] Roberts was subsequently confirmed, for no one could find fault with his views. However, others have not been so lucky. In 1987, Robert Bork was nominated for the Supreme Court by President Ronald Reagan. During his confirmation hearings, he was asked about the Ninth Amendment. He claimed it was unimportant and that the "right to privacy"[529] described in Griswold v. Connecticut had no constitutional support. After expressing these views, Bork was not confirmed. Senator Daniel Patrick Moynihan said of his decision not to confirm Bork that "it is his restricted vision of privacy which troubles me most. I cannot vote for a jurist who simply cannot find in the Constitution a general right of privacy...its importance is such that I cannot support anyone for a Supreme Court appointment who would not recognize it."[530] Only 22 years after that right was put into words in the case of Griswold v. Connecticut and it was already a fundamental American principle. This proves that the rights protected by the Ninth Amendment are indeed natural rights, those rights that "are not annexed to us by parchments and seals. They are created in us by the decrees of Providence, which establish the laws of our nature. They are born with us; exist with us; and cannot be taken from us by any human power without taking our lives. In short, they are founded on the immutable maxims of reason and justice."[531]

In the course of daily life, one does many things that are like second nature. Breathing the air, sitting, climbing trees, hugging a friend, singing, dancing, acting, gossiping, writing, painting, playing sports, wearing jewelry, eating, drinking, shopping, reading, standing, skipping, running, jumping—all these are unregulated freedoms Americans possess. While someone is standing around reading a book, they do not expect to be told to stop. They know they have a right to be doing so; but where does it guarantee them that right? The only place Americans are guaranteed their inherent natural rights is the Ninth Amendment which states that "the enumeration in the Constitution, of certain rights, shall not be construed to deny or disparage others retained by the people." Yet, when the Constitution was first drafted, Americans truly feared that these rights would be denied them by the new national government. Alexander Hamilton expressed this passionate and commonly held belief with true eloquence: "The sacred rights of mankind are not to be rummaged for among old parchments or musty records. They are written, as with a sunbeam, in the whole volume of human nature, by the hand of the divinity itself, and can never be erased or obscured by mortal power."[532] The American people protested the Constitution's lack of an enumeration of their basic rights, convincing Congress that they must 'expressly declare the great rights of mankind secured under this Constitution."[533] Thus began the struggle to form a comprehensive Bill of Rights that would satisfy the needs of the vastly different poles of the country, as well as one that wouldn't endanger any rights left unlisted. It was a monstrous task, which James Madison valiantly undertook. Madison, faced with over one hundred proposed amendments, a disinterested Congress and a desire to please as many people as possible, came up with an ingenious compromise. This was the Ninth Amendment, an expansive, unclear, and completely comprehensive solution to all these problems. Its inclusion in the Bill of Rights made it agreeable to everyone and all thirteen states ratified the Constitution in 1791. For years the Ninth Amendment sat around until the Supreme Court unexpectedly resuscitated it in 1965. Since then, it has become the basis for the "right to privacy"[534] Americans now list among their fundamental rights. It has also spawned controversy concerning the extent to which it should be interpreted. Through this exhaustive journey it has remained a symbol of everything that this country stands for: liberty, justice and independence. The Founding Fathers provided for themselves and their posterity with the Ninth Amendment by foreseeing a future that they could not predict, and making sure that the fundamental freedoms they enjoyed as Americans would never be denied anyone who claimed citizenship under the Star-Spangled Banner.

Bibliography

Bailyn, Bernard, ed. The Debate on the Constitution: Federalist and Anti-Federalist Speeches, Articles, and Letters During the Struggle over Ratification, Part Two. New York: Library of America, 1993.

Balko, Radley. "For Independence Day, Supreme Court Slams Founders". 06 July 2005. Fox News. http://www.foxnews.com/printer_friendly_story/0,3566,161422,00.html

Cornell, Saul. The Other Founders: Anti-Federalism and the Dissenting Tradition in America, 1788-1828. Chapel Hill: University of North Carolina Press, 1999.

Goldberg, Justice Arthur J. "Concurring Opinion: Supreme Court of the United States: 381 U.S. 479: Griswold v. Connecticut" no.469 (1965). dKosopedia: The Free Political Encyclopedia, http://www.dksospedia.com/index.php?title=Griswold_v._

Connecticut-Concurrence_Goldberg

"Griswold v. Connecticut". dKosopedia: The Free Political Encyclopedia. http://www.dkosopedia.com/index.php/Griswold_v._Connecticut

Jefferson, Thomas. "Declaration of Independence". The Declaration of Independence, http://www.ushistory.org/declaration/document/index.htm

Levy, Leonard W. Origins of the Bill of Rights. New Haven: Yale University Press, 1999.

"Ninth Amendment Resurfaces" (2002), TalkLeft: The Politics of Crime, http://talkleft.com/new_archives/000140.html

Patterson, Bennett B. The Forgotten Ninth Amendment. Indianapolis: Bobbs-Merrill, 1955.

Rakove, Jack N. Original Meanings: Politics and Ideas in the Making of the Constitution. New York: Vintage, 1996.

"Roberts: Roe 'Settled as Precedent'". The Baltimore Sun, 14 September 2005, http://baltimoresun.com/news/nationworld/bal-te.roberts14sep14,1,81975.story?   coll=bal-home-utility

"Roe v. Wade". http://en.wikipedia.org/wiki/Roe_v._Wade

The Paradox of the Ninth and Tenth Amendments

By
Kate McFarland

The Ninth and Tenth Amendments of the United States Constitution represent the greatest paradox in American constitutional history. The Ninth Amendment states that Americans are guaranteed rights not listed in the Constitution, while the Tenth Amendment reserves rights to the states not specifically addressed in the Constitution. The two amendments have sparked social change, countless Supreme Court cases, and cultural transformations in America's history. While the Tenth Amendment was prominent in early American history, over time, the Ninth Amendment has had a larger impact on the United States politically, socially, and economically.

After the Revolutionary War, Americans saw the need to create a new system of government. On November 15, 1777, representatives from New Hampshire, Massachusetts, Rhode Island, Connecticut, New York, New Jersey, Pennsylvania, Delaware, Maryland, Virginia, North Carolina, South Carolina and Georgia gathered together to form such a government, meeting in what has been called the Continental Congress. Because the colonists were fighting against British rule, most representatives did not want to have a government that mirrored that of their oppressors. Therefore, the Continental Congress, as a whole, debated the extent to which the central government should have power while preserving the effectiveness of state's rights. The Continental Congress, after four years of controversy, established a national government with limited powers. A legislative body called the Congress of the Confederation was designed to operate the government with representation from every state to regulate foreign affairs, Indians, maintain an army, and control western regions.[535] "The Articles of Confederation and Perpetual Union" were ratified by all thirteen states on March 1, 1781.[536]

Problems ensued soon after ratification of the Constitution concerning issues of economy and interstate relations. Because each state had different currencies and policies of transaction, sales between states were arduous and impracticable. Without necessary resources flowing between states, each region was lacking essential resources. Disputes could not be settled because there was no national Supreme Court system establishing and enforcing laws. In addition, regions west of the Appalachian Mountains were tempted to leave the Union due to wealth they hoped to accumulate if they joined Spain's North American territories. A treaty between Spain and the Western regions would lessen the burden of expensive exports because goods traveling through the Spanish- controlled Mississippi River would be exempt from taxes. If an agreement with the Spanish were reached, the territories would receive invaluable protection from the Spanish militia against the ongoing threat of Indians and the British in the Ohio River Valley. Factions began to form, based on divisions of wealth and region. During an economic depression in 1786, farmers in Massachusetts rebelled against the creditors who took their land because of policies deterring debtors. This act, Shay's Rebellion, sparked fear in the elite class and ultimately a change in the United States government.

On May 14, 1787, representatives from twelve states met in Philadelphia to discuss changes to the Articles of Confederation. Little did they know they would ultimately abolish the Articles completely and form a new constitution. Factions developed between larger and smaller states. Issues such as representation in Congress created two groups, those who favored the Virginia Plan and those who favored the New Jersey Plan. The former stated that representation should be population-based, while the New Jersey Plan argued that each state should have equal representation. To compromise, a plan was developed where there would be one house based on population and one in which each state would be represented equally. Factions divided increasingly as the Federalists and Anti-Federalists fought over the ratification of the Constitution. While Federalists supported a national government with great influence limited only by checks and balances within itself, Anti-Federalists saw a central government as a threat to the power of the people. Anti-Federalists firmly believed that a president would quickly resemble a monarch. "But we are told that we need not fear; because those in power, being our representatives, will not abuse the powers we put in their hands" stated a sarcastic Anti- Federalist Patrick Henry.[537] The arguments between these two parties as well as the arguments surrounding the Virginia and New Jersey plans essentially began the debate of state versus national government power.

Another constitutional issue which caused tremendous strife within the Continental Congress was the proposed Article I, Section 8, Clause 18 of the Constitution, called the "necessary and proper clause." Clause 18 states; "To make all Laws which shall be necessary and proper for carrying into Execution the foregoing Powers, and all other Powers vested by this Constitution in the Government of the United States, or in any Department or Officer thereof."[538] The purpose of this clause was to give the national government the flexibility and power to deal with future problems such as laws defining punishment, federal taxes, and interstate commerce. "Practically every power of the National Government has been expanded in some degree" is a statement showing the broad nature of this clause to allow for federal government supremacy.[539] This "elastic clause" threatened Anti- Federalists because it could potentially give the federal government tremendous power. Federalists, however, saw it as completely essential to ensure the contemporary nature of the Constitution. This also caused controversy between the two groups and led to a compromise for the feuding parties.

Ratification of the Constitution was doubtful due to regional and ideological debates among leaders. Federalists Alexander Hamilton, John Jay, and James Madison fully supported the Constitution in its rough form. They showed their belief in the document through the new nation's first media campaign, a series of articles named "The Federalist Papers." Initially developed to rally support from New York citizens for the Constitution, the papers ultimately led to a wider audience and more support throughout the states. Anti-Federalists were less than pleased and sought support through their own series of counter-papers. The main sticking issue with the Constitution as the Anti- Federalists saw it was a powerful central government located in New York with a lack of sentiment for states' or people's rights.

To appease Anti- Federalists and hasten the ratification process, James Madison developed a Bill or Rights to ensure freedoms were guaranteed to the people. The idea of a Bill of Rights had originally come from John Locke and the Enlightenment era. Framers of the Constitution considered natural laws, as described by Alexander Hamilton, as "the sacred rights of mankind (that) are not to be rummaged for, among old parchments, or musty records. They are written, as with a sun beam in the whole volume of human nature,...and can never be erased or obscured."[540] Framers also desired equality and justice. The Bill of Rights is a list of rights and freedoms to which Americans were entitled and to be protected by and from the government. The Bill of Rights today are the first ten amendments to the Constitution, among which are amendments nine and ten. These amendments were written specifically to counteract the "necessary and proper clause," Article 1, Section 8, Clause 18 of the Constitution. James Madison states:

> "It has been said that in the federal government they are unnecessary, because the powers are enumerated, and it follows that all that are not granted by the constitution are retained... I admit that these arguments are not entirely without foundation; but they are not conclusive to the extent which has been supposed."[541]

Madison argued the final amendments to the Bill of Rights were completely necessary as they added those rights that went beyond the Constitution and eased the worries of Anti- Federalists. On September 17, 1787, the Constitution was ratified by the Constitutional Convention in Philadelphia, largely due to the inclusion of the Ninth and Tenth Amendments.

The Ninth Amendment reads; "The enumeration in the Constitution, of certain rights, shall not be construed to deny or disparage others retained by the people."[542] The Ninth Amendment refers to rights, not necessarily listed in the Constitution, which belong to the people. "The Ninth Amendment served as a precautionary reminder that there were limits to the national government's powers that were not explicitly stated in the Constitution and these unenumerated rights were, indeed, retained by the people in their respective states."[543] This amendment was designed to lessen the worry of some that rights not listed "might lead the government to take away or trample on any rights that weren't listed."[544] It was also used to limit the federal government. "The amendment is designed to protect the rights of the minority from the will of the majority."[545]

Anti-Federalists, still fearful of losing their state and individual rights, pressured the Continental Congress to include one more amendment, the Tenth Amendment. "The powers not delegated to the United States by the Constitution, nor prohibited by it to the states, are reserved to the states respectively, or to the people."[546] This amendment has also been called the "reserve clause," as it saves all powers not specifically listed in the Constitution to the states and to the people. Though some interpret the Tenth Amendment to be merely a reiteration of the limits of Federal government as addressed by the Ninth Amendment, it actually serves as a debate over national powers. This amendment sets up the controversial topic of state government's conflicting powers with the federal government. While the amendment caused much controversy, it did, however provide a balance between state and national governments, preventing one or the other from becoming too powerful.

The Ninth and Tenth Amendments were intentionally written by Madison to be vague. They are incredibly confusing and could relate to many or no issues in particular. The circular nature of both articles was provided to allow future lawmakers flexibility based on issues of the time. Because Madison predicted the Constitution would serve as the cornerstone of the evolving American political process, he wanted to allow for progress and change of the political system in future years. Supreme Court Justice Robert Jackson declared, however, "The Ninth Amendment rights which are not to be disturbed by the Federal Government are still a mystery to me," shows the confusion the well intentioned vague amendments have caused.[547]

The first significant impact of these amendments came in the Supreme Court case McCullough vs. Maryland in 1819. This case stemmed from a decision in 1791 by the federal government to form a national bank. The national bank was allowed to operate on a trial basis and was to expire twenty years later. After those twenty years, it was renewed by Congress. The state of Maryland attempted to tax the federal bank in 1818. When the Baltimore branch of the national bank did not pay its taxes, the state of Maryland sued James McCulloch, a cashier at the bank.[548] The Maryland high courts favored the state; however, the U.S. Supreme Court decided that states did not have the authority to sue federal entities. This case set the precedent that the federal government was supreme to the state governments. Chief Justice Marshall, who presided over the case, declared, "the [federal] government of the United States, though limited in its power, is supreme within its sphere of action."[549] To support his decision, Marshall cited the implied powers of the Constitution that regulated the Tenth Amendment and the powers reserved to the states. As a result of the decision, the Tenth Amendment lost part of its meaning and importance.

States have attached the Tenth Amendment to campaigns of secession in several cases. On December 15, 1814, delegates from New England met at the Hartford Convention to discuss problems in the area due to the War of 1812. Issues, such as the Embargo Act of 1807, which had caused an economic downturn in the North but was not affecting the South, were discussed. As a result, representatives throughout the New England area met in secret to fix the problems that "Mr. Madison's War" had created.[550] The delegates debated the possibility of seceding from the United States but, ultimately, decided to remain part of the country as long as certain conditions were met. This proposal resulted in a major reevaluation of the Tenth Amendment. The federal government recognized the importance of states' rights as outlined in the Tenth Amendment.

The Hartford Convention was not the only attempt at secession by individual states prior to the Civil War. On December 19, 1828, the South Carolina legislature attempted to secede from the United States.[551] John C. Calhoun, vice president under Andrew Jackson, resigned due to his opposition to the Tariff of 1828, one which negatively affected Southern farmers. "Calhoun wrote an essay about this conflict, *The South Carolina Exposition and Protest,* in which he asserted nullification of federal laws."[552] As a result, South Caroline nullified the "Tariff of Abominations" and attempted to secede. These two attempts at secession highlight the ongoing regional tensions within the United States. In addition, the desire for more states' rights was clear as states sought to use the "reserve clause" to provide them with more power and control because the federal government had overstepped its boundaries by allowing a tax that negatively affected South Carolina. Calhoun believed economic issues were reserved to the state, not the federal government.

These two attempts to secede by states soon became a reality in 1860. South Carolina seceded from the Union and commenced the Civil War. As issues such as slavery, regional divisions, and states' rights became nonnegotiable, tensions rose within the federal government. Abraham Lincoln, as President, had no intention of granting the rebellious Southern states more rights. The Union crumbled and Civil War broke out. The cause of the Civil War was not merely an issue of slavery or presidential status, but from the South's point of view, the disregard of the Tenth Amendment. The federal government was usurping all powers, even those not listed in the Constitution. Commercial and political issues unique to the South were decided upon by Northern politicians who had their own best interests in mind. Instead of reserving certain powers to the states such as economics and social status, the national government had taken control of everything. The South saw this as Congress using "exercises of powers not delegated and thus unconstitutional."[553] Southerners seceded because of the Bill of Rights and fought in an effort to defend their Constitutional rights. The president of the Confederacy, Jefferson Davis, justified the secession by declaring "the Constitution did not give the federal government any powers to regulate secession, the Tenth Amendment must grant the power of secession to the states."[554] Ironically, though, as a result of the war, the national power strengthened during the time of Reconstruction and further limited the Tenth Amendment.

In the 1900s, the federal government continued to extend its power over the states by ignoring the Tenth Amendment. First, in 1908, the Employers' Liability Cases declared "every carrier engaged in interstate commerce liable to any employee, including those whose activities related solely to intrastate activities, for injuries caused by negligence."[555] States rights activists believed the federal government overstepped its boundaries by ruling on laws related to commerce. Since this law was enacted during the Gilded Age, a period when commerce was perpetuated by lasseizfaire capitalism and corruption, employers defended their rights with the Tenth Amendment because they did not want to lose their profitable businesses. By requiring employers to be responsible for accidents incurred by employees on the job, the federal government no longer allowed employers to fire injured employees and immediately replace them with healthy workers. Employers were held responsible for the injured employee. This drastic change in the workplace caused tremendous economic and social change. Secondly, limitations of the Tenth Amendment were extended by Child Labor Laws. This "interference" by the federal government caused the most opposition within the states. Employers claimed that attempts "to regulate the conditions of employment, [was] a power reserved to the state."[556] The Supreme Court dismissed their case and re-established federal supremacy. Eventually, this ruling was overturned in 1918 with the Hammer v. Dagenhart case, which declared that Congress had no right to make law on child labor issues, strengthening the Tenth Amendment. The Slaughter-House Cases of 1872 strengthened the Tenth Amendment even further. The series of cases was started by butchers and livestock producers who sued the state for giving exclusive rights to livestock production to one New Orleans Company.[557] The court voted in favor of the state saying "a state's power to regulate its own affairs 'were essential to the perfect working of our complex form of government."[558] During the Reconstruction Era through the late 1930s several attempts were made by the states to utilize and strengthen the Tenth Amendment; however, they were, for the most part, struck down by the Supreme Court.

After 175 years of inactivity, the Ninth Amendment became lively during the twentieth century. During the Depression, the Ninth Amendment was prevalent in cases such as Ashwander v. Tennessee Valley Authority in 1936. This case was unique in that it discussed rights not protected. Established in the ruling was "while the people may have rights that are not spelled out in the Constitution, no such rights can interfere with the government's right to do what the Constitution specifically says it may do."[559] This case, joined by Tennessee Electric Power Co. v. Tennessee Valley Authority (1939) specifically stated that "the Ninth Amendment did not prevent the federal government from controlling the retail price of its electrical energy."[560]   Other Depression Era laws that dealt with the Ninth Amendment included the 1933 New Deal Regulatory Acts and, in 1937, government regulation of the economy.

Many significant social transformations were caused as a result of the Ninth Amendment. In Griswold v. Connecticut (1965) the right to privacy was established. In this case, Estelle Griswold was arrested for giving contraceptive advice to a married couple at her branch of Planned Parenthood. When her case reached the Supreme Court, the concept of illegal contraception was overruled as a part of the right to privacy. This decision extended American freedoms over the next forty years, including numerous other rights such as the right for parents to raise their children in a manner they find suitable and the right to privacy in homosexual relationships. This case has expanded the Ninth Amendment and allowed the Supreme Court to take more liberties when granting rights not specifically addressed in the Constitution. Some have even used the Ninth Amendment to validate affairs as an excuse that the government can no longer dictate "bedroom business." As issues such as privacy have permeated American culture, the Ninth Amendment has gained importance as it allows for such culture altering Supreme Court cases.

Perhaps, the most controversial case involving the Ninth Amendment was the 1973 case Roe v. Wade. Norma McCorvey, a Texas resident, decided she needed to terminate the pregnancy of her second child as she could not provide for her first. Since abortions were not permitted in the state of Texas, McCorvey, who used the name Jane Roe to protect her identity, argued that, under Griswold v Connecticut, she was entitled to privacy to make her own decision about abortion. Her claim was ruled constitutional, leading to giant leaps for women's rights. Since Roe v. Wade, cases such as Webster v. Reproductive Health Services (1989), Rust v. Sullivan (1991), and Planned Parenthood v. Casey (1992) have granted even more rights to women and their reproductive health under the Ninth Amendment.

The Ninth Amendment has also played a large role in court procedures.   The landmark case Gideon v. Wainright (1963) determined an important aspect of the judicial process. Gideon, a man convicted in Florida, was not granted a lawyer to help him defend his case because he could not afford one. He appealed his case to the Supreme Courts and, through the Ninth Amendment, established the precedent that all defendants have the right to a lawyer.

Since President John F. Kennedy's administration, the Tenth Amendment has had a revival. This can especially be seen in the health care arena. States have established their dominance over health care instead of the federal government by providing for their residents. States are responsible for offering accessible health insurance to customers at a low rate. Although this is a power given to the federal government, because of fiscal problems and budget deficits the federal government has lacked the leadership necessary to take on this complex issue.[561] Therefore, the states have controlled an aspect of government granted to the federal portion and have risen above the level of "reserved" rights. As Chief Justice Harlan F. Stone argues, "the [tenth] amendment states but a truism that all is retained which has not been surrendered."[562]

The Tenth Amendment has had a short term impact on the American economy.

In the 1976 Supreme Court case of National League of Cities v. Usery (1976) disputes over minimum wage and maximum hours for employees was argued. In this case, states received the power to determine their own rates for wages and hours. This power greatly strengthened support for the Tenth Amendment though the ruling was later overturned in Garcia v. San Antonio Metro (1985). "Congress may regulate interstate commerce directly, but it may not 'regulate state governments' regulation of interstate commerce."[563] An additional recent use of the Tenth Amendment was seen in 1992 when states were mandated by the federal government to change their disposal of waste systems to adhere to the federal Low-Level Radioactive Waste Management Act amendments. States, such as New York, were angered by this ruling because the state felt that the national government had no authority to issue such an act. In New York v. United States (1992), the Supreme Court upheld two parts of the act claiming "Congress had the authority under the Commerce Clause to use financial rewards and access to disposal sites as incentives for state waste management."[564] Justice Sandra Day

O'Connor wrote a dissenting opinion, however, citing the violation of the Tenth Amendment.

> "Either type of federal action would 'commandeer' state governments into the service of federal regulatory purposes, and would for this reason be inconsistent with the Constitution's division of authority between federal and state governments.' This last provision violated the Tenth Amendment."[565]

The influence of the two amendments has broadened and changed substantially in the past ten years. From a modern perspective, the Ninth Amendment has served to adapt rights and serve as a reflection of society. The right to privacy is the most important aspect of the Ninth Amendment in modern history.[566] Important rights granted by the amendment extend far beyond those two. Significant rights include the right to a clean environment, education, medical care, a job, and housing.[567] As these rights became guaranteed throughout the past 40 years, society has changed in direct relationship. Adequate housing, for example, has been increasingly provided for those who are homeless.

Rights guaranteed by the Tenth Amendment to the people and states have also increased in recent years. "Such initiatives demonstrate that the idea of divided powers expressed in the Tenth Amendment still influences our system of government."[568] These rights include: marriage, divorce, commerce with the state, drinking and driving ages, and maintenance of roads.[569] The drinking age has been an especially interesting battle concerning states rights. Since Congress knew that it could not regulate the drinking age because it was a right specifically reserved to the states to determine, Congress developed the Surface Transportation Act of 1982, allowing Congress to withhold funds for transportation from states that did not raise their drinking age to 21.[570] This deceptive attempt by Congress to circumnavigate the Tenth Amendment worked and all states changed their legal drinking age limit by 1989. However, it also showed the importance of the Tenth Amendment. Congress was aware of the strength of the amendment and how far states were willing to go to protect the rights given to them. If Congress believed the Tenth

Amendment was not popular and under-supported, it would have changed the drinking age as a matter of federal law. Because of strong sentiments for states' rights in recent years, Congress knew this approach would force states to accept the national legislation, while still allowing for states' rights.

Gun control has become a major issue in the late twentieth century and an area where the Tenth Amendment can state its authority. The Brady Handgun Violence Act of 1994 was a federal mandate declaring that local law enforcement must do a background check on firearm purchasers before allowing the use of the gun. Jay Printz of Ravalli County, Montana, argued against the Brady Act in the Supreme Court Case Printz v. U.S. (1997) that his Tenth Amendment rights had been violated by Congress. Congress had put the burden of background checks on the police department and did not cover the expensive costs the local law enforcement had incurred as a result. The Supreme Court agreed with Printz in a statement supported by the Tenth Amendment and the Federalist Papers.

> "The Framers rejected the concept of a central government that would act upon and through the States, and instead designed a system in which the State and Federal Governments would exercise concurrent authority over the people. The Federal Government's power would be augmented immeasurably and impermissibly if it were able to impress into its service- and at no cost to itself- the police officers of the 50 states."[571]

This statement not only established guidelines on gun control, but also established limitations on federal mandates, acts legislated by Congress that states must obey, but are not supported financially by the national government. It is significant that this case established limits on the national government so it did not become too powerful and usurp further control from the states. The Tenth Amendment asserted its power, maintaining the states' rights to control gun purchases as well as providing limits on federal mandates.

While the Tenth Amendment was prominent in early American history, the Ninth Amendment has had a larger impact on the United States politically, socially, and economically in the past century.

One constant reflects both the Ninth and Tenth Amendments. Both amendments have evolved and, more recently, have become significant. While the Tenth Amendment was used during the nineteenth century to instigate the Civil War and allow for several acts passed by Congress, it did not protect rights reserved to the state as much as it did during the later twentieth century on a political and economic basis. The Ninth Amendment did not have an effect on the political or economic spectrum, but had a tremendous impact on culture as it reflected changing values of the twentieth century. While the Tenth Amendment had a large impact politically and economically, the Ninth Amendment had an equally large impact socially on the United States during the late twentieth century. Both evolved to reflect changing views of the citizens and have expanded over the past 200 years. The greatest paradox in Constitutional history comes alive through the vague rights that the Ninth and Tenth Amendments allow.

Bibliography

Clause 18. Necessary and Proper Clause. 2 November 2005.http:// caselaw.lp.findlaw.com/data/constitution/article01/44.html#4.

De Rosa, Marshall. The Ninth Amendment and the Politics of Creative Jurisprudence.November 2005. <http://www.mises.org/ misesreview_detail.asp?control=8&sortorder=issue.>

Edwards, George C and Martin P. Wattenberg and Robert L. Lineberry. Government inAmerica. New York: Longman, 1998.

Gustavson, Robert. A Biography of John Caldwell Calhoun. 1 November 2005.http://odur.let.rug.nl/~usa/B/calhoun/jcc.htm. 5 May 2005.

Halbrooks, Jacob. "The Anti-Federalist Struggle for the Bill of Rights." 31 October2005 <http://www.geocities.com/libertarian_ press/antifeds.html>.

Hartford Convention. 1 November 2005.http://www.bartleby. com/65/ha/HartfordC.html.

Henderson, Harry. Gun Control. New York: Facts on File, Inc, 2005.

Holder, Angela and John Holder. The Meaning of the Constitution. Hauppauge, NewYork: Barons, 1997.

Feinburg, Barbara Silberdick. Constitutional Amendments. New York: Twenty FirstCentury Books, 1996.

Finkelman, Paul and Melvin Urofsky. Landmark Decisions of the United StatesSupreme Court. Washington D.C: CQ Press, 2003.

James Madison Proposes Bill of Rights. 31 October, 2005,http://www.jmu.edu/madison/gpos225-madison2/madprobll.htm#useless.

Krull, Kathleen. A Kid's Guide to America's Bill of Rights. New York: Avon Books,INC., 1999.

Lieberman, Jethro K. A Practical Companion to the Constitution. Los Angeles, CA:University of California Press, 1999.

Lindop, Edmund. The Bill of Rights and Landmark Cases. New York: Franklin Watts,1989.

New York v. United States. 3 November 2005<http://www.oyez.org/oyez/resource/case/644/>

Pendergest, Tom and Sara Pendergest and John Sousanis. ConstitutionalAmendments.Detroit: U.X.L., 2001.

Tenth Amendment-Reserved Powers. 2 November 2005.<http://www.gpoaccess.gov/constitution/html/amdt10.html.>

The Bill of Rights and Beyond. D.C: Library of Congress, 1991.

The Fourteenth Amendment
And
Same-Sex Marriages

By
Beth King

No issue involving family law and civil rights is more prevalent in modern global and national politics and ethics than same-sex marriage. Four countries, Canada, Spain, Belgium, and the Netherlands have already legalized the marriage of two members of the same gender, and other countries considering such legislation include South Africa, the United Kingdom, New Zealand, the Czech Republic, Finland, Luxembourg, Portugal, Spain, Switzerland, and Taiwan. Currently, Massachusetts is the only state within the United States in which same-sex marriage is legal, but as of 2003, those states which have experienced or are experiencing lawsuits concerning the right of gay people to get married include Alaska, Arizona, California, Colorado, the District of Columbia, Florida, Georgia, Hawaii, Indiana, Kentucky, Minnesota, Nebraska, New Jersey, New York, Ohio, Pennsylvania, Vermont, Washington, and Wisconsin.[572] The galvanized activity of anti-gay organizations has indicated that our country is at the height of the debate over equality in marriage. In fact, anti-gay groups spend about four times the amount of money than gay rights organizations in the ever-intensifying struggle.[573]

In 1996, President Clinton signed the Defense of Marriage Act into law, leaving the legality of same-sex marriage up to the states. As of 2004, thirty-nine states have passed similar anti-gay marriage laws, ensuring that the full faith and credit of the Constitution, requiring each state to respect the court decisions and legal proceedings of other states, would not apply to recognition of gay marriages. Opponents of such marriages are attempting to alter the federal Constitution to incorporate the Federal Marriage Amendment, which would legally define marriage as consisting "only of the union of a man and a woman." An exploration of the history shaping the debate over same-sex marriages, gay equality and their relevance to the Constitution will demonstrate that, in accordance with the Fourteenth Amendment and decisions of the Supreme Court, the wishes of two consenting adults to socially and legally contract in the form of marriage should not be denied on the basis of gender.

The longstanding, historical tradition of equality in the United States is a source of great pride for Americans, one which is routinely reinforced and celebrated in public schools and national holidays. It is arguably the theme of the nation, set forth by the pen of Thomas Jefferson at the birth of the country and emphasized in nearly all aspects of national history since. Unfortunately, this tradition is accompanied by a lengthy record of injustice and prejudice. Homosexuals have endured just as much hatred and inequity as any other minority group, yet the legacy of antigay discrimination is relatively obscure and seldom documented. Antigay sentiment reached its peak in the 1950s, when homosexuals, particularly men, bore the stigma of perversion, psychopathy, and pedophilia. In several states, individuals convicted of sexual misconduct, such as sodomy, were required to undergo psychiatric treatment. In 1953, President Eisenhower issued an executive order banning homosexuals from employment in the government and required companies with government contracts to ferret out and fire gay, or "sexually perverted" employers. Thus, in the midst of the McCarthy era, more homosexuals lost their jobs and reputations due to government harassment than Communists. Gay individuals had no right to public assembly, nor were bars and restaurants allowed to serve homosexuals or cater to the gay population. Many government officials enacted nationwide "cleansing" campaigns, in which the police raided the headquarters of the few gay organizations in existence, arrested their leaders and stole their membership lists.[574] Similarly, the Hays Code, a set of rules governing movie production created in 1930 and abandoned in 1967, prevented Hollywood films and music from depicting or even inferring to the existence of homosexuality.[575]

The homosexual "Cultural Revolution" developed in the 1970s when, in 1975, the ban on gay federal employees was lifted. However, gay organizations showed more interest in the individual rights of gay people, such as in employment, than in the rights of gay couples. Several events are responsible for the birth of the desire of same-sex couples to marry. In previous decades, the idea of homosexual marriages was absurd, largely due to the negative reputation of gay people but this view changed as the visibility of gay individuals in popular culture and acceptance of gay people increased. As an unprecedented number of people "came out of the closet" to their loved ones, people were forced to reconsider their preconceived notions about the nature of homosexuals. Many gay couples themselves were unconcerned with their legal marital status until the AIDS epidemic of the 1980s caused the tragic death of their partners. In addition to the loss of their loved ones, the surviving partner had to face the harrowing ordeal of legal discrimination. Because their partnership was not recognized by law, they were often denied the right to visit their significant other in the hospital, make medical decisions for their sick partner, secure funeral arrangements, take bereavement leave, sue for wrongful death or malpractice, collect on insurance, and inherit shared housing or property, or a myriad of other rights automatically given to heterosexual spouses. In a similar vein, the emergence of what some call the "lesbian baby boom" increased gay awareness of the benefits of marriage. As more and more gay couples, particularly lesbians, began to raise children, several issues arose concerning legal parenting and custody. If the lesbian couple were to separate, the biological mother could deny her previous female partner visitation or custody rights on the basis that their relationship was not legal, despite the fact that her ex-partner raised the child from birth. Similarly, if the biological mother were to die, the child could be separated from the second adult he or she had been raised by and placed in different households or with distant relatives.[576] Since the 1980s, gay Americans have made significant advancements. The presidential election of 1992 was the first to feature gay issues in national debate. Under the Clinton administration, the federal government forbade employment discrimination based on sexual orientation among its agencies, prompting private employers to quickly follow suit.

The overall improvement of the reputation of gay people in today's society is especially evident in our youth. Despite the teenage practice of referring to that which is profoundly unacceptable as 'gay,' an unprecedented number of young people accept different sexual preferences as easily as they accept different ethnic backgrounds. According to the Gay and Lesbian Straight Education Network, nearly one in every ten high schools boasts a Gay Straight Alliance on its club roster. The University of California, Los Angeles' 2004 survey of college freshmen indicates that 57% favor same-sex marriage and similar research has affirmed a decline in the use of negative epithets such as "faggot" and "queer." Today's gay teenager faces a palpably smaller amount of negative responses to his or her sexuality than previous generations.[577] Whether they view homosexuality as sinful behavior or not, many Americans clearly view homophobia in the same light as racism, sexism, and anti-Semitism.

This brings us to the history of marriage itself. The institution of marriage is by no means stable or subject to the confines of tradition; it fluctuates in response to changes in culture and law. Most of these changes were at one point in history challanged on the basis that they were unnatural, a threat to family order and social stability, and contrary to the will of God. Correspondingly, marriage is a tool often used to perpetuate oppression and limit the freedoms of a particular group of people. The marriages of American slaves were never permitted or recognized and Nazi Germany forbade the marriage of a Jewish person to a non-Jew. Realistically, the state no longer holds any power to deny a request for divorce and a woman's legal identity is no longer absorbed by her husband upon entrance into a contractual marriage, her rights as an individual and a citizen preserved. Similarly, racial background is now irrelevant in the decision to grant marital status. In fact, the events surrounding the debate of interracial marriage parallel those surrounding gay marriage in several ways. In the 1870s, judges in support of anti-miscegenation laws argued the following: that the regulation of marriage belongs to the individual states, that interracial marriage violates the will of God, that interracial marriages are unnatural, and that because both whites and blacks were punished under these laws, anti-miscegenation legislation does not violate the Fourteenth Amendment. These are exactly the same arguments being used to deny gay equality in marriage today. Those who supported the legalization of interracial marriage used the Fourteenth Amendment to prove their case, just as those who support the legalization of same-sex marriage do. Interestingly enough, in 1843, Massachusetts was the first state to strike down its own anti-miscegenation law, just as it was the first state to legalize marriage between two members of the same gender.[578] For the same reasons that the state may not deny marital status based on race, the state should not be able to deny marital status based on gender.

The twentieth century brought into play three major contemporary changes in marriage which have convinced gay couples of their right to be married. The most important aspect of Western marriage: every citizen has the right to choose his or her partner in marriage. This is the most fundamental and implicitly understood basic right concerning modern marriage. Heterosexual people need not obtain the permission or approval of their partner from their friends, family, or the state to enter a civil marriage. Secondly, the roles of husbands and wives have irrevocably changed, due in large part to women's liberation. The historical marital structure in which the husband is the head of family and is responsible for the provision of food and money and the wife raises the children and cares for the physical and emotional needs of her family is no longer strictly applicable. The typical American household displays a blur in the lines of historically patriarchal and matriarchal responsibilities, meaning that the duties of contributing to the financial progress of the family, caring for the children, and making important family decisions are often equally shared between both the woman and the man. This is a new kind of liberalness in the definition of marriage, one which makes marriage more inviting and imaginable for gay couples. [579]

> "All persons born or naturalized in the United States, and subject to the jurisdiction thereof, are citizens of the United States and of the state wherein they reside. No state shall make or enforce any law which shall abridge the privileges or immunities of citizens of the United States; nor shall any state deprive any person of life, liberty, or property, without due process of law; nor deny to any person within its jurisdiction the equal protection of the laws."

> Section 1, Amendment XIV

Since the original framing of the Constitution, no provision has helped to significantly define the structure and attitude of the United States more than the Fourteenth Amendment. After the passage of the Thirteenth Amendment, which outlawed slavery within the United States, many southern states established Black Codes and Jim Crow laws, which attempted to, and were often successful in, returning freed slaves to their former condition. In response to these laws, Congress passed the Fourteenth Amendment, which broadly redefined the requirements for citizenship and the rights of said citizens. The framers of this amendment intended it to be used to secure the protection of the rights of black people and all other races within the United States, including voting rights. In the years following the Civil War, the Fourteenth Amendment has been subject to broader interpretation by the courts and has been effectively used to strike down laws denying civil rights. The equal protection clause of the Fourteenth Amendment has been used to end segregation laws, federal employment discrimination laws, anti-miscegenation laws, and many other laws which systematically oppressed minority groups.[580] The credibility of same-sex couples' contention that their inability to marry one another denies them civil rights is rooted in the first section of the Fourteenth Amendment.

The word "marriage" carries two separate connotations. The first describes a religious and social status, encompassing the ceremonies and marital rules dictated by a particular faith that couples choose to observe. Western societal norms require that two married adults love and commit to each other, but this does not prevent marriages based on financial gain or citizenship. The second connotation refers to the civil and legal status recognized by the government, in which marriage is a contract made between a couple and the state. In the same-sex marriage debate, it is important to distinguish between civil marriage and religious marriage. Civil marriage is an institution owned and regulated by the government. The "sanctity" of religious marriage is not threatened by equality in civil marriage. It is performed by legally designated officials and involves a slew of legal repercussions. In a report from 2004, the General Accounting Office found that there are approximately 1,138 federal rights that accompany civil marriage.[581] A list of the rights, privileges, and responsibilities allotted to heterosexual married couples and denied to homosexual couples include, but are in no way limited to, the entitlement to bereavement leave, the ability to file wrongful death claims, the right to draw Social Security payments of a deceased partner, automatic inheritance of shared property, debt responsibility, access to courts regulating separation involving property, custody, child support, and alimony, entitlement to medical leave, hospital visitation rights, eligibility for Medicare or Medicaid coverage, rights involving residency and family unification laws, access to joint home, auto, or health insurance, automatic rights involving joint parenting, adoption, foster care, and visitation for non-biological parents, nationwide acknowledgment and recognition of the relationship, the right not to testify against one another in judicial proceedings, and protection against domestic violence.[582] The majority of these rights are unobtainable for gay and lesbian partners, no matter how many legal documents a couple might acquire. By denying gay couples access to the purely legal institution of civil marriage, the government clearly both abridges the privileges and immunities of homosexual citizens and denies these individuals and their relationships the equal protection of the law.

It is currently commonplace for antigay organizations and individuals to claim that gay people seek not equal rights, but "special rights." These organizations contend that, because no one can legally marry a member of the same sex, anti-gay marriage litigation does not violate the Fourteenth Amendment. In other words, homosexuals can enjoy the benefits of marriage just as a heterosexual can as long as said homosexual marries a member of the opposite sex. Clearly, this argument mimics that which was made in support of anti-miscegenation laws. Straight people have the right to marry the informed, consenting adult of their choice, gay people do not. In the 1996 case of Romer v. Evans, the state of Colorado attempted to use just such an argument to justify its "Amendment 2" referendum, which prohibited branches of the government from adopting policies that would protect the status of people based on homosexual orientation, behavior or conduct. The Colorado Supreme Court rejected the state's argument that such an amendment placed gays and lesbians "in the same position as all other persons" as "implausible."

Another tactic of antigay entities is to insist that gay marriage is not an issue of civil rights at all, that civil rights pertain only to discrimination based on "unchangeable physical characteristics."[583] A quick check of the online reference site, dictionary.com, provides us with the following definition of civil rights:

"The rights belonging to an individual by virtue of citizenship, especially the fundamental freedoms and privileges guaranteed by the 13th and 14th Amendments to the U.S. Constitution and by subsequent acts of Congress, including civil liberties, due process, equal protection of the laws, and freedom from discrimination."

What the definition does not say is "freedom from discrimination based on physical characteristics." Ignoring this, the state denies marriage applications based on the gender of the two parties. Whether one believes that sexual orientation is not a voluntary choice, as the American Psychological Association does[584], or you do, gender is an undeniably "unchangeable physical characteristic."

As we learned from Loving v. Virginia, the 1967 Supreme Court case involving the arrest of a white man and his black wife, "marriage is one of the basic civil rights of man, fundamental to our very existence..." Consider the following words from Coretta Scott King, an outspoken supporter of gay people's freedom to marry;

"My husband, Martin Luther King Jr., understood that all forms of discrimination and persecution were unjust and unacceptable for a great democracy. He believed that none of us could be free until all of us were free, that a person of conscience had no alternative but to defend the human rights of all people... The civil rights movement that I believe in thrives on unity and inclusion, not division and exclusion. All of us who oppose discrimination and support equal rights should stand together to resist every attempt to restrict civil rights in this country."

Many deeply religious people fear that the legalization of same-sex marriage will jeopardize their constitutionally protected religious freedom. The answer to this is, simply, that this right is constitutionally protected. The First Amendment to the Constitution is likely the most respected and prized pillar of American law and any attempt to jeopardize the freedoms enumerated within it would be met with steadfast opposition. Just as the legalization of abortion has not prevented pro-life advocates from vocalizing their religious objections to abortion, so the legalization of same-sex marriage will not prevent those who morally disapprove of homosexuality from verbally dissenting. This is where the distinction between religious marriage and civil marriage is especially crucial. Individual faiths will not be forced to recognize or perform such marriages and private schools and organizations will not be required to endorse acceptance of homosexuality or homosexual marriage, simply because to do so would be illegal. Let us also remember that "freedom of religion" implies "freedom from religion." The religious beliefs of some faiths that homosexuality is a sin ought not dictate the legal validity regarding the recognition of gay people's relationships.

A multitude of other reasons for denying civil marriage rights to gay couples have been presented by antigay entities, most of them largely unfounded. For example, "Same-sex marriage will lead to the destruction of traditional families." It is neither the duty nor the place of the state to regulate "tradition" in family or society. Slavery was a tradition. Female subjugation was a tradition. Tradition is irrelevant. How one chooses to structure and interact with one's family is entirely up to the individual, and who is to say that one kind of family is inferior to another?

"Children suffer when raised by gay couples": Many of these antigay entities enjoy consistently parading the hundreds of studies and expert opinions contending that children do better when raised by a mother and a father. However, these studies simply reaffirm that children are, on average, more well-adjusted when raised by two parents; it has never been conclusively proven that children raised by two parents of the same gender fare worse than their peers raised by one man and one woman. In fact, there are several studies and expert opinions which conclude that it is the quality of a child's relationship with his or her parents which determine overall welfare, not the sex of the parents themselves.[585]

"Procreation and species perpetuation are the basis of marriage": In the Massachusetts Supreme Court decision legalizing same-sex marriage, the Commonwealth attempted to argue that the purpose of marriage is procreation, and that it is, therefore, pointless for gay couples to get married, a contention dismissed as false. If this argument were relevant, infertile heterosexual couples and couples with no desire to have children would be similarly prevented from gaining marital status.

"The legalization of same-sex marriage would inevitably lead to legalized incest, polygamy, bestiality, pedophilia and other horrors:" It is absurd, and moreover offensive, to compare the legal union of two consenting adults to sexual relations with animals and relatives and child molestation. Incest is a crime; homosexuality is not. This line of thinking likely stems from the old stigma that homosexuality equals pedophilia and perversion. Several countries have legalized same-sex marriage, none has legalized bestiality.

"Homosexual behavior is unnatural:" For a behavior that's supposedly unnatural, homosexuality sure does occur in nature often. Many species, especially orangutans and other primates closely biologically related to humans, include members of the race who consistently seek out individuals of the same sex for sexual gratification or courting rituals. Just as humans sometimes do, two same-sex members of a species are capable of pair-bonding for long periods of time.[586]

In the discussion of the legality of same-sex marriages, we are unavoidably required to address the subject of civil unions/domestic partnerships. Many of those who are discomforted by the prospect of gay marriage but do no wish to appear cruel or intolerant find refuge in the support of civil unions. The foreign countries which offer the choice of a civil union for same-sex couples are Sweden, France, Germany, Finland, Switzerland, and Great Britain. Currently, Vermont and Connecticut are the only states which have approved same-sex civil unions, while California provides the option of a same-sex domestic partnership.[587] These civil unions bear resemblance to marriage, but fall short on several factors. For example, there are 200-300 legal rights that accompany Vermont civil unions, a number significantly lower than those which accompany civil marriage. Who makes the distinction between rights that gay couples deserve and those they do not? Furthermore, a Vermont civil union is recognized only in Vermont. A Californian domestic partnership is recognized only in California. Quite simply, civil unions aren't good enough. It seems that only the word "marriage" itself has the capability to open the doors to all 1,138 federal rights given to heterosexual married couples. Essentially, the establishment of civil unions opens the doors of the national marriage bus to gay couples, but delegates that they remain in the back. We tried the whole "separate but equal" thing before; it didn't work. The Massachusetts Supreme Court realized this, when, after deciding that denying gays and lesbians legal marital benefits created second-class citizens and violated the Constitution, it rejected the notion that civil unions fulfilled this edict.

Realistically, there is no compelling argument as to why gay couples ought to be continuously denied legal recognition and marital status, and there is no rational evidence as to how gay marriage would be detrimental to marriage, families, or society in any way. What it all boils down to is that the opposition to same-sex marriage is founded solely on the belief that homosexuality is 'bad' and, as the Supreme Court explains in its decision in Lawrence v. Texas, "moral disapproval of a group does not justify discrimination."

At its base, the case for the legalization of same-sex marriages relies simply on equality. Straight people have rights that gay people do not. The policy of nearly every state to deny applications for marriage licenses based on gender is a form of governmental discrimination, expressly forbidden by the Constitution. If same-sex marriages were to be legalized, it would breed a new atmosphere of social tolerance, for the issue of marriage equality is not just that of legal proceedings; it is a matter of giving our fellow citizens and their personal choices the dignity and respect they deserve.

The Fifteenth Amendment

It Took a Long Time
By
Rebecca Boucher

In 1870, the Fifteenth Amendment was passed by congress guaranteeing African-Americans a voice in their government. Despite the rights guaranteed to blacks in the Fifteenth Amendment, they did not truly have the right to vote until the Voting Rights Act of 1965. For those ninety-five years, African-Americans had to fight for their right to vote, battling against discrimination and violation of their constitutional rights.

One law passed by the Civil War congress was the Military Construction Act of 1867, which allowed Confederate states to be readmitted into the Union if they adopted universal male suffrage in their state constitutions and laid groundwork for the Fifteenth Amendment. One of three Civil War amendments, the Fifteenth Amendment was framed in early 1869 and proposed to the legislatures of several states by the 40th Congress. In order to be ratified, twenty of the 37 states had to agree with the proposal. Finally ratified on February 3, 1870, the Fifteenth Amendment stated, "The right of citizens of the United States to vote shall not be denied or abridged by the United States or by any state on the account of race, color, or previous condition of servitude."[588] This meant that black male citizens had the same voting rights as all other citizens of the United States. Section two of the amendment gave Congress the power to enforce the amendment by appropriate legislation. Before the amendment was even a year old, Congress passed several civil rights laws using its power from section two.

The major laws passed were known as the Enforcement Acts, which, "were criminal codes that protected blacks' rights to vote, hold office, serve on juries, and receive equal protection of laws."[589] The first, passed in May 1870, stopped political officials from discriminating against voters on the basis of color in the application of local election laws. The second act, or Force Act, came in February 1871, and placed congressional elections that were being held in cities with a population over 20,000 under direct supervision of the federal government. However, the most important law regarding civil rights did not come until April 1871, and was called the Ku Klux Klan Act. This act was created to stop southern violence directed against blacks but was later modified to punish only the crime of denying equal protection under the law. One positive part of the act was that it did authorize the President to suspend the writ of habeas corpus and to use military power against conspiracies concerning civil rights. All three acts were passed to enforce the Fifteenth Amendment.

These acts did have many other positive affects, but the southern states found ways to take them away. Immediately after the Civil War ended, only five states let blacks vote on the same basis as whites. The states legally used literacy or education tests to disenfranchise African-Americans and, since few southern whites wanted blacks to vote, the literacy test was used frequently to deny them this right. Most blacks were illiterate because of slavery so it made it that much easier for southern whites to use literacy tests to disenfranchise blacks. One of the first literacy tests, used in South Carolina, was called the "eight-box" because it required voters to put a ballot in a different box for every position that was up for election.[590] If the voter did not put the ballot in the correct box the vote would not count. Knowing that most blacks could not read the boxes they even shuffled them so they could not memorize the order. Another method was the secret or Australian ballot. Before the adoption of the secret ballot, one would get a ballot from the political parties with the candidate's names already on it. This way of voting didn't force voters to read, so officials switched to the secret ballot. The secret ballot had all of the candidates' names on it and the voter would have to make his choice in private, forcing the voter to read it on his own. This way of voting was an easy and legal way to discriminate against illiterate blacks. The first use of the secret ballot was in 1888 and was immediately adopted everywhere. Some of the literacy requirements were so difficult to understand that even literate blacks would fail them, so it left no hope for those illiterate ones.

Many states had their own literacy requirements. Between 1870 and 1924, most states required which required the voter, "be able to read the constitution in English and write his name."[591] The Constitution then and now is a difficult piece to read, especially with no formal education. Only a few exemptions were made and the most common one was for people with disabilities. Even though a lot of poor whites could not pass the literacy tests, the states still carried them out. One way poor whites found their way around the literacy tests was the "understanding clause," which meant if a white man could read a certain passage to a registrar's satisfaction, he was eligible to vote. The states also found other ways around the literacy tests. The "grandfather clause" was enacted on February 8, 1898, for voting purposes. The clause was a legal mechanism passed during Reconstruction by seven southern states. This was used to protect poor illiterate whites having to take the literacy tests while keeping blacks from voting. The clause stated that any person or any of their descendants who had voted before 1867 was exempt from tax, property, and educational requirements. This allowed whites whose grandfathers had voted before 1867 to vote without taking the literacy test. Since no blacks had voted before 1867, no blacks qualified under the "grandfather clause." In 1915, during Guinn v. United States, the Supreme Court declared the "grandfather clause" unconstitutional because it violated the equal voting rights granted in the Fifteenth Amendment.[592] However, Oklahoma responded by passing a law that required those who had not voted to register in 12 days or forfeit the franchise. The Supreme Court also struck down that law in 1939. These decisions did not affect the legality of the literacy test but made it illegal to exempt whites from it..

Another way states legally disenfranchised black voters was by the issue of a poll tax, a fee a voter must pay before voting. The tax was high enough that it kept the poor from voting. The poor that the states intended to disenfranchise were the blacks. Most blacks had not yet gotten good paying jobs because of discrimination in the south. Most poll taxes throughout the U.S. were between $1 and $2. However, some even reached as high as $4.[593] Now, that may not seem like a lot of money but, more than 100 years ago, that was a lot of money to poor blacks with low paying jobs.

Georgia was the first to use the poll tax in 1871 and the state made it cumulative in 1877, which meant all citizens were required to pay back taxes before being allowed to vote. In 1937, a white man filed suit against Georgia and its poll tax alleging violation of the Fourteenth and Nineteenth Amendments. He argued that women should have to pay poll taxes, too. The case, Breedlove v. Suttles, was decided by the Supreme Court, which rejected the white man's arguments, ruling the poll tax was made to create revenue and taxation and was not a concern of the Nineteenth Amendment.

One legal way the states could discriminate but not direct it toward blacks and look obvious was residency requirements. Many states had residency requirements for suffrage. There were two parts to residency requirements. The first was that blacks had to have lived in the state for a certain amount of time. At that time, many blacks moved frequently and did not live in one place for very long. Between 1870 and 1923, most states required at least six months and as much as two years residency in the voter's state in order to be eligible to vote. The second part of the residency requirement was that their property had to be worth a certain amount in order to vote. This "property value" requirement was usually extreme and was very difficult to meet for poor blacks. In March, 1972, the Supreme Court declared lengthy voting requirements unconstitutional. To comply with the ruling, many states had to change their residency requirements. Now, most states have no length of residency requirements.

Since some ways of disenfranchisement were being rejected, southerners found another way to discriminate against blacks: the all-white primary. Thanks to the Supreme Court's decision in Newberry v. United States, holding a primary is not a real part of the election process so it was legal for states to pass an all- white primary law.[594] Texas was one of the first states to pass a law forbidding blacks from participation in Democratic primaries. The Supreme Court, however, struck down the Texas law in Nixon v. Herndon arguing it was a violation of the Fourteenth and Fifteenth amendments. Texas tried again by passing a law saying that the party was a private association that was not subject to the two amendments, which only applied to states. Once again the Supreme Court rejected the law in Nixon v. Condon because the candidates were to represent Texas, so it did concern the states. The state Democratic convention met and passed a resolution which limited party membership to whites. The Supreme Court did not disagree with this decision and upheld the exclusion of blacks in Grovey v. Townsend. Finally, after going back and forth with Texas officials, the Supreme Court put an end to the all-white primary in Terry v. Adams, which only ended white primaries in Texas. The court's decision in United States v. Classic made the right to vote secure in the Constitution and confirmed that Congress had the right to regulate primaries. The decision by the Supreme Court was the official downfall of the all-white primary.

Most southern states used all types of suppressive election procedures. Many states had complicated or misleading election procedures such as "multiple ballots." Some elections required voters to cast a ballot in several different locations and Democratic officials, who did not want the blacks to vote, often failed to inform black voters of the complicated procedures. If the confusing procedures were not followed correctly, the ballots would be disqualified. Southern states also created difficult registration requirements by "requiring frequent re-registration, long terms of residence in a district, and registration at inconvenient times."[595] Uninformed, blacks usually did not complete all parts of the registration and therefore were not qualified to vote.

Gerrymandering is the process by which state legislatures redraw election boundaries to create a clear majority of similar voters in an area. So, in areas with a heavy black influence, gerrymandering was the answer to get whites what they wanted. In the end, the whites would have the majority in the city and the blacks would be a part of the surrounding counties that had little influence. One example of gerrymandering took place in Tuskegee, Alabama, where a lot of blacks lived. The number of blacks was a threat to the white control of the city so the state legislature redrew the boundaries of the city. However, the blacks did not go down without a fight. In 1960, the Supreme Court heard the case Gomillion v. Lightfoot which included racial gerrymandering. The court ruled in favor of the blacks deciding that the state legislature's actions were a violation of the Fifteenth Amendment.

One of the last legal ways states disenfranchised blacks was by amending their state constitutions. After the Civil War, most southern states were required to rewrite their state constitutions giving blacks their newly granted rights. All states did rewrite them but, not too long after, amended the changes. A few southern states even passed amendments taking away most black voting rights which they had just granted. If the southern states did not amend the state constitution, they passed laws negating the rights given.

From 1868-1888, violence and fraud were the major illegal ways that southern whites disenfranchised blacks. From 1889 to 1930, 3,700 men and women were lynched in the United States, most of them southern blacks. In Mississippi, a plan to control black votes and to regulate their economic and public lives with uncontrolled violence was used. It was called the Mississippi Plan and whites used it to brutally devastate the black vote. Those who did get to vote voted Democratic because they feared the wrath of the whites if they did not. The second Mississippi Plan was not as violent as the first but still was marked by rewriting the state constitution and passing anti-black legislation. The Ku Klux Klan and the Knights of the White Camellia were anti-black terrorist organizations that tried to stop the black community from getting stronger. The Ku Klux Klan, which was the most well known anti-black group in the United States, formed between 1865 and 1866, organized waves of violent assaults and acts of intimidation and assassinations against African Americans who might vote. The fear alone that the Klan caused kept blacks from even thinking about voting. One of the biggest cases involving violence and voting was United States v. Cruikshank. In April, 1873, an army of Klansmen stormed a Louisiana courthouse killing 60 freedmen. A federal grand jury indicted 97 of the attackers on various charges, including violation of constitutional rights. The trial took two months and a six- week jury deliberation to acquit one of the nine defendants and fail to reach a verdict on the others. During a retrial, only three defendants were convicted of conspiracy and all remaining defendants were acquitted of the murder charges. The Klan was known for its intimidation, burning crosses and vandalizing homes. Threats were made almost daily toward blacks who were thinking about voting. Many leaders were assassinated during the Civil Rights movement. The assassinations were done to stop the movement's momentum, but they only helped accelerate it.

The most famous assassination was of Dr. Martin Luther King Jr. in Memphis, Tennessee. He was the nonviolent leader of the Civil Rights movement. Although his followers were stricken with grief, his death helped accelerate the movement.

Fraud was another major illegal way to disenfranchise blacks all over the South, Democratic officials found legal means of disenfranchisement. There were many ways to commit electoral fraud, one of them being ballot box stuffing. Officials would fill out multiple ballots for the Democratic candidate and put them in the box. Other forms of fraud included throwing out non-Democratic votes or counting them for the Democrats even though they were for the opposition. In the eleven years between 1880 and 1901, Congress seated 26 Republican or Populist candidates who had been cheated by the different ways of fraud. Finally, people started to speak up about fraud and a case was made against two Kentucky election inspectors who were accused of refusing to receive and count votes for a black elector, a violation of the Enforcement Act of 1870. The case United States v. Reese was brought before the Supreme Court which dismissed the indictments.

Black women had major roles in getting their right to vote. When people refer to blacks they are speaking about black men. However, black women had to fight just as hard to get their Fifteenth Amendment rights, which did not give any women the right to vote until they won suffrage. Black women were discouraged from taking part in women's suffrage movements because of the discrimination. Even some white women did not want African-American women to participate. Ida B. Wells-Barnett, however, was a journalist who led an anti-lynching campaign and was an advocate for women's suffrage in 1913. She got a group of black women together to march in Washington, D.C. for women's rights but when she got there she was discriminated against by her fellow demonstrators. They asked her to stand at the back of the march and not with the white women. White women feared that if they let black women participate in the suffrage movement they would lose the support of southern whites. Wells-Barnett and her followers refused to march in the parade because of the discrimination. Only a couple of years later, in 1920, did women get the right to vote. The Nineteenth Amendment was proposed in June of 1919 and was signed into a law by August 1920. The amendment was almost exactly the same as the Fifteenth Amendment except voting could not be denied because of gender. It was not until 1957 when the same number of women voted as men. However, black women now had to face the same discrimination as black men had since the passing of the Fifteenth Amendment.

Black women waited until 1968 to see the first black woman in the House of Representatives, Shirley Chisholm of New York. This was a big step for the women's rights movement and there were many women before her who set the path. Rosa Parks, one of the most well known Civil Rights activists, refused to give up her seat to white people on a bus. Her refusal led to the Montgomery Bus-Boycott, which went on for 381 days. Finally, the Supreme Court ruled in 1956 that segregation on public transportation was unconstitutional and Rosa Parks became a symbol for the rights of both blacks and women. [596]

Blacks fought both the legal and illegal ways of discrimination that whites threw at them. Slowly, blacks got the rights that they were promised in the Fifteenth Amendment when Congress passed legislation that contained voting-related provisions. The first came in 1957 by way of President Eisenhower and was aimed to increase the number of black voters. The Civil Rights Act of 1957 was primarily a voting rights bill and was the first legislation passed since Reconstruction. The 1957 act created, "the Civil Rights Division within the Department of Justice and the Commission on Civil Rights." Authority was given to the Attorney General, "to intervene in and institute lawsuits seeking injunctive relief against violations of the Fifteenth Amendment." However, even if someone violated the act they faced a trial by a jury which would have been all white in the south. The act was largely opposed by southern Senators because they did not want such sweeping changes. Strom Thurmond, a Senator who opposed the bill, took part in the longest filibuster in congressional history. After his twenty-four hour and eighteen minute speech was finished, a vote was allowed and the bill passed in the Senate. President Eisenhower signed the bill into law. Next to come was the Civil Rights Act of 1960. Signed by President Dwight D. Eisenhower, the act established, "federal inspection of local voter registration rolls and introduced penalties for anyone who obstructed someone's attempt to register to vote or actually vote."[597]

The two acts did not impress civil rights leaders as being very effective. They were deemed ineffective because it only added an extra three percent to the black voter rolls. Many people accused Eisenhower of passing on his difficult issues to his successor. Eisenhower was also criticized for admitting that he did not understand some parts of the act. The only positive that some saw in the two acts was the federal recognition of a problem.

In 1939, Congress started to try to get rid of the poll tax, but most of the country, especially the South, was not behind it. However, the Twenty-fourth Amendment was proposed by the Eighty-seventh Congress in 1962. In less than six months, the amendment passed through the Senate and the House and two years later, on January 23, 1964, the Twenty-fourth Amendment was ratified. Section 1 gave the right to citizens to vote in any election for President, Vice President, Senator, or Representative in Congress without paying a poll tax. The amendment eliminated poll taxes everywhere. Section 2, as in the Fifteenth Amendment, gave power to Congress to pass legislation to uphold the rights given in the amendment. Even though it was passed after both the Civil Rights Act of 1957 and 1960, it was the first law that had an actual impact on the civil rights of blacks. The amendment's impact went only so far because only five states still used a poll tax when the amendment was passed.

> "Rarely are we met with a challenge... to the values and the purposes and the meaning of our beloved Nation. The issue of equal rights for American Negroes is such an issue... the command of the Constitution is plain. It is wrong-deadly wrong- to deny any of your fellow Americans the right to vote in this country."[598]

The passage is from President Johnson's speech to Congress when he was trying to introduce the idea of a voting rights act. President Johnson was serious about the issue and that forced Congress to act. The Voting Rights Act of 1965 was passed by July, 1964. Finally the act was signed into a law by President Lyndon B. Johnson on August 6, 1965, and is considered the most successful piece of legislation in civil rights history. Section 4 basically outlawed literacy tests as requirements to vote and specifically outlawed literacy tests in six southern states where voter registration was less than fifty percent in the 1964 Presidential election. Also, in Section 5, no voting changes could be made without the approval of a three-judge court. Other provisions included federal examiners who would investigate voting conditions. Since the act made such an impact, it was challenged in the Supreme Court several times. The first was in South Carolina v. Katzenbach when the state brought an injunction against the enforcement of the act by the Attorney General. The Supreme Court upheld the act. Another case was Allen v. State Board of Elections where a change in procedures for casting write-in ballots was questioned. The Supreme Court held the changes because they were covered in Section 5. The law made a major impact and was renewed in 1970, 1975, and 1982.

In 1970 and 1975, there were amendments to the act extending it for five years in 1970 and seven in 1975. During the hearings, Congress heard testimony from blacks who had suffered through gerrymandering and other types of discrimination. Due to the blacks' testimony, Congress added protection from voting discrimination for language minority citizens.[599] In 1980, the Supreme Court decided, in Mobile v. Bolden, that, "it required that any constitutional claim of minority vote dilution must include proof of a racially discriminatory purpose." This requirement made it a lot more difficult to prove such claims.

There was another amendment in 1982 that added special provisions to the act regarding Section Five. Congress decided to review the records of voting discrimination in order to decide whether the act should be continued. Congress made the decision that they still needed that section because it would protect voting rights. The amendment extended coverage of that section for 25 more years and altered Section Two so that a plaintiff did not have to prove discriminatory purpose to establish violation. In 2007, the extended act will be up for review in Congress, but the actual act itself is a permanent right and will never expire.

The impact of the Voting Rights Act of 1965 in black voter registration was huge. The first major impact was that blacks were being elected to public offices. In 1964, there had been only 16 black state legislators in the south but, by 1966, there were 37. Southern voters also sent two blacks to Congress in 1972 and a third in 1974. They were the first in Congress in more than 70 years. Before the Voting Rights Act of 1965, the number of whites registered to vote outnumbered the blacks. In Alabama, only 19.3% of the black population was registered to vote whereas 69.2% of the white population was registered. By the end of 1965, 250,000 more black voters had been registered, and by the end of 1966, only 4 out 13 southern states had fewer than 50% of blacks registered to vote.[600]

Voter Registration Rates (1965 vs. 1988)

	March 1965			November 1988		
	Black	White	Gap	Black	White	Gap
Alabama	19.3	69.2	49.9	68.4	75.0	6.6
Georgia	27.4	62.6	35.2	56.8	63.9	7.1
Louisiana	31.6	80.5	48.9	77.1	75.1	-2.0
Mississippi	6.7	69.9	63.2	74.2	80.5	6.3
North Carolina	46.8	96.8	50.0	58.2	65.6	7.4
South Carolina	37.3	75.7	38.4	56.7	61.8	5.1
Virginia	38.3	61.1	22.8	63.8	68.5	4.7

Twenty-three years later in Alabama, 68.4% of blacks were registered to vote and 75% of whites were registered, showing that the Voting Rights Act of 1965 had made a major impact on the number of black voters.[601]

The Fifteenth Amendment was passed in 1870 to give blacks the same voting rights as whites. However, it took ninety-five years for legislation to be passed in order to ensure those rights. For all those years, blacks had to endure many hardships just to try to live normally. Fighting against literacy tests, which discriminated against illiterate blacks, poll taxes, which took advantage of poor blacks in the south, residency requirements, gerrymandering, fraud, violence and many more tactics, blacks thought they would never truly have the right to vote even though it was given to them in the Fifteenth Amendment. Finally, the legislation that secured their rights was the Voting Rights Act of 1965, signed into law by Lyndon B. Johnson. Blacks across the United States finally got to use the right to vote without fear of being attacked or discriminated against. The increase in number of black voters shows that the Voting Rights Act of 1965 was the piece of legislation that blacks were waiting for to allow them to use their rights.

Bibliography

Americans.net. "Voting Rights Act of 1965," 1996. http://www. historicaldocuments.com/VotingRightsActof1965.htm.

Barker, Lucius J., and Twiley W. Barke Jr. Civil Liberties and the Constitution, seventh ed. Englewood Cliffs, New Jersey: Prentice Hill, 1994.

Dunn, John M. The Civil Rights Movement. San Diego, California: Lucent Books, 1998.

Keyssar, Alexander. The Right to Vote: The Contested History of Democracy in the United States. New York: Basic Books, 2000.

Meltzer, Milton. There Comes a Time. New York: Random House, 2001

"Race, Voting Rights, and Segregation: Direct Disenfranchisement," http://www.umich.edu/~lawrace/ disenfranchise1.htm.

.Rosenberg, Jonathan, and Zachary Karabell. Kennedy, Johnson, and the Quest for Justice. New York: W.W. Norton & Company, 2003.

Trueman@pavilion.co.uk. "The 1965 Voting Rights Act," May, 2005. http://www.historylearningsite.co.uk/1965_voting_rights_act. htm.

United States Department of Justice. "Introduction To Federal Voting Rights Law," March 28, 2005. http://www.usdoj.gov/crt/ voting/intro/intro_c.htm

Wormser, Richard. "The Enforcement Acts," PBS. http://www. pbs.org/wnet/jimcrow/stories_events_enforce.html

The Sixteenth Amendment

Is The
Income Tax Legal?

By

Lauren Williams

April Fifteenth is the day that income taxes are due, the day that is forever engraved into one's head. The Sixteenth Amendment created the income tax, which gives the government the right to tax the money one earns every year. The income tax is an easy way for the government to raise money as well as provide it with a constant revenue source. Most people don't realize that there is a debate over whether the income tax is constitutional or not. Over the years, there have been rulings declaring that the income tax is unconstitutional, as well as rulings declaring it constitutional. Which one is it? There are lots of theories on this. Some say the rulings are different because the Constitution needs to adapt over time.[602] This is a very controversial issue since everyone is directly affected by this amendment. Some might even go as far to say that this is the most important amendment since it plays such an important role in every life.

Many believe that the income tax was created in the United States but they would be mistaken because it has been around for hundreds of years. A form of income tax originated with the ancient people of Greece and Rome. The citizens of the communities gave payment to the government, not in money, but in a share of their crops. Later, the idea of the tax spread to the British. William Pitt was the prime minister of Britain when he created the income tax as a way to create revenue for the Napoleonic Wars. In 1799, it came into effect in order to help pay for equipment, such as weapons for the war. The income tax ranged from less than a percent to ten percent. William Pitt estimated that he would be able to raise ten million dollars. However, the tax only brought in six million dollars to the country. Britain has also had the income tax disappear and reappear in its history. The income tax lasted for three years until Henry Addington became prime minister and he abolished it during peacetime. Although the British went a year without it, it was then reintroduced and it lasted until 1816, when tensions with other countries arose. It once again appeared, for the last time, in 1842 by Robert Peel when he realized he needed a way to earn revenue for the budget. Britain was the first country to enforce the income tax under law.[603]

The reason the income tax first appeared in the United States was a need for revenue. Before the Revolutionary War, the United States earned most of the money it needed through imports and exports. When the Articles of Confederation were written in 1781, no tax system was created since the purpose was not to create a strong national government. The way the government raised revenue was by having the state governments donate money. This didn't provide the government with constant revenue, since the states were not forced to provide funds.[604]

When the Constitution was written in 1789, the founders knew they needed a way to raise revenue. The first article, eighth section says, "The Congress shall have Power To lay and collect Taxes, Duties, Imposts and Excises, to pay the Debts and provide for the common Defense and general Welfare of the United States; but all Duties, Imposts, and Excises shall be uniform throughout the United States;" [605] This gave congress the right to tax people in order to bring in revenue. The following years, the government continued to tax imports and exports, as well as various other products; however, the income tax was never presented. There are several strong words in this section. The clause states to pay for debts, as well as provide for the defense of our country. As one looks later in history, the income tax was created as a way to finance war as well as to pay debts. Whenever the income tax appeared in the United States it was to finance a war, or to solve an economic crisis.

There were two direct taxes before the Civil War began. One was in 1798, when the United States was having problems with France. A direct tax was made on houses, land and other property to the government. Direct taxes were abolished in 1802 for ten years until the War of 1812. In that year, Congress added extra taxes to raise money, although the tax was abolished in 1817, and for the next forty-four years no taxes for the federal government were collected. [606]

The first income tax appeared in the United States during the Civil War. The government was in debt, so the tax provided a way to raise money for the debt and to finance the war. It also helped to calm the citizens, especially the poor and middle class who supported the war by fighting, while the wealthy did not. The wealthy would pay others to go in their place in battle to fight. The income tax helped to get the wealthy involved in the war. The tax was three percent of incomes of people who made over eight hundred dollars a year.[607]

Congress passed the Revenue Act of 1861 which created the income tax. The act stated, "there shall be levied, collected, and paid, upon annual income of every person residing in the U.S. whether derived from any kind of property, or from any professional trade, employment, or vocation carried on in the United States or elsewhere, or from any source whatever." The tax however, didn't go into effect until 1862. President Lincoln divided the areas that the Union had into districts in order to control collection of the taxes. There was also a new office created called the Internal Revenue Service in the Treasury Department, which controlled the way the taxes were counted. People were hired to control the district collections, assure that everyone was paying his taxes, by assessing his property. The act was followed by another in 1864 which raised. the tax rate. If one made more than ten thousand dollars, the tax would be ten percent of income, five thousand to ten thousand dollars was seven point five percent, and six hundred to five thousand dollars was five percent. The act made it mandatory that people pay their taxes and, if they refused, there was a penalty. [608]

In Ulysses S Grant's first inaugural address to the nation, he discussed the debt of the United States. He stated,

"A great debt has been contracted in securing to us and our posterity the Union. The payment of this, principal and interest, as well as the return to a specie basis as soon as it can be accomplished without material detriment to the debtor class or to the country at large, must be provided for. To protect the national honor, every dollar of Government indebtedness should be paid in gold, unless otherwise expressly stipulated in the contract. Let it be understood that no repudiator of one farthing of our public debt will be trusted in public place, and it will go far toward strengthening a credit which ought to be the best in the world, and will ultimately enable us to replace the debt with bonds bearing less interest than we now pay. To this should be added a faithful collection of the revenue, a strict accountability to the Treasury for every dollar collected, and the greatest practicable retrenchment in expenditure in every department of Government."[609]

In this speech, he states reasons why the income tax needs to be exact. However, Grant's administration abolished the income tax in 1872, and went back to having exports and imports provide revenue. All tax offices were shut down and records sent to an office to be stored. [610]

Between the years of 1868 and 1881, the U.S. Supreme Court heard challenges to the constitutionality of the taxes on real estate and inheritances. Some of the cases were Pacific Insurance Company vs. Soule, Veazie Bank vs. Femno, and also Scholy vs. Rezv. One case was Springer vs. U.S. In this case, the plaintiff, William Springer, argued whether the government taxing his profit earned was legal, and whether it was a direct tax. The court decided that the direct tax could be considered a capitation tax; therefore it did not affect him. A capitation tax would be a poll tax. [611]

Resulting from the Civil War cases, there were several exceptions for deductions on taxes. Some of the exceptions were losses on real estate, interest paid, taxes on local, state, and national level, along with rent being paid. In addition to the deductions, all the salaries of officers, or payment to those in the government were free of tax. The taxes for the federal government became exempt in 1863. Justice Rodger Taney of the Supreme Court wrote a letter to the Secretary of Treasury stating that the taxation on his paycheck was unconstitutional, since it violated the doctrine of separation of power. In 1864, the law was changed so all federal salaries were exempt from taxation. [612]

During the following years, revenue was raised through other taxes. The income tax reappeared once again in 1894. This was in response to the Panic of 1893. The Panic of 1893 was caused by not having enough gold, railroads became bankrupt, and banks failing. In Grover Cleveland's second inaugural address, 1893, he discussed the income tax in a manner of disgust. He stated, "When we tear aside the delusions and misconceptions which have blinded our countrymen to their condition under vicious tariff laws, we but show them how far they have been led away from the paths of contentment and prosperity. When we proclaim that the necessity for revenue to support the Government furnishes the only justification for taxing the people, we announce a truth so plain that its denial would seem to indicate the extent to which judgment may be influenced by familiarity with perversions of the taxing power. And when we seek to reinstate the self-confidence and business enterprise of our citizens by discrediting an abject dependence upon governmental favor, we strive to stimulate those elements of American character which support the hope of American achievement." [613]Later, however, under his administration the Revenue Act of 1894 (Wilson-Gorman Tariff Act) was created. The tax called for two percent of incomes over four thousand dollars. Even though Cleveland didn't support the law, he allowed it to pass, although he did not sign it.

However, this was the shortest time the income tax appeared. One year later, in 1895, the tax was challenged in the Supreme Court. There were two hearings for the Pollock vs. Farmers' Loan and Trust Company. On March 7, 1895, the first case went before the Supreme Court. The case at the time was very big news, since the public had a huge interest in the decision. The lawyers defending the income tax were James C. Carter, Richard Olney, and Edward B. Whitney. The lawyers challenging the income tax were William D. Guthrie, Clarence Seward, George Edmunds, and Joseph Hodges Choate. Both teams had very respected and famous lawyers. The arguments were presented in front of a panel of eight judges for the first trial, and in front of nine judges in the second.[614]

The lawyers defending the income tax argued that the income tax was not a direct tax. They believed that the only criterion that the tax had to meet was its uniform applicability. In other words, the tax had to be the same everywhere and it could not change based on the location in which one lived. In addition, Congress would have to tax all people in the same bracket the same amount. Carter told the Court that this should not be a decision left to the Court to make, but one for Congress to decide. He stated, "Nothing could be more unwise and dangerous - nothing more foreign to the spirit of the Constitution - than an attempt to baffle and defeat a popular determination by a lawsuit. When the opposing forces of sixty millions of people have become arrayed in hostile political ranks upon a question which all men feel is not a question of law, but as legislation, the only path of safety is to accept the voice of the majority as final."[615] The lawyers argued a very strong case in support of the income tax.

The opposing side fought back with just as much passion. They asked the Court to destroy the legislation under the Fourteenth Amendment equal protection clause. Seward asked the Court to correct the error by looking at what the writers of the Constitution felt was a direct tax. Seward stated, "There is a tradition in the legal profession that once when a suggestion was made to Mr. Lincoln that a judicial decision settled a question, he responded with some firmness that in this country nothing was settled until it was settled right."[616] In Choate's final statement he said, "If it be true, as my learned friend said in closing, that the passions of the people are aroused on the subject, if it be true that a mighty army of sixty million citizens is likely to be incensed by this decision, it is the more vital to the future welfare of this country that this court again resolutely and courageously declare, as Marshall did, that it is has the power to set aside an act of Congress violative of the Constitution, and that it will not hesitate in executing the power, no matter what the threatened consequences of popular or populistic wrath may be."[617] With this strong speech, the lawyers concluded a five day presentation in front of the Supreme Court.

On April 8, 1895, the Supreme Court announced a six-man majority stating that the income tax was unconstitutional. The Constitution, in Article one, Section two, Clause three, states, "Representatives and direct Taxes shall be apportioned among the several States which may be included within this Union..."[618] Under Article I, section nine, clause four states "No Capitation, or other direct, Tax shall be laid, unless in Proportion to the Census or Enumeration herein before directed to be taken." [619]Under these two statements in the Constitution, the justices declared the Revenue Act of 1894 unconstitutional. The court believed the income tax to be a direct tax. It believed that the founders thought the direct tax should only be imposed during times of war or national emergencies. However, the Supreme Court did not strike down the entire law. The justices were divided four to four, leaving some parts still intact. In this ruling, they declared that all the tax statements be destroyed. The records of all the income taxes were burned, leaving the country without important records of its history.[620]

All the justices gave a short speech after the verdict was announced by Chief Justice Melville Fuller, stating their reasons for their vote. Justice Field agreed with Fuller calling the income tax unconstitutional. He said, "The present assault upon capital is but the beginning. It will be but the stepping-stone to others, larger and more sweeping, till our political contests will become a war of the poor against the rich; a war constantly growing in intensity and bitterness."[621] He gave a frightening look at what he said could be America's future. However, Justice Edward White disagreed with Fuller and Field. He believed the case should not have even been brought before the Court, saying that it violated the jurisdictional guidelines Congress made. There were very different views in the first case, which made the answer of the case questionable.

The case of Pollock vs. Farmers' Loan and Trust Company did not satisfy either side. Guthrie asked to have a rehearing on the issues that the Court left intact. However, the only way it was allowed to be retried was if the Court looked at whether it was constitutional once again. On May 6, 1895, the Court gathered once again to reevaluate the income tax. This time the Court gained another justice, Howell Jackson, who was ill, but said he would participate so there would not be another tie. Choate once again proved to be an outstanding speaker, asking the Court to vote down income tax on personal property. Choate asked the court to finish what the last court case had started. The opposing side once again tried to argue that the income tax was constitutional. Olney stated, "Unless the Court can be induced to reconsider the question, what remains of the law is hardly worth preserving."[622] They tried to persuade the justices to reconsider whether it was constitutional, since, with most of the law gone, it was "useless." Arguments ended on May eighth, lasting only three days. On May 20, 1895, the justices reported back with their decision. Fuller immediately began by reading a statement. He said, "Whenever this Court is required to pass the validity of an act of Congress as tested by the people, the duty imposed requires in its discharge the utmost deliberation and care, and invokes the deepest sense of responsibility. This is especially so when the question involves the exercise of a great governmental power."[623] He continued on by saying that this time the court found the income tax on all accounts unconstitutional. He said that he believed the writers to have thought the state governments would get their revenue by direct taxation, and the federal government would get its revenue by tariffs and by other indirect taxes. Fuller later described the court case as, "a slow and deliberate process, which gives time for mere hypothesis and opinion to exhaust themselves, and for sober second thought of every part of the country to be asserted."[624] The justices took a lot of consideration into the matter, and interpreted the case as they saw it.

One of the justices, Henry Brown, read his opinion to the Court. He stated, "If the question what is, and what is not, a direct tax, were now, for the first time, presented, I should entertain a grave doubt whether, in view of the definitions of a direct tax given by the courts and writers upon political economy during the present century, it ought not to be held to apply not only to an income tax, but to every tax the burden of which is borne, both immediately and ultimately, by the person paying it. It does not, however, follow that this is the definition had in mind by the framers o the Constitution."[625] Justice Brown along with Justice Harlan, Justice White, and Justice Jackson all voted against the Chief Justice. However, there were more votes supporting the chief justice. This was a very close vote, closer than the vote in the first trial. It shows that even the top court officials had mixed feelings on the issue. It was far from being a one-sided argument.

That was not the end of the income tax. Some politicians worked to bring back the idea. The only possible way for the income tax to be reinstated was for an amendment to be created to override the Pollock case. Between 1895 and 1909, there were thirty-three income amendments proposed in congress, each of which was destroyed by special interest groups. The main leaders who pushed for the income tax were Woodrow Wilson, William Jennings Bryan, William Taft, and Theodore Roosevelt. Theodore Roosevelt was a big advocate for the income tax and urged other Congressmen to endorse it. In a speech to Congress he said, "When our tax laws are revised the question of an income tax and an inheritance tax should receive the careful attention of our legislators. In my judgment both of these taxes should be part of our system of Federal taxation. I speak diffidently about the income tax because one scheme for an income tax was declared unconstitutional by the Supreme Court; while in addition it is a difficult tax to administer in its practical working, and great care would have to be exercised to see that it was not evaded by the very men whom it was most desirable to have taxed, for if so evaded it would, of course, be worse than no tax at all; as the least desirable of all taxes is the tax which bears heavily upon the honest as compared with the dishonest man. Nevertheless, a graduated income tax of the proper type would be a desirable feature of Federal taxation, and it is to be hoped that one may be devised which the Supreme Court will declare constitutional."[626] They worked hard to push the bill in Congress as well as to outside groups.

When the tax was first proposed, Taft was president, although it wasn't passed until Wilson became president. Taft was picked by Roosevelt to be his successor, so the work of the income tax would continue. However, Taft supported the idea of a corporate tax, rather than an income tax, since it was less controversial. Later, Taft said that he would support an amendment which would create an income tax. President Wilson worked very hard in campaigning for the tax. He went around to special interest groups in order to get the amendment passed. Wilson happened to be a great admirer of the British Parliament, which may have contributed to his efforts in creating the income tax.

Senator Norris Brown of Nebraska presented the income tax amendment. The words were revised later by the Finance Committee.

The sixteenth amendment states, "The Congress shall have the power to lay and collect taxes on incomes, from whatever source derived, without apportionment among the several states, and without regard to any census or enumeration."[627] Senator Kay Bailey of Texas, suggested that the amendment be approved by the state conventions, instead of the legislatures; however, that idea was defeated. Getting the amendment passed did not cause a problem. The income tax was passed in the senate with a vote of 77 to 0. In the House of Representatives, it passed with a vote of 318 to 14. The amendment was ratified on February 3, 1913.

Even after the Sixteenth Amendment was ratified that didn't stop people from challenging it. In 1916, in Brushaber vs. Union Pacific Railroad, the constitutionality of the income tax was once again challenged. Frank Brushaber went to the Supreme Court calling it a direct tax and the Supreme Court stated that the amendment prevented it from being called a direct tax. The Supreme Court ruled it to be an indirect tax. There have been many more cases that have been presented in front of the Supreme Court, all holding that amendment as constitutional.[628]

The argument that the Sixteenth Amendment is not constitutional is not the only argument. There are also people who believe that the Sixteenth Amendment was never properly ratified. People have lots of different theories on this topic. Some look at the details, such as what letters are capitalized, the spelling, along with the punctuation of the bills that ratified it in the different states. Some claim that Ohio was not a state at the time, and Ohio helped to ratify the amendment. One of the last arguments is that it implies the power for the income tax, but does not directly give the power.[629]

In 1909, the Sixteenth Amendment was sent to the state legislatures to be ratified. For the amendment to be ratified, three-fourths of the forty-eight (only 48 states existed at that time) had to ratify the amendment. It took until 1913 for the required number of states to ratify it. Secretary Philander Knox received thirty-eight responses ratifying the amendment, along with four responses not approving it. The remaining six did not respond. According to some people, they believe that only twenty states properly validated the

Sixteenth Amendment, therefore leaving it far short of the three-fourths requirement.[630]

One case that appeared before the Seventh Circuit Court of Appeals was U.S. vs. Thomas. This case argued whether the Sixteenth Amendment was ever ratified. The court said,

"Thomas insists that because the states did not approve exactly the same text, the amendment did not go into effect Secretary Knox considered this argument. The Solicitor of the Department of State drew up a list of the errors in the instruments and-taking into account both the triviality of the deviations and the treatment of earlier amendments that had experienced more substantial problems - advised Secretary that he was authorized to declare the amendment adopted. The Secretary did so.....Secretary Knox declared that enough states had ratified the Sixteenth Amendment. The Secretary's decision is not transparently defective. We need not decide when, if ever, such a decision may be reviewed in order to know that Secretary Knox's decision is now beyond review."[631]This made it clear that if any court case came up declaring that the amendment was never ratified it would be thrown out. The court cases are seen as trivial, and are thrown out. In addition to the arguments of the constitutionality of the Sixteenth Amendment, there have also been cases determining what income can be taxed. In 1926, Collector Bowers v. Kerbaugh-Empire Co. went before the Supreme Court for a ruling on what income could be taxed. At this point, it was not a question of the legality of the tax itself but what kind of income can be taxed that doesn't count as a direct tax. Justice Pierce Butler states,

"(It) was not the purpose or the effect of that amendment to bring any new subject within the taxing power. Congress already had the power to tax all incomes. But taxes on incomes from some sources had been held to be "direct taxes" within the meaning of the constitutional requirement as to apportionment. The Amendment relieved from that requirement and obliterated the distinction in that respect between taxes on income that are direct taxes and those that are not, and so put on the same basis all incomes "from whatever source derived". "Income" has been taken to mean the same thing as used in the Corporation Excise Tax of 1909 (36 Stat. 112), in the Sixteenth Amendment, and in the various revenue acts subsequently passed. After full consideration, this court declared that income may be defined as gain derived from capital, from labor, or from both combined, including profit gained through sale or conversion of capital."[632] Justice Pierce Butler stated very clearly that income from labor, capital, or profit can be taxed.

Another court case was Commissioner vs. Glenshaw Glass Co. in 1955. This was another court case which helped to define income. The definition the court gave was that taxes can be levied on "accessions to wealth, clearly realized, and over which the taxpayers have complete dominion."[633] This states that wages, benefits, bonuses are all under income. The only exceptions would be those made by Congress.

The income tax can be seen as a great addition to our government. The income tax allows the government to continue running, by providing it with a constant revenue. The income tax also helps to keep the American people involved in their government. Since everyone is directly affected by the income tax, people pay more attention to what the government does with the money. As a result, people become more active with the government, truly creating a government by the people.

The income tax has created a lot of controversy in the United Sates over the years. There have been debates on whether it was ever ratified, if it is constitutional, as well as what the government has the right to tax. There have been hundreds of court cases involving the income tax, all with very different outcomes. However, past cases have helped to set a precedent for cases today. Even chief officials in the government as well as the highest law officials have very different ideas on the subject. It makes it very hard to say one view is right and the other view is wrong. There has never been a clear cut decision on the income tax. The legislature even had to go above the courts in order to create the tax. They had to create an amendment to the constitution with which the courts could not argue. The question still remains, is the income tax legal or not? The only people who know exactly what the direct tax meant are our Founding Fathers. As Abraham Lincoln once said, "We the people are the rightful masters, both of Congress and the Courts, not to overthrow the Constitution, but to overthrow the men who pervert the Constitution."[33] This will be a fight in society for years and years to come. The question is which side is right?

Prohibition - Morality by Law?

By
Katherine Stone

The Eighteenth Amendment had its antecedents in a broad Progressive movement whose members believed that religion and government could improve mankind. The Eighteenth Amendment and its successor, the Volstead Act, prohibited the manufacture, sale, and transportation of liquor. The Progressive Movement evolved in the late 1800s and early 1900s, when many reforms began taking place to ameliorate abuse in various aspects of America life.

Americans for whom faith was a major part of their lives generally believed that alcohol had a deleterious effect on families and communities. Those who supported prohibition efforts came to be known as "dries," and those opposed to the efforts became known as "wets." American society had gone through a period of laissez-faire and progressives argued that a correction was needed in social and economic policy. Prohibition was one reform in this broad effort to improve Americans.

Even before the Progressive Movement, some people had been uncertain about the presence of alcohol in their society. The idea of the Temperance Movement was created in Ireland in the early 1800s, and later moved to Scotland and Britain. The first temperance societies in the United States appeared in New York in 1808, and were followed by movements in Massachusetts in 1813. By the 1830s, there were more than 6,000 temperance groups.[634]

One of the first movements for prohibition in the United States was the Women's Christian Temperance Union. This group's antecedents rested in the British temperance societies, and the WCTU quickly became popular in the Midwest. The Union undertook the arduous task of attempting to start a large-scale prohibition movement.

The Prohibition movement had been dominated by states and localities from its earliest years, long before the amendment was passed in 1917. In 1697, New York passed a law stating that saloons must close on Sundays. In 1735, Georgia passed a statewide prohibition law. This attempt at statewide prohibition failed and was abandoned in 1742.

There was a belief among certain people of faith that the use of alcohol was not conducive to the Christian life. The Women's Christian Temperance Union, and later the Anti-Saloon League, grew out of this understanding. The WCTU believed that alcohol was a bad influence on families and, therefore, a bad influence on women. Frances E. Willard, arguably the leading anti-alcohol crusader in the late 1800s, campaigned with the motto "Agitate, Educate, Legislate," and used the white ribbon to symbolize purity.[635]

The Temperance Movement encouraged moderation in consumption of liquors or even abstinence. From the beginning, the Temperance Movement supported a number of causes relating to the welfare of women and children, such as women's suffrage, equal pay, birth control, child labor reform, an eight-hour workday, and environmental conservation. Supporters of this group were mostly women (and their children) who had suffered at the hands of drunken husbands. They blamed alcohol for society's difficulties, health problems, destitution, and crimes. They fought against drug traffic, the use of alcohol, tobacco, drugs, white slavery, child labor, and army brothels. Liberals and conservatives both supported Temperance causes at different times in the country's history.[636]

The Temperance Movement supported local and state governmental action. The WCTU felt that by dominating the local governments, the nation would turn dry. Thus, in 1851, Maine proposed a statewide prohibition that succeeded. It was such a success that, by 1855, twelve additional states became dry. By 1900, more than half of America was dry.[637]

Prohibition laws passed by Maine and the states that followed had a rather large loophole; the federal government, not the state, ran the postal service. This meant that liquor could be mailed from state to state, or liquor could be shipped from a wet state to a dry state. To solve this problem, the Wilson Original Packages Act was passed in 1890. This Act made it illegal to send liquor to any dry state. However, punishment was not enforced and shippers disregarded the law. In 1913, the Interstate Liquor Act was passed, which attempted to reinforce the Packages Act. The Interstate Liquor

Act also failed to include government enforcing and had the same results. Finally, in 1917, the Reed Amendment was passed, which provided for a $1,000 fine for transporting liquor into a dry state.[638] All of these efforts were based on the idea that states and localities should be protected if they wanted to become dry. The creation of a truly national prohibitionist policy, however, required a much more muscular political effort.

Founded in Cleveland, Ohio in November of 1874, the Women's Christian Temperance Union geographically and economically appealed largely to the middle two-thirds of the country from the Appalachians westward. The Union began with two hundred women from seventeen states. Dr. Dio Lewis, who lectured them on the importance of non-violent protests, inspired them.[639] Such protests occurred in Fredonia, New York and Hillsboro and Washington Court House, Ohio, where the women prayed while kneeling in front of saloons. These acts succeeded in getting two hundred and fifty communities to outlaw liquor in only three months.[640]

The WCTU was in the vanguard of the women's rights movement, which started by supporting the banning of alcohol. Other chapters soon broadened their views to include tobacco, drugs, and unfair labor practices as the enemy of women and children. Many local organizations in the WCTU supported a host of economic and social reforms, including the protection of women and children at home and work, women's right to vote, shelters for abused women and children, the eight-hour work day, equal pay for equal work, the founding of kindergartens, assistance in founding the PTA, federal aid for education, stiffer penalties for sexual crimes against girls and women, uniform marriage and divorce laws, dress reform, travelers' aid, prison reform and police matrons, women police officers, homes and education for wayward girls, promotion of nutrition, pure food and drug act, legal aid, labor's right to organize, passive demonstrations and world peace.[641] Of all these causes, the campaign against alcohol had the broadest appeal to women. Alcohol played a key role in many of the abuses against women and children, and many women agreed that prohibition of alcohol would be the best place to start.

The WCTU found one technique of truly lasting significance: they preached to many public schools about the dangers of alcohol.[642] Thirty years later, a new political mindset emerged in the generation that had been lectured so successfully by the WCTU and its associates.

From the beginning, the WCTU members had a less altruistic impetus for the anti-alcohol movement which including being anti-immigrant as well. One of their earlier mottoes was "For God, for Home, and Native Land." Although they later changed the words "Native Land" to "Every Land," the WCTU clearly had a commonality with the Nativist desires. The Nativists were anti-immigrant in the sense that they were against immigrants who were not like them. Many immigrants of the time were from southern and eastern Europe, where alcohol was a common part of their culture. They were typically characterized as owning saloons and, therefore, spreading immorality through drinking.

The WCTU's focus on local and state government action had accomplished much, but some politicians viewed Prohibition as a cause for national action. Prohibition became an issue in the 1884 presidential campaign between Republican James Gillespie Blaine and Democrat Grover Cleveland. Blaine had an impressive political resume but it had not featured Prohibition. He was born in West Brownsville, Pennsylvania, and was graduated from Washington College (now known as Washington and Jefferson) in 1847. In 1859, he became a Republican representative in the Maine legislature. In 1863, he was elected to Congress, and soon became Speaker of the House.

In 1876, he was elected to the Senate, and supported "hard money programs and protective tariffs." He failed to win the upcoming election due to his involvement with the railroad scandal. Instead, he supported James A. Garfield in the election of 1880, and became Secretary of State. After Garfield's assassination, Blaine resigned.[643]

During his 1884 campaign against democrat Grover Cleveland, Blaine came to New York State looking for votes in that very close race. His campaign manager decided to highlight his support for Prohibition in a speech delivered to New York. The reaction against Blaine was so fierce it crippled his campaign. Irish and German-

Americans, and others who felt maligned, reacted loudly to Blaine's support of Prohibition and turned out to vote for Grover Cleveland. Clearly, while some politicians believed Prohibition was a national issue, its time on the national stage had not yet arrived.

Conservative Christians who held anti-drug and anti-communist views founded the Prohibition Party in 1869. This party is the third oldest political party in America. John Bidwell, who was the party's presidential nominee in 1892, received a total of 273,000 votes (2.3%), and came in fourth place. This was the best year for the party in any political race. Earl F. Dodge was the party's presidential nominee in 1984, 1988, 1992, 1996, 2000, and 2004. The year 2000 was the worst for the party, receiving only 208 votes.[644]

Members of the Prohibition Party did more than just run for president. Other Prohibition Party politicians include Sidney Catts, the governor of Florida in 1916, Kittel Halverson of Minnesota, a member of Congress in 1890, and Charles Randall of California, also a member of Congress in 1914, 1916, and 1918. Reverend Robert P. Shuler ran for Senator in California in 1932, and succeeded in receiving 560,088 votes, or 25.8%.[645] None of the politicians who saw Prohibition as a national issue were able to move the prohibition campaign to the federal level until 1913.

The WCTU's early anti-immigrant tendencies and Blaine's blunder showed that immigration was an important aspect of the issue. Many of the new immigrants settled in the growing cities and congregated in neighborhoods served by saloons. At the same time, many farmers were migrating towards cities, causing further conflict. The emigrants from rural America were not like the new immigrants from other lands. Their rural roots emphasized a dry, white, non-Roman Catholic society. Conflict was inevitable. Into this situation stepped the Anti-Saloon League.

Soon, America realized that the state and local forces were not impacting the national government strongly enough. The Anti-Saloon League believed that the Women's Christian Temperance Union was not being aggressive enough in its actions and stepped up the action, beginning non-violent protests.

Founded in 1893 in Ohio by Dr Howard Russell, a Protestant clergyman, the Anti-Saloon League campaigned vigorously, and sometimes violently, against the sale of alcoholic beverages. Its main goal was to end liquor traffic by destroying saloons, thereby cutting off the resources for the sale and distribution of alcohol. The Anti-Saloon League's early efforts focused on helping dry localities keep alcohol out. They built on the Wilson Original Packages Act of 1890, which prohibited the importation of alcoholic beverages into dry areas, by authoring the Webb-Kenyon Bill (passed on March 1, 1913). Webb-Kenyon reinforced the Packages Act, but still lacked penalties for violation.

Dr. Russell's efforts coincided with the activities of Carry Amelia Nation, who was arguably one of the most active members of the Anti-Saloon League. She was born on November 25, 1846, to George Moore and Mary Campbell in Gerrard County, Kentucky. She grew up reading and living off of the words of the Bible. In 1867, she married Charles Gloyd in Belton, Missouri. He was a heavy drinker, and their child Charlien was born sick. Soon after, she left her husband because of his drinking problem and his inability to bring in a steady income. In 1877, she married David Nation. After the wedding, they moved to Texas and, in 1889, to Medicine Lodge, Kansas. David became pastor of the Christian Church, and Carry taught Sunday school. In 1880, Kansas had voted for statewide prohibition, and Carry felt it would be a safer place to live. However, the saloons ignored the law.

Carry soon joined the Women's Christian Temperance Union; her chapter was anti-drinking and tobacco, and pro women's rights, especially modest dress. Carry claimed she had visions, and felt a sense of divine protection. This belief appeared to be true when a devastating town fire in 1889 destroyed everything except her home.

As an active WCTU member, she prayed in front of the saloons starting in 1890. On June 1, 1900, she used rocks and bricks to attack saloons for the first time. Soon, the hatchet became her weapon of choice. With her change from non-violent to violent protests, she succeeded in closing all the saloons in Medicine Lodge.

In 1901, she divorced David who died two years later. She bought land in Eureka Springs, Arkansas, and a farm named Hatchet Hall, hoping it would become a school of prohibition.

Carry continued her protests and traveled to many towns where alcohol was legal. She was jailed numerous times for "disorderly conduct" and "disturbing the peace," and the government began fining the sale of hatchets.

Besides the hatchet and her violent protesting, Carry was also a very effective spokesperson, and went on speaking tours through 1920. In January of 1921, while giving her last speech, she fell to the floor. She died in June of that year, and was buried in Belton, Kansas.[646]

Members of the middle class, rural residents, and Protestants of northern European ancestry, as well as various church and temperance societies supported Carry Nation's Anti-Saloon League. Even John D. Rockefeller is recognized for donating over $350,000 to the League.

At the beginning of World War I, the Anti-Saloon League suddenly changed into a powerful anti-immigrant (anti-German) pre-war party that portrayed alcohol as a symbol of all evil in the world. The League believed that if their country were to preserve European Protestants and the nation, the saloons must be abolished. They accused the saloons of "annually sending thousands of our youths to destruction, for corrupting politics, dissipating workmen's wages, leading astray 60,000 girls each year into lives of immorality, and banishing children from school" and the saloon owner as "a profiteer who feasted on death and enslavement."[647]

In 1913, the League altered its goal from local to national prohibition. On December 10, 1913, 4,000 protesters marched down Pennsylvania Avenue singing temperance songs. They congregated at the steps of the Capital, and were met by Congressman Richard Hobson of Alabama, and Senator Morris Sheppard of Texas. The leader of the march, League Superintendent Purley Baker, gave both copies of the proposed 18th Amendment.

Wayne Wheeler, at one point, was the legislative lawyer of the League. It was his idea to "send letters, telegrams, and petitions to Congressmen and Senators in Washington,"[648] to support national action. These efforts in 1914 led to the "Dries" gaining seats in the 1914 Congressional elections.

In addition to social policy, the entry of America into World War I also greatly helped the cause of prohibition. Woodrow Wilson had not campaigned as a prohibitionist candidate in when first elected in 1912 and the cause was never featured in his successful campaign for re-election in 1916. However, Wilson did favor American involvement in the Great War that had raged in Europe since August, 1914. The vast core of the nation from the Appalachians to the Rockies was not pro-war, and Wilson needed some wartime hysteria against all things foreign. When the war abroad broke out, many people at home felt threatened by German-Americans. Ironically, most of the brewers supported this rationale. Many people began to suspect that bars were connected with spying for their home country, or for selling pure Americans poisoned beer. "Dries," thus, argued that beer was now un-American, and the Anti-Saloon League portrayed prohibition as an act of patriotism.[649] This anti-foreign sentiment, which harkened back to the earlier Nativist sentiments of the WCTU, provided a subtle but clear link between the argument of the "Dries" and support for the War. "Prohibitionist propaganda characterized the liquor industry as foreign-controlled and pointed out that German-Americans owned and managed many of the nation's breweries."[650] Wayne Wheeler was an early twentieth-century version of a "spin doctor" whom politicians of a later time employed. Wheeler spun the war effort as a war against one evil: "Kaiserism abroad and booze at home must go."[651]

Further impetus for a nationalized prohibition policy appeared in the centralization of government power that was characteristic of wartime governmental action. At the direction of the Wilson Administration, "...the federal government took over railroads and factories, passed a conscription act, and curtailed liberty and free speech. As an outgrowth of this centralization of power in Washington, D.C, many Americans increasingly viewed the federal government as the upholder of American morality, temperance, and sobriety. In their minds, the federal government should limit individual freedoms for the sake of higher social responsibilities."[652]

The "Wets," however, argued that prohibition was not fair. They claimed that the men were away fighting the war and that the woman voted prohibition into law while the men were away. The "Dries" shot back that elections were held months before the men left, and that women did not yet have the right to vote.

The "Dries" main argument was that a key ingredient in beer was grain. The more beer made, the less grain there was for Americans and soldiers to eat. The brewers, and Germans, were accused of using raw materials and laborers who could be used in the war efforts.[653]

It was not until 1917 that the Eighteenth Amendment banned the manufacture, sale, or transportation of beverages with an alcohol content of 80 proof (40%) or higher. The amendment was passed by Congress in 1917, and sent to the states for ratification. Mississippi was the first state to sign on January 8, 1918, and Nebraska the last on January 16, 1919.[654] Many Americans supported the amendment because it did not eliminate the glass of wine or bottle of beer with dinner.

However, supporters of Prohibition were not satisfied with the terms of the amendment, because it did not ban all alcohol. They decided to draft more restrictive legislation. The National Prohibition Act was crafted by Wheeler, and sponsored by Andrew Volstead.[655]

Soon after the end of World War I, a powerful political man emerged. Andrew Volstead was arguably a bridge between the state and local efforts, and a national prohibition policy.

Andrew Volstead was a prohibitionist and protestant Midwesterner of northern European ancestry. Representing Minnesota's Seventh District, Volstead understood that his constituency regarded alcohol as something of a national menace.

He was born in Kenyon, Minnesota on October 31, 1860, to Norwegian immigrants. He attended school at Decorah Institute, Iowa. After graduating, he became the city attorney and, later mayor, in Granite Falls, Minnesota, in 1886 through 1902. In 1903, he became a Republican member of Congress. He was against lynching.

In 1922, he failed to win his congressional election, so he returned to Minnesota and worked as a lawyer. He died in Granite Falls, Minnesota on January 20, 1947.[656]

During his twenty-one years as a Congressman, Volstead introduced the most effective Act of National Prohibition. In October of 1919, the Volstead Act passed over President Wilson's veto and took effect on January 20, 1920. The act banned all alcohol with ½% alcohol content (all alcohol, except some non-alcoholic beverages). Those who agreed to the Eighteenth Amendment because it did not rid them of their glass of wine, felt betrayed. Veterans of World War I were also upset because, abroad, liquor was a part of their everyday routine.[657]

There was a rather large loophole in the Volstead Act, which affected the Church and medical practices. Alcoholic beverages were allowed for medical and sacramental use. It was not illegal for the Catholic Church to serve real wine during mass. Doctors were recorded in 1928 to have prescribed over $40 million for whiskey.[658]

Another loophole was that Section 29 of the Volstead Act allowed for home production of fermented fruit juices (wine). This made winemakers very happy, and it quite possibly saved the vinegar and California grape industries. Winemakers even made a grape jelly that would turn to wine, after adding water and letting it stand for two months. Selling wine to churches also saved many wineries. Between 1922 and 1924, the demand by churches of wine increased by 800,000 gallons.[659]

The purpose of Prohibition, the elimination of drinking, fell far short of reaching its goal. The failure was due in part to the loopholes in the law: religious and medical exceptions, fermented juices and home brewing, and the inverse relationship between the Prohibition goal and the desires of many Americans. As Prohibition laws became more commonplace, the availability of alcohol decreased. When Prohibition laws were adopted nationally and alcohol had become illegal, the demand remained the same, if not grew stronger.

The effect of prohibition on the "Wet" community was astronomical. While the availability of alcohol was low, the demand skyrocketed. Illegal drinking rose to 22.8 gallons a person per year, which was five times greater than in 1850. Not only did the consumption rate increase, but the number of people drinking also rose.[660] Making and selling alcohol became a very lucrative hobby.

A moonshiner is a nickname for one who distilled alcohol illegally. Their homemade stills were often located in their barns or basements, or even backyard forests.

Because there were not any Pure Food and Drug regulations on the production of alcohol, there were many safety concerns. With the often unknown additions of lye, rubbing alcohol, wood alcohol, paint thinner, bleach, formaldehyde, embalming fluid, chemical fertilizers, and manure,[661] there were many reported cases of blindness and neurological damage, or paralysis.

Bootleggers were the ones daring enough to actually import and sell the alcohol. Because alcohol was so rare and the demand for it so high, prices rose dramatically. The price of beer rose 700%, brandy 433%, and spirits 270%, and the overall potency rose by 150% during Prohibition.

The effects of alcohol hit the drinkers hard. At the beginning of the prohibition period (1920), there were 1,064 deaths from alcohol poisoning. By 1925, there were 4,154 deaths from alcohol poisoning and the homicide rate increased by 5.6%. This murder figure could be linked to the 78% increase in general crime. The competition for profits from selling alcohol became the beginning of organized crime.[662]

Chicago was the center of crime and violence at this time, and Al Capone is most commonly associated with gangsterism. Alphonse Capone was born in Brooklyn, New York, in 1899. Johnny Torrio recruited him at age 22 to get customers for Torrio's bootleg business. After 3 years, Capone took over Torrio's business, and had 161 chapters. However, Capone's business was different from his competitors in the respect that he killed competitors.

The start of gang rivalry began in 1926, with the murder of Chicago's main provider of alcohol, Dion O'Banion. Shortly after, eight cars went to Capone's "headquarters" and the occupants of the cars shot at everything with machine guns. This event led to many more gang shootings, which resulted in a total of more than 500 gangsters being killed in Chicago.

Capone's most notorious attack on one of his competitors is known as the St. Valentine's Day Massacre, which occurred on Valentines' Day in 1929. Capone's men dressed as policemen and claimed to be raiding Bugs Moran "headquarters". After lining six of the leading members against a wall, Capone's men shot them all.

Capone is known for having profited hugely from his illegal acts. He earned over sixty million dollars from illegal sales of alcohol, twenty five million from gambling, ten million from vice, and another ten million from miscellaneous investments. He did not hide his wealth, and once even stated, "I make my money by supplying a public demand. If I break the law, my customers who number hundreds of the best people in Chicago, are as guilty as I am. The only difference is that I sell and they buy. Everybody calls me a racketeer. I call myself a businessman."[663]

Capone was eventually jailed in 1928 for eleven years, but on grounds of tax evasion, not murder. In 1939, he was released, but the prohibition period had ended and his illegal services were no longer needed. He died in 1947, twenty-eight years after the Eighteenth Amendment was enacted.

The amendment was brought about by a series of broad trends that came together in the late 19th century and early 20th century. The conservative religious churchgoers believed that alcohol was the root of all evil and the social reformers' believed that alcohol damaged society by harming the most vulnerable. Both of these beliefs were compounded by a sense that the ill effects of alcohol were being imported into the country by immigrants who did not understand the American culture and society. Politicians brought these attitudes together and various organized groups found new ways to exert pressure on the political system. They were aided by World War I, which focused on anti-immigrant tendencies, and the belief in the inherent superiority of the American culture on this issue.

Those in support of the Eighteenth Amendment, the religious conservatives, and those who profited from the amendment, the gangsters, bootleggers, and moonshiners, were at direct odds. The gangsters epitomized everything that a good religious conservative was against: drugs, violence, murder, alcohol, gambling, etc. Although the vast majority of Americans were against those illegal offences, they did not consider alcohol to be a criminal act. For any law to be effective, it cannot offend the majority of the people.

The Twenty-first Amendment was passed by Congress on February 20, 1933, and ratified by the states by December 5 of the same year, fourteen years after the original ratification of the Eighteenth Amendment. The Twenty-first Amendment allowed citizens to transport or import intoxicating liquors into any state, territory, or possession of the United States. Thus, the conservative religious groups and World War I served to catapult the government into passing the Eighteenth Amendment on Prohibition, but organized crime and the desires of a majority of the American adult population to have the freedom to consume alcohol, led to its repeal in the form of the Twenty-first Amendment.

Bibliography

Adams, Cecil. 2001. What did the Catholic Church use for altar wine during Prohibition? Straight Dope Science Advisory Board. http://www.straightdope.com/mailbag/maltarwine.html. October 5, 2005.

Andrew, David, Evan, and Gary. Last updated 2005. Prohibition Laws. http://library.thinkquest.org/04oct/00492/Prohibition_Laws. htm. September 25, 2005.

Chernoff, Eric. Manning, Michael. Smith, Sarah. Moonshining and Prohibition. http://www.ibiblio.org/moonshine/sell/prohibition. html. September 25, 2005.

Encyclopedia Britannica, Inc.1999. Temperance Movement. http://search.eb.com/women/articles/temperance_movement.html. October 2, 2005.

Gunzburger, Ron. 2004. Prohibition Party. Directory of U.S. Political Parties. http://www.politics1.com/parties.htm. September 25, 2005.

Jankowski, Ben. 1994. The Making of Prohibition - Part I: The History of Political and Social Forces at Work for Prohibition in America. Brewing Techniques, November/December. http://www. brewingtechniques.com/library/backissues/issue2.6/jankowski. html. October 5, 2005.

Minnesota Historical Society. 2005. Prohibition and the Volstead Act. Minnesota Historical Society. http://www.mnhs.org/library/ tips/history_topics/103prohibition.html. September 25, 2005.

Online Highways. 2005. James G. Blaine 1830-1893. http://www. u-s-history.com/pages/h726.html. October 1, 2005.

Online Highways. 2005. The Temperance Movement. http://www. u-s-history.com/pages/h1054.html. October 2, 2005.

Online Highways. 2005. The Temperance Movement: Carry A. Nation 1846-1911. http://www.u-s-history.com/pages/h1058.html. October 1, 2005.

Prohibition Party History. http://www.prohibitionists.org/History/ history.html. September 25, 2005.

Schaffer, Clifford A. History of Alcohol Prohibition. Schaffer Library of Drug Policy. http://www.druglibrary.org/schaffer/ LIBRARY/studies/nc/nc2a.htm. October 5, 2005.

Spartacus Educational. Last updated 2005. Al Capone. http://www. spartacus.schoolnet.co.uk?USAcapone.htm. September 20, 2005.

Spartacus Educational. Last updated 2005. Anti-Saloon League. http://www.spartacus.schoolnet.co.uk/USAsaloon.htm. October 5, 2005.

Spartacus Educational. Last updated 2005. Volstead Act. http:// www.spartacus.schoolnet.co.uk?USAvolstead.htm. September 20, 2005.

Thornton, Mark. 2005. Alcohol Prohibition was a Failure. CATO Institute. http://www.cato.org/pubs/pas/pa-157.html. September 27, 2005.

Weinhardt, Beth. 2005. History of the Anti-Saloon League 1893-1933. http://www.wpl.lib.oh.us/AntiSaloon/history/. September 27, 2005.

Women's Christian Temperance Union. 2005. Women's Christian Temperance Union: Early History. http://womenshistory.about.

com/gi/dynamic/offsite.htm?zi=1/XJ&snd=womenshitory&zu-http%3A%2F%2Fwww.wctu.org%2Fearlyhistory.html. September 29, 2005.

Wow Essays. Prohibition: The Power is in the People. 2004. http://www.wowessays.com/dbase/aa2/1pf260.shtml. October 7, 2005.

Zimmerman, Woody. 2003. When the Dream Becomes a Nightmare: Reliving Prohibition. Atlantic Highland Herald, October 30. http://www.ahherald.com/atlarge/2003/031030_prohibition.html. September 25, 2005.

Zywocinski, Joan Rapczynski Florence. 2005. Prohibition as a Reform. Yale-New Haven Teachers Institute. http://www.yale.edu/ynhti/curriculum/units/1978/3/78.03.03.x.html. September 25, 2005.

The Twenty-third Amendment
And Statehood
For the
District of Columbia
By
Diana Burk

More than two hundred years ago, in 1791, the Founding Fathers first proposed an idea to create a "Federal District[664] to be the center of national governmental proceedings and consist of citizens once living in Maryland and Virginia. Since the district's creation, citizens of this district, denied their right to vote due to various legislative acts of Congress, have unearthed the buried battle cry "No Taxation without Representation," and petitioned Congress in an effort to be recognized as legal voters. Finally, in 1812, Congress allowed D.C. residents to elect their own local government but the citizens of Washington D.C. wanted more. They pushed until the Twenty-third Amendment was passed in 1961, giving D.C. residents the right to vote in national elections and allowing them to choose nonvoting Electoral College members (fixed at 3). D.C. residents are now using this amendment as a stepping-stone, claiming they deserve the same rights as state residents, and that D.C. should become a state. But how could the national government possibly recognize D.C. as a state when this would not only cause massive fiscal federal coordination problems and drastically complicate the lives of many working Americans but would throw Congressional balance into a tailspin?

The argument for D.C. rights has traces much older than the Twenty-third Amendment that are important to understanding why the "D.C. Statehood Green Party", a conglomeration of the D.C. statehood party founded by civil rights activists in 1970 and the Green Party, is so adamant about Washington D.C. becoming the fifty-first state of the United States. [665] The Founding Fathers debated the structure of the original federal district, which consisted of five separate provinces, Washington City, Georgetown, Washington

County in Maryland, and Alexandria and the county of Arlington in Virginia. One bill gave residents no self-government and left legislation to the national government while another option granted partial home-rule and a local legislature. In 1801, Congress passed emergency legislation dividing the District into two counties, Washington County where Maryland laws would apply, and Alexandria County where Virginia laws would apply (The Virginia part of the District was returned to Virginia in 1846).[666] The Organic Act of 1801 was the first act of D.C. "disenfranchisement" which stated that D.C. residents could not vote in the states where the district had been created.[667] In 1803, a bill was proposed to give Georgetown back to Maryland because the federal government was not utilizing it at the time. The bill failed and Georgetown and Washington later consolidated against the wishes of the citizens who lived there. In 1871, Washington residents elected their first government, which consisted of a governor and a bicameral legislature modeled after the national legislature. This first step towards state autonomy proved to be a failure as the government was corrupt and could not legislate effectively and the political infrastructure was basic and weak. Congress soon stepped in and placed the power in the hands of three presidentially appointed commissioners.[668] D.C. residents could no longer elect even their local government officials, which was the main impetus for the passage of the Twenty-third Amendment.

As originally proposed on June 17th, 1960, by Senator Kenneth Keating of New York, the Twenty-third Amendment would have granted Washington D.C. as many Congressional votes as a state with equal population and would have equal representation as any state. Congressman Emmanuel Celler of New York had to alter the amendment to secure passage by the House Judiciary Committee. Instead, D.C. would have only the same number of representatives as the least populous state and would, therefore, have a constricted number of three representatives. The representation would consist of a Delegate to the House of Representatives, who could only vote in committee and draft bills, and two non-voting Senators who could lobby and show interest in certain issues.[669] The Amendment became effective on March 29, 1961.

Following the passage of the amendment, the "District of Columbia Home Rule Act" was passed in December 1973, which increased the political sway D.C. residents had over local politics. D.C. residents were given the ability to elect a mayor and a council, the Council of the District of Columbia. Residents elected a council as well as an Advisory Neighborhood Commission in the fall of 1974. The Commissioners would represent every 2,000 residents and would advise the Council on smaller, community interests.[670] Although voters were initially satisfied with this advancement in home rule because of the seemingly hopeful wording of the document, they soon discovered the D.C. Council they had elected was still subject to the approval of Congress. A Segment of the Home Rule Act stated,

> "....Subject to the retention by Congress of the ultimate legislative authority over the nation's capital granted by Article I, Section 8, of the Constitution, the intent of Congress is to delegate certain legislative powers to the government of the District of Columbia; authorize the election of certain local officials by the registered qualified electors in the District of Columbia; grant to the inhabitants of the District of Columbia powers of local self-government; modernize, reorganize, and otherwise improve the governmental structure of the District of Columbia; and, to the greatest extent possible, consistent with the constitutional mandate, relieve Congress of the burden of legislating upon essentially local District matters." [671]

Voters were deluded by the words "grant to the inhabitants of the District of Columbia powers of local self-government," and missed the words "subject to retention by Congress." Not surprisingly, the limitations set by Congress on the District are longer and much more detailed than the powers actually granted by the act. Additionally, it is made explicitly clear that the Act is not to contradict the Constitution since the Constitution states Congress has the power, "To exercise exclusive Legislation in all Cases whatsoever, over such District (not exceeding ten Miles square)," [672] which gives the impression that the 93rd Congress believed they were almost overstepping the legislative boundary by giving D.C. such power. However, voters did not agree and have yet to cease the push towards statehood.

In 1790, when the District was first established, only about 3,000 citizens lived in the area--far less than the 50,000 required for statehood.[673] By 1975, the District population reached almost 10 times that number. [674] In 1978, Congress passed what was called the Voting Rights Amendment, which would have given the District voting representation in Congress (consisting of two senators and a congressman), had the rest of the nation not let it sit unattended past the allotted seven-year ratification period. The amendment finally died in 1985 because only sixteen states ratified the amendment, and thirty-eight were necessary for the amendment to go into effect. Had the amendment succeeded, the Twenty-third Amendment would have been repealed and the District would have been granted the full voting rights of any other state and full representation in Congress in addition to its already established members of the Electoral College during presidential elections.[675] The amendment was a monumental step forward for D.C. statehood but the fact that it sat for almost ten years waiting to be ratified signified the lack of support for D.C. statehood by other U.S. states. Undiscouraged, residents still pushed for statehood, and have yet to cease their pledge.

One of the main arguments D.C. residents attempt to make is the right of residents to vote because they pay the same local and federal taxes as other states yet they are not represented in the federal government. However, residents don't realize the state of financial turmoil the District would find itself in had the system been configured differently. According to Dennis Kucinich, member of the House Government Reform Committee, "We must provide for increased infrastructure, jobs, education, and health care spending....D.C. residents pay enough annually in federal taxes to support a state. In fact, they pay more federal taxes than several states and have per capita tax payment that is above the national average."[676] Yet, how many states have approximately fifty percent of their real estate exempt from taxation? Of course their per capita payment would be above the national average, considering residents pay for the services to run the entire District, including the public services within government owned property. The D.C. Apple seed

Center estimated a loss of $690 million in 1995, about 10% of the total yearly D.C. budget, due to the fact that all Government organizations, foreign embassies, or nonprofit organizations are exempt from taxation.[677] In effect, the current tax rates are still not high enough to pay for the services needed to run D.C. even with the additional funding from national federal taxes. Although D.C. residents dearly want their district to become a state, they do not realize supporting this feat is a financial impossibility.

Capital investment is essential to keeping any major city up-to-date, but is especially vital to the District. In 1995 and 1996, D.C. infrastructure was unsupported financially and the District plummeted into a period of intense debt. The Financial Control Board was created in 1996 after the Government Accountability Office (GAO) published a prediction of increased deficits. The District government became a mere puppet of the national government, as the Financial Control Board consisted of five members appointed by the President (Clinton, when created in 1996). The Board, which still exists today, has the ability not only to reject the city budget as proposed by the Mayor and his Council but can also impose its own spending plans and overrule various agreements and contracts that deal with finances. Almost any issue can be drawn into a financial issue, giving the board power to overrule almost any decision made by the mayor and council. Of course, Congressmen agree that the power is necessary, according to Republican representative James Walsh, chairman of the House subcommittee on the District of Columbia, "The board's power is absolute and it is absolutely necessary. This authority needs to have control." [678] The chairman claimed to speak in the best interests of D.C. finances, as the District had yet to handle its own finances responsibly without major involvement by Congress through a forced direct linkage between Congress, in the form of the Financial Control Board, and the Mayor and Council of D.C.

After the installation of the Financial Control Board, the District made a remarkable financial turnaround. In March 1998, the District reversed its debt and concluded the year with a surplus of over $1 billion.[679] The main source of surplus, however, was the federal assumption of debt. Although an easy solution to a growing problem, this act made the District even more dependent on federal financial aid. Essentially, sufficient funds were provided so the District could manage its own budget without hiking taxes; however in effect, Congress now wields a stronger influence over District finances than before. The District was left dependent on Congress for stability and could never become a state in its current financial status. [680]

Additionally, a District financial report states the nature of the surplus was not due to an improvement in local governmental proceedings but the nature of the market and federal aid, which demonstrates the inability for the District to control its own finances even while a city, let alone as a state. The National Association to Restore Pride In America's Capital presents a reflection on the numerical data supporting this fact.

"Spending from local revenue sources was modestly below expectations in government direction ($4M), in economic development ($5M); public safety ($9M); human support services ($8M); human resource development ($5M); and interest on short-term borrowing ($6M). In some cases, however, these "savings" apparently resulted from the inability of the city to consummate planned procurements--i.e., poor management rather than good management." [681]

Essentially, D.C. is not ready to be placed in the driving seat of its own budget. This can be illustrated by the recent distribution of funds by Mayor Anthony Williams, who, instead of focusing on Medicare and improvement of the dilapidated D.C. school system, has placed his efforts into buying a baseball team and creating a new stadium, forcing many residents from their homes with little means of relocating themselves. [682] Williams has claimed this is an attempt to renew a rundown portion of D.C., but cannot support his long-term plan with numerical evidence that would outweigh the benefits of direct funding for school and welfare. [683]

However, the federal government should release the District from its state of financial dependency and focus on creating a strong tax base for the district to utilize for funds. Another method by which the federal government controls the D.C. government financially is through federal payments to the district instead of creating a strong tax base. Because much of the district land is non-taxable, federal payments are made in lieu of taxes to support District programs. These federal payments place the District in a state of dependency because the District always lacks the money necessary to support its citizens. Yet the District is still not fully supported by the federal government, which means the District is constantly desperate for financial support. This financial void is due mainly to a small financial tax base because of tax cuts for the wealthy citizens.[684] A solution to this problem would be to end tax cuts on the wealthy and focus on creating a government supported directly by its own citizens. D.C. citizens would not only benefit directly from their input into their local government, but the possibility of D.C. responsibly taking charge of its own financing would finally emerge.

Yet, the full transformation of D.C. from district to state would add an immense burden to the list of problems already plaguing residents and workers in D.C. Having the third worst traffic rate in the nation, according to a study completed by the Texas Transportation Institute, local commuters spend an average of seventy hours a year sitting in traffic jams. [685] With statehood comes transformed infrastructure, more politicians, workers, more office buildings, and more cars on the roads. This would further exacerbate the traffic problem and bog down the land-locked city that is becoming increasingly crowded within the city and around its borders. Additionally, Washington D.C. is the only city that is prohibited from taxing commuters from other states. However, were the District to become a state, this law would have to be repealed in order to maintain consistency with inter-state commerce. [686] In summary, the hard working citizens of both Maryland and Virginia who commute to the District every day and already pay taxes would be forced to pay additional taxes and suffer through increased traffic and frustration.

Adding the state of New Columbia[687] as the fifty-first state of America would drastically impact the Congressional political structure. New Columbia would have the second smallest state population (of 572,000 residents), after Wyoming, which has a population of 494,423. [688] Currently in the 109th House and Senate there is a dominant Republican force. Within the House, there are 231 Republicans, 202 Democrats, and 1 Independent, all of whom are voting members of Congress. In the Senate, there are fifty five

Republicans, forty four Democrats, and one Independent. [689] The District currently has 1 non-voting representative and 2 non-voting senators, all of whom are Democrats due to the overwhelmingly large Democratic voting population within the city. Granting statehood to the District would immediately give the Democratic Party two safe seats in the Senate and one in the House of Representatives.[690] This is the basis for the Democratic D.C. Statehood Green Party effort to make D.C. a state while the Republican Party is resolved to keep D.C. from statehood. President George W. Bush plugs against every attempt by D.C.'s non-voting delegate, Democrat Eleanor Holmes Norton, to introduce legislation to create the state of New Columbia.

There is a strong partisan nature of adding direct representation of the small District of Columbia, which is why politicians attempting to maintain any sense of equality within Congress so adamantly fight the addition of these votes. Although registered as members of a political party, members of Congress do not always vote according to their party affiliation. Many decisions on environmental and public health issues are close because there are differing opinions within parties. [691] Only in the past election did Republicans regain control of the Senate in contrast to the 107th Congress, in which the Republican Party held only 49 seats. The addition of two consistently Democratic senatorial votes could affect close votes in a future Congress in which there is not a clear dominating party. [692]

In addition to affecting close decisions, the addition of two Democratic senators would transform certain committees and subcommittees. Currently, there are three "shadow" members of the senate elected by D.C. residents, meaning they have limited ability to influence congressional legislation. The current D.C. shadow senators are Paul Strauss and Ray Browne.[693] They are allowed participation in committees and subcommittees and listen to hearings, yet they cannot vote or shape decisions except through effective lobbying. By allowing them to vote, the outcome of committee decisions could be affected by the steady Democratic vote, thereby seriously affecting the main course of congressional legislation.

A recent development in gaining voting representation for the District is the re-introduction of the D.C. Fairness in Representation

Act, which would grant citizens one voting representative in Congress. Introduced by Republican Tom Davis of Virginia and chairman of the House Committee on Government Affairs, this bill would give one seat in the House to the District of Columbia, justifying it by giving the other seat to Utah. Because Utah voted strongly in support of the Republican candidate, George W. Bush in the presidential election of 2004, Davis justified political balance of the Democratic District vote with the presumed Republican representative from Utah. The expansion of the House to 437 seats would be only temporary until 2012, when the representation would be divided based on population as recorded in the 2010 Census, at which time the District would retain its one seat and the other 435 seats would be divided among the fifty states. This legislation is currently under discussion in Congress.[694]

Although these representatives reflect the opinion of thousands of Americans, if almost any large city were to be isolated from its state, the majority would be overwhelmingly Democratic.[695] This being said, the District ranked twenty-first in population according to the 2000 Census, behind Memphis, Jacksonville, San Diego, among other cities. [696] If D.C. should get its own voting representation in Congress with only 572,000 residents, why shouldn't New York City separate from the rest of New York State, as nearly 8 million people live in New York City alone? The answer is that the citizens of New York City are already represented by New York representatives and senators who, unlike District representatives, can vote.

The current status of the District is unique and, therefore, cannot be compared with any other large city and must be taken with a unique outlook. Indeed, there are many problems with the current status of the District and the micromanagement of Congress overpowering all home- rule. Many actions taken by Congress have worsened financial and social troubles among D.C. residents. For example, in 2001, Mayor Williams privatized the D.C. General Hospital under orders of the Financial Control Board. The hospital is the only full-service public health facility in the city and privatizing these services caused a major health care crisis. [697] In 1998, the D.C. electorate passed Initiative 59, which would have made medical marijuana legal in the District. Against the wishes of both the Mayor and D.C. voters, who had voted 69% in support of the bill, Congress overturned this initiative and it never passed. [698] The residents of Washington D.C. are entitled to voting representation as a right of the Constitution and are being denied this right. However there is a much more plausible and intelligent solution to this dilemma than statehood.

One solution proposed by activists of the historically weighted slogan, "No Taxation without Representation," is to exempt D.C. residents from federal taxes in place of representation. [699] This "solution" is almost comical, as it would probably cause chaos within the District within months of enactment. Rather, the effort should be made to increase the tax base. The tax base is already too small to efficiently support the District without financial aid from the federal government, and forcing the federal government to foot the entire cost of maintaining D.C. would be financially impossible and the entire District infrastructure would crumble.

Completely dissolving the federal district has been considered as well, although the impact this action would have on the federal government and its freedom from the whim of the public would be gargantuan and would transform the nature of the natural scope of politics unimaginably, as the residents and workers in D.C. would be able to force their will directly upon government officials. Local residents would then have the power to hold major protests with fewer restrictions because the District would no longer have control over the area around the federal buildings, which could possibly lead to chaos. The formation of the District is based on this notion: in 1783, when Philadelphia was the capital and the states were under the Articles of Confederation, Congress was in session when hundreds of Pennsylvania militiamen surrounded Independence Hall, demanding payment for unpaid wages from the American Revolution. Congress ordered the Pennsylvania governor to remove the soldiers but because they lacked local control over the area, the governor did not comply. Although the quarrel ended peacefully, the framers of the Constitution later decided to create a federal territory under control of the federal government, thereby keeping Congress separate from a state and in its own district.[700] Dissolving the District at its current state and returning the entire plot of land to

Maryland and Virginia would reinstate the subjectivity to unwanted infiltration by the populous.

While there are several proposed alternatives to statehood, there is one that stands above the rest in practicality and outcome. A reasonable way to allow for both representation of District residents and protection of the federal government would be to decrease the size of the District to only federal territory. Washington D.C. would be divided between federal buildings and residences. The District would only include the government owned areas not subject to taxes, such as the offices of government officials, the National Mall and non-profit organizations with offices within the District. The result? A federal enclave created for the purpose of law creation and enforcement and purposeful jurisdiction, similar in structure to a military base.

The neighborhoods would be returned to Maryland in a fashion similar to that of the city of Alexandria being returned to Virginia in the early 19th century. Beginning at that time, the national capital developed mostly on the Maryland side of the District, which was the main impetus for the return of what are now Arlington County and the city of Alexandria to Virginia.[701] A similar action is now necessary for the residents of the District who are being denied their right to federal representation because they live too close to the White House.

However, adding a section of D.C. to Maryland would affect the means by which D.C. residents were represented. Maryland's representation in Congress would increase with the increase in population caused by the addition. This would cause another seat to be taken from another state in return, because the number of seats remains constant unless there is a legislative addition of seats, which only happens when there is an increase in overall national population.[702] This is the tradeoff. D.C. residents would no longer gain direct representation, as the power of the overwhelming Democratic majority would be watered down by the other residents of Maryland. This means the political balance of congress would no longer be in jeopardy, as there would no longer be two guaranteed Democratic seats. Yet, Maryland could possibly take the vote from a republican state, thereby disrupting the nature of the congressional party system once again; however, this is unlikely. By adding Washington, the number of electoral votes of Maryland would increase by one. The District currently has three votes (Democratic) in presidential elections. The Republicans would gain electoral votes if the votes were taken from the District, as the District always votes Democratic. In the end, the Congressional balance is somewhat maintained by transferring the D.C. neighborhoods to Maryland jurisdiction.

This is also illustrated in the senate, as increasing Maryland population would have no effect on the Senate, yet D.C. residents would be fully represented by the Maryland Senators they would elect in Maryland elections. Because the ratio of the state populations of California and the District is about 70:1,[703] it is difficult to justify the reason why the District deserves its very own voting senators, when voters could be allowed to participate in the election of Maryland senators.

Renaming part of D.C. "Maryland" would also resolve the issue of commuter tax. The neighborhoods ceded to Maryland would become a represented suburbia analogous to Alexandria, Virginia. The Maryland section of the district would be renamed and labeled as a city within Maryland. Additionally, commuters would not be taxed to work within the area because it is a city within a state.

Currently, D.C. finances are poorly split between federal jurisdiction and the neighborhoods within the District, making it difficult for financial needs to be met, especially in certain areas such as public health and schooling. Physical separation of neighborhoods from federal offices will allow local officials to more accurately cater to the needs of the citizens many of whom currently live in desperate poverty. These people would pay Maryland and federal taxes and would be supported by a stronger, more effective state legislature that would exert its own power over local laws and the division of the budget. State funding would apply to the D.C. citizens in Maryland and children would benefit from in-state public school benefits and other financial assistance. Taxpayers would also see their dollars directly applied into the needs in their own communities under more effective legislation.

Finally, returning residential neighborhoods to Maryland would improve the overcrowding of suburbs adjacent to Washington D.C. In the past fifty years, D.C. has lost nearly half its population, as hundreds of thousands of residents have moved out of the District since 1950. [704] They have moved into the suburbs for many reasons, including crime, and poor school systems, (which stem from the financial deficit caused by the dependency on the federal government), but the main reason being lack of representation. A move two miles across the Potomac River is not far to gain constitutional rights denied for years. This exodus of residents results in the poorest of the poor being left behind, or those who do not have the means to move. Thus, the amount of wealth and education within the city decreases and the problems of meeting financial needs and supporting local infrastructure are intensified. By minimizing the District into a merely functional government territory, citizens will have little desire to uproot themselves when granted representation in their own home as well as the promise of support of a centralized state government.

The Twenty-third Amendment served as merely a step towards solving the problem of representing the 572,000 residents who were not considered in the original formation of the Constitution. The District was not intended to become a location of residency; as written in Article I of the Constitution; it is merely described as the core of the American government.[705]

The original framers of the Constitution misjudged the District when foreseeing it as only the federal center of the national government, as thousands of Americans now call the District their home. In order for a change in representation for the District to take place, the Twenty-third Amendment must be repealed and replaced by more intricate legislation allowing representation in Congress in addition to national elections. As it stands, the Twenty-third Amendment makes it evident that D.C. is not a state and that it does not act as a state, as it's electors are only, "… considered, for the purposes of the election of President and Vice President, to be electors appointed by a state,"[706] only equal in theory to those appointed by actual states.

Today, the D.C. Statehood Green Party continues to push adamantly for D.C. statehood. The D.C. Statehood Party was founded by civil rights activists in 1970 and merged with the D.C. Green Party in 1999 to form the D.C. Statehood Green Party after it adopted the cause for D.C. statehood as a civil rights battle.[707] The argument of the Green Party is that the majority of the non-represented D.C. residents are minorities and, therefore, this battle for statehood is not only political but racial as well. In current battles, this has tied many minority activists to the cause of D.C. statehood, aggravating the debate and uprooting passionate arguments on both sides of the issue among Congressmen and local politicians.

Because of the intricate social and political nature of the issue of D.C. statehood, many politicians in support of statehood are outspoken in their support while those against it tend to remain quieter. Gaining votes is most important to politicians and, therefore, their support or lack thereof for such a cause can make or break an election.

The question of D.C. statehood has pervaded the minds of many politicians, from the D.C. Mayor to the President of the United States. Financially, the District of Columbia could not handle supporting its residents and infrastructure as a state, as it receives much support from the national government in grants as well as management of the budget. Congressional micromanagement has caused certain problems for residents; however, these same actions have saved the District countless times from economic and structural downfall. The conversion of the District into "New Columbia," would change the lives of thousands of working Americans, for the worse. Increased traffic and financial strain would ensue and plague the already hectic lives of those who commute to D.C. each day. The implications of creating a state from the national capital would affect congressional balance intended to reflect the majority opinion of the nation as a whole.

Yet, citizens of the United States are being denied their right to representation in Congress, a right guaranteed by the U.S. Constitution, a right so robustly fought for by American colonists during the American Revolution. The District must be divided for this injustice to end. The residential neighborhoods must be rightfully returned to Maryland where they can flourish and finally become part of the nation they fund. The people within the District denied representation must be granted their right. Only then will the residents cease their migration to the suburbs surrounding the District; only then will the budget correlate to the actual needs of D.C. residents through state legislation. The District will finally be able to serve its intended purpose: to be the heart of the national government as intended by the original framers of the U.S. Constitution.

Bibliography

Davis, Tom. "Statement of Representative Tom Davis, Chairman, Committee on Government Affairs on the introduction of the DC FAIR Act." 109th Cong., May 3, 2005.

Encyclopedia of the American Constitution, 2nd ed. S.v. "Twenty-third Amendment."

Frey, William. "Census 2000 Reveals New Native-Born and Foreign-Born Shifts Across U.S." PSC Research Report. Report No. 02-520. August 2002.

Goldberg, Jonah. "Eliminate Federal Taxes for D.C. Residents." Townhall.com Columns. 20 April 2001.

Government by the People, 17th ed. S.v. "Twenty-third Amendment."

http://en.wikipedia.org/wiki/District_of_Columbia_Voting_Rights_Amendment

http://www.abfa.com/ogc/hrtall.htm

http://www.dccouncil.washington.dc.us/history.html

http://www.dcist.com

http://www.dc.gov/

http://www.dcvote.org/media/media.cfm?mediaID=167

http://www.dcvote.org/trellis/denial/argumentsforandagainst.cfm

http://www.dcvote.org/trellis/denial/
10mythsaboutthedistrictofcolumbia.cfm

http://www.dcvote.org/trellis/denial/dcvotingrightshistoricaltimelin
e.cfm

http://www.dcstatehoodgreen.org/testimony/testimony.php?annc_
id=1&section_id=1

http://www.drugpolicy.org/statebystate/washingtondc/

http://www.fairfaxcountyva.com/9/history.asp

http://www.fff.org/freedom/fd0211d.asp

http://www.gp.org/press/states/dc_2005_01_26.html

http://www.house.gov/Constitution/Constitution.html

http://www.narpac.org/BUDI.HTM#budturn

http://www.narpac.org/FOI.HTM

http://www.norton.house.gov/

http://www.opensecrets.org/politicians/candlist.
asp?Sort=N&Cong=108

http://www.prb.org/

http://www.senatordc.wdcnet.net/

http://www.themilitant.com/1995/5918/5918_23.html

http://tti.tamu.edu/

http://www.ushistory.org/presidentshouse/history/faq.htm

http://www.washingtonpeacecenter.org/articles/incomeinequality.
html

http://www.washingtonpost.com/wp-dyn/articles/A38235-
2005Mar15.html

Judis, John. "Majority Rules." The New Republic Online. 5 August
2002.

Do Young Americans Deserve The Twenty-sixth Amendment?

By
Bailey Disselkoen

It is equivalent to driving at sixteen: voting rights for young adults are being taken for granted. It is surprising to many that this amendment was ratified in a record time of 107 days, [708] but almost did not exist. Politicians strongly opposed it for various reasons and, yet, the Twenty-sixth Amendment which states: "The right of citizens of the United States, who are eighteen years of age or older, to vote shall not be denied or abridged by the United States or any State on account of age,"[709] passed easily. It is not studied in schools; the names of the leaders in favor of it are not implanted in students' heads or in stone. Hollywood has yet to make a movie about it. When Abbie Hoffman and Jerry Rubin[710] die they will not lie in state, nor will they be remembered for their roles in a turning point of 20th century America. This amendment created a split on the Supreme Court and in an already splintered country.

The late 1960s and early 1970s are remembered as the time of 'sex, drugs, and rock and roll.' The Grateful Dead, Malcolm X, the Pill, and Timothy Leary were all "highlights" of the era.[711] The creation of the feminist, civil rights, and anti-war movements were in full swing and, more than ever before, the youth were not only involved but were making a statement.

A riot on the campus of Kent State University in Ohio can be evaluated as a pivotal point in the intensity of student involvement. On May 1st, 1970, the students of Kent State gathered to express their opposition to the war in Vietnam and President Nixon's invasion of Cambodia. The typical protests of singing songs, burning flags, and making speeches, slowly escalated into the burning of the campus JROTC building. On May 4, Governor Leroy Satrum declared a state of emergency and called in the National Guard. Bricks were thrown, rifles were fired, screams were heard, and chaos ensued. Eleven seconds later, four students lay dead. Ironically, only two of them had been involved in the protest.[712]

The issue of lowering the voting age was sparked by the fact that the youth of America was playing a more active role in the affairs of their country. Georgia had already lowered its voting age to eighteen,[713] and nineteen–year-olds were granted the right to vote in Massachusetts, Minnesota, and Montana.[714] In 1970, Senator Birch Bayh took it to the next step, proposing that 18 year olds be allowed to vote nationwide, in federal and local elections. He raised the controversial question, asking "[How] can we in good conscience expect youth to work within the system, when we deny them that very opportunity?"[715] This was timely, as the Voting Rights Act of 1965 was up for renewal.[716] The act was met by strong resistance, and declared unconstitutional by many people;[717] yet in the end, not only was it part of the act, but became a Constitutional Amendment.

From the eyes of the more conservative and older generation, the youth were seen as promiscuous, irresponsible, and rebellious and, it was believed, their vote would skew the political system. Many citizens backed President Nixon and his opposition to the amendment; in the Public Opinion Poll of 1970, he had a majority of support.[718]

With the newfound passion for sex and drugs, young adults helped feed negative stereotypes. The Young International Party of 1968 originated as a joke but soon grew to be one of the largest movements of the time period as a youth movement. Leader Abbie Hoffman remembers, we were all stoned...rolling around on the floor...Yippie!

...and so the YIPPIE party was born, the Youth International Party

...All you do is change the H in hippie to the Y in Yippie and you've got it.[719]

The party dealt mainly with anti-war protests but soon earned a bad reputation for violence. During the Democratic convention in Chicago, youth threatened to put LSD into Chicago's water supply to 'turn on' citizens to the steps they believed the Government needed to take.[720] Police were armed with tear gas and guns and prepared to keep the peace regardless of the fight that was sure to ensue. Officials added to the image of the youth immaturity and rebellion through various statements such as "we feel that the insane antics shown by some groups are getting out of hand. We want the public to know this and back the policemen in the fight."[721]

It can be generalized that majority of young adults, ages 18-21, fell to the left of the political spectrum. As a result, there was also a strong Republican backlash. It was estimated that, if granted suffrage, 25 million 18-25 year olds would be eligible to vote[722] and that all the new liberal votes would go to the Democratic Party, substantially weakening the Republican Party.

In order to stop the vote, President Nixon signed, with resignation, the following act on June 22, 1970. The Act was as follows,

> The Congress finds and declares that the imposition and application of the requirement that a citizen be 21 years old and as a precondition to voting in any primary or any election denies and abridges the inherited constitutional rights of citizens 18 years old but not yet 21 years old to vote, a particularly unfair treatment of such citizens in view of the national defense responsibilities imposed on such citizens.[723]

Many states complied immediately and lowered the age bar, but Oregon, Iowa, and Texas filed suit with the Supreme Court asking that it to be overturned. They stated, "Congress has exceeded its authority in enacting a provision in conflict within state control."[724] In October, 1970, the cases were combined into one large suit, "Oregon vs. Mitchell."[725] The states argued that they were protected from following federal law and, therefore, concluded that the voting age was the states' decision. The Government argued in return, when assessing the Fourteenth Amendment, "No state shall make or enforce law which shall abridge the privileges or immunities of citizens of the United States," that clearly stated the eighteen-year-old vote could not be denied.[726] The count ruled by a 5-4 majority that the act was constitutional.[727] The case created judicial upheaval as it was decided by one vote. Justice Burger, Justice Blackmun, Justice Harlan, and Justice Stewart, were all against it.[728] Justices

Brennan, Douglas, Marshall, and White, were in favor of it. Justice Hugo L. Black served as the tie breaker.[729] He was alone in his belief that the legislative power over local elections was constitutional during federal elections. He wrote that, "... Congress is empowered to establish laws governing federal elections but that state and local elections must be regulated by themselves."[730]

Despite resistance and its close Court vote, the eighteen year old vote was declared legal, by law. Yet, it soon became apparent that states would not properly enforce it. Revisions were already being made to keep out the amateur voters.[731] Congress decided to perform the inevitable and in January, 1971, Senator Arthur Vandenberg and Representative Jennings Randolph proposed a Twenty-sixth Amendment.[732] It reached the floor in March of 1971 and was unanimously passed by the Senate. The House of Representatives then passed the amendment with a 400-19 vote. Three months later, the Twenty-sixth Amendment was ratified by enough states to pass.[733]

Contrary to the conventional wisdom of the day, however, passage of the Twenty-sixth Amendment did not mean the death of the Republican Party, especially when it came to the 1972 Presidential election. The New York Times rightfully predicted that,

> A third of the Democrats-twice the usual rate-say they will defect and vote for President Nixon; of this group, more than half the Whites say that minorities, particularly Blacks have been getting 'too much' attention.[734]

An estimated 25 million 18-29 year olds were eligible to vote in the 1972 election; 11 million of them, because of the 26th Amendment. However, only 48% of young adults in this age bracket actually voted, creating a record low voter turnout.[735]

Going against popular wisdom, Nixon and the Republicans did just as much canvassing and outreach for the youth vote in the 1972 election as Democrats did. In fact, when assessing the votes of college students, their vote split evenly between the two parties. However, as the Department of Commerce statistics proved, most 18-21 year olds weren't in college but, rather, were "white, single, and living in a family, not going to school but having a high school diploma, holding a job, and living in a metropolitan city."[736] Regardless, the immense Democratic majority among young people turned out to be merely myth. More recently, as if to prove the point, only forty-five percent of 18-29 year olds voted for President Bush in 2004.[737]

VOTE BY AGE	BUSH		KERRY	NADER
TOTAL	2004	2000	2004	2004
18-29 (17%)	45%	n/a	54%	0%
30-44 (29%)	53%	+4	46%	1%
45-59 (30%)	51%	+2	48%	0%
60 and Older (24%)	54%	+7	46%	0%

[738]

Others, however, were in favor of the amendment. Student organizations were founded to campaign for the right to vote. They were structured by more respectable and fundamental means than marijuana. V. O. T. E., Voter Opportunities To Eighteen year olds based itself in Florida; Michigan was home to the Committee of Total Citizenship. "18x72" (lowering the voting age to 18 by 1972) was formed in Massachusetts, and in California I. N. V.O. L. V.E [739] Former Chairman Edmund J. Bonnett of the LUV-18 committee (Let Us Vote at 18), states the main feelings of the youth at the time.

Our contention was that if 18 year olds were permitted to vote in Federal Elections in Georgia and Kentucky, and Alaska and Hawaii had voters under age 21, then we in New Jersey and other states not afforded that same privilege, were not receiving the same equal protection of the U.S. Constitution. We were being taxed by the

Federal Government, sent off to fight in foreign lands, yet denied the right to participate in the selection of that Government.[740]

This double standard of having to fight for the government that youth were not allowed to vote for, provoked the phrase "hell no, we won't go."[741] In addition to the Vietnam argument, and Bonnett's previous point that there should be a state standardization when it came to the voting rights, there were as many reasons in favor of the eighteen year old vote as against it.

A popular prediction was that in allowing eighteen year olds the right to vote, the crime rate and violent protests would decrease. Many thought that by enabling the right to vote, youth would put all their energy into electoral politics as opposed to violent rebellions to express their political opinion.

Other reasoning for ratification came from the fact that eighteen year olds were treated like adults and given responsibilities in other areas. They could legally get married, facilitate contracts, buy property, pay taxes, and even be tried as an adult for criminal acts at eighteen.[742] The twenty-one-year old age barrier had originated as those younger were thought to be unqualified. However, in 1970, this had changed. More than 80% of the 18 year olds had graduated from high school.[743]

Lastly, the eighteen-year-old vote was considered as beneficial to the political process itself. Harvard Law Professor Paul Fruend explained, "We need to channel the idealism, honesty, and open hearted sympathies of these young men and women, and their informed judgments, into responsible political ideals."[744] A wider diversity of voters would help to form a more accurate testimony as to what was needed to propel the United States government forward.

This amendment should be evaluated as a large accomplishment of the youth of America. Only eight states refused to ratify it, including Florida, Kentucky, Mississippi, Nevada, New Mexico, North Dakota, South Dakota, and Utah.[745] Out of the ten thousand amendments proposed in the United States Senate over the past two hundred years, this amendment was one of the thirty three suggestions to make it out of the Senate, and one of the twenty six to become an amendment.[746]

President Nixon welcomed the Twenty-sixth Amendment with the following,

Some 11 million young men and women who have participated in the life of our nation through their work, their studies, and their sacrifices for its defense, are now to be fully included in the electoral process of our country. I urge them to honor this right by exercising it- by registering and voting in each election.[747]

It can be seen by the elections since 1972, his wishes were ignored. Nineteen eighty-four was named the 'Year of the Yuppie' (Young Urban Professional);[44] the turbulence of the 1960s and 1970s had come to an end in part because of the Twenty-sixth Amendment and the end of the Vietnam war. Ex-radicals were moving into cities, refurbishing apartments, popping collars, and making money.[748] Jerry Rubin, after spending four years in jail, re-emerged as an investment banker.[749] The "baby boomer"[750] generation was growing up. Though some Yippie ideals were carried over to Yuppies, the strong political bond was lost. Professor Hendrick Hertzberg commented, "Yuppiedom carried over from hippiedom as an appreciation for things deemed 'natural,' an emphasis on personal freedom, and self absorption of that part of the counterculture known as the human potential movement."[751] Thus, the need to vote and remain politically active was not emphasized as a natural right. The focus shifted toward material belongings, "entrepreneurship, not political activism, marked the path to personal liberation and social transformation."[752]

The decline of political activism continued, starting a trend in young voters. Since 1972, a steady decline can be seen in the percent of eligible 18-24 year old voters. From 1972 to 1976, the number dropped form 62% to 50.1%. [753] The lowering in number can be directly compared to the voter turnout as a whole population. In 2004, only 17% voted, an all time low.[754]

Organizations now work to bring back the political involvement of America's youth, remembered for its lasting impact on the 20th century. The Close-Up Foundation is an organization which places the blame on teachers and parents for pushing students to look inward at their own personal problems as opposed to the problems of the country. "[We] work with educators and others to reconnect young people, democracy's next generation, to civic participation… the goal is simple…every student should leave high school with a diploma in one hand and a voter registration card in the other."[755]

Another organization, Rock the Vote lead by Patrick J. Lippert, works to increase the numbers of 18-24 year olds who vote. The organization helped to push for the National Voter Registration Act (NVRA) of 1993, ('motor voter' law) which allows for young people to register to vote as they obtain their drivers license. Before the NVRA, voter registering was a long and arduous process.[756] Rock the Vote has continued to work with young people, even after the passage of the act. Teamed with celebrities from Madonna, to Shop Dog, to the OC's Seth Cohen, teen celebrities use their high profile to help the cause.[757] Dartmouth Junior Alisha Levine explained, "I think that Rock the Vote, P. Diddy, and Outcast are doing a great job making the concept of voting attractive to college age voters. They are all super cool—if they are doing it [voting], then it must be the cool thing to do."[758]

High school students, in addition to college- age students, are also working to increase voter turnout. Teenage Republicans and Young Democrats work side by side with local delegates, help with canvassing, work the polls, and make an effort to get their presence felt in their local community. Both groups work to set-up voter registration at schools, to make it even more manageable for students. The Teenage Republicans and Young Democrats have made it their goal to provide support for candidates at local and federal levels, to teach young people how the democratic system works, to promote young people's involvement in politics, to aid the Democratic/ Republican parties, and to teach leadership values in the youth of the community.

Not only do organizations work to increase voter turnout, a growing movement exists to lower the voting age yet again. In California, for example, it was suggested to lower the voting age to fourteen. The bill would have allowed for 14-15 year olds to be given a quarter vote, and for 16-17 year olds to be given a half vote.[759] Not unlike 1972, the movement has sparked a large debate. Comparably, 16 and 17 year olds in England have worked to lower the voting age to 16.[760] The issues have remained more or less the same as they were less than forty years ago.

Advocates for a lower voting age argue that sixteen year olds are allowed several adult responsibilities including jobs, taxation, and marriage. In addition, 16 year olds are more mature and educated than the 18 year olds of 1972, and it would benefit national politics to increase voter representation. The opposing arguments also remain the same: 16 year olds do not have enough experience and, therefore, cannot be trusted with the responsibility to vote for the best candidate.[761]

The Twenty-sixth Amendment, which created tension during its birth, is losing support with each 18-21 year old who chooses not to vote. Although organizations are working to fix this problem and have brought together the young and old, Republicans and Democrats, rappers and senators alike in the process, the problem still exists. Yes, there are movements to lower the voting age, and yes, Young Democrats and Teenage Republicans are proving to be influential in their communities. But there is an obvious lack of communication. In 2004, only 17% of 18-24 year olds voted, the lowest of any other age bracket. The last generation put itself on the line to be blasted by hoses, thrown in jail and bitten by dogs, some even died, to give youth a right that they don't seem to have the time, heart, or passion, to secure. President Nixon, against the amendment from its start, told young people "to honor this right by exercising it,"[762] to take advantage of the opportunity to shape their country, their future, and their lives, into the world they want. The Twenty-sixth Amendment to the Constitution of the United States gave young people a voice; all they have to do is use it.

Bibliography

"1970." <u>Congress and the Nation.</u> Vol. III. Washington DC: Congressional Quarterly Service, 1973. 498-505.

<u>26 Amendment</u>. 8 Nov. 2005 <http://http://thomas.loc.gov/cgi-bin/query/z?r102:E26NO1-B157>.

Archer, Jules. <u>The Incredible Sixties</u>. New York, New York: Harcourt Brace Jovanovich, 1986.

<u>Close Up Foundation</u>. 8 Nov. 2005 <http://www.closeup.org/amend.pdf >.

<u>Dems Face off in 'Rock the Vote'</u>. 8 Nov. 2005 <http://http://www.cnn.com/2003/ALLPOLITICS/11/04/elec04.prez.rock.vote/>.

Faber, Doris, and Harold Faber. <u>We the People</u>. New York, New York: Charles Scribner's Sons, 1987.

<u>Lower the Voting Age</u>. 8 Nov. 2005 <http://crf-usa.org/youthsite/lowering_the_voting_age.htm>.

Orbuch, Steven. "In the Granite State, Dartmouth Rocks the Vote." <u>The Dartmouth</u> 22 Oct. 2004. 8 Nov. 2005 <http://www.thedartmouth.com/section.php?section=mirror&date=2004-11-08>.

Palmer, Kris E. "26 Amendment." <u>Constitutional Amendments</u>. 571-576.

Rosenthal, Jack. "The 'Secret' Key Issue." <u>New York Times</u> 6 Nov. 1972: 47.

Schulman, Bruce J. <u>The Seventies</u>. New York, New York: The Free Press, 2001.

US President/National/Exit Poll. 8 Nov. 2005 <http://http://
www.cnn.com/ELECTION/2004/pages/results/states/US/P/00/
epolls.0.html>.

Wright, Mike. What They Didn't Teach You About the 60's.
Novato, California: Presidio Press, 2001.

Youth Rights. 8 Nov. 2005 <http://www.youthrights.org/forums/
showthread.php?t=117>.

Presidential Impeachment

By
Rikki Wagner

"Now, for the first time in the history of the world, has a nation brought before its highest tribunal its chief magistrate for trial and possible deposition from office upon charges of maladministration of the powers and duties of that office. In other times and in other lands it has been found that despotism could only be tempered by assassination, and nations living under constitutional governments even have found no mode by which to rid themselves of a tyrannical, imbecile, or faithless ruler, save by overturning the very foundation and framework of the Government itself. And but recently, in one of the most civilized and powerful governments of the world, from which our own institutions have been largely modeled, we have seen a nation submit for years to the rule of an insane king, because its constitution contained no method for his removal."[763]

Benjamin F. Butler's opening statement in the Senate trial of the impeachment of Andrew Johnson, quoted above, cites the importance of impeachment in the United States government. When presidents take an oath before they enter office, they become bound to an agreement that "they shall be removed from office on impeachment for, and Conviction of, Treason, Bribery, or other high Crimes and Misdemeanors."[764] The president should be subject to similar laws as all U. S. citizens are to insure a fair and trustworthy administration. Furthermore, the president should also be prevented from gaining too much power while in office. The impeachment process is fair, and remains today as originally established by the founders of the Constitution, who created a basis for the process of impeachment.

The presidential impeachment process is based on a system of checks and balances in order to make the removal of a president justifiable. When the Congress feels there are grounds for impeachment, the House of Representatives issues articles of impeachment to bring the president to trial. The president then proceeds through a trial in the Senate, with the Chief Justice of the

Supreme Court presiding. Therefore, all three of the branches of government play a role in the impeachment process, which prevents one branch from obtaining too much power; this is a key foundation of the United States government.

At the Constitutional Convention many of the Founding Fathers had a fear of an "out-of-control" executive remaining in office, thus the idea of removal of the president on certain grounds became evident. On June 2, 1787, Delegate Hugh Williamson of North Carolina called for the "removable on impeachment and conviction of malpractice or neglect of duty"[765] of an executive. This motion was strongly supported by other delegates, but on June 19th Morris suggested that if terms were given to the president, there was no need for the legislature to have the ability to impeach a president. This comment made by Morris caused controversy among the delegates, which resulted in a strong response from Elbridge Gerry, Edmund Randolph, Benjamin Franklin, and James Madison, "Impeachment was a safeguard against punishments and abuses of powers."[766]

After the issue of impeachment was passed to the Committee of Detail at the Convention, the grounds for impeachment became treason, bribery, or corruption. The first step of the process to remove an executive was for the House of Representatives to impeach the president, and then the Supreme Court would hold a trial for the conviction of removal of office. Morris objected to the Courts' involvement, and believed that the Senate conduct the conviction hearing with the Chief Justice present. This suggestion was supported, and on September 4 the Committee of Postponed Matters reached the conclusion that the impeachment process should consist of a three part recommendation: impeachment by the House, trial by Senate, with Chief Justice present, and impeachment on grounds of treason or bribery.[767] Madison objected because corruption was not included and added "other high crimes and misdemeanors," which passed. Only two more corrections were made to the process of impeachment; that to convict a president of impeachment, two-thirds of the Senate was required, and that this process of impeachment also applied to the Vice President and all civil officers of the United States.[768]

There have been no major changes to the process of impeachment, but the Constitution only provides the framework for the act. The procedures and regulations of this process rely on the rules of the internal regulations of both the House of Representatives and the Senate. There have only been two impeachment trials, although a third impeachment was inevitable for Nixon, which resulted in his resignation from presidency.

The first impeachment trial in the United States was Andrew Johnson's in 1868. Johnson was Abraham Lincoln's Vice President from Tennessee; so he assumed office after Lincoln was assassinated. Johnson developed a plan for reconstruction of the South on his own, which was to pardon all rebels of the southern states, excluding the Confederate Army leaders. All property was returned to rebels as well, with the exception of their slaves. The plan allowed for rebel states to reenter the Union by holding a convention for white delegates to make a new State Constitution.[769] This plan, which he put into action, upset the Radical Republicans, who were in control of Congress. They thought that Congress should have been responsible for developing and enacting a reconstruction plan for the South.

Congress passed a Freedmen's Bureau Bill to provide for the protection of blacks in courts, establish schools, and give land to newly freed African Americans. Johnson vetoed this bill, and Congress was unable to override his veto. Congress made strides insuring rights for ex-slaves by passing the Civil Rights Act in 1866, which gave property rights, the ability to make contracts, and the right to serve as witnesses in a court of law to African Americans. This act was also vetoed by Johnson, but was overridden by Congress. This was the first time Congress overrode a President's veto in American history. All vetoes in the past were unable to receive a majority in Congress and pass after the initial veto by the President. Congress also ratified the Fourteenth Amendment in 1866, which defined citizenship for any person born on US territory and overrode Johnson's veto of a second Freedmen's Bureau Bill. [770]

Congress passed a reconstruction act after many violent crimes occurred, including the New Orleans Massacre, which had been "written with a steel pen made out of a bayonet" which was once again vetoed by the President but overridden by Congress.[771]

This new law forced much tighter restrictions on southern states. Congress passed several reconstruction acts, which were all vetoed by Johnson, but then overridden by Congress. All of the vetoes of important reconstruction legislature frustrated and angered the Radical Republicans, which led to the development of the Tenure of Office Act. This act forced the President to receive the Senate's approval before firing any appointed government official, including his cabinet members but the act was vetoed by Johnson and overridden again by Congress.[772] This act was established to prevent Johnson from becoming too controlling and powerful in the view of the congressmen.

The Tenure of Office Act led to the impeachment of President Johnson. He fired his Secretary of War, Edward Stanton, because he was appointed by Lincoln and was not supportive of Johnson. This action of Johnson violated the Tenure of Office Act because he did not receive the Senate's approval. The House of Representatives impeached Johnson in 1868 on the grounds of high crimes or misdemeanors and for the violation of the Tenure of Office Act. The underlying reason for his impeachment however, was that he failed to cooperate or compromise with the Radical Republicans in Congress on reconstruction or African American rights issues.[773] The House of Representative voted on party line -126 to 47 in favor of impeachment, and composed eleven articles of impeachment.[774] The first Article of Impeachment stated that Johnson was

> "Unmindful of the high duties of his oath of office and of the requirements of the Constitution, that he should take care that the laws be faithfully executed, did unlawfully, in violation of the Constitution and laws of the United States, issue an order in writing for the removal of Edwin M. Stanton from the office of Secretary of the Department of War."[775]

This article states Johnson's violation of the Tenure of Office Act. Article three of the impeachment articles was another charge regarding the violation of the Tenure of Office Act, stating that Johnson "did commit, and was guilty of a high misdemeanor in office, in this: That without authority of law, while the Senate of the United States was then and there in session, he did appoint one

Lorenzo Thomas to be Secretary for the Department of War, ad interim, without the advice and consent of the Senate."[776] Articles one through nine all responded to Johnson's violation of the Tenure of Office act by firing Stanton and hiring Lorenzo Thomas.

Articles 10 and 11 were based on Johnson's failure to cooperate with Congress because he "design[ed] and intend[ed] to set aside the rightful authorities and powers of Congress, did attempt to bring into disgrace, ridicule, hatred, contempt and reproach, the Congress of the United States."[777]

The Senate trial began with opening statements from Benjamin F. Butler from Massachusetts. He stated that:

> "These and his concurrent acts show conclusively that his attempt to get the control of the military force of the Government, by the seizing of the Department of War, was done in pursuance his general design if it were possible, to overthrow the Congress of the United States; and he now claims by his answer the right to control at his own will, for the execution of this very design, every officer of the Army, Navy, civil, and diplomatic service of the United States. He asks you here, Senators, by your solemn adjudication, to confirm him in that right, to invest him with that power, to be used with the intents and for the purposes which he has already shown."[778]

Butler argued for the impeachment of Johnson because he felt that it was his duty, as a member of Congress, to protect the country from an "insane" president, who had gained too much power and was now a threat to the people.

Butler's opening statement was followed by Benjamin Curtis's argument supporting the president. He believed that the president has a right to have or to appoint anyone in his administration during his presidency. Lincoln, not Johnson, had appointed Stanton, and therefore Stanton did not support Johnson who favored the Southern States. The Radical Republicans in Congress did not support Johnson either and did not want him to have the ability to remove any administrators appointed by Lincoln; therefore they passed the Tenure of Office Act.

During Johnson's impeachment trial, numerous Senators spoke, a majority of whom supported the impeachment of Andrew Johnson, and several witnesses testified. These witnesses included Burt Van Horn, James Moorhead, Samuel Wilkson, and George Karsner in favor of impeachment, known as the managers, and Lorenzo Thomas in support of the president. [779] The witnesses discussed their relation to the president and the articles of impeachment. Closing arguments from both sides were heard and the Senators cast their votes. The Chief Justice stated the final result on May 26, 1868, that "upon the question of adjournment, without day, the yeas are 34 and the nays are 16. So the Senate sitting as a court of impeachment for the trial of Andrew Johnson upon articles of impeachment presented by the House of Representatives stands adjourned without day."[780] Therefore, the Senate found that there were not sufficient grounds to remove the president from office for articles one through ten.

Andrew Johnson escaped charges of impeachment for Article 11 by one vote; Edmund G. Ross, a Radical Republican, did not give into the pressure of the other Radical Republicans and voted not guilty. This resulted in a final tally of 35 Radical Republicans to 19 Democrats, which was one shy of the two-thirds majority required and Johnson was able to stay in office.

The impeachment process works to ensure the power of the president does not become abusive to either the people or the government. The branches of the government worked together to insure that the founder's request for impeachment was met; however, in this case, the Congress was not pleased with the actions of the president. Congress passed laws to protect the actions they wanted and acted on this to attempt to impeach the president, but was unsuccessful because the system of checks and balances prevented one branch of government from becoming too powerful. In this case, the President's impeachment was the result of political differences, but it was justified by the violation of the Tenure of Office act, which was created to protect the Radical Republicans in Congress.

Richard Nixon resigned from office before his impeachment trial took place. He was advised that if his case were taken to trial there was no possible way he would remain president. Thus, to retain his dignity and to escape from a long, and possibly embarrassing trial, he resigned.

On June 17, 1972, a team known as "the plumbers," who did Nixon's dirty work in his campaigns, entered the Watergate Hotel in Washington, D.C., which was the headquarters of the Democratic National Committee. These six burglars took pictures of documents, placed wiretaps on telephones, and looked for information which could possibly hurt the Democratic Party or the nominee in the next presidential election. They were caught red-handed by the police after a security guard, Frank Willis, noticed tape on the garage door to hold it open, and then notified the police. G. Gordon Liddy and E. Howard Hunt, who were hired and oversaw the burglars, carefully destroyed all of the evidence. This scandal led to uncovering of executive abuse of power and eventually Nixon's resignation.

Nixon's attempt to cover up his and the White Houses connection to the Watergate scandal action was eventually uncovered in the trials concerning this case. The cover-up was an instinctive action by the administration, although it led to further crimes, which seemed to continue increasing. Nixon's crimes included perjury, and obstruction of justice, and this cover-up kept the Watergate scandal from becoming influential in the presidential election in November 1972. The president aided and supported the cover-up and, therefore, was guilty of the crimes as well.

Congress created a committee to research and investigate Watergate, which lead to the discovery that the White House was holding audiotapes concerning the scandal. These tapes gave sufficient evidence that Nixon was, indeed, involved in the cover-up. On February 6, 1974, the House passed House Resolution 803 by 410-4, which allowed the Judiciary Committee to form a discussion on opening a case of impeachment against Nixon.[781] The Committee of the Judiciary adopted three articles of impeachment, but they were never voted on in the House because Nixon resigned before it took place.

The first Article of Impeachment stated, "... in violation of his constitutional duty to take care that the laws be faithfully executed, has prevented, obstructed, and impeded the administration of justice."[782]   According to the Committee, Nixon broke the law by withholding evidence, making false statements, attempting to influence testimony of witnesses, misusing the CIA, and making false statements to the public. The second Article of Impeachment stated that Nixon misused his executive power by using the CIA inappropriately, and the third article discussed Nixon's failure to comply with subpoenas to provide the tapes to the police.[783]

On August 8, 1974, he gave a speech to the people of the United States announcing his resignation and apologizing for his actions:

> "In the past few days, however, it has become evident tc me that I no longer have a strong enough political base in the Congress to justify continuing that effort. As long as there was such a base, I felt strongly that it was necessary to see the constitutional process through to its conclusion, that to do otherwise would be unfaithful to the spirit of that deliberately difficult process and a dangerously destabilizing precedent for the future. But with the disappearance of that base, I now believe that the constitutional purpose has been served, and there is no longer a need for the process to be prolonged... To have served in this office is to have felt a very personal sense of kinship with each and every American. In leaving it, I do so with this prayer: May God's grace be with you in all the days ahead."[784]

The Founders of the Constitution wanted the impeachment articles to protect the people from a tyrannical executive holding a position above the law. Nixon's acts were against the law and he abused his power as president, therefore, the system of checks and balances was successful by having a president remove himself when his actions exceeded the boundary of executive power. Nixon attempted to win his last election by discrediting other opponents and political parties, which is an action the founders wanted to prevent.

The most recent trial of impeachment for a president in the United States was William Jefferson Clinton's. Clinton was forced to undergo an impeachment trial after he was exposed for having an affair and then committing perjury. The series of scandals of Bill Clinton took place before he entered the White House. In 1978 he, his wife, Hillary Rodham Clinton, and their friends, James and Susan McDougal, borrowed $203,000 to start a vacation home development company, the Whitewater Development Corporation, which could have been involved in illegal financial activities.[785] Later McDougal received a loan to create the Madison Guaranty, which supplied money to Clinton's governor's campaign.[786] Then Clinton, Hillary, and some of their friends were involved in further financial investigations. After Clinton was elected president, information about Whitewater began to appear. A congressional committee was established to investigate the Whitewater situation, and Ken Starr was appointed to lead an independent investigation of the Clintons.

The investigation began to focus on the President's personal conduct after complaints by Paula C. Jones, an Arkansas state clerical worker, of sexual harassment in 1991.[787] The White House attempted to tarnish the name of Jones, which resulted in civil lawsuit charges against Clinton; who then attempted to delay the trial. During the investigation of Jones, information involving an affair between Monica Lewinsky and Clinton was discovered. Lewinsky, a young White House intern, had several sexual encounters with the President in the White House over a period of 18 months. Linda Tripp, a friend of Lewinsky, taped over 20 hours of telephone conversations of Lewinsky, which gave details of the affair. When Clinton was asked questions about the affair in depositions and later in speeches to the American people he claimed the accusations were non-existent, and then attempted to persuade Lewinsky not to provide testimony against him. These were the grounds for the impeachment trial.[788]

Lewinsky provided a dress with stains from sexual encounters on it in exchange for immunity to prove that Clinton had lied under oath. He later stated that "Indeed, I did have a relationship with Ms. Lewinsky that was not appropriate. In fact, it was wrong. It constituted a critical lapse in judgment and a personal failure on my part for which I am solely and completely responsible."[789]

The House of Representatives felt that this action of committing perjury was enough justification for impeachment. On December 12, 1998 the House Committee on the Judiciary resolved four Articles of Impeachment based on the violation of high crimes and misdemeanors. The first Article of Impeachment charged Clinton with committing perjury, giving false or misleading information, and attempting to influence a witness. The first article expanded to say, "In doing this, William Jefferson Clinton has undermined the integrity of his office, has brought disrepute on the Presidency, has betrayed his trust as President, and has acted in a manner subversive of the rule of law and justice, to the manifest injury of the people of the United States."[790] This article explains how he violated his trust and obligations of presidency, which the founders wanted to be considered pure and trustworthy.

The second Article of Impeachment gives specific dates in which the president committed perjury under oath. The third Article of Impeachment states Clinton's attempts to persuade a witness from telling the truth or give misleading information, "corruptly engaged in, encouraged, or supported a scheme to conceal evidence that had been subpoenaed in a Federal civil rights action brought against him,"[791] and he supported his attorney to give misleading information. The fourth and final Article of Impeachment states Clinton's violation of his duties as President of the United States.

After a long, vigorous, and humiliating trial, Clinton was found not guilty. To be found guilty of impeachment two-thirds majority vote of the Senate must occur, but only 45 out of the needed 67 guilty votes were received for Article 1 of Impeachment. All 45 Democrats and 10 Republicans voted not guilty of the charges against Clinton in Article 1, and in Article Two, obstruction of justice, 50 votes were guilty, and 50 not guilty. Once again, all of the Democrats and 5 of the Republicans voted not guilty, this lead to the final decision of not guilty, freeing Clinton of all charges and allowed him to remain as president.

With regard to the impeachment trial of Bill Clinton, the verdict of not guilty corresponds with the intentions of the framers of the Constitution of the power of impeachment. In this case, Clinton was not abusing his powers in a way to bring harm to the people of the United States, so the investigation shifted from financial to personal conduct, which, although not honorable, was not illegal. This changed however, after he committed perjury to hide the truth, thus becoming a crime. The founders of the Constitution wanted to prevent any president from becoming too powerful, and abusing his executive powers in a way to harm the peoples' or the government's rights. Therefore, although Clinton's actions were inexcusable, they did not threaten his actions and decisions he made as President.

The intent of the framers of the Constitution was to prevent a similar situation that had previously occurred with a leader abusing his power. In colonial America, the British monarch had power over the colonies and abused his power, which ultimately hurt and angered the people of the colonies. The founders wanted to prevent this from happening by using a system of checks and balances, and impeachment is one of the congressional checks on the executive branch.

In the three impeachment requests by the Committee of the Judiciary, including Nixon, political differences led to Congress applying pressure to impeach the president; which was not the intention of the Founders. The founders a did not want the Congress to impeach the president because of political differences, which is why the Chief Justice presides over the hearing and two-thirds majority is required to remove the President from office. For example, Andrew Johnson's impeachment resulted from an angry Congress, because Johnson's actions made it extremely difficult for them to achieve any laws, acts, or amendments they had wanted to pass.

As a result of the power to impeach a President given to Congress, the people are being protected from future possible abusers of executive power. This is an important right to have because it prevents a tyrannical ruler from forming and controlling the people or other governmental institutions. Robert F. Drinan, a professor of law and a member of the House committee investigating the charges against Clinton, wrote:

> "The framers of the Constitution devised the impeachment process in order to provide a safety net for extreme situations where the removal of a president is the only way to curtail a major abuse of power. But the founding fathers knew that in an extreme case there would be a need to remove a president before the time of his re-election. This was especially true since the writers of the Constitution feared (long before the time when a president was limited to eight years in office)

that a president could aggregate power to himself and stay in office as if he were a member of a royal family."[792]

This "safety net" is one of the qualities of the government, which makes the United States of America unique, by providing back-up procedures if any situation gets out of control, which often occurs in other countries. Therefore, it is a necessary and fair process, by watching over the president's actions to insure the safety of the country.

Bibliography

"Bill Clinton." Online. Home page on-line. Available from http://www. Historyplace. com/ United States /impeachments/ clinton. htm. Internet; accessed 28 October 2005.

Barr, Bob. The Meaning of IS. Atlanta, Georgia: Stroud & Hall Publishers, 2004.

Cohen, Daniel. The Impeachment of William Jefferson Clinton. Brookfield, Connecticut: Twenty-First Century Books, 2000.

Constitutional Rights Foundation. "The Impeachment of Andrew Johnson." Constitutional Rights Foundation Weblesson. Home page on-line. Available from http://www.crf-usa.org/impeachment/impeachment1.html. Internet; accessed 26 October 2005

Fremon, David K. The Watergate Scandal in American History. Springfield, NJ: Enslow Publishers, Inc., 1998.

Harpweek. "Articles of Impeachment." Harpweek Online. Home page on-line. Available from http://www.impeach andrewjohnson. com/13ArticlesOfImpeachment/Articles Of ImpeachmentI.htm. Internet; accessed 25 October 2005.

Jurist: The Law Professors' Network, "Testimony of Father Robert F. Drinan, S.J. Professor of Law, Georgetown University Law Center," Jurist: The Law \ Professors' Network Online. Home page on-line. Available from http://jurist.law.pitt.edu/drinan.htm. Internet; accessed 3 November 2005.

Library of Congress. "Research Guide on Impeachment." Library of Congress Online. Home page on-line. Available from http://memory.loc.gov/ammem/amlaw/Impeachment-Guide.html. Internet; accessed 25 October 2005.

Milkis, Sidney M., and Michael Nelson. The American Presidency Origins and Development. Washington, D.C.: Congressional Quarterly Inc, 1994.

Olson, Keith W. Watergate: The Presidential Scandal that Shook America. Lawrence, Kansas: University Press of Kansas, 2003.

"Opening Argument of MR. Benjamin F. Butler of Massachusetts." Online. Home page on-line. Available from http://www.law.umkc. edu/faculty/ projects/trials/impeach /ButlerOpening.html. Internet; accessed 24 October 2005.

Pika, Joseph A., and Norman C. Thomas. The Politics of the Presidency. Washington, D.C.: Congressional Quarterly Inc, 1997.

Teaching American History. "Articles of Impeachment." Teaching American History Online. Home page on-line. Available from http://teachingamericanhistory.org/library/index. asp?document=456. Internet; accessed 1 November 2005.

"Testimony in the Impeachment Trial of Andrew Jackson." Online. Home page on-line. Available from http://www.law.umkc.edu/ faculty/projects/ trials/ impeach/testimony.html. Internet; accessed 25 November 2005.

Watergate. info. "Articles of Impeachment Adopted by the Committee on the Judiciary." Watergate. Info Online. Home page on-line. Available from http://watergate.info/impeachment/ impeachment-articles.shtml. Internet; accessed 27 October 2005.

Watergate. info. "Nixon Resignation Speech." Watergate. Info Online. Home page on-line. Available from http://watergate. info/ Nixon /resignation-speech.shtml. Internet; accessed 28 October 2005.

THE ISSUES OVER THE YEARS

The Louisiana Purchase
Was It Constitutional?

By

Justine Jensen

The territory that is west of the Mississippi River was not always part of the United States of America. It was not until the government bought this territory from France in 1803 that it became United States territory and was subsequently split up into the states with which we are familiar with today. Although the people of the United States have now accepted the Louisiana Purchase in full, the government did not have the constitutional right to purchase this territory from France. Additionally, France did not have the right to repurchase this territory from Spain. The French were too preoccupied with the dream of attaining a global empire to worry about the consequences of turning back on the Treaty of Paris of 1763. Thomas Jefferson, on the other hand, was concerned with regaining the loss of the American right of deposit at the Mississippi River to worry about whether or not purchasing the Louisiana Territory fell under the guidelines of the Constitution. As a result, James Monroe, who was sent to Paris to negotiate with the French, agreed to purchase the Louisiana Territory without the authorization of the government to do so.

The United States had to deal with two major constitutional issues that came along with owning the territory. One important issue was how this new territory was going to be governed since the Constitution did not set up guidelines on how to set up a government in a new territory. The only model that was available to do so was the Northwest Ordinance, which could not be applied to land as large as the Louisiana Territory. The second issue was the integration of the residents of Louisiana into the United States. The Constitution's regulations on naturalization simply would not be sufficient for the number of new people who had yet to be naturalized.

The land west of the Mississippi River and the northern territories of Canada were owned by France in the mid 1600s. In addition to this land, the French also wanted to claim the Ohio Valley; in other words, land that was east of the Mississippi River, north of the Ohio River, and west of the Appalachian Mountains. However, France was not the only country interested in this land. The English, too, were well aware of the fertile land in this region and wanted to claim the territory for themselves. The conflict between these two nations over who got to settle the land was eventually decided by war, called the Seven Years War in Europe or French and Indian War in The New World. During the last two years of the war, the Spanish allied with the French against their common enemy, the British. It was during the last two years of the war that the British overthrew the French territories in Quebec, soon ruling all of Canada, the Caribbean islands, and the land west of the Appalachian Mountains and east of the Mississippi River. [793]

The war came to an end in 1763 with the Treaty of Paris. In this treaty, the French gave up their claim to all of their territories in the new world. They ceded their claims in Canada to the British and their territory to the west of the Mississippi River to Spain.

When the Spanish had controlled the territory west of the Mississippi, they had granted the United States, under Pinckney's Treaty, "the navigation of the said River [Mississippi] in its whole breadth from its source to the Ocean shall be free only to his (the Spanish king's) Subjects and the Citizens of the United States".[794] This was critical for the prosperity of the United States economy since the United States could now more easily transport goods from the west to the east via the Mississippi and the Gulf Coast. Without the Mississippi River, the citizens who lived in the west (west of the Appalachian Mountains and east of the Mississippi River), had to transport their goods across the mountain range, extending the time, labor and cost to transport goods to the eastern portion of the United States. With access to the Mississippi River, the goods could easily be put on a boat and reach their destination months earlier.

However, this privilege came to an abrupt end when the Spanish engaged in a secret treaty with the French. In the Treaty of San Ildefonso "His Catholic Majesty [the Spanish King] promises and undertakes on his part to retrocede to the French Republic...the colony or province of Louisiana, with the same extent that it now has in the hands of Spain and that it had when France possessed it..." [795]

Upon the signing of the Treaty of San Ildefonso, Pinckney's Treaty, which had granted the United States unlimited, tariff free access to the Mississippi River, was nullified.

One of the reasons that the Spanish had granted the United States this access to the Mississippi was because they did not care about the river as a source of transportation. Instead, they saw the river as a barrier to keep the British colonists out of their silver mines in Mexico.[796] The French did not have the same attitude towards the river as the Spanish did. They saw it as another piece of property they could add to their growing global empire. As a result, the French would not allow the Americans the same privileges as the Spanish in regards to the Mississippi River. Contrary to the Spanish, the French saw the river as a way to earn money from the citizens of the United States by levying high tariffs on American ships that transported their goods on the river.

When the Treaty of Ildefonso was signed, the French owned the land but the Spanish still governed it. The outline of the treaty gave Spain the ability to decide when they would hand over the land to France: "His Catholic Majesty will give the necessary orders for the occupation of Louisiana by France."[797] Because the French did not govern the land, the Spanish could have stopped the French from imposing their restrictions on the Americans with regards to the Mississippi River. The Spanish did not do this for the simple reason that they did not believe it would be in their best interest to challenge the authority of the French. The Spanish saw no need to start a conflict over an issue that could lose them the profit they would make when they sold the land.

Technically, the French had given up the right to buy this land from Spain when they had ceded this same territory to the Spanish King. In the Treaty of Paris of 1763, the French ceded the land "...in full right, and guaranties to..."[798] the Mississippi River, its port, and the land to the west of the Mississippi River. Therefore, the French had permanently, not temporarily, relinquished control of the land to Spain. The mere act of repurchasing the Louisiana Territory on the part of the French was prohibited by the Treaty of Paris of 1763. The repurchasing of this territory would later cast doubt on the French and their loyalty in this regard. Consequently, if the French could not legally repurchase this land they could not legally sell it to the United States. In effect the United States could not legitimately purchase the territory from France and admit it to its Union.

Thomas Jefferson's main interest in obtaining the Louisiana Territory was not for the land, as the Spanish had been, but for access to the Mississippi River. If the United States could secure ownership of the river, nobody else could impose tariffs or restrictions on American ships that needed to navigate it. The land was just a bonus.

To obtain ownership of the Mississippi River, Thomas Jefferson was willing to go beyond the Constitution and deal with the ramifications of his proposal later. Jefferson addressed the cession of the Louisiana Territory to Spain in numerous messages to Congress. On January 11, 1803, Thomas Jefferson wrote a message to the Senate in which he nominated Robert R. Livingston and James Monroe to negotiate with France in "...securing our rights in the river Mississippi..."[799] In accordance with this message, Livingston and Monroe were sent to negotiate terms with France.

News that Livingston and Monroe had arrived in France quickly made its way to the office of Napoleon Bonaparte, who Bonaparte wasted no time in setting a meeting with Mr. Livingston. It was Foreign Minister Talleyrand, a French officer, who wound up receiving Monroe and Livingston, who argued that if the French did not sell New Orleans and the Floridians to the United States, then the Americans would gain the territory when the imminent war between the French and British finally broke out.[800] Based on the success that America had in the negotiations in the Treaty of Paris, the French chargé d'affaires surmised that Monroe "will go to London if he is badly received in Paris."[801] This would be a problem because, should Livingston go to London, he would, no doubt, inform the English that the French occupation of the Louisiana Territory would put the English position in Canada in peril. The Americans would easily convince the British that the French have a habit of breaking their promises. The retrocession of the Louisiana Territory was a good example of this because the Treaty of Paris of 1763 forbade it. Therefore, it would be wise to assume that the French could also reclaim the Canadian territories that had been ceded to the British in the same treaty.

The French were well aware of their precarious position and they knew that both the British and Americans were not displeased about their territorial claims in the new world - the Americans because of their loss of the Mississippi River, and the English because of the threat that the French would attempt to take back their territory in Canada. To top it off, there were slave revolts in Santo Domingo, a French - owned colony off the coast of Florida, as well as an outbreak of yellow fever. The French had sent troops to calm the rebellion but were having little luck. While the prospects of attaining a global empire were quickly dwindling, the French could no longer afford to pacify the revolts in Santo Domingo and keep the Louisiana Territory. As a result, the French decided to sell the entire territory to the United States of America, not just the port of New Orleans as had been requested. The French not only needed the money but also saw no rational point in keeping Louisiana without the port at New Orleans.[802]

This became a problem for Monroe and Livingston. They were sent to France to negotiate for the port of New Orleans and Florida, not the entire territory of Louisiana. Monroe knew that they did not have the authority from the American government to purchase the entire Louisiana Territory from France, only the specified portions. He was, therefore, forced to make the hard decision on whether or not to accept the French offer without permission of the government. Monroe knew that, should he hesitate too long, he may lose the opportunity to make any sort of deal with France. Should this happen, the United States would lose not only the land that they did not want but also the land that they did. As a result, sending a message to Jefferson requesting permission to purchase the land was not an option because it would take too long for a response to arrive in Paris. Therefore, he decided that as "minister extraordinary," he had the power vested in him to make a decision as long as it reflected the best interests of the Unites States. He decided to go ahead and purchase the land.[803]

When Monroe made his decision, he believed that he was making it in the best interests of the United States. This decision, however, brought up many constitutional realities that the United States was unprepared to handle, such as the naturalization of the residents of Louisiana and a governmental system under which the new territory would be run. When Monroe made his decision, he was not taking into consideration these issues and how they would be handled by the Constitution. It would have been wise of Monroe to wait and make an agreement with the French when he knew that the government would support not only him but the programs that would have to be put in place to allow for the successful integration of the territory. Without this authorization, Monroe's agreement with France was illegal. He was not making this agreement with the support of the United States government because purchasing the entire Louisiana Territory was not at all what he was sent to negotiate. The Constitution does not allow for one person to make such decisions on his own, which is what Monroe did. At the time the Treaty between the United States and the French Republic was signed, Congress had yet to affirm the request to purchase this territory. The treaty between the United States and the French Republic was signed on April 30, 1803. On October 31, 1803, the House of Representatives and Senate stated that the "…President of the United States be, and he is hereby authorized to take possession of, and occupy the territory ceded by France to the United States…"[804]

A total of six months passed before permission was given by the Senate to purchase the land. The system of checks and balances that was set up in the Constitution was clearly ignored.

It is the role of Congress to make decisions that represent those of the majority of the United States population. To make this possible, the Constitution set up a bicameral Congress composed of the House of Representatives and the Senate.

The House of Representatives is elected "by the People of the several States."[805]. This is designed to ensure that the people of the United States are equally represented by allowing the citizens to elect those officials whom they feel will best represent them. The elected officials will then get to comprise the House of Representatives. The Senate, on the other hand, was state legislators, meaning that the senators represent the states, not the people. In order for the members of the Senate and House to get reelected they must make decisions not for themselves, but for the American people. If the American people feel that they are not being fairly represented, then they will not reelect those officials back to office.

One of the jobs of the legislative branch is to give permission to the President on various issues affecting the United States. If Congress does not think that the President is looking out for the best interests of the American people, then they have the power to forbid the president to continue that course of action. This process is called the checks and balances system. When Thomas Jefferson went ahead and sent Monroe to purchase the requested territories before the approval of Congress to acquire these territories, he was in direct violation of the Constitution. Without the authorization of Congress, there was no way of knowing whether or not the people agreed with this course of action. The President was making this decision based on his own beliefs and conceptions. The separation of powers helps to ensure that no one section of the government, whether it is judicial, legislative, or executive, ever gets too much power. When the treaty between the United States and the French Republic was signed, the executive branch of the government had exceeded its constitutional powers.

Thomas Jefferson knew that his request to purchase the Louisiana Territory was not an enumerated constitutional right. Therefore, he could not say that he had the implied power to purchase the land. In order for the implied powers of the Constitution to stand, there has to be enumerated rights listed in the Constitution that cannot be otherwise obtained. Therefore, it was not possible for Thomas Jefferson to claim that he had the implied constitutional right to purchase the Louisiana Territory. To make his request meet the constitutional standards, he started and abandoned the following amendment to the Constitution:

> "Louisiana, as ceded by France to the U S. is made a part of the U S. Its white inhabitants shall be citizens, and stand, as to their rights & obligations, on   the same footing with other citizens of the U S. in analogous situations."[806]

This amendment would have overridden all the technical problems of integrating the people of the Louisiana Territory into the United States as well as erase all the speculation over the constitutionality of the purchase. This amendment would be void when debating the purchase of similar territories since it specifically addresses the Louisiana Territory and would be void when debating other similar issues.

Jefferson abandoned the amendment because he did not feel that such an amendment was necessary or possible.[807] Despite this, Jefferson was not about to give up on the successful integration of the Louisiana Territory into the United States. He knew how important the land was to the nation's economy and was well aware that, with the purchase of the Louisiana Territory, came access to the Mississippi River.

The problem with the Louisiana Territory was not the geographic expansion of the land but the demographic expansion. The Louisiana Territory was not geographically defined. Rather, the land that the United States accumulated was the land that fell under the political jurisdiction of the French. [808] Therefore, the exact amount of land that was being purchased by the United States government was unclear to them. When the government purchased the land, it had no idea how many people were residing there. When Article III of the treaty between the United States and the French republic was written, the United States had not yet realized the immense number of people who were residing in this territory.

The inhabitants of the ceded territory shall be incorporated in the Union of the United States and admitted as soon as possible according to the principles of the <u>federal Constitution</u> to the enjoyment of all these rights, advantages and immunities of citizens of the United States, and in the mean time they shall be maintained and protected in the free enjoyment of their liberty, property and the Religion which they profess.[809]

The only two pieces of land that the United States had asked for, after all, had been the port of New Orleans and the territory of Florida. Therefore, there was a much larger population that had to be naturalized than originally thought and no way to accomplish this. Congress had previously relied on the Northwest Ordinance to create the Mississippi Territory. However, this plan was not sufficient to provide for naturalization of the residents of the Louisiana Territory or for an adequate system of government.

Up until then, the Northwest Ordinance had served as the blueprint for creating new states. The Northwest Ordinance allowed Congress to divide the land "into two districts"[810] as they saw fit. Congress also appointed "…, a governor, … a secretary,…a court to consist of three judges, any two of whom to form a court, which shall have a common law jurisdiction,…"[811] However, this was written for substantially smaller territories and could not easily be applied to a larger territory that had such ambiguous boundaries. Therefore, the Congress had to think of another way to govern the Louisiana Territory. Their solution was to set up the Governance Act of 1804.[812]

Under the Governance Act, the residents of the Louisiana Territory were educated on what they needed to know to successfully integrate into the United States. Mostly, they were taught the basics of the American political and economic beliefs. Advocates of the act believed that the people of the Louisiana Territory would come to think of themselves as Americans if they were treated like Americans under the law. They argued that they would lose their traditional political and social beliefs and realize the benefits of those of the United States. Federalists, however, did not agree with this perspective and thought that, no matter what, the residents of the Louisiana Territory would always consider themselves as foreigners and never consider themselves as American citizens no matter how they were treated under the law.[813]

In the end, the Federalists were right. The Louisianans did not respond as positively to the American presence as the Americans had hoped. Their response to the Governance Act was not one of compassion towards the United States but one of contempt. The Louisianans complained that the Governance Act "does not 'incorporate us in the union,' that it vests us with none of the 'rights,' gives us no advantages, and deprives us of all the 'immunities' of American citizens."[814]   One major setback of the Governance Act was that there were no elected officials to govern the territory. This is just one of the major differences between the Northwest Ordinance and the Governance Act. The Northwest Ordinance set up a political system in the districts that allowed for the people to be treated as if they were a part of the states while the Governance Act did not. As a result, the people in the Louisiana Territory felt that they were the dumping grounds for the American economy. There was nobody there for them if they were to need financial, judicial, or economic assistance and no one in Congress represented them and their needs. A group of Louisianans got together and formed the Remonstrance, the goal of which was to gain recognition from the government and secure the rights they deserved as a part of the nation. The response that this group received was varied.   Republicans in Congress supported the people of the Louisiana Territory because they had thought that these people were similar to themselves.   However, William Palmer, a Federalist senator from Vermont, stated that the Louisianan's are "all Frenchmen…they resemble New England men more than Virginians."[815] Furthermore, when the Remonstrance went to speak to the House of Representatives they were welcomed by a warning statement that the Remonstrance "may contain expressions that the House will have to pardon, ascribing them to the feelings of the inhabitants so peculiarly situated, and not to any want of respect for the Government of the Union."[816] The tone of the meeting was set. The House of Representatives was now expecting to hear something that they were not going to agree with even before the Remonstrance group got up to speak. This statement alone could have clouded the judgment of the people sitting on the committee and caused them to view the statements made by the Remonstrance in a way that they, otherwise, may not have. The committee of the House chosen to investigate the claims of the Remonstrance was very critical and found the claims of the Remonstrance to be "manifest absurdity," stating that they "appreciated too much highly the rights which have been secured to them [Louisianans] by the treaty of cession."[817]

The committee of the House chosen to look into the complaints of the Louisianans failed. The Louisiana Territory was a part of the United States and, therefore, deserved to have their concerns carefully listened to by the Congress of the United States. This did not happen. The concerns of the Remonstrance were not heard with open ears. Instead, they were criticized without a second thought because, as Palmer stated, they were more like Frenchmen that Americans. When the cession treaty between the French and the United States was written up it was understood that the residents of the Louisiana Territory would be integrated into the United States with a government that would consider the "manors...necessities...customs..."[818] of the people. In the end, however, it was their different culture that set them apart from the rest of the Union.

In order for Jefferson to officially take the office of The President of the United States, he had to "solemnly swear (or affirm) that I will faithfully execute the Office of President of the United States, and will to the best of my Ability, preserve, protect and defend the Constitution of the United States."[819] Jefferson did not keep this promise. Under his presidency, he allowed Monroe to purchase the Louisiana Territory without the consent of Congress. When Monroe went ahead and agreed to purchase the Louisiana Territory without the consent of Congress to do so, he was in direct violation of the Constitution. The constitutional consequences of Monroe's decision to accept this territory were immense. Monroe not only lacked the authorization of the Congress to make such a decision but he also made this decision not for the American people but for the American economy. In making this decision, the government was forced to take into consideration all the related issues, such as how to incorporate the citizens already living in this part of the nation. Another important issue that had to be decided was how to govern this new land. Now, however, there is no question as to the legitimacy of this purchase. In fact, it is often referred to as one of Jefferson's many presidential successes. The reality is that the purchase of the Louisiana Territory was not the constitutional blessing that it is portrayed as now.

Bibliography

Authority Given to the President to Take Possession of the
Territory of Louisiana, http://www.yale.edu/lawweb/avalon/
statutes/2us245.htm

Annals of Congress, 8th Cong., 2d sess. (1804-05), 727-28 quoted
in Peter J Kastor, The Nation's Crucible. (Yale University, 2004),
60.

Cerami, Charles A. Jefferson's Great Gamble. Illinois:
Sourcebooks Inc., 2003.

Constitution of the United States of America http://www.house.
gov/Constitution/Constitution.html.

 Fleming, Thomas. The Louisiana Purchase. New Jersey: John
Wiley & Sons, Inc., 2003.

Kastor, Peter J. The Nation's Crucible. Yale University, 2004.

Kukla, Jon. A Wilderness So Immense. New York: Knopf, 2003.

McCulloch v. State of Maryland, et al. February Term, 1819, http://
www.tourolaw.edu/patch/McCulloch/.

Naturalization Act of June 18, 1798, http://uscis.gov/graphics/
aboutus/history/attacha.htm.

Northwest Ordinance; July 13, 1787, section 1, http://www.yale.
edu/lawweb/avalon/nworder.htm.

Pichton to Talleyrand, February 18, 1803, Lyon, Louisiana in
French Diplomacy, 202-3 as quoted in Jon Kukla. A Wilderness So
Immense. (New York: Knopf, 2003), 268.

Pulmer, Memorandum of Proceedings in Senate, 222, quoted in Peter J Kastor, The Nation's Crucible. (Yale University, 2004), 59.

"Remonstrance of the People of Louisiana against the Political System Adopted by Congress for Them," ASP, Misc, 1:396, quoted in Peter J Kastor, The Nation's Crucible. (Yale University, 2004), 58.

This Month in Immigration History: March 1790, http://uscis.gov/graphics/aboutus/history/mar1790.htm.

Thomas Jefferson's Proposed Amendment to the Constitution, July 1803, http://press-pubs.uchicago.edu/founders/documents/a2_2-3s25.html.

Thomas Jefferson, Message to the Senate of January 11, 1803 Regarding Louisiana http://www.yale.edu/lawweb/avalon/presiden/messages/tj003.htm.

Treaty Between the United States of America and the French Republic, Article III, http://www.yale.edu/lawweb/avalon/diplomacy/france/louis1.htm.

Treaty of Friendship, Limits, and Navigation Between Spain and The United States; October 27, 1795, http://www.yale.edu/lawweb/avalon/diplomacy/spain/sp1795.htm.

Treaty of Paris 1763, http://www.yale.edu/lawweb/avalon/paris763.htm.

Treaty of San Ildefonso : October 1, 1800, http://www.yale.edu/lawweb/avalon/ildefens.htm.

Wheelan, Joseph. Jefferson's War America's First War on Terror 1801-1805. New York: Carrol & Graf Publishers, 2003.

The Civil War

Did It Really Start in Philadelphia?
By
Sarah Merchant

The Civil War was a watershed, a turning point for America, lasting from 1861 until the year 1865. The war is defined as, "A conflict between the Union and Confederate states over the issues of slavery and states' rights."[820] Both sides had their own views, the north felt that slavery should be abolished, whereas the south felt that slavery was an integral part of their economy.

On one side of the fence, the southern senator from South Carolina, John C. Calhoun, felt slavery was essential. He stated, "I hold that in the present state of civilization the relation now existing in the slave-holding states between the two [races] is, instead of an evil, a good-a positive good."[821] However, Congressman David Wilmot of Pennsylvania felt that slavery should be abolished. He proposed, "... that slavery be excluded from the lands acquired from Mexico after the Mexican War."[822] Calhoun and many other southern senators were outraged, claiming, "The Constitution forbade Congress from passing such a law. It was up to the citizens of each state or territory to decide."[823]

These disputes caused Senator Stephen A. Douglas of Illinois to introduce the Kansas-Nebraska Act, "Law that allowed the question of slavery in the Nebraska Territory to be decided by popular sovereignty and which created the Kansas and Nebraska territories."[824] He thought the idea of "territorial governments" would open the new territory to slavery, but that people living within their own territories would decide on whether or not to permit slavery. This "principle of popular sovereignty," which soon repealed the Missouri Compromise of 1820, the act allowing Missouri to become a slave state and Maine a free state and attempted to settle the question of slavery's spread by allowing slavery only in specific southern territories. Douglas did not think that his proposal would create a great uproar, but rather prevent one. He was wrong. Many northerners who opposed his bill were outraged, and "grew more bitter." Soon, trouble broke out in Kansas.

There were many attacks on the antislavery settlers (free soilers) who lived in Kansas by those who believed in slavery. As they fought, they became known as "guerrillas" or irregular soldiers. This fighting promoted an eastern newspaper to coin the phrase, "Bleeding Kansas." Although there was continual controversy and states continued to hold strongly to the belief of slavery, the Constitution, itself declared the equality of all people.

Despite the fact that the Fifth Amendment states, "No person shall… be deprived of life, liberty, or property…" southerners believed that slaves were not people, but property. The South had always depended on agriculture and the growing of cotton, whereas the North had several industries and many factories that manufactured their goods. The production of cotton was intensive labor, and required many slaves.

More than 4 million blacks were slaves in the South, and the South felt that if the North continued trying to abolish slavery, it would have an enormous negative economic impact on the Southern Economy. Without the slaves, there would be no cotton production. Those in the North (the abolitionists) were outraged since they felt that slaves were people. They felt that anyone who kept slaves was committing an unconstitutional act because the slaves were being deprived of their constitutional rights, such as life and liberty, which is previously stated in the Fifth Amendment. These arguments between the North and South eventually led to the Civil War.

"Disputes of slavery between the North and the South were one of the leading causes leading to the Civil War. The anti-slavery movements in the North were seen as threats to the economy and way of life in the South."[825] Northern states believed that slavery was against the ideas of the Revolution. This theory reduced the number of slaves within the North, making it easier to abolish slavery. Not only did the fewer number of slaves help in the abolition of slavery in the North, but the economy in the North also helped. It did not require the slave labor as required in the South. **"There were plenty of free white men to do the sort of labor slaves performed. In fact, the main demand for abolition of slavery came not from**

those who found it morally wrong but from white working-class men who did not want slaves as rivals for their jobs."[826]

In order to help save the Union and to express both viewpoints, whether it was abolishing slavery or not, many court cases were presented around this time. The case of Dred Scott v. Sanford began when a slave, Dred Scott, was purchased by John Emerson to be used as Emerson's servant. While serving in the Army, Emerson was transferred from many different states, all of which were "free states." It was by traveling into these "free states," according to Scott, that he became a free man. "Scott argued that since slavery had been banned in Illinois by state law, he had become free when Emerson brought him to that state. Furthermore, slavery was also illegal in the Wisconsin Territory because Wisconsin was in the northern part of the Louisiana Purchase. Slavery had been banned there by Congress in the Missouri Compromise of 1820. In other words, Scott claimed that when he returned to the state of Missouri, he was no longer a slave. Since he "had not been re-enslaved he was still free."[827]

This case moved from one court to the next over several years. Not only did the Missouri Supreme Court rule against Scott in 1852, but so did Roger B. Taney, Chief Justice of the Supreme Court. "'Negroes,' he said were 'a subordinate and inferior class of beings.' They had 'none of the rights and privileges' of citizens of the United States. Scott was not a citizen. Therefore he had no right to bring suit in a federal court even if he had been free!" This one statement by Taney kept Scott a slave, which became known as the Dred Scott Decision, "Scott was still a slave despite living in a free state for a time."[828]

"Under Articles III and IV, argued Taney, no one but a citizen of the United States could be a citizen of a state, and that only Congress could confer national citizenship. Taney reached the conclusion that no person descended from an American slave had ever been a citizen for Article III purposes."[829] "Taney reasoned that the Missouri Compromise deprived slaveholding citizens of their property in the form of slaves and that therefore the Missouri Compromise was unconstitutional."[830] Was this case and ruling a foreshadowing of issues yet to be presented?

"The decision increased antislavery sentiment in the North and fed the sectional antagonism that burst into war in 1861."[831] Many people were still outraged by the ruling in the Dred Scott case, still creating controversy between the North and the South. President James Buchanan was one of the leading factors of this continual struggle between the states because he tried to get Congress to accept and pass the Lecompton Constitution - a proposed constitution in the state of Kansas that supported slavery. Buchanan wanted Kansas to be a slave territory but many residents of Kansas strongly disagreed with his thinking. Senator Stephen Douglas was one of the many who opposed the Lecompton Constitution. This proposed Constitution failed and Kansas was considered a free state.

Stephen Douglas, like Buchanan, was a Democrat. In 1858, Douglas was running for reelection for the U.S. Senate. At this time, after the rejection of the Lecompton Constitution in Congress, it was very hard for him to gain support. Many supporters of the document felt that it was Douglas' fault that the proposal was rejected so they no longer supported him.

Douglas' opponent for the seat in the Senate was Abraham Lincoln. Each man had his own views, which were expressed in the Lincoln-Douglas debates of 1858. "Historians have traditionally regarded the series of seven debates between Stephen A. Douglas and Abraham Lincoln during the 1858 Illinois state election campaign as among the most significant statements in American political history."[832] The main issue that was covered during these sequential debates was that of slavery.

Lincoln said: "... The real issue in this controversy - the one pressing upon every mind - is the sentiment on the part of the class [the Republicans] that looks upon the institution of slavery as a wrong, and of another class that does not look upon it as wrong.

...They [the Republicans] look upon it as being a moral, social, and political wrong; and...they insist that it should, as far as it may be, be treated as a wrong; and one of the methods of treating it as a wrong is to make provision that it shall not grow larger.... It is the eternal struggle between these two principles - right and wrong - throughout the world. They are the two principles that have stood face to face from the beginning of time; and will ever continue to struggle...."[833]

Lincoln was just standing up for the Republican Party, by stating that slavery was wrong, and it should not spread to new territories. Douglas then responded by stating: "We ought to extend to the negro race...all the rights, all the privileges, and all the humanities which they can exercise consistently with the safety of society. Humanity requires that we should give them these privileges; Christianity commands that we should extend those privileges to them. The question then arises. What are those privileges, and what are the nature and the extent of them? My answer is, that that is a question each State must answer for itself...If the people of all the States will act on that great principle, and each State mind its own business, attend to its own affairs, take care of its own negroes, and not meddle in with its neighbors, then there will be peace throughout the North and the South, the East and the West, throughout the whole Union."[834]

This exchange between Lincoln and Douglas is often called "The Great Debate". "Douglas tried to persuade the voters that Lincoln and the Republicans were dangerous radicals. He accused them of being abolitionists and of favoring equality. Lincoln 'thinks the Negro is his brother,' the Little Giant sneered. As for the western territories, Douglas claimed that all were destined by climate and soil conditions to be free. Allowing slave owners to settle in Kansas would not in fact mean that they would do so."[835]

Many Illinois voters had the same view on slavery as Douglas did. "But Lincoln insisted, all people had 'natural rights' described in the Declaration of Independence: the right to life, liberty, and the pursuit of happiness. On the question of slavery in the territories Lincoln took a firm stand. He put Douglas in a difficult political position by asking him if people of a territory could exclude slavery before the territory became a state. After all did not the Dred Scott decision mean that slavery could not be banned in any territory?"[836]

These questions were presented to Douglas in the debate in Freeport, Illinois. Douglas' response to Lincoln's question is known as the Freeport Doctrine. He said:

"It matters not what way the Supreme Court may ... decide.

...The people have the lawful means to introduce or exclude [slavery] as they please, for the reason that slavery cannot exist ... unless it is supported by local police regulations."

Douglas' theory was a strong one which allowed him to win the seat in the Senate, but the position as president in the upcoming election of 1860 was going to go to Lincoln. The argument that Douglas made in this debate helped him win votes in Illinois, but not in slave states. His main goal was reached, allowing people to believe that popular sovereignty could be spread throughout territories despite the Dred Scott decision.

As the election of 1860 neared, many of the Democrats were split, both for and many against Douglas. The Republican candidate in this election was Lincoln. Once again the two men were running against each other for a position. With Lincoln as the Republican candidate, many southerners threatened to secede. However, those who stood for "the Constitution and the Union," but those not necessarily in favor of Lincoln, formed the Constitutional Unionist Party. The majority of the Constitutional Unionist Party nominated another man for president, John Bell. Now, there were four candidates running for the position of president.

"Lincoln received 1,866,000 votes, nearly all in the northern states. Douglas got 1,383,000 also mostly in the North. Breckinridge received 848,000 and Bell 593,000. But Lincoln won a solid majority of the electoral votes, one hundred and eighty of the three hundred and three cast. What had happened was this: In the Free states where the election was between Lincoln and Douglas, it was a fairly close contest, with Lincoln winning in every state. Despite his large popular vote, Douglas got only 12 electoral votes. In the slave states, Breckinridge and Bell divided the votes. Breckinridge had a majority in all the states of the Deep South and Bell carried the border states of Tennessee, Kentucky, and Virginia."[837]

"Although he got much less than half the popular vote, Lincoln had been legally elected president."[838] As President of the United States of America, Abraham Lincoln was neither for nor against slavery. "Although he was not an abolitionist and thought slavery unassailably protected by the Constitution in states where it already existed, Lincoln also thought that America's founders had put slavery on the way to 'ultimate extinction' by preventing its spread to new territories."[839] This caused Lincoln to be a man with many internal struggles.

His main objective was to save the Union; slavery was not the issue for him. Whether it was continued or abolished was not Lincoln's primary focus. "My paramount object in this struggle is to save the Union, and is not either to save or to destroy slavery. If I could save the Union without freeing any slave I would do it, and if I could save it by freeing all the slaves I would do it; and if I could save it by freeing some and leaving others alone I would also do that."[840] The survival of the Union was more important to Lincoln than one man in slavery or a thousand men in slavery. He felt that it was his "Constitutional responsibility"[841] to uphold the Union in order for the country to survive. Without this existence, the country would be in chaos, as evident with the onset of the Civil War because of the separation of states.

"When he was elected President in 1860, seven Southern states left, or seceded, from the United States."[842] These states then formed the Confederate States of America, becoming a separate union (a confederacy). By leaving the Union as created by the founding fathers, southerners, "...hoped to protect not only slavery but what they considered their whole way of life. The southern states based their right to leave the Union on the fact that the original 13 states had existed separately before they joined together to form the United States Constitution. Surely each had the right to cancel its allegiance if its citizens so desired. This was the doctrine of states' rights, first argued by Jefferson in the 1790s."[843] As defined by Garraty, states' rights are, "Doctrine that holds that the states not the federal government have the ultimate power." Though states' rights were an issue, that was not why the southern states seceded. "They seceded because of the matter of southern regionalism - loyalty to the region and to the slave system."[844] Southerners felt that they could no longer be a part of the Union because they felt that the president of the union, Lincoln, was against slavery. He was quoted as saying, "If slavery is not wrong, nothing is wrong." Southerners saw this as a "slap in the face." Southerners would not accept the fact that the practice of owning slaves was wrong. Therefore, when Lincoln became president, the southern states left the Union and formed their own.

In forming this new union, the Southern states elected a new president and created a new constitution, The Constitution of the Confederate States of America. In the original Constitution of America there were only certain restrictions. However, in writing the constitution for governing the Confederacy, there were additional restrictions.

In comparing these two documents regarding the provision of the nomination of a president, The Constitution of the Confederate States of America was rephrased to say, "**No Person except a natural born Citizen [or a Citizen of the United States]** *of the Confederate States, or a citizen thereof,* **at the time of the Adoption of this Constitution,** *or a citizen thereof born in the United States prior to the 20th of December, 1860,* **shall be eligible to the Office of President...**"[845] **This means, "Anyone (even foreign born) who was a citizen of the Confederate States of America at the time of the adoption of the Constitution, was eligible. Also anyone who would become a citizen – but was born in the United States prior to December 20, 1860 was eligible. In either case the person must have had fourteen years residency in the Confederate States of America."[846]** In the original constitution it states, "No person except a natural born Citizen, or a Citizen of the United States, at the time of the Adoption of this Constitution, shall be eligible to the Office of President ..."[847] The underlying difference in this provision shows how The Confederate Constitution was more exclusionary in who was "accepted." This ethnocentric philosophy is apparent in its belief that slavery is an acceptable practice. "Their constitution also specifically mentioned slavery and guaranteed the rights of the citizens to own slaves. Congress was forbidden to pass any law 'denying...the right of property in negro slaves.'"[848]

Taking into consideration all the restrictions that were previously laid out in their new constitution, the people of the Confederacy elected a president to run their union. Right after the Confederates had finished creating the constitution, they elected Jefferson Davis of Mississippi. With two presidents in one country, there were bound to be problems. One such problem was Fort Sumter, located in Charleston Harbor, where Major Anderson and some of his men were stationed and on watch.

Lincoln soon faced a problem with Fort Sumter, a problem he inherited from President Buchanan. "Major Anderson and his men could not hold out forever without fresh supplies. After considering the question for a month, Lincoln decided to send food to the besieged garrison but no troop reinforcements or ammunition. He informed the governor of South Carolina of his intention. The Confederates would not accept even his small 'invasion' of what they considered their territory. On April 12, acting on orders from President Davis, they began to bombard Fort Sumter. By the next day the fort was in ruins. When his ammunition was almost exhausted, Major Anderson and his weary troops laid down their arms and surrendered. The Civil War had begun."[849] Though slavery was the ultimate cause for this war, people no longer were just fighting to abolish slavery, but they were fighting to save the Union.

For several years, neither side was winning. This all changed in April 1862, when Congress abolished slavery in the District of Colombia, leading Lincoln to believe that all slaves could be free or emancipated. Therefore, he issued a document called the Emancipation Proclamation. "This proclamation stated that after January 1, 1863, 'all persons held as slaves within any states... in rebellion against the United States shall be...forever free.'"[850] When that day came, the slaves were indeed freed. Finally the war was being fought for not just saving the Union, but also for freedom.

The aftermath of the war was great, both beneficial and detrimental. By the end of the war, more than four million blacks were freed from slavery, even though their way of living was not defined yet. This was known as the Thirteenth Amendment - the official abolishment of slavery. However, the war had also caused damage to the South's economy. The plantations in the South, where the slaves had once worked had been destroyed, and much of the wealth of Southern planters was gone.

Though slaves had become free because of the war, Southerners still segregated blacks from whites. Black Codes were passed in order to keep blacks in a semi-slavery condition. Blacks were only allowed to maintain jobs that involved housework or farming.

When Northerners heard about this they were alarmed, and alerted Congress. Congress passed the Civil Rights Act, which made blacks legal citizens of the United States of America. "It was necessary to state this specifically because the Dred Scott decision had declared that even free blacks were not American citizens."[851]

President Andrew Johnson vetoed the bill that Congress had passed. He felt that it was a mistake to make the blacks citizens. He said, "It is unconstitutional to give blacks safeguards which go infinitely beyond any that the ...Government has ever provided for the white race." "Before the war, he once said that he wished every white family in America could have one slave 'to take the drudgery' out of life!"[852] Congress again passed the Civil Rights act, obtaining the two-thirds majority in order to override the president's veto. The Civil Rights Act then became law.

Similar to the Civil Rights Act, the Fourteenth Amendment was passed, which made blacks citizens of the United States, guaranteeing them civil rights, and equal protection of the laws. Not only was the Fourteenth Amendment passed, but a Fifteenth Amendment was soon passed allowing all citizens (including African Americans) to vote.

These amendments were part of the Reconstruction period, and helped give blacks their freedoms, thus being named the Civil War Amendments. Is that not what the Civil War was about, two different parts of the country fighting to save the Union, but also trying to abolish or maintain slavery?

Several court cases were linked to these amendments. These court cases became known as the Civil Rights Cases. Though these amendments were passed in order to provide more equality between blacks and whites, there were still some racial issues, as seen in one court case, Plessy v. Ferguson.

Homer Adolf Plessy, a light-skinned black man from Louisiana was arrested for sitting in a "White" railroad car. This car was reserved by Louisiana law for whites only. Plessy went to court and argued that the separation of railroad cars is breaking the Thirteenth and Fourteenth Amendments. Though this was true, Justice Henry Brown, however, wrote:

"That [the Separate Car Act] does not conflict with the Thirteenth Amendment, which abolished slavery ... is too clear for argument ... A statute which implies merely a legal distinction between the white and colored races -- a distinction which is founded in the color of the two races, and which must always exist so long as white men are distinguished from the other race by color -- has no tendency to destroy the legal equality of the two races ... The object of the [Fourteenth] Amendment was undoubtedly to enforce the absolute equality of the two races before the law, but in the nature of things it could not have been intended to abolish distinctions based upon color, or to enforce social, as distinguished from political equality, or a commingling of the two races upon terms unsatisfactory to either."[853]

Before the Civil War broke out, the nation as a whole was slowly falling apart. It was no longer the complete puzzle it once was. America had been a nation that was united and strong. After the Revolutionary War, everyone was happy to celebrate their independence. With this in mind, many of those who were against slavery and wanted to abolish it believed now, that all people, even those who were slaves should have their freedom. Controversy soon arose when many southerners still believed that African Americans were inferior and beneath them.

The South depended on slaves to do its labor, whereas the North had factory workers to do the labor. Many Northerners also felt that if they continued to own slaves, then there would be competition between white and black workers. The white working men felt that slavery was not necessary. These two contrasting views soon caused the nation to split apart, leaving the Union and the Confederacy. America was now weak and people were not willing to accept change, this being a lead factor of the Civil War.

The Civil War was a catastrophic event. The numbers of dead on both sides attest to its impact. Though, with this entire catastrophe, slaves were freed by Lincoln's Emancipation Proclamation and by the Civil War amendments.

The Civil War showed just how vulnerable the nation was and how slavery was a major issue. It also showed how people were willing to stand up for what they believe in, as present when southern states seceded from the Union because they continued to want to practice slavery.

"Slavery was undoubtedly the immediate fomenting cause of the woeful American conflict. It was the great political factor around which the passions of the sections had long been gathered - the tallest pine in the political forest around whose top the fiercest lightning was to blaze and whose trunk was destined to be shivered in the earthquake shocks of war."[854]

Bibliography

Garraty, John A., The Story of America ,Holt, Rinehart and Winston, Inc., Orlando, 1991

Justice Henry Billings Brown, "Majority opinion in *Plessy v. Ferguson*," Desegregation and the Supreme Court, ed. Benjamin Munn Ziegler (Boston: D.C. Heath and Company, 1958) 50-51. as cited in, http://www.watson.org/~lisa/blackhistory/post-civilwar/notes.html #5
http://www.civilwarhome.com/gordoncauses.htm
http://www.civilwarhome.com/csconstitution.htm
http://www.usconstitution.net/const.html
http://www.kidport.com/RefLib/UsaHistory/CivilWar/CivilWar.htm
http://sc94.ameslab.gov/TOUR/alincoln.html

Speech at Alton, Illinois, October 15, 1858 by Stephen A. Douglas as cited in, The Story of America http://www.answers.com/main/ntquery;jsessionid=23kk9w0qatm4g?method=4&dsid=2222&dekey=Lincoln-Douglas+debates+of+1858&gwp=8&curtab=2222_1&sbid=lc05a&linktext=Lincoln%20and%20Douglas%20debate

Speech at Alton, Illinois, October 15, 1858 by Abraham Lincoln as cited in, The Story of America http://www.answers.com/main/ntquery;jsessionid=23kk9w0qatm4g?method=4&dsid=2222&dekey=Dred+Scott+v.+Sandford&gwp=8&curtab=2222_1&sbid=lc05a&linktext=Dred%20Scott%20decisionm
http://www.oyez.org/oyez/resource/case/101/
http://www.freemaninstitute.com/scott.htm
http://www.kidport.com/RefLib/UsaHistory/CivilWar/Slavery.htm
http://www.civilwarhome.com/slavery.htm

Ward, Geoffrey C., The Civil War an Illustrated History, Alfred A. Knopf, Inc., New York, 1990 http://showcase.netins.net/web/creative/lincoln/speeches/greeley.htm

ENDNOTES

[1] Government in America (Textbook)

[2] Federalist Papers 17 and 45

[3] Federalist 45

[4] Federalist No. 45

[5] Cato

[6] Government in America

[7] Kentucky Resolutions

[8] Kentucky Resolutions

[9] Government in America

[10] Government in America

[11] Government in America

[12] http://en.wikipedia.org/wiki/Tenth_Amendment_to_the_United_States_Constitution

[13] Government in America

[14] Cato

[15] http://www.law.umke.edu/faculty/projects/ftrials/conlaw/tenth&elev.htm

[16] Federalist No 45

[17] Marvin Meyers. *The Mind of the Founder Sources of the Political Thought of James Madison.* (University Press of New England 1973) p 69._

[18] Doris and Harold Faber. *The Early Years of the United States The Birth of a Nation.* (Charles Scribner's Son's New York 1989) p. 70

[19] Marvin Meyers. *The Mind of the Founder Sources of the Political Thought of James Madison.* (University Press of New England 1973) p 18

[20] Ian Finseth. *The Rise and Fall of Alexander Hamilton.* <http://xroads.virginia.edu/~CAP/ham/hampltcs.html#2> 1/2/2006

[21] Richard B. Morris. *Witnesses at the Creation Hamilton, Madison, Jay, and the Constitution.* (Holt, Rinehart and Winston New York, 1985) p 103

[22] <www.odur.let,rug.nl/`usa/B/gmason/gmas05.htm> 1/2/2006

[23] <www.lexrex.com/bios/phenry.htm> 1/2/2006

[24] <www.stradfordhall.org/richard.html?HISTORY> 1/2/2006

[25] James Roger Sharp. *American Politics in the Early Republic The New Nation in Crisis.* (Yale University Press,1993) p 23

[26] John C. Miller. *The Federalist Era.* (Harper & Row Publishers, 1960) p 30

[27] Ian Finseth. The Rise and Fall of Alexander Hamilton. <http://xroads. virginia.edu/~CAP/ham/hampltcs.html#2> 1/2/2006

[28] James Roger Sharp. *American Politics in the Early Republic The New Nation in Crisis.* (Yale University Press, 1993) p 24.

[29] Robert Bryan Haskins. <http://home.earthlink.net/~haskman/history. htm#VI>

[30] James Roger Sharp. *American Politics in the Early Republic The New Nation in Crisis.* (Yale University Press, 1993) p 24.

[31] Herbert J. Strong. *The Anti-Federalist Writings of the Opponents of the Constitution.* (The University of Chicago Press, 1981) p 39

[32] Herbert J. Strong. *The Anti-Federalist Writings of the Opponents of the Constitution.* (The University of Chicago Press, 1981) p 74

[33] Herbert J. Strong. *The Anti-Federalist Writings of the Opponents of the Constitution.* (The University of Chicago Press, 1981) p 208

[34] Alexander Hamilton and James Madison. *Federalist No. 52 The House of Representatives.* (From the New York Packet 1788)

[35] Marvin Meyers. *The Mind of the Founder, Sources of Political Thought of James Madison.* (University Press of New England, 1973) p 78

[36] Alexander Hamilton and James Madison. *Federalist No. 52 The House of Representatives.* (From the New York Packet) 1788

[37] Alexander Hamilton and James Madison. *Federalist No. 53 The Same Subject Continued: The House Of Representatives.* (From the New York Packet) 1788

[38] Doris and Harold Faber. *The Early Years of the United States The Birth of a Nation.* (Charles Scribner's Son's New York 1989) p. 72

[39] Alexander Hamilton. The Powers of the Judiciary Federalist No. 80.

[40] Alexander Hamilton. The Judiciary Branch, Federalist Paper No. 78.

[41] Brutus. *Anti-Federalist No. 78-79.* (New York Journal 1788)

[42] Alexander Hamilton. *The Executive Department Federalist No. 67.* (From the New York Packet) 1788

43 Alexander Hamilton. *The Executive Department Federalist No.67* (From the New York Packet) 1788

44 Letters from Cato. *Various Fears Concerning the Executive Department Anti Federalist No 67.* (The New York Journal) 1788

45 Letters from Cato. *Various Fears Concerning the Executive Department Anti Federalist No 67.* (The New York Journal) 1788

46 Alexander Hamilton or James Madison. *The Senate, Federalist No. 62* (For the Independent Journal.)

47 Alexander Hamilton or James Madison. *The Senate, Federalist No. 62* (For the Independent Journal.)

48 Alexander Hamilton or James Madison. *The Senate, Federalist No. 62* (For the Independent Journal.)

49 Brutus. *On the Organization and Powers of the Senate-Part 1 Anti-Federalist No. 62* (The New York Journal) 1788

50 Brutus. *On the Organization and Powers of the Senate-Part 1 Anti-Federalist No. 62* (The New York Journal) 1788

51 Brutus. *On the Organization and Powers of the Senate-Part 1 Anti-Federalist No. 62* (The New York Journal) 1788

52 Brutus. *On the Organization and Powers of the Senate-Part 1 Anti-Federalist No. 62* (The New York Journal) 1788

5354 Ferris, Robert G., The Signers of the Constitution, First Edition, Interpretive Publications Inc., Flagstaff, AZ, 1976, pp.172-174

55 Bradford, M.E., Second Edition Revised, Founding Fathers, University Press of Kansas, 1994, pp. 40-48

56 Morris, Richard B., First Edition, Witnesses At The Creation, Holt, Rinehart, and Winston, New York, NY, 1985, pp. 17-37

57 Lind, Michael, First Edition, Hamilton's Republic, The Free Press, New York, NY, pp. 218

58 Chidsey, Donald B., First Edition, Mr. Hamilton and Mr. Jefferson, International and Pan-American Conventions, Nashville, Tennessee, 1975, pp. 14-25

59 Lind, Michael, First Edition, Hamilton's Republic, The Free Press, New York, NY, pp. 127-133

60 Lind, Michael, First Edition, Hamilton's Republic, The Free Press, New York, NY, pp. 120-123

[61] Lind, Michael, First Edition, <u>Hamilton's Republic</u>, The Free Press, New York, NY, pp. 56, 153-155

[62] Lind, Michael, First Edition, <u>Hamilton's Republic</u>, The Free Press, New York, NY, pp. 218

[63] Helen Hill Miller, <u>George Mason the Man Who Didn't Sign</u> (Board of Regents of Gunston Hall, 1987) 1.

[64] Pauline Maier, <u>American Scripture</u> (New York: Alfred A. Knopf, 1997) 133.

[65] Maier 133.

[66] Maier 133.

[67]Donald Senese, <u>George Mason and the Legacy of Constitutional Liberty</u> (Fairfax: Fairfax County History Commission, 1989) 117.

[68] Senese 117.

[69] Robert Ferris and James Charleton, <u>The Signers of the Constitution</u> (Flagstaff: Interpretive Publications Inc, 1986) 33.

[70] "About the Founding Fathers," Oak Hill Publishing Company, http://www.constitutionfacts.com/Founding_Fathers/AboutFF.htm (accessed October 28, 2005)

[71] Gunston Hall, "George Mason and the Constitution," Gunston Hall, http://www.gunstonhall.org/georgemason/constitution.html (accessed October 25, 2005)

[72] "George Mason and the Constitution."

[73] Senese 118.

[74] Ferris 69.

[75] Miller 11.

[76] Miller 11.

[77] Miller 12.

[78] Robert Rutland, <u>The Papers of George Mason 1725-1792 Volume III</u> (Chapel Hill: University of North Carolina Press, 1970) 978.

[79] "George Mason and the Constitution."

[80] Rutland 989.

[81] Ferris 72.

[82] "George Mason and the Constitution."

[83] Rutland 991.

[84] Rutland 978.

[85] Senese 120.

[86] "George Mason and the Constitution."

[87] "George Mason and the Constitution."

[88] Rutland 991.

[89] Miller 13.

[90] Edmund Morgan, The Birth of the Republic 1763-89 (Chicago: The University of Chicago Press, 1992) 153.

[91] Carter Pittman, "Our Bill of Rights and How it Came to Be," http://www.constitution.org/gmason/amd_gmas.htm (accessed October 20, 2005).

[92] Miller 13.

[93] Miller 13.

[94] "George Mason and the Constitution."

[95] "George Mason and the Constitution."

[96] Ferris 85.

[97] "George Mason and the Constitution."

[98] "George Mason and the Constitution."

[99] Morgan 154.

[100] "George Mason and the Constitution."

[101] "George Mason and the Constitution."

[102] "Constitutional Topic: The Bill of Rights," The U.S. Constitution Online, http://www.usconstitution.net/consttop_bor.html (accessed October 20, 2005).

[103] "Constitutional Topic: The Bill of Rights."

[104] "Constitutional Topic: The Bill of Rights."

[105] "Constitutional Topic: The Bill of Rights."

[106] Senese 121.

[107] "About the Founding Fathers."

108 "Notes on the Amendments," The U.S. Constitution Online, http://www.usconstitution.net/constamnotes.html (accessed October 20, 2005).

[109] "Notes on the Amendments."

[110] Rutland 993.

[111] "Popular Election of Senators," http://www.gpoaccess.gov/constitution/pdf/con028.pdf (accessed October 22, 2005).

[112] "Popular Election of Senators."

[113] Rutland 993.

[114] "George Mason Quotes," Gunston Hall Plantation, http://gunstonhall. org/geogemason/quotes.html (accessed November 4, 2005).

[115] "Amendment I," *The Declaration of Independence and the Constitution of the United States of America* (Washington, D.C.: Cato Institute, 2000), 43.

[116] David Barton, *Original Intent: The Courts, the Constitution, & Religion* (Aledo: WallBuilder Press, 1997), 125-126.

[117] Ibid.

[118] Ibid.

[119] Ibid., 139-143.

[120] "Religion and the Founding of the American Republic," *Library of Congress*, http://www.loc.gov/exhibits/religion/rel04.html

[121] Barton, *Original Intent,* 92-93.

[122] Ibid., 93.

[123] Gregory Schaaf, Ph.D., *Franklin, Jefferson, & Madison on Religion and the State* (Santa Fe: CIAC Press, 2004), 83-84.

[124] "Franklin Requests Prayers in the Constitutional Convention," *Library of Congress.*

[125] "Amendment I," *The Declaration of Independence and the Constitution of the United States of America*, 43.

[126] John W. Whitehead, *The Second American Revolution* (Westchester: Crossway Books, 1982), 98.

[127] Ibid.

[128] Ibid.

[129] Barton, *Original Intent,* 28.

[130] Ibid.

[131] Ibid.

[132] Ibid.

[133] Ibid., 31.

[134] Whitehead, *The Second American Revolution,* 98.

[135] Barton, *Original Intent,* 45.

[136] Maureen Harrison and Steve Gilbert, *Freedom of Religion Decisions of the United States Supreme Courts* (San Diego: Excellent Books, 1996), 1.

[137] Barton, *Original Intent,* 43-44

[138] Ibid., 45-46.

[139] Whitehead, *The Second American Revolution*, 99-100.

[140] Barton, *Original Intent,* 25.

[141] Ibid., 44.

[142] Ibid.

[143] Whitehead, *The Second American Revolution,* 100.

[144] Barton, *Original Intent*, 25.

[145] Harrison and Gilbert, *Freedom of Religion Decisions,* 5.

[146] Ibid.

[147] Barton, *Original Intent,* 47.

[148] Ibid.

[149] Harrison and Gilbert, *Freedom of Religion Decisions*, 33.

[150] Barton, *Original Intent*, 367.

[151] Harrison and Gilbert, *Freedom of Religion Decisions*, 40.

[152] Victoria Sherrow, *Freedom of Worship* (Brookfield: The Millbrook Press, 1997), 9.

[153] Harrison and Gilbert, *Freedom of Religion Decisions*, 41.

[154] Barton, *Original Intent*, 13.

[155] Ibid., 14-15.

[156] Sherrow, *Freedom of Worship*, 8.

[157] "Religion and the Founding of the American Republic," *Library of Congress.*

[158] Roger Newman, *The Constitution and its Amendments: Volume 3* (New York: Macmillan Reference USA, 1999), 60

[159] Kris Palmer, *Constitutional Amendments 1789 to the Present* (Farmington Hills, IN: Gale Group Inc., 2000), 20

[160] Newman, *The Constitution Vol. 3*, 59.

[161] Chairman Warren Burger, *The Bill of Rights and Beyond,* (Washington D.C.: The Commission on the Bicentennial of the U.S. Constitution, 1991) 22

[162] Roger Newman, *The Constitution and its Amendments Volume 2* (New York: Macmillan Reference USA, 1998), 88

[163] Newman, *The Constitution Vol. 2,* 90

[164] David G. Savage, *The Supreme Court and Individual Rights 4th Edition* (Washington D.C.: CQ Press, 2004), 46,47

[165] Jethro Liberman, *A Practical Companion to the Constitution* (London: University of CA Press, Ltd., 1999), 196

166 U.S. v. Cruikshank et al. Supreme Court of the United States October Term, 1875

[167] Richard Hanes and Daniel Brannen, *Supreme Court Drama Volume 1* (Canada: UXL, Gale Group, 2001) 7

[168] Lorraine Glennon, *The 20th Century: An Illustrated History of our Life and Times* (North Dighton, MA: JG Press, Inc., 1999) 138

[169] Liberman, *Companion*, 196

[170] Newman, *The Constitution Vol. 3*, 59

[171] Savage, *The Supreme Court*, 37

[172] Palmer, *Constitutional Amendments*, 20

[173] Savage, *The Supreme Court*, 31

[174] Liberman, *Companion*, 141

[175] Savage, *The Supreme Court*, 48

[176] Savage, *The Supreme Court*, 48

[177] Hanes and Brannen, *Supreme Court Drama*, 17

[178] Savage, *The Supreme Court*, 49

[179] Savage, *The Supreme Court*, 49

[180] Liberman, *Companion*, 141

181 Anne and Heidi, "Women's March on D.C.," Documents from the Women's Liberation Movement, 29 November 1971, < http://scriptorium. lib.duke.edu/wlm/wom/> (7 November 2005)

[182] Savage, *The Supreme Court*, 50

[183] *Judy Madsen et al. v. Women's Health Center, Inc. et al* Supreme Court of the United States, 512 U.S. 753 1994

[184] Savage, The *Supreme Court*, 50

[185] "Skokie, Illinois" *Wikipedia, the Free Encyclopedia,* 4 November 2005 <http://en.wikipedia.org/wiki/Skokie,_Illinois> (5 November 2005)

[186] Palmer, *Constitutional Amendments*, 18

[187] Liberman, *Companion*, 347

[188] Palmer, *Constitutional Amendments*, 17

[189] Savage, *Supreme Court*, 47

[190] Palmer, *Constitutional Amendments*, 19

[191] *Lloyd Corporation v. Tanner* Supreme Court of the United States, 407 U.S. 551 1972

[192] Liberman, *Companion*, 347

[193] Palmer, *Constitutional Amendments*, 20

[194] *Saia v. The People of New York* Supreme Court of the United States, 334 U.S. 558 1948

[195] Palmer, *Constitutional Amendments*, 19

[196] Palmer, *Constitutional Amendments*, 20

[197] Lowell, James Russell. "V. Cooper.", A Fable for Critics. 1848

[198] Milton, John. Areopagitica: A speech of Mr. John Milton for the liberty of unlicensed printing to the Parliament of England. November 23, 1644.

[199] U.S. Const. Bill of Rights, Amendment I. 1791.

[4] Linder, Doug. *The Trials of Lenny Bruce*, http://www.law.umkc.edu/faculty/projects/ftrials/bruce/bruce.html (2003)

[200] Ibid

[201] Ibid

[202] Ibid

[203] Ibid

[204] Ibid

[205] Ibid

[206] Ibid

[207] Ibid

[208] Ibid

[209] Ibid

[210] Ibid

[211] Ibid

[212] Ibid

[213] Ibid

[214] Ibid

[215] Ibid

[216] Ibid

[217] Assistant District Attorney Vincent Cuccia, http://www.colonytheatre.org/shows/Lenny.html

[218] Doug Linder, *The Trials of Lenny Bruce*, http://www.law.umkc.edu/faculty/projects/ftrials/bruce/bruce.html (2003)

[219] Hustler Magazine v. Falwell, 485 U.S. 46, (1988).

[220] Ibid

[221] "Court, 8-0, Extends Right to Criticize Those in Public Eye," *New York Times*, 25 February 1988, sec. A, p. 1

[222] set by *New York Times Company v. Sullivan*, 376 U.S. 254 (1964) ruled that "actual malice" must be found for libel charges, i.e. the publisher must knowingly print falsities as fact, knowing they are not.

[223] Harrison, Maureen, Gilbert Steve, ed. "VULGAR SPEECH: Cohen v. California", *Freedom of Speech Decision of the United States Supreme Court*, Excellent Books, San Diego, 1996.

[224] Ibid

[225] Harrison, Maureen, Gilbert Steve, ed. "FILTHY WORDS: The FCC v. Pacifica Foundation", *Freedom of Speech Decision of the United States Supreme Court*, Excellent Books, San Diego, 1996.

[226] Ibid

[227] Ibid

[228] *The People vs. Larry Flynt*. Milos Forman. Columbia Pictures, 1996.

[229] Evans, J. E. Freedom of the Press. 1st ed. Vol. 1. Minneapolis: Lerner Publications Company, 1990. 19-20.

[230] Ibid.

[231] Jensen, Carl, and Project Censored. 20 Years of Censored News. 1st ed. Vol. 1. New York City: Seven Stories P, 1997. 39-40, 109-110, 195, 271-272, 331-332.

[232] Evans, J. E. Freedom of the Press. 1st ed. Vol. 1. Minneapolis: Lerner Publications Company, 1990. 8.

[233] Lindop, Edmund. The Bill of Rights and Landmark Cases. 1st ed. Vol. 1. New York City: Franklin Watts, 1989. 95.

234 Lindop, Edmund. The Bill of Rights and Landmark Cases. 1st ed. Vol. 1. New York City: Franklin Watts, 1989. 78-82.

235 Lindop, Edmund. The Bill of Rights and Landmark Cases. 1st ed. Vol. 1. New York City: Franklin Watts, 1989. 79.

236 Ibid. 75-78

237 Stewart, John. America. 1st ed. Vol.1. New York City: Warner Bros, 2004. 155.

238 Jensen, Carl, and Project Censored. 20 Years of Censored News. 1st ed. Vol. 1. New York City: Seven Stories P, 1997. 9-10.

239 Jensen, Carl, and Project Censored. 20 Years of Censored News. 1st ed. Vol. 1. New York City: Seven Stories P, 1997. 9.

240 Jensen, Carl, and Project Censored. 20 Years of Censored News. 1st ed. Vol. 1. New York City: Seven Stories P, 1997. 28-29.

241 "Indonesia's New Phase." The New York Times 22 Dec. 1965. 17 Oct. 2005 <http://pqasb.pqarchiver.com/nytimes/>.

242 Jensen, Carl, and Project Censored. 20 Years of Censored News. 1st ed. Vol. 1. New York City: Seven Stories P, 1997. 30-31.

243 Ibid. 30

244 Ibid. 29.

245 Jensen, Carl, and Project Censored. 20 Years of Censored News. 1st ed. Vol. 1. New York City: Seven Stories P, 1997. 29.

246 Jensen, Carl, and Project Censored. 20 Years of Censored News. 1st ed. Vol. 1. New York City: Seven Stories P, 1997. 29.

247 Ibid.

248 Ibid. 16-19.

249 Jensen, Carl, and Project Censored. 20 Years of Censored News. 1st ed. Vol. 1. New York City: Seven Stories P, 1997. 17

250 Jensen, Carl, and Project Censored. 20 Years of Censored News. 1st ed. Vol. 1. New York City: Seven Stories P, 1997. 68-68

251 Roderick T. Long, "Philosophy Page," http://praxeology.net/seneca. htm (accessed September 2, 2005).

252 Carl T. Bogus, "The Hidden History of the Second Amendment," Violence Policy Center, http://www.vpc.org/fact_sht/hidhist.htm (accessed September 2, 2005).

253 S. Marvin Tuomala, "The Right to Bear Arms," http://www. spiritcaller.net/quotes/guns.htm (accessed September 2, 2005).

[254]Ibid.

[255]Herbert M. Levine, *American Issues Debated; Gun Control*, ed. Kathy DeVico, Shirley Shalit (Austin, TX: Vaughn Company, Steck, 1998), 65.

[256]Ibid.

[257]Bogus, The Hidden History of the Second Amendment," http://www.vpc.org/fact_sht/hidhist.htm.

[258]John R. Lott Jr., "Clinton Lies About the Assault Weapons Ban," 1998, http://www.tsra.com/Lott2.htm (accessed September 2, 2005).

[259]Levine, *American Issues Debated; Gun Control*, 30.

[260]Levine, *American Issues Debated; Gun Control*, 29.

[261]Levine, *American Issues Debated; Gun Control*, 9.

[262]"Map & Graph: Countries by Crime: Murders with Firearms," December, 2005, nationmaster.com, http://www.nationmaster.com/graph-T/cri_mur_wit_fir_cap.

[263]"Q&A: Brazil Arms Referendum," October 23, 2005, BBC News, http://news.bbc.co.uk/2/hi/americas/4356728.stm (accessed November 1, 2005).

[264]"Firearms and Violence," July 9, 2005, DAWN; the Internet Edition, http://www.dawn.com/2005/07/09/ed.htm (accessed November 1, 2005).

[265]Steve Centanni, "DC Gun Law Under Fire," December 2, 2002, Fox News, http://www.foxnews.com/story/0,2933,71750,00.html (accessed September 2, 2005).

[266]Levine, *American Issues Debated; Gun Control*, 28.

[267]Levine, *American Issues Debated; Gun Control*, 30.

[268]Saul Cornell, "The Second Amendment Under Fire: The Uses of History and the Politics of Gun Control," January, 2001, George Mason University, http://historymatters.gmu.edu/credits.html (accessed September 2, 2005).

[269]Ibid.

[270]"Editorial: Lax Gun Laws Serving Interests of Terrorists," March, 2005, San Antonio Express-News, http://www.mysanantonio.com/opinion/editorials/stories/MYSA2031405.04B.terror-guns2ed.12b210f7d.html.

[271]Amy Goldstein, "House Passes Ban on Gun Industry Lawsuits," *The Washington Post*, 21 October 2005, 7(A).

[272]Ibid.

[273]Ibid.

[274]"Bush Administration Statement On Senate Bill Repeats Lies Of The National Rifle Association," July 26, 2005, The Brady Campaign, http:// http://www.bradycampaign.org/press/release.php?release=670 (accessed September 2, 2005).

[275]"Gun Lobby Endangers Workers in its Push to Force Businesses to Allow Guns in the Workplace," August 2, 2005, The Brady Campaign, http://www.bradycampaign.org/press/release.php?release=678 (accessed September 2, 2005).

[276]Dave Montgomery, "Interest in Renewing '94 Weapons Ban is Low," August 12, 2004, Detroit Free Press, http://www.freep.com/news/nw/ guns12e_20040812.htm (accessed September 2, 2005).

[277]Susan Jones, "Ad Campaign Warns Tourists About New Florida Gun Law," September 28, 2005, CNSNews.com, http://www.cnsnews.com/ ViewCulture.asp?Page=%5CCulture%5Carchive%5C200509%5CCUL2 0050928a.html.

[278]Spencer S. Hsu, "House GOP Proposes to Repeal D.C. Gun Bans," *Washington Post*, 14 September 2005, 1(A) [newspaper on-line]; available from http://www.washingtonpost.com/wp-dyn/articles/A18935- 2004Sep13.html; Internet.

[279]Mark Souder, "Issues: Second Amendment," U.S. House of Representatives, http://souder.house.gov/Issues/Issue/?IssueID=664.

[280]Spencer S. Hsu, "House Votes to Repeal D.C. Gun Limits," *Washington Post*, 30 September 2005, 1(B) [newspaper on-line]; available from http://www.washingtonpost.com/wp-dyn/articles/ A60034-2004Sep29.html; Internet.

[281]Ibid.

[282]David Vacca, "David Vacca's Suitcase Full of Good Ideas," September 16, 2005, http://www.radix.net/~vacca/ (accessed September 2, 2005).

[283]Ibid.

[284]Long, Philosophy Page," http://praxeology.net/seneca.htm.

[285]Tom Sargis Jr., "Famous Quotes from Famous Americans (and others...)," October 14, 2005, http://www.ycsi.net/users/gunsmith/quotes. htm (accessed October 14, 2005).

[286] Wikipedia. 2005. <http://en.wikpdia.org/wiki/Second_Amendment_ to_the_United_States_Constitution>

[2] Wikipedia. Second Amendment

3 <www.BradyCampaign.org/facts/issues>

4 http://www.constitution.org/cmt/tmc/pcl.htm

5 "Whether the Second Amendment Secures an Individual Right", 2004. <http://www.usdoj.gov/olc/secondamendment2.htm>

6 "Whether the Second Amendment..."

7 <http://www.enotes.com/gun-violence-article/>

8 Stephen P. Halbrook, "Guns and Prohibition, in Al Capone's day and Now". The Wall Street Journal. April11, 1989, A22 as found online @ www.stephenhalbrook.com/articles/guns&prohibition.html

9 <http://www.plu.edu/≈gunvlnce/history2.html#MFA>

10 Freya Ottem Hanson. The Second Amendment. Enslow Publishers, Inc. Springfield, NJ.1998. Pp 34-35.

11<http://www.gunlawnews.org/ffa.38.html>

12 <http//proliberty.com/observer/20040805.htm>

13 <www.jpfo.org/miller.html>

14 Hanson, 37.

15 <http://thomas.loc.gov/cgi-bin/bdquery/z?d099:SN00049: @ @@D&summ2=m>

16 Hanson, 50.

17 <http://en.wikipedia.org.wiki/United_States_v._Lopez>

18 <www.BradyCampaign.org/facts/issues>

19Clark Staten, "Three Days of Hell in Los Angeles",1992.
        <www.emergency.com/la-riots.htm>

20Second Amendment Foundation, "SAF Demands Answers For Gun Ban at FEMA Relief Center Outside Baton Rouge", 2005.
        <http://www.saf.org/viewpr-new.asp?id=164

287United States of America v. Emerson, 270 F.3d 203, 220, 260 (5th Cir. 2001).

288Article I, Section 8 of the United States Constitution.

289The Right to Keep and Bear Arms," A Report of the Subcommittee on the Constitution of the United States Committee on the Judiciary, 97th Cong. 2nd Session (1982). Page 11.

290Id., at pages 11-12.

291The Second Amendment and the Historiography of the Bill of Rights by David T. Hardy, 4 J. of L. & Pol. 1-62 (1987) found at www.hardylaw. net/historiography.html

[292]"The Right to Keep and Bear Arms," A Report of the Subcommittee on the Constitution of the United States Committee on the Judiciary, 97th Cong. 2nd Session (1982). Page 7, Found at http./ www.constitution.org/ mil/rkba1982.htm

[293]Id., at page 2.

[294]A Century of Lawmaking for a New Nation: U.S. Congressional Documents and Debates, 1774 - 1875. Annals of Congress, House of Representatives, 1st Congress, 1st Session

Pages 451 & 452.

[295]Id., at p.5.

[296]http://en.wikipedia.org/wiki/Second_Amendment_to_the_United_ States_Constitution, page 7.

[297]Id.

[298]Id.

[299]Id.

[300]The Embarrassing Second Amendment by Sanford Levinson, 99 Yale Law Journal pp.637-659 found in www.guncite.com/journals/embar. html, page 5.

[301]United States v. Emerson, 270 F.3d 203, 220, 260 (5th Cir. 2001).

[302]The Right to Keep and Bear Arms," A Report of the Subcommittee on the Constitution of the United States Committee on the Judiciary, 97th Cong. 2nd Session (1982).

[303] Is the Second Amendment an individual or a collective right: United States v. Emerson's revolutionary interpretation of the right to bear arms. St. John's Law Review, Spring 2003 by Michael Busch

[304]United States v. Emerson, 270 F.3d 203, 220, 260 (5th Cir. 2001).

[305] Levinson, 99 Yale Law Journal pp.637-659 found in www.guncite. com/journals/embar.html

[306]Id., at page 4.

[307]The Second Amendment and the Historiography of the Bill of Rights

by David T. Hardy, 4 J. of L. & Pol. 1-62 (1987) found in www.hardylaw. net/historiography.html

[308]Whether the Second Amendment Secures an Individual Right, Memorandum Opinion for the Attorney General, August 24, 2004, p.15 found at www.usdoj.gov/olc/secondamendment2.htm

[309]http://www.bradycampaign.org/facts/issues/?page=second, Brady Campaign to Prevent Gun Violence, The Second Amendment.

[310] http://www.saf.org/ThePeopleUS.html, The People in the United States Constitution.

[311]The Embarrassing Second Amendment by Sanford Levinson, 99 Yale Law Journal pp.637-659 found in www.guncite.com/journals/embar.html

[312]Emerson at 24.

[313]"Whether the Second Amendment Secures an Individual Right, Memorandum Opinion for the Attorney General, August 24, 2004, p.15 found at www.usdoj.gov/olc/secondamendment2.htm

[314]The Right to Keep and Bear Arms," A Report of the Subcommittee on the Constitution of the United States Committee on the Judiciary, 97th Cong. 2nd Session (1982). Id., at page 11.

[315]United States v. Miller, 307 U.S. 174 (1937)

[316]Is the Second Amendment an individual or a collective right: United States v. Emerson's revolutionary interpretation of the right to bear arms. St. John's Law Review, Spring 2003 by Busch, Michael

[317]The Second Amendment and the Historiography of the Bill of Rights by David T. Hardy, 4 J. of L. & Pol. 1-62 (1987) found at www.hardylaw.net/historiography.html

[318] Amendments to the Constitution. 2004. United States House of Representatives. http://www.house.gov/Constitution/Amend.html (accessed September 2005)

[319] Schulz, Nancy. 2001. The E-Files. Washington Post. April 29, sec. G.

[320] Li, Xing. 2005. FanFiction.Net. Fanfiction.Net. http://www.fanfiction.net/ (accessed September 2005)

[321] Dilucchio, Patrizia. 1997. Multimedia: Get with the Programs of the Cultish World of Fan Fiction, Stars of Competing TV Shows Mix It Up—and Censors Don't Exist. Entertainment Weekly. September 26.

[322] Chandler-Olcott, Kelly and Mahar, Donna. 2003. Adolescents' anime-inspired "fanfictions": An exploration of multiliteracies. Journal of Adolescent & Adult Literacy. April 1.

[323] Mayo, Tracy. 2003. Taking Liberties with Harry Potter Thousands of Spin-offs of J. K. Rowling's Novels - Many with Graphic Sex – can be Read on the Internet. But Why Is This Fan Fiction, Often of Questionable Legality, Allowed to Flourish? The Boston Globe. June 29, sec. Magazine.

[324] On the extraordinary growth of fanorama and why it is here to stay. 2003. The Spectator. June 14.

[325] Plagiarism. 2005. Wikipedia. http://en.wikipedia.org/wiki/Plagiarism (accessed October 22, 2005)

[326] Cha, Ariana Eunjung. 2003. Harry Potter and the Copyright Lawyer. The Washington Post. June 18, sec. A.

[327] Copyright Infringement. 2005. http://en.wikipedia.org/wiki/ Copyright_infringement (accessed October 22, 2005)

[328] Interview with the author. Shinjin, Shirou. October 22, 2005. E-mail interview.

[329] Li, Xing. 2005. FanFiction.Net. Fanfiction.Net. http://www.fanfiction. net/ (accessed September 2005)

[330] Abas, Zoraini Wati. 2003. Helping kids to pick up writing skills. New Straits Times. September 25, sec. Outlook Web Watch.

[331] Li, Xing. 2005. FanFiction.Net. Fanfiction.Net. http://www.fanfiction. net/ (accessed September 2005)

[332] On the extraordinary growth of fanorama and why it is here to stay. 2003. The Spectator. June 14.

[333] Gray, B Allison. 2005. Good Conversation! A Talk with Tamora Pierce. School Library Journal. March 1.

[334] On the extraordinary growth of fanorama and why it is here to stay. 2003. The Spectator. June 14.

[335] Mayo, Tracy. 2003. Taking Liberties with Harry Potter Thousands of Spin-offs of J. K. Rowling's Novels - Many with Graphic Sex – can be Read on the Internet. But Why Is This Fan Fiction, Often of Questionable Legality, Allowed to Flourish? The Boston Globe. June 29, sec. Magazine.

[336] Gray, B Allison. 2005. Good Conversation! A Talk with Tamora Pierce. School Library Journal. March 1.

[337] Interview with the author. Shinjin, Shirou. October 22, 2005. E-mail interview.

[338] Schulz, Nancy. 2001. The E-Files. Washington Post. April 29, sec. G.

339 Interview with the author. Shinjin, Shirou. October 22, 2005. E-mail interview.

340 Mayo, Tracy. 2003. Taking Liberties with Harry Potter Thousands of Spin-offs of J. K. Rowling's Novels - Many with Graphic Sex – can be Read on the Internet. But Why Is This Fan Fiction, Often of Questionable Legality, Allowed to Flourish? The Boston Globe. June 29, sec. Magazine.

341 Buechner, Maryanne Murray. 2002. Pop Fiction Stars and storybook characters are inspiring more teens to write for the Web. Is this a good thing? Time. March 4.

342 Weeks, Linton. 2004. IT was a dark+stormy Nite... The Washington Post. February 1, sec. Style.

343 Li, Xing. 2005. FanFiction.Net. Fanfiction.Net. http://www.fanfiction.net/ (accessed September 2005)

344 Cha, Ariana Eunjung. 2003. Harry Potter and the Copyright Lawyer. The Washington Post. June 18, sec. A.

345 Li, Xing. 2005. FanFiction.Net. Fanfiction.Net. http://www.fanfiction.net/ (accessed September 2005)

346 Interview with the author. Shinjin, Shirou. October 22, 2005. E-mail interview.

347 MediaMiner.Org. 2005. MediaMiner.Org. http://www.mediaminer.org/fanfic/ (accessed September 2005)

348 Interview with the author. Shinjin, Shirou. October 22, 2005. E-mail interview

349 Cha, Ariana Eunjung. 2003. Harry Potter and the Copyright Lawyer. The Washington Post. June 18, sec. A.

350 Interview with the author. Shinjin, Shirou. October 22, 2005. E-mail interview.

351 Potter, Andrew. 2004. Will it be free, or feudal? National Post. May 15, sec. Books.

352 Salamon, Julie. 2001. The cult of Buffy. New York Times Upfront. May 5.

353 Potter, Andrew. 2004. Will it be free, or feudal? National Post. May 15, sec. Books.

354 Interview with the author. Shinjin, Shirou. October 22, 2005. E-mail interview.

355 Li, Xing. 2005. FanFiction.Net. Fanfiction.Net. http://www.fanfiction. net/ (accessed September 2005)

356 Mayo, Tracy. 2003. Taking Liberties with Harry Potter Thousands of Spin-offs of J. K. Rowling's Novels - Many with Graphic Sex – can be Read on the Internet. But Why Is This Fan Fiction, Often of Questionable Legality, Allowed to Flourish? The Boston Globe. June 29, sec. Magazine.

357 Schulz, Nancy. 2001. The E-Files. Washington Post. April 29, sec. G.

358 Darbyshire, Peter. 2005. Classic characters never die: They're just reinvented by modern-day writers. Vancouver Providence. September 11, sec. Unwind.

359 Chandler-Olcott, Kelly and Mahar, Donna. 2003. Adolescents' anime-inspired "fanfictions": An exploration of multiliteracies. Journal of Adolescent & Adult Literacy. April 1.

360 Potter, Andrew. 2004. Will it be free, or feudal? National Post. May 15, sec. Books.

361 Mayo, Tracy. 2003. Taking Liberties with Harry Potter Thousands of Spin-offs of J. K. Rowling's Novels - Many with Graphic Sex – can be Read on the Internet. But Why Is This Fan Fiction, Often of Questionable Legality, Allowed to Flourish? The Boston Globe. June 29, sec. Magazine.

362 Schulz, Nancy. 2001. The E-Files. Washington Post. April 29, sec. G.

363 Buechner, Maryanne Murray. 2002. Pop Fiction Stars and storybook characters are inspiring more teens to write for the Web. Is this a good thing? Time. March 4.

364 Scodari, Christine and Felder, Jenna L. 2000. Creating a pocket universe: "Shippers," fan fiction, and the X-Files online. Communication Studies. October 1.

365 Cha, Ariana Eunjung. 2003. Harry Potter and the Copyright Lawyer. The Washington Post. June 18, sec. A.

366 Li, Xing. 2005. FanFiction.Net. Fanfiction.Net. http://www.fanfiction. net/ (accessed September 2005)

367 Shepherd, Robert E, Dec. 1999. "The Juvenile Court at 100 Years: A Look Back." Juvenile Justice Bulletin. Page 13-21. Retrieved October 24, 2005 from SIRS Researcher.

368 Ibid

[369] Shepherd, Robert E, Dec. 1999. "The Juvenile Court at 100 Years: A Look Back." Juvenile Justice Bulletin. Page 13-21. Retrieved October 24, 2005 from SIRS Researcher

[370] http://www.juvenilejusticefyi.com/history_of_juvenile_justice.html

[371] Shepherd, Robert E, Dec. 1999. "The Juvenile Court at 100 Years: A Look Back." Juvenile Justice Bulletin. Page 13-21. Retrieved October 24, 2005 from SIRS Researcher

[372] Pardeck, John T. Children's Rights: Policy and Practice. New York: The Haworth Social Work Press, 2002. Page 12

[373] http://www.juvenilejusticefyi.com/history_of_juvenile_justice.html

[374] IBID

[375] Pardeck, John T. Children's Rights: Policy and Practice. New York: The Haworth Social Work Press, 2002. Page 12

[376] IBID

[377] http://www.youthrights.org/inregault.shtml

[378] Ibid

[379] In Re Gault, 387 U.S. 1 (1967)

[380] Ibid

[381] White, Susan O. Handbook of Youth and Justice. New York: Plenum Publishers, 2001.

[382] Jost, Kenneth, April 23, 2003. "Children's Legal Rights." CQ Researcher. Page 339-354. Retrieved October 24, 2005 from SIRS Researcher.

[383] Ibid

[384] Roberts, Albert R. Juvenile Justice Sourcebook. New York: Oxford University Press, 2004.

[385] www.tjpc.state.tx.us/publications/reviews/02/02-2-13.htm

[386] Ibid

[387] Ibid

[388] Roberts, Albert R. Juvenile Justice Sourcebook. New York: Oxford University Press, 2004. pg. 263

[389] Roberts, Albert R. Juvenile Justice Sourcebook. New York: Oxford University Press, 2004. pg. 265

[390] Ibid

[391] Snyder, Howard N. and Sickmund, Melissa, Dec. 1999. "The Juvenile Justice: A Century of Change." Juvenile Justice Bulletin. Page 1-20. Retrieved October 24, 2005 from SIRS Researcher.

[392] Grisso, Thomas. Youth on Trial. Chicago: University of Chicago Press, 2000. Pg 14

[393] White, Susan O. Handbook of Youth and Justice. New York: Plenum Publishers, 2001 pg. 386

[394] Leiberman, Jethro K. The Evolving Constitution. New York: Random House, Inc., 1992. pg 291

[395] Ibid

[396] Maryam, Ahrajani, Youth Justice in America. Washington D.C.: CQ Press, 2005 pg. 33

[397] Maryam, Ahrajani, Youth Justice in America. Washington D.C.: CQ Press, 2005 pg. 33

[398] Maryam, Ahrajani, Youth Justice in America. Washington D.C.: CQ Press, 2005 pg. 153

[399] Jost, Kenneth, April 23, 2003. "Children's Legal Rights." CQ Researcher. Page 339-354. Retrieved October 24, 2005 from SIRS Researcher.

[400] Richey, Warren, Feb. 1, 2000. "Teens and the Death Penalty: In Executing Youths, U.S. Stands Alone." Christian Science Monitor News Service. Retrieved October 24, 2005 from SIRS Researcher.

[401] Ibid

[402] Roberts, Albert R. Juvenile Justice Sourcebook. New York: Oxford University Press, 2004 pg. 311

[403] Grisso, Thomas. Youth on Trial. Chicago: University of Chicago Press, 2000 pg. 267

[404] Roberts, Albert R. Juvenile Justice Sourcebook. New York: Oxford University Press, 2004 pg. 51

[405] Grisso, Thomas, Youth on Trial. Chicago: University of Chicago Press, 2000 pg. 287

[406] Richey, Warren, Feb. 1, 2000. "Teens and the Death Penalty: In Executing Youths, U.S. Stands Alone." Christian Science Monitor News Service. Retrieved October 24, 2005 from SIRS Researcher.

[407] Ibid

[408] Grisso, Thomas. Youth on Trial. Chicago: University of Chicago Press, 2000 pg. 287

[409] Grisso, Thomas. Youth on Trial. Chicago: University of Chicago Press, 2000 pg. 287

[410] Pardeck, John T. Children's Rights: Policy and Practice. New York: The Haworth Social Work Press, 2002 pg- 14

[411] Ibid

[412] Roberts, Albert R. Juvenile Justice Sourcebook. Oxford University Press, New York: 2004 pg. 475

[413] George C. Edwards III, Martin P. Wattenberg, and Robert L Lineberry, Government in America: People, Politics and Policy. (New York: Longman, 1998), 572.

[414] Ibid.

[415] Kris E. Palmer, Constitutional Amendments: 1789 to the Present. (New York, Gale Group, 2000), 67.

[416] Roger K. Newman, The Constitution and Its Amendments, Volume 3, from the First Amendment: Libel and Defamation to the Thirteenth Amendment. (New York, Macmillan Reference USA, 1999), 72.

[417] Ibid.

[418] Kris E. Palmer, 82, 83.

[419] Kris E. Palmer, 83.

[420] Ibid.

[421] Roger K. Newman, 76.

[422] Ibid.

[423] Roger K. Newman, 76, 77.

[424] K. B. Melear, "From In Loco Parentis to Consumerism: A Legal Analysis of the Contractual Relationship Between Institution and Student," *NASPA Journal* 40 (2003).

[425] Andre A. Moenssens, "Do School Children Have Fourth Amendment Rights?," *Forensic-Evidence.com*: University of Missouri-Kansas City School of Law 2004. <http:// www.forensic-evidence.com/site/Police/ school_4th.html> (7 October 2005).

[426] Touro Law Center, "TINKER ET AL. v. DES MOINES INDEPENDENT COMMUNITY SCHOOL DISTRICT ET AL," *Touro Law Center:* Bringing Law to Life 2005. <http://www.tourolaw.edu/ patch/Tinker/> (7 October 2005).

[427] Ibid.

[428] Kris E. Palmer, 68.

[429] Andre A. Moenssens.

[430] Ibid.

[431] Kris E. Palmer, 68.

[432] Ibid.

[433] Roger K. Newman, 80.

[434] Lucius J. Barker, Twiley W. Barker, Jr., Michael W. Combs, Kevin L. Lyles, H. W. Perry, Jr.,

Civil Liberties and the Constitution: Cases and Commentaries. (Upper Saddle River, New Jersey, 1998), 793.

[435] Kris E. Palmer, 68.

[436] Lucius J. Barker, Twiley W. Barker, Jr., Michael W. Combs, Kevin L. Lyles, H. W. Perry, Jr., 794.

[437] Kris E. Palmer, 68.

[438] Andre A. Moenssens

[439] Kris E. Palmer, 68.

[440] Ibid.

[441] Andre A. Moenssens

[442] Lucius J. Barker, Twiley W. Barker, Jr., Michael W. Combs, Kevin L. Lyles, H. W. Perry, Jr., 796.

[443] Ibid.

[444] Lucius J. Barker, Twiley W. Barker, Jr., Michael W. Combs, Kevin L. Lyles, H. W. Perry, Jr., 798.

[445] Andre A. Moenssens

[446] Ibid.

[447] Alschuler, Albert. *Impact*, John Kasich, The O'Reilly Factor, June 27 2002. Fox New Network, 2002.

[448] Ibid.

[449] Samuel Walker. *In Defense of American Liberties: A History of the ACLU*, (Edwardsville, Illinois: Southern Illinois University Press, 1999), 131.

[450] Scott Canon, "Debate over right to privacy roils a nation and its courts," *Knight Rider Newspaper*, sec. 1, October 15, 2005.

[451] Jay Bookman, "Privacy Right Unlisted but Perfectly Clear," *Atlanta Journal-Constitution*, sec. 1, October 18, 2005.

[452] US Constitution, 4th amendment.

[453] Amitai Etzioni. *The Limits of Privacy.* New York: Basic Books, 1999.

[454] U.S. Government, "Privacy," http://privacy.gov.us/privacy%5Frights/

[455] Ibid., 4.

[456] Constitution of the United States, *Fourth Amendment*

[457] Elaine Cassel. *The War on Civil Liberties: How Bush and Ashcroft Have Dismantled the Bill of Rights*, (Chicago, Illinois: Lawrence Hill Books), 2004.

[458] Walker, 131.

[459] Bookman, 1.

[460] Thomson Find Law, "Ninth Amendment- Unenumerated Rights" U.S. Constitution: 9th Amendment, http://caselaw.lp.findlaw.com/data/constitution/amendment09/ (accessed October 25, 2005)

[461] Bookman, 1.

[462] Charles Sykes, *The End of Privacy: Personal Rights in the Surveillance Society*, (New York: St. Martin's Press, 1999), 29.

[463] Canon, 2.

[464] Etzioni, 192.

[465] Ibid., 193.

[466] Ibid., 193.

[467] NIH, "Privacy Act of 1974," http://www.nih.gov/icd/od/foia/privact74.htm (accessed October 30, 2005.)

[468] Ibid., 2.

[469] Dr. Tom O'Connor, "Right of Privacy," Constitutional Law, http://faculty.nwc.edu/toconnor/325/325lect.04.htm (accessed October 24, 2005)

[470] Simson Garfinkle, *Database Nation: The Death of Privacy in the 21st Century* (Sebastopol, CA: O'Reilly and Associates, 2000), 6.

[471] Christina Parenti, *The Soft Cage: Surveillance in America from slave passes to the war on terror* (Cambridge, MA: Basic Books, 2003), 2.

[472] Etzioni, 140.

[473] Ibid., 140.

[474] Ibid., 141.

[475] Cassel, 11.

[476] Ibid., 11.

[477] Ibid., 13.

[478] Ibid., 13.

[479] Herbert N. Foerstel, *Refuge of a Scoundrel: The Patriot Act in Libraries* (Westport, CT: Libraries Unlimited, 2004), 15.

[480] Ibid., xiii

[481] Ibid., 15.

[482] Cassel, 13.

[483] Ibid., 14.

[484] Ibid., 15.

[485] Richard C Leone and Greg Anrig, JR. ed., *The War on Our Freedoms: Civil Liberties in an Age of Terrorism,* (New York: Public Affairs, 2003), 130

[486] Ibid., 130.

[487] Ibid., 131.

[488] Ibid., 17.

[489] Ibid., 16.

[490] Canon, 2.

[491] Leonard W. Levy, *Origins of the Bill of Rights* (New Haven: Yale University Press, 1999), 241.

[492] Jack N. Rakove, *Original Meanings: Politics and Ideas in the Making of the Constitution* (New York: Vintage, 1996), 289.

[493] Justice Arthur J. Goldberg, "Concurring Opinion: Supreme Court of the United States: 381 U.S. 479: *Griswold v. Connecticut*" no.469 (1965). dKosopedia: The Free Political Encyclopedia, http://www.dksospedia.com/index.php?title=Griswold_v._Connecticut-Concurrence_Goldberg

[494] Bennett B. Patterson, *The Forgotten Ninth Amendment* (Indianapolis: Bobbs-Merrill, 1955).

[495] Thomas Jefferson, *Declaration of Independence*, 1.

[496] Levy, 249.

[497] George Mason, in Rakove, 288.

498 John Leland, "John Spencer to James Madison, Enclosing John Leland's Objections" in *The Debate on the Constitution: Federalist and Anti-Federalist Speeches, Articles, and Letters During the Struggle over Ratification*, Part Two, ed. Bernard Bailyn, 268 (New York: Library of America, 1993).

499 Mercy Otis Warren, "A Columbian Patriot", ed. Bailyn, 294.

500 Alexander Hamilton, in Levy, 245.

501 James Wilson, in Levy, 246.

502 James Madison, in Levy, 246.

503 Noah Webster, "Giles Hickory III", ed. Bailyn, 311.

504 James Madison, in Rakove, 289.

505 "Amendments Proposed by the Virginia Convention, June 27, 1788", in Levy, 275.

506 James Madison, in Goldberg, http://www.dksospedia.com/index.php?title=Griswold_v._Connecticut-Concurrence_Goldberg

507 James Madison, "Amendments Offered to Congress by James Madison, June 8, 1789", in Levy, 282-283.

508 Levy, 249.

509 Justice Joseph Story, in Goldberg, http://www.dksospedia.com/index.php?title=Griswold_v._Connecticut-Concurrence_Goldberg

510 Levy, 249.

511 Levy, 247.

512 Levy, 242.

513 Robert H. Jackson, in Levy, 241.

514 Justice William O. Douglas, in "Griswold v. Connecticut", dKosopedia: The Free Political Encyclopedia, http://www.dkosopedia.com (accessed October, 30, 2005).

515 Goldberg, http://www.dksospedia.com/index.php?title=Griswold_v._Connecticut-Concurrence_Goldberg

516 Goldberg, http://www.dksospedia.com/index.php?title=Griswold_v._Connecticut-Concurrence_Goldberg

517 Douglas, in "Griswold v. Connecticut", http://www.dkosopedia.com/index.php/Griswold_v._Connecticut

518 Douglas, in "Griswold v. Connecticut", http://www.dkosopedia.com/index.php/Griswold_v._Connecticut

519 Douglas, in "Griswold v. Connecticut", http://www.dkosopedia.com/index.php/Griswold_v._Connecticut

520 Justice Harry Blackmun, in "Roe v. Wade", Wikipedia, http://en.wikipedia.org/wiki/Roe_v._Wade (accessed October 30, 2005).

521 Levy, 251.

522 Goldberg, http://www.dksospedia.com/index.php?title=Griswold_v._Connecticut-Concurrence_Goldberg

523 Justice Stewart Potter, in "Griswold v. Connecticut", http://www.dkosopedia.com/index.php/Griswold_v._Connecticut

524 Justice Hugo L. Black, in Levy, 243.

525 Levy, 256.

526 "Ninth Amendment Resurfaces"(2002), TalkLeft: The Politics of Crime, http://talkleft.com/new_archives/000140.html

527 Douglas, in "Griswold v. Connecticut", http://www.dkosopedia.com/index.php/Griswold_v._Connecticut

528 John Roberts, in "Roberts: Roe 'Settled as Precedent'", *The Baltimore Sun*, 14 September 2005, http://baltimoresun.com/news/nationworld/bal-te.roberts14sep14,1,81975.story?coll=bal-home-utility

529 Douglas, in "Griswold v. Connecticut", http://www.dkosopedia.com/index.php/Griswold_v._Connecticut

530 Daniel Patrick Moynihan, in "Ninth Amendment Resurfaces", http://talkleft.com/new_archives/000140.html

531 John Dickinson, in Levy, 250.

532 Alexander Hamilton, in Levy, 250.

533 James Madison, in Levy, 246.

534 Douglas, in "Griswold v. Connecticut", http://www.dkosopedia.com/index.php/Griswold_v._Connecticut

535 Lieberman, Jethro. A Practical Companion to the Constitution. (Los Angeles, CA: University of California Press, 1999), 58.

536 Lieberman, A Practical Companion to the Constitution, 58.

537 Halbrooks, Jacob. "The Anti-Federalist Struggle for the Bill of Rights." 31 October 2005 < http://www.geocities.com/libertarian_press/antifeds.html>.

538 Lieberman, A Practical Companion to the Constitution, 316.

[539] Clause 18. Necessary and Proper Clause. 2 November 2005. http://caselaw.lp.findlaw.com/data/constitution/article01/44.html#4.

[540] Lieberman, A Practical Companion to the Constitution, 314.

[541] James Madison Proposes Bill of Rights. 31 October, 2005, http://www.jmu.edu/madison/gpos225-madison2/madprobll.htm#useless.

[542] Lieberman, A Practical Companion to the Constitution, 580.

[543] De Rosa, Marshall. The Ninth Amendment and the Politics of Creative Jurisprudence. 2 November 2005. < http://www.mises.org/misesreview_detail.asp?control=8&sortorder=issue.>

[544] Pendergast, Tom, Pendergast, Sara, Sousanis, John. Constitutional Amendments. (Detroit: U.X.L., 2001), 181.

[545] Holder, Angela, Holder, John. The Meaning of the Constitution. (Hauppauge, New York: Barron's Educational Series, 1997), 83.

[546] Lieberman, A Practical Companion to the Constitution, 580.

[547] Krull, Kathleen. A Kid's Guide to America's Bill of Rights. (New York: Avon Books, INC, 1999), 181.

[548] Edwards, George, Wattenberg, Martin, Lineberry, Robert. Government in America. (New York: Longman, 1998), 61.

[549] Edwards, George, Wattenberg, Martin, Lineberry, Robert. Government in America. 61.

[550] Hartford Convention. 1 November 2005. http://www.bartleby.com/65/ha/HartfordC.html.

[551] The Bill of Rights and Beyond. (D.C.: Library of Congress, 1991), 55.

[552] Gustavson, Robert. A Biography of John Caldwell Calhoun. 1 November 2005. http://odur.let.rug.nl/~usa/B/calhoun/jcc.htm. 5 May 2005.

[553] The Bill of Rights and Beyond. 54.

[554] Pendergest, Tom. Constitutional Amendments. 206.

[555] Tenth Amendment-Reserved Powers. 2 November 2005. <http://www.gpoaccess.gov/constitution/html/amdt10.html.>

[556] Lieberman, A Practical Companion to the Constitution, 506.

[557] Pendergest, Tom. Constitutional Amendments. 208.

[558] Pendergest, Tom. Constitutional Amendments. 208.

[559] Pendergest, Tom. Constitutional Amendments. 186.

[560] Pendergest, Tom. Constitutional Amendments. 186.

[561] Edwards, George. Government in America. 64.

[562] Krull, Kathleen. A Kid's Guide to America's Bill of Rights. 192.

[563] Lieberman, a Practical Companion to the Constitution, 506.

[564] New York v. United States. 3 November 2005.<http://www.oyez.org/oyez/resource/case/644/>

[565] New York v. United States. 3 November 2005.<http://www.oyez.org/oyez/resource/case/644/>

[566] Lindop, Edmund. The Bill of Rights and Landmark Cases. 28.

[567] Krull, Kathleen. A Kid's Guide to America's Bill of Rights. 182.

[568] The Bill of Rights and Beyond. 54.

[569] Krull, Kathleen. A Kid's Guide to America's Bill of Rights. 193.

[570] Edwards, George. Government in America. 59.

[571] Henderson, Harry. Gun Control. (New York: Facts on File, Inc, 2005), 84.

[572] Davina Kotulski, Ph.D., *Why You Should Give a Damn About Gay Marriage.* (Los Angeles: Advocate Books, 2004), 9-10, 132.

[573] Cahill, Sean, Ph.D., *Same-Sex Marriage in the United States Focus on the Facts.* (Lanham, Maryland: Lexington Books, 2004), 20.

[574] David K. Johnson, *The Lavender Scare: The Cold War Persecution of Gays and Lesbians in the Federal Government.* (Chicago: University of Chicago Press, 2004), Chapter 6, 119-146.

[575] Gregory Black, *Hollywood Censored: Morality Codes, Catholics, and the Movies.* (Cambridge: Cambridge University Press, 1994), 21-49.

[576] George Chauncey, *Why Marriage? The History Shaping Today's Debate Over Gay Equality.* (New York: Basic Books, 2004), 95-111.

[577] John Cloud, "The Battle Over Gay Teens," *Time Magazine* 166, no. 15 (October 10, 2005) 42-51.

[578] Peggy Pascoe, *Why the Ugly Rhetoric Against Gay Marriage is Familiar to this Historian of Miscegenation.,* History News Network, http://hnn.us/articles/4708.html.

[579] George Chauncey, *Why Marriage? The History Shaping Today's Debate Over Gay Equality.* (New York: Basic Books, 2004), 59-71.

[580] *Wikipedia*

[581] Davina Kotulski, Ph.D., *Why You Should Give a Damn About Gay Marriage.* (Los Angeles: Advocate Books, 2004), 3.

582 Evan Wolfson, *Why Marriage Matters America, Equality, and Gay People's Right to Marry.* (New York: Simon & Schuster, Inc.), 13-15.

583 James Dobson, Ph.D., *Marriage Under Fire: Why we Must Win This Battle,* (Sisters, Oregon: Multnomah Publishers), 96.

584American Psychological Association, *Answers to Your Questions About Sexual Orientation and Homosexuality,* American Psychological Association Online, http://www.apa.org/pubinfo/answers. html#whatcauses.

585Eileen Durgin-Clinchard, Ph.D., *Bibliography of Articles on Gay and Lesbian Parenting,* January 1996, http://www.bidstrup.com/parenbib. htm.

586 James Owen, *Homosexual Activity Among Animals Stirs Debate,* 23 July 2004, http://news.nationalgeographic.com/news/2004/07/0722_ 040722_gayanimal.html.

587 Spain Legalizes Same-Sex Marriage, *The Washington Post,* 1 July 2005, p A15; available from http://www.washingtonpost.com/wp-dyn/ content/article/2005/06/30/AR2005063000245.html.

588Lucius J. Barker, and Twiley W. Barker Jr., *Civil Liberties and the Constitution,* seventh ed. (Englewood Cliffs, New Jersey: Hall Inc., Prentice, 1994), 755.

589Richard Wormser, "The Enforcement Acts," http://www.pbs.org/wnet/ jimcrow/stories_events_enforce.html (accessed November 5, 2005).

590"Race, Voting Rights, and Segregation: Direct Disenfranchisement," http://www.umich.edu/~lawrace/disenfranchise1.htm.

591Alexander Keyssar, *The Right to Vote: The Contested History of Democracy in the United States* (New York: Basic Books, 2000), 362-367.

592Barker and Barker Jr., *Civil Liberties and the Constitution,* 553.

593Alexander Keyssar, *The Right to Vote: The Contested History of Democracy in the United States* (New York: Basic Books, 2000). Table A.10.

594Barker and Barker Jr., *Civil Liberties and the Constitution,* 553.

595Barker and Barker Jr., *Civil Liberties and the Constitution,* 551.

596Milton Meltzer, *There Comes A Time* (New York: Random House, 2001).

597"Civil Rights Act of 1960," http://en.wikipedia.org/wiki/Civil_Rights_ Act_of_1960 (accessed October 31, 2005).

[598]trueman@pavilion.co.uk, "The 1965 Voting Rights Act," May, 2005, http://www.historylearningsite.co.uk/1965_voting_rights_act.htm (accessed November 1, 2005).

[599]United States Department of Justice, "Introduction to Federal Voting Rights Law," March 28, 2005, http://www.usdoj.gov/crt/voting/intro/intro_c.htm (accessed November 4, 2005).

[600]Americans.net, "Voting Rights Act of 1965," 1996, http://www.historicaldocuments.com/VotingRightsActof1965.htm.

[601]Barker and Barker Jr., *Civil Liberties and the Constitution*, 553.

[602]Wikipedia. "Income Tax." http://en.wikipedia.org/wiki/Income_tax

[603] Wikipedia. "Income Tax."

[604] U.S. Treasury. "Fact Sheets: Taxes." http://www.Treas.gov/education/fact-sheets/taxes/ustax.shtml

[605]http://www.house.gov/Constitution/Constitution.html

[606]U.S. Treasury

[607]U.S. Treasury

[608]Fox, Cynthia. "Income Tax Records of the Civil War Years." NARA; http://www.archives.gov/publications/prologue/1986/winter/civil-war-tax-records.html

[609]Hunt, John Gabriel, *The Inaugural Addresses of the Presidents*. New York; Gramercy Books, 1997.

[610]Fox, Cynthia

[611]Find Law. "Springer vs. U.S.." http://caselaw.lp.findlaw.com/scripts/getcase.pl?navby=case&court=us&vol=102&page=586

[612] Fox, Cynthia

[613]Hunt, John Gabriel

[614]Johnson, John W., *Historic U.S. Court Cases*. New York: Rutledge, 2001.

[615] Johnson, John W

[616] Johnson, John W

[617] Johnson, John W

[618] U.S Constitution

[619] U.S Constitution

[620] Johnson, John W

[621] Johnson, John W

[622] Johnson, John W

[623] Johnson, John W

[624]Johnson, John W

[625]Legal Information Institute. "Brown, J. Dissenting Opinion."http://supct.law.cornell.edu/supct/html/historics/USSC_CR_0158_0601_ZD1.html

[626]Tax History Museum. "1901-1932: The Income Tax Arrives." http://www.tax.org/Museum/1901-1932.htm

[627]U.S Constitution

[628]Wikipedia. "Sixteenth Amendment to the United States Constitution." http://en.wikipedia.org/wiki/Sixteenth_Amendment_to_the_United_States_Constitution

[629] We The People. "How Some States did not legally ratify the 16th Amendment."http://www.givemeliberty.org/features/taxes/notratified.htm

[630]We The People

[631]Wikipedia. "Sixteenth Amendment to the United States Constitution."

[632]Wikipedia. "Sixteenth Amendment to the United States Constitution."

[633] Wikipedia. "Sixteenth Amendment to the United States Constitution."

[33]   Hart, Phil. "The Purpose of the 16th Amendment." News With Views; http://www.newswithviews.com/money/money4.htm

[634] Spartacus Educational. Last updated 2005. Anti-Saloon League. http://www.spartacus.schoolnet.co.uk/USAsaloon.htm. October 5, 2005.

[635] Women's Christian Temperance Union. 2005. Women's Christian Temperance Union: Early History. http://womenshistory.about.com/gi/dynamic/offsite.htm?zi=1/XJ&snd=womenshitory&zu-http%3A%2F%2Fwww.wctu.org%2Fearlyhistory.html. September 29, 2005.

[636] Online Highways. 2005. The Temperance Movement. http://www.u-s-history.com/pages/h1054.html. October 2, 2005.

[637] Andrew, David, Evan, and Gary. Last updated 2005. Prohibition Laws. http://library.thinkquest.org/04oct/00492/Prohibition_Laws.htm. September 25, 2005.

[638] Schaffer, Clifford A. History of Alcohol Prohibition. Schaffer Library of Drug Policy. http://www.druglibrary.org/schaffer/LIBRARY/studies/nc/nc2a.htm. October 5, 2005.

[639] Zywocinski, Joan Rapczynski Florence. 2005. Prohibition as a Reform. Yale-New Haven Teachers Institute. http://www.yale.edu/ynhti/curriculum/units/1978/3/78.03.03.x.html. September 25, 2005.

[640] Women's Christian Temperance Union. Early History.

[641] Ibid

[642] Encyclopedia Britannica, Inc.1999. Temperance Movement. http://search.eb.com/women/articles/temperance_movement.html. October 2, 2005.

[643] Online Highways. 2005. James G. Blaine 1830-1893. http://www.u-s-history.com/pages/h726.html. October 1, 2005.

[644] Gunzburger, Ron. 2004. Prohibition Party. Directory of U.S. Political Parties. http://www.politics1.com/parties.htm. September 25, 2005.

[645] Prohibition Party History. http://www.prohibitionists.org/History/history.html. September 25, 2005.

[646] Online Highways. 2005. The Temperance Movement: Carry A. Nation 1846-1911. http://www.u-s-history.com/pages/h1058.html. October 1, 2005.

[647] Schaffer. History of Alcohol Prohibition.

[648] Weinhardt, Beth. 2005. History of the Anti-Saloon League 1893-1933. http://www.wpl.lib.oh.us/AntiSaloon/history/. September 27, 2005.

[649] Zywocinski. Prohibition as a Reform.

[650] Online Highways. Temperance Movement.

[651] Andrew, David, Evan, and Gary. Prohibition Laws.

[652] Ibid

[653] Schaffer. History of Alcohol Prohibition.

[654] Ibid

[655] Minnesota Historical Society. 2005. Prohibition and the Volstead Act. Minnesota Historical Society. http://www.mnhs.org/library/tips/history_topics/103prohibition.html. September 25, 2005.

[656] Spartacus Educational. Anti-Saloon League.

[657] Andrew, David, Evan, and Gary. Prohibition Laws.

[658] Adams, Cecil. 2001. What did the Catholic Church use for altar wine during Prohibition? Straight Dope Science Advisory Board. http://www.straightdope.com/mailbag/maltarwine.html. October 5, 2005.

[659] 2,139,000 gallons in 1922, 2,503,000 gallons in 1932, 2,944,700 gallons in 1924

[660] Wow Essays. Prohibition: The Power is in the People. 2004. http://www.wowessays.com/dbase/aa2/1pf260.shtml. October 7, 2005.

[661] Chernoff, Eric. Manning, Michael. Smith, Sarah. Moonshining and Prohibition. http://www.ibiblio.org/moonshine/sell/prohibition.html. September 25, 2005.

[662] Wow Essays. Prohibition: Power in the People.

[663] Spartacus Educational. Anti-Saloon League.

[664] http://www.dcvote.org/trellis/denial/dcvotingrightshistoricaltimeline.cfm

[665] http://www.dcstatehoodgreen.org

[666] ""History of Self- Government in the District of Columbia." http://www.dccouncil.washington.dc.us/history.html

[667] http://www.dcvote.org/trellis/denial/dcvotingrightshistoricaltimeline.cfm, pg. 1

[668] Ibid, pg. 2.

[669] *Encyclopedia of the American Constitution*, 2nd ed. S.v. "Twenty-third Amendment." Pg. 2743

[670] "History of Self- Government in the District of Columbia."

[671] "District of Columbia Home Rule Act." http://www.abfa.com/ogc/hrtall.htm

[672] "U.S. Constitution." http://www.house.gov/Constitution/Constitution.html

[673] "History of Self- Government in the District of Columbia."

[674] "DC Voting Rights and Representation" http://about.dc.gov/statehood.asp

[675] "District of Columbia Voting Rights Amendment." http://en.wikipedia.org/wiki/District_of_Columbia_Voting_Rights_Amendment

[676] "DC Statehood." http://www.kucinich.us/issues/dc_statehood.php

[677] "City Finances." http://www.narpac.org/FOI.HTM

[678] "FCB to Run D.C. Government." http://www.themilitant.com/1995/5918/5918_23.html

[679] "City Budget." http://www.narpac.org/BUDI.HTM#budturn

[680] Ibid.

[681] Ibid.

[682] http://www.fff.org/freedom/fd0211d.asp

[683] http://www.dc.gov/

[684] http://www.washingtonpeacecenter.org/articles/incomeinequality.html

[685] http://tti.tamu.edu/

[686] "Statehood Greens to Bush." http://www.gp.org/press/states/dc_2005_01_26.html

[687] http://www.dcvote.org/

[688] http://www.prb.org/

[689] http://usgovinfo.about.com/blbalance.htm

[690] http://www.norton.house.gov/

[691] http://www.washingtonpost.com/wp-dyn/articles/A38235-2005Mar15.html

[692] http://www.opensecrets.org/politicians/candlist.asp?Sort=N&Cong=108

[693] http://about.dc.gov/statehood.asp

[694] Davis, Tom. "Statement of Representative Tom Davis, Chairman, Committee on Government Affairs on the introduction of the DC FAIR Act." 109th Cong., May 3, 2005.

[695] Judis, John. "Majority Rules." *The New Republic Online.* 5 August 2002.

[696] http://www.dcvote.org/trellis/denial/argumentsforandagainst.cfm

[697] "Statehood Greens to Bush."

[698] " Reform in Washington D.C." http://www.drugpolicy.org/statebystate/washingtondc/

[699] Goldberg, Jonah. "Eliminate Federal Taxes for D.C. Residents." *Townhall.com Columns.* 20 April 2001.

[700] http://www.ushistory.org/presidentshouse/history/faq.htm

[701] http://www.fairfaxcountyva.com/9/history.asp

[702] http://www.dcist.com/

[703] Frey, William. "Census 2000 Reveals New Native-Born and Foreign-Born Shifts Across U.S." *PSC Research Report.* Report No. 02-520. August 2002.

[704] http://www.dc.gov/

[705] "U.S. Constitution."

[706] Ibid.

[707] http://www.dcstatehoodgreen.org/testimony/testimony.php?annc_id=1&section_id=1

[708] Faber, Doris, and Harold Faber. We the People. New York, New York: Charles Scribner's Sons, 1987.

[709] Faber, 205.

[710] Abbie Hoffman and James Rubin are credited with the funding of the YIPPIES, the Youth Independent Party in the early 1970's.

[711] Wright, Mike. What They Didn't Teach You About the 60's. Novato, California: Presidio Press, 2001.

[712] Wright, 325-326.

[713] Close Up Foundation. 8 Nov. 2005 <http://www.closeup.org/amend.pdf>.

[714] Palmer, Kris E. "26 Amendment." Constitutional Amendments. 571-576.

[715] Palmer, 574.

[716] Faber, 203-205.

[717] Palmer, 575.

[718] http://thomas.loc.gov/cgi-bin/query/z?r102:E26NO1-B157

[719] Wright, 210.

[720] http://thomas.loc.gov/cgi-bin/query/z?r102:E26NO1-B157

[721] Wright, 121.

[722] Congress and the Nation, 498-505.

[723] Faber, 204.

[724] Faber, 205.

[725] Palmer, 569.

[726] Faber, 204-205.

[727] www.closeup.org/amend.pdf

[728] Congress and the Nation, 498-505.

[729] Palmer, 569.

[730] Congress and the Nation, 1005.

[731] http://thomas.loc.gov/cgi-bin/query/z?r102:E26NO1-B157

[732] www.closeup.org/amend.pdf

[733] www.closeup.org/amend.pdf

[734] Rosenthal, Jack. "The 'Secret' Key Issue." New York Times 6 Nov. 1972: 47.

[735] Congress and the Nation, 1006.

[736] Congress and the Nation, 1006.

[737] http://www.cnn.com/ELECTION/2004/pages/results/states/US/P/00/epolls.0.html

[738] http://www.cnn.com/ELECTION/2004/pages/results/states/US/P/00/epolls.0.html

[739] http://thomas.loc.gov/cgi-bin/query/z?r102:E26NO1-B157

[740] http://thomas.loc.gov/cgi-bin/query/z?r102:E26NO1-B157

[741] Congress and the Nation, 574.

[742] www.closeup.org/amend.pdf

[743] www.closeup.org/amend.pdf

[744] www.closeup.org/amend.pdf

[745] Congress and the Nation, 498-505.

[746] Faber, 205.

[747] www.closeup.org/amend.pdf

[748] Schulman, Bruce J. The Seventies. New York, New York: The Free Press, 2001.

[749] Schulman, 246.

[750] Baby Boomer refers to the large number of children born in the late 1940s and early 1950s. This was caused by the men returning home from World War II. It was the baby boomer generation that grew up to be hippies.

[751] Schulman, 243.

[752] Schulman, 244.

[753] http://www.closeup.org/amend.pdf

[754] www.youthrights.org/forums/showthread.php?t=117

[755] http://www.closeup.org/amend.pdf

[756] Congress and the Nation, 568.

[757] http://www.cnn.com/2003/ALLPOLITICS/11/04/elec04.prez.rock. vote/

[758] Orbuch, Steven. "In the Granite State, Dartmouth Rocks the Vote." The Dartmouth 22 Oct. 2004. 8 Nov. 2005 <http://www.thedartmouth. com/section.php?section=mirror&date=2004-11-08>.

[759] Dems Face off in 'Rock the Vote'. 8 Nov. 2005 <http://http://www. cnn.com/2003/ALLPOLITICS/11/04/elec04.prez.rock.vote/>.

[760] www.crf-usa.org/youthsite/lowering_the_voting_age.htm

[761] www.crf-usa.org/youthsite/lowering_the_voting_age.htm

[762] www.closeup.org/amend.pdf

[763] "Opening Argument of MR. Benjamin F. Butler of Massachusetts," Online [home page on-line]; available from http://www.law.umkc.edu/ faculty/projects/ftrials/impeach/Butler Opening.html; Internet; accessed 24 October 2005.

[764] The Constitution of the United States of America, Article II section 4.

[765] Sidney M. Milkis and Michael Nelson, The American Presidency Origins and Development (Washington, D.C.: Congressional Quarterly Inc, 1994), 37.

[766] Ibid

[767] Ibid., 37.

[768] Ibid., .38.

[769] Constitutional Rights Foundation Weblesson, "The Impeachment of Andrew Johnson" Constitutional Rights Foundation Weblesson Online; available from http://www.crf-usa.org/impeachment/ impeachment1. html; Internet; accessed 26 October 2005.

[770] Ibid.

[771] Ibid.

[772] Milkis and Nelson, The American Presidency Origins and development, 178.

[773] The Impeachment Of Andrew Johnson

[774] Library of Congress, "Research Guide on Impeachment" Library of Congress Online; available from http://memory.loc.gov/ammem/amlaw/ Impeachment-Guide.html; Internet; accessed 25 October 2005.

[775] Harpweek, "Articles of Impeachment" Harpweek Online [home page on-line]; available from http://www.impeach-andrewjohnson.

com/13ArticlesOfImpeachment /ArticlesOfImpeachmentI.htm; Internet; accessed 25 October 2005.

776 Ibid.

777 Ibid.

778 "Opening Argument of MR. Benjamin F. Butler of Massachusetts".

779 "Testimony in the Impeachment Trial of Andrew Jackson" *Online* [home page on-line]; available from http://www.law.umkc.edu/faculty/ projects/ trials/impeach/testimony .html; Internet; accessed 25 November 2005.

780 Ibid.

781 Watergate. info, "Articles of Impeachment Adopted by the Committee on the Judiciary," *Watergate. info Online* [home page on-line]; available from http://watergate.info/impeachment/impeachment-articles.shtml; Internet; accessed 27 October 2005.

782 Ibid.

783 Ibid.

784 Watergate. info, "Nixon Resignation Speech," *Watergate. info Online* [home page on-line]; available from http://watergate. info/ Nixon / resignation-speech.shtml; Internet; accessed 28 October 2005.

785 "Bill Clinton," *Online* [home page on-line]; available from http:// www.historyplace.com/unitedstates /impeachments/ clinton.htm; Internet; accessed 28 October 2005.

786 Ibid.

787 Ibid.

788 Ibid.

789 Ibid.

790 Teaching American History, "Articles of Impeachment," *Teaching American History Online* [home page on-line]; available from http:// teachingamerican history.org/library/index.asp?document=456; Internet; accessed 1 November 2005.

791 Ibid.

792 Jurist: The Law Professors' Network, " Testimony of Father Robert F. Drinan, S.J. Professor of Law, Georgetown University Law Center" Jurist: The Law Professors Network [home page on-line]; available from http://jurist.law.pitt.edu/drinan.htm; Internet; accessed 3 November 2005.

[793] Kukla, Jon. First edition. A Wilderness So Immense. Alfred A. Knopf, division of Random House, Inc. New York, 2003. pp32

[794] Treaty of Friendship, Limits, and Navigation Between Spain and The United States; October 27, 1795. Article IV. ***http://www.yale.edu/lawweb/avalon/diplomacy/spain/sp1795.htm***

[795] Treaty of San Ildefonso : October 1, 1800, Article3 http://www.yale.edu/lawweb/avalon/ildefens.htm

[796] Kukla, Jon. First edition. A Wilderness So Immense. Alfred A. Knopf, division of Random House, Inc. New York, 2003. pp33

[797] Treaty of San Ildefonso : October 1, 1800, Article 4 http://www.yale.edu/lawweb/avalon/ildefens.htm

[798] Treaty of Paris 1763 Article I sec VII http://www.yale.edu/lawweb/avalon/paris763.htm

[799] Thomas Jefferson - Message to the Senate of January 11, 1803 Regarding Louisiana http://www.yale.edu/lawweb/avalon/presiden/messages/tj003.htm

[800] Kukla, Jon. First edition. A Wilderness So Immense. Alfred A. Knopf, division of Random House, Inc. New York, 2003. pp269

[801] Pichton to Talleyrand, February 18, 1803, Lyon, *Louisiana in French Diplomacy,* 202-3.

[802] Cerami, Charles A. *Jefferson's Great Gamble.* Sourcebooks, Inc. Naperville, Illinois. 2003, pp199.

[803] Ibid

[804] Authority Given to the President to Take Possession of the Territory of Louisiana, http://www.yale.edu/lawweb/avalon/statutes/2us245.htm

[805] Constitution of the United States of America, Article I, section 2 clause 1 http://www.house.gov/Constitution/Constitution.html

[806] Thomas Jefferson's Proposed Amendment to the Constitution, July 1803, http://press-pubs.uchicago.edu/founders/documents/a2_2_2-3s25.html

[807] Kastor, Peter J. The Nation's Crucible. Yale University Press. 2004, pp46.

[808] Kastor, Peter J. *The Nation's Crucible*, Yale University Press, New Haven & London, 2004, pp 42

[809] Treaty Between the United States of America and the French Republic, Article III, http://www.yale.edu/lawweb/avalon/diplomacy/france/louis1.htm

[810] Northwest Ordinance; July 13, 1787, section 1, http://www.yale.edu/lawweb/avalon/nworder.htm

[811] Ibid, section 4

[812] Kastor, Peter J. *The Nation's Crucible*, Yale University Press, New Haven & London, 2004, pp 50.

[813] Ibid

[814] "Remonstrance of the People of Louisiana against the Political System Adopted by Congress for Them," *ASP*, Misc, 1:396.

[815] Pulmer, *Memorandum of Proceedings in Senate*, 222.

[816] *Annals of Congress*, 8th Cong.,2d sess. (1804-05), 727-28.

[817] Ibid., 1014-15

[818] *Annals of Congress*, 8th Cong., 2d sess. (1804-05), 727-28

[819] Constitution of the United States of America Article 2 section 1 clause 8, http://www.house.gov/Constitution/Constitution.html

[820] Garraty, John A., *The Story of America*, Holt, Rinehart and Winston, Inc., Orlando, 1991, pg. 1155

[821] Ward, Geoffrey C., *The Civil War an Illustrated History*, Alfred A. Knopf, Inc., New York, 1990, pg. 16

[822] Garraty, John A., *The Story of America*, Holt, Rinehart and Winston, Inc., Orlando, 1991, pg. 516

[823] IBID

[824] IBID, pg. 1164

[825] From, http://www.kidport.com/RefLib/UsaHistory/CivilWar/Slavery.htm

[826] From, http://www.civilwarhome.com/slavery.htm

[827] Garraty, John A., *The Story of America*, Holt, Rinehart and Winston, Inc., Orlando, 1991, pg. 525

[828] IBID, pg 527

[829] http://www.oyez.org/oyez/resource/case/101/

[830] http://www.freemaninstitute.com/scott.htm

[831]From, http://www.answers.com/main/ntquery;jsessionid=23kk9w0qat m4g?method=4&dsid=2222&dekey=Dred+Scott+v.+Sandford&gwp=8 &curtab=2222_1&sbid=lc05a&linktext=Dred%20Scott%20decision

[832]From, http://www.answers.com/main/ntquery;jsessionid=23kk9w0qat m4g?method=4&dsid=2222&dekey=Lincoln-Douglas+debates+of+1858 &gwp=8&curtab=2222_1&sbid=lc05a&linktext=Lincoln%20and%20D ouglas%20debate

[833] From Speech at Alton, Illinois, October 15, 1858 by Abraham Lincoln as cited in, *The Story of America*

[834] From Speech at Alton, Illinois, October 15, 1858 by Stephen A. Douglas as cited in, *The Story of America*

[835]Garraty, John A., *The Story of America ,*Holt, Rinehart and Winston, Inc., Orlando, 1991, pg. 531

[836]IBID

[837]Garraty, John A., *The Story of America ,*Holt, Rinehart and Winston, Inc., Orlando, 1991, pg. 537

[838]IBID

[839] From, http://sc94.ameslab.gov/TOUR/alincoln.html

[840] From, http://showcase.netins.net/web/creative/lincoln/speeches/greeley.htm

[841] IBID

[842] From, http://www.kidport.com/RefLib/UsaHistory/CivilWar/CivilWar.htm

[843]Garraty, John A., *The Story of America,* Holt, Rinehart and Winston, Inc., Orlando, 1991 pgs. 538-539

[844] IBID, pg. 539

[845] From http://www.civilwarhome.com/csconstitution.htm

[846] IBID

[847] From, http://www.usconstitution.net/const.html

[848] Garraty, John A., *The Story of America ,*Holt, Rinehart and Winston, Inc., Orlando, 1991, pg. 544

[849] Garraty, John A., *The Story of America ,*Holt, Rinehart and Winston, Inc., Orlando, 1991, pg. 548

[850]IBID, pg. 570

[851]Garraty, John A., *The Story of America*, Holt, Rinehart and Winston, Inc., Orlando, 1991, pgs. 595-596

[852] IBID, pg. 596

[853] From, Justice Henry Billings Brown, "Majority opinion in *Plessy v. Ferguson*," <u>Desegregation and the Supreme Court</u> , ed. Benjamin Munn Ziegler (Boston: D.C. Heath and Company, 1958) 50-51. as cited in, http://www.watson.org/~lisa/blackhistory/post-civilwar/notes.html#5

[854] From http://www.civilwarhome.com/gordoncauses.htm